Genesis and Validity

Also by Martin Jay

The Dialectical Imagination: A History of the Frankfurt School and the Institute of Social Research, 1923–1950 (1973 and 1996)

Marxism and Totality: The Adventures of a Concept from Lukács to Habermas (1984)

Adorno (1984)

Permanent Exiles: Essays on the Intellectual Migration from Germany to America (1985)

Fin de Siècle Socialism and Other Essays (1988)

Force Fields: Between Intellectual History and Cultural Critique (1993)

Downcast Eyes: The Denigration of Vision in Twentieth-Century French Thought (1993)

Cultural Semantics: Keywords of Our Time (1998)

Refractions of Violence (2003)

La Crisis de la experiencia en la era postsubjetiva, ed. Eduardo Sabrovsky (2003)

Songs of Experience: Modern American and European Variations on a Universal Theme (2005)

The Virtues of Mendacity: On Lying in Politics (2010)

Essays from Edge: Parerga and Paralipomena (2011)

Kracauer l'exilé (2014)

Reason After Its Eclipse: On Late Critical Theory (2016)

Splinters in your Eye: Frankfurt School Provocations (2020)

Genesis and Validity

The Theory and Practice of Intellectual History

Martin Jay

PENN

UNIVERSITY OF PENNSYLVANIA PRESS

PHILADELPHIA

Copyright © 2022 University of Pennsylvania Press

All rights reserved. Except for brief quotations used
for purposes of review or scholarly citation, none of this
book may be reproduced in any form by any means without written
permission from the publisher.

Published by
University of Pennsylvania Press
Philadelphia, Pennsylvania 19104-4112
www.upenn.edu/pennpress

Printed in the United States of America
on acid-free paper

10 9 8 7 6 5 4 3 2 1

Library of Congress Cataloging-in-Publication Data
Names: Jay, Martin, author.
Title: Genesis and validity : the theory and practice of intellectual history / Martin Jay.
Other titles: Intellectual history of the modern age.
Description: Philadelphia : University of Pennsylvania Press, [2021] | Series: Intellectual history of the modern age | Includes bibliographical references and index.
Identifiers: LCCN 2021003508 | ISBN 9780812253405 (hardcover)
Subjects: LCSH: Intellectual life—History. | History—Philosophy.
Classification: LCC D16.9 .J35 2021 | DDC 901—dc23
LC record available at https://lccn.loc.gov/2021003508

For my students at Berkeley

INTELLECTUAL HISTORY OF THE MODERN AGE

Series Editors

Angus Burgin
Peter E. Gordon
Joel Isaac
Karuna Mantena
Samuel Moyn
Jennifer Ratner-Rosenhagen
Camille Robcis
Sophia Rosenfeld

CONTENTS

Introduction   1

Chapter 1. Impudent Claims and Loathsome Questions:
Intellectual History as Judgment of the Past   28

Chapter 2. Historical Explanation and the Event:
Reflections on the Limits of Contextualization   34

Chapter 3. Intention and Irony: The Missed Encounter
Between Hayden White and Quentin Skinner   48

Chapter 4. Walter Benjamin and Isaiah Berlin:
Modes of Jewish Intellectual Life in the Twentieth Century   62

Chapter 5. Against Rigor: Hans Blumenberg on Freud and Arendt   78

Chapter 6. "Hey! What's the Big Idea?": Ruminations on the
Question of Scale in Intellectual History   93

Chapter 7. Fidelity to the Event? Lukács's *History and
Class Consciousness* and the Russian Revolution   106

Chapter 8. Can Photographs Lie? Reflections on a
Perennial Anxiety   124

Chapter 9. Sublime Historical Experience, Real Presence,
and Photography   140

Chapter 10. The Heroism of Modern Life and the Sociology of
Modernization: Durkheim, Weber, and Simmel   155

Chapter 11. Historical Truth and the Truthfulness of Historians   174

Chapter 12. Theory and Philosophy: Antonyms in
Our Semantic Field?   193

Chapter 13. The Weaponization of Free Speech   204

Notes   219

Index   283

Acknowledgments   297

Introduction

There is no more contentious and perennial issue in the history of Western thought—and perhaps not it alone—than the vexed relationship between the genesis of an idea or value in a specific context, and its claim to validity beyond it.[1] Can ideas or values transcend their spatial and temporal origins, earning abiding respect for their intrinsic merit, or do they necessarily reflect them in ways that belie their universal pretensions? Are discrete contexts, however they are defined, so incommensurable and unique that the intact passage of ideas from one to the other is inevitably impeded? Can ideas survive their voyages away from home in ways that enable meaningful transcultural comparison? Are historical epochs so radically different that no standards of progress or development (or regression and decay) can grant the present the right to weigh the merits of past ideas or values by criteria that transcend the moment of their promulgation? Are we inevitably compelled to judge based on the standards of our own cultural standpoint, contrary to the familiar French proverb *Tout comprendre c'est tout pardoner*. In short, to borrow the elegant metaphor of the American intellectual historian John Diggins, is it possible to extract the oyster entirely from the pearl that excreted it?[2]

These questions have, in fact, been around for a very long time. At least since the invention of writing, the possibility of surviving the place and moment of enunciation has enabled the claim of what is enunciated to transcend its origins. But as soon as isolated cultural systems, unreflectively secure in their assumptions, were challenged from without by contact with competing systems or undermined from within by heterodox doubts, absolute claims of truth or unbending standards of moral virtue were haunted by the specter of contextual relativity. Although anticipated in even the most apparently self-assured of premodern cultures—the Hebrew Bible, for example, records an often awkward and contentious if nonetheless inspiring struggle to ground universal claims in the contingent narrative of a particular people[3]—such qualms came to a head only in the modern period, when time-honored theological, ontological, and moral verities were subjected to sustained and intensified scrutiny. No longer was it easy to assume objective notions of "the good" resided in ontological truths available through rational contemplation or divine revelation, leaving many to conclude that subjectively grounded, culturally bound "values" were the only viable alternative. The question then inevitably arose: who was the privileged subject whose values or worldview could claim transcendent validity?

In our own time, still further erosion of confidence followed the global decentering of the West, which found itself vulnerable to the charge that it had imposed its ideas and values on the rest of a world no longer willing to accept its hegemony. The "provincializing" of Europe by postcolonial historians, who challenged the dominant Eurocentric narrative of world history, inevitably led to the concomitant provincializing of European ideas.[4] Putatively species-wide "human" rights, for example, were now judged as illegitimate projections of the values of one culture onto others. Western aesthetic norms were challenged by defenders of alternative traditions from other parts of the world.[5] The Western monopoly on defining such putatively universal ideas as "reason" was broken by voices from hitherto marginalized cultures.[6]

One result of the loss of confidence in traditional verities has been the call for a "global intellectual history," challenging the hegemony of European or Western thought, effacing the spatial hierarchy dividing center from periphery, and upending the temporal hierarchy of "advanced" and "backward" cultures.[7] But including hitherto neglected, marginalized, or denigrated traditions of thought, while enriching our appreciation of human differences, does little to buttress the universal or absolute claims of any of them (including the respect for difference as itself a universal value). Nor does it resolve the question of whether a totalizing global perspective can ever emerge from a comparative commensuration of different local narratives. It would therefore seem to tip the balance toward genesis over validity, by making all cultures provincial, and denying to anyone a privileged role as hegemonic.

Paradoxically, however, the adoption of a global or "transnational" perspective also devalues specific locations as the relevant genetic context of ideas. For if microhistory lends itself to saturated contextualization much more easily than its macro counterpart,[8] then diminishing the importance of local or even national discursive communities may well undercut the purchase of concrete genetic explanations. Or at best it displaces them to less geographically grounded alternatives such as transnational archives or cyberspace functioning across parochial national or even regional boundaries and beyond specific moments in time.⁹ But because these may be too diffuse and unfocused to exercise strong genetic determination, the result is a tacit refocusing of attention on the validity of the ideas themselves.

Complicating the issue still further is that fact that from the onset it has taken on political coloration. The putative links between one or another position and a specific political inclination, however, have never been conclusively demonstrated. In the eighteenth and nineteenth centuries, it was typical of "progressive" advocates of the Enlightenment tradition to be in favor of universal transcendence and cosmopolitan disembeddedness, while "conservative" devotees of diversity, including many Romantics, championed the rootedness of ideas in the specific soil of different cultures and historical periods. Defending the value of long-lasting traditions and the habitual acceptance of their wisdom, the latter balked at wiping the slate clean in the name of abstract and untested principles, which threatened to obliterate the lessons of diverse historical experience.

But by the late twentieth century, when the hegemony of the West came under increased attack, it was often right-wing thinkers who sounded the tocsin against the undermining of putatively universal values by narrowly tribal contextualists.¹⁰ Conflating the assault on cross-cultural truths on the part of previously marginalized groups with the alleged postmodernist ethic of "anything goes," they lamented the erosion of binding standards grounded in a normative notion of reason or nature. Against the attack on historical "metanarratives," which left in tatters any hopes for a unified story of human development such as the one told by "modernization" theory, they doggedly advocated the spread of ideas and practices that would benefit humankind as a whole (as exemplified by the campaign waged by American neoconservatives during the administration of George W. Bush to export capitalist democracy to the rest of the world).

It would, however, be wrong to conclude that only contemporary conservatives have challenged relativist contextualization. Drawing on the Frankfurt School's Critical Theory, the intellectual historian Peter Gordon has charged that "much of the prestige of contextualism arises from a logical fallacy of collapsing validity into genesis."¹¹ Theodor W. Adorno's distinction between ideological and utopian ideas and his belief in the negative, critical potential of thought to transcend the status quo implies that ideas cannot be entirely reduced to—or in his vocabulary, are nonidentical with—their genetic context.¹² Similarly, Jürgen Habermas's contention that the speech act of asserting validity claims reaches beyond any local context and expresses universal aspirations also suggests that historians will betray the illocutionary intention of such assertions by reducing them entirely to the discursive milieu of their initial utterance. "For it is the paradoxical truth inherent in the very meaning of critical reflection," Gordon argues, "that situated thinking exceeds its own situation."[13]

Ambiguous political implications aside, the perennial tension between genesis and validity has been expressed in many different, often only imperfectly congruent, vocabularies. At times, it has appeared in the distinction between an objective Mind holding eternal ideas and the finite, subjective minds that may or may not discover or share them. Truth, so it is asserted, is a quality of ideas in relation to the reality they reference, whereas mere "certainty" involves only the beliefs of always fallible humans (expressed as well in the distinction between objective notions of the "good" and mere human "values"). The "logicism" of those who uphold this position—which is often buttressed by invoking the allegedly universal truths of syllogistic logic—is invidiously compared with the reductive "psychologism" of those who insist that ideas cannot transcend their origins in the psyches or social situations of those who generate or defend them.[14] In linguistic terms, a similar contrast pits an allegedly universal metalanguage, understood, for example, in mathematical symbols, which can express truths seemingly unrefracted through the vehicle of their expression, against the discrete vernacular languages that require imperfect translation to compensate for the inevitable limits of each.[15]

At other times, the tension between genesis and validity plays out in a stark, sometimes tendentiously drawn opposition between "history" (or alternatively "culture") and "nature." Here "nature" becomes a placeholder for universality and eternity—as in natural law or natural rights—and "history" signifies the vagaries of temporal change and local situation. Although "historicism" has occasionally been defined as the positing of developmental laws that aspire to absolute status across cultures, by and large the term has signified the unique, ephemeral, and contingent, rather than the repeated and necessary.[16] To historicize thus means to attend to the specific temporal and spatial situations out of which ideas come and into which they are inserted, which can imply they are not timeless or applicable everywhere. What became known in the 1920s as the "crisis of historicism," which has taken many different forms and never really ended, was generated by the fear of "anything goes" relativism that the term connoted.[17] For even if validity has at times been grounded in tradition or habitual repetition, such defenses are more vulnerable to skeptical critique than ones drawing on the authority of an allegedly immutable nature presumed to survive the flow of time and contingency of spatial location.[18]

Still another variant of the genesis/validity opposition can be found in the distinction between immanence and transcendence.[19] Typically, the former signifies embeddedness in particular cultures or epochs, themselves understood to be self-sufficiently grounded and resistant to external critique, while the latter values the capacity to rise above local contexts and seek more general validity beyond their boundaries. Although within an immanent context there are often internal tensions, even contradictions—thus the idea of "immanent critique" that pits the norms of a culture against their imperfect realization in actual practice[20]—the transcultural validity of those norms cannot be assumed. As Wittgenstein argued with his concept of a "form of life," each culture follows tacit rules, like those of a game, that underlie their operations. Nor, according to those who challenge metanarratives of progress, can rules that govern present forms be retrospectively foisted on earlier eras, especially when it comes to normative values, although perhaps to cognitive assumptions as well.[21] So doing, critics worry, is to impose on the past what the British historian E. P. Thompson famously called "the enormous condescension of posterity."[22]

The boundaries of immanence can, however, also be extended, as they have by recent theological critics of secularization,[23] beyond a specific culture or epoch to denote a more general innerworldly, secular, naturalist, species-wide humanism. In this expansive version of the "immanent frame" argument, the transcendent alternative is relocated to a supernatural realm generating values that cannot be grounded humanistically within the given world. Here immanence implies earthbound horizontality and transcendence celestial verticality. Although it is possible to trace the genetic origins of a religion in a specific time and place, believers in their transcendent value insist that they reveal truths or values that are valid absolutely. Pushing back against the modern transformation of objective notions of the "good" into subjective "values," they seek firmer foundations for their normative investments, which they claim reflect an inherent hierarchy beyond human choice.[24]

The target of this theologically informed defense of transcendence is often the perceived arrogance of positivist scientism. Ironically, a similar unease with the limits of an immanent frame can be discerned among defenders of the validity of scientific knowledge itself, who claim it transcends the limits of the context out of which it emerged. What the philosopher of science Karl Popper called "the myth of the framework,"[25] underlying, for example, Thomas Kuhn's deflationary argument for the succession of incommensurable paradigms of scientific theories, fails to account for the cumulative learning enabled by the scientific method.[26] Although Popper acknowledged human fallibility and the impossibility of ever reaching a perfectly true view of reality, he argued for progressively closer approximations of that truth and scorned the relativism he saw in the sociology of science. However indebted theories might be to the cultural situations of the theorists who generate them, it is possible to test their validity—in Popper's terms more by falsification than verification—across cultures. To reduce scientific ideas to their local "context of discovery" rather than stressing their survival in the more cross-cultural "context of justification" would be to commit what had been dubbed "the genetic fallacy" in 1934 by Morris Raphael Cohen and Ernest Nagel in their *Introduction to Logic and Scientific Method*.[27]

When, however, the frame surrounding immanence is more modestly circumscribed and identified with a specific historical period or culture, it is possible to understand the outside of the frame as horizontally related and redefine "transcendence" as something other than absolute. One way to uncouple transcendence from universal and ahistorical validity is suggested by Reinhart Koselleck, the leading exponent of "the history of concepts." Noting that there are some structures of meaning that recur over generations, he argues that "such phenomena of repetition that go beyond everyday experience might be called 'transcendental' . . . . They are 'transcendent,' not in the sense of otherworldliness, but in the sense that they reach beyond and undergird multiple generations." He then ventures a more ambitiously universalist argument of his own: "All groups with shared experiences possess a certain minimum need for transcendence: without it, there is no final explanation—however provisional it might be—and it would be impossible to translate experience into knowledge."[28]

It can likewise be argued that without some possibility of ideas remaining meaningful—and also potentially persuasive—beyond their context of origin, posterity would be unable to make any sense out of them at all. Even if we eschew the problematic ideal of rational reenactment promulgated by the philosopher of history R. G. Collingwood,[29] there must be some overlap, some common ground, between usages to enable whatever interpretative exercise allows understanding across even epochal thresholds. Not every act of temporal translation requires, after all, the chance discovery of a Rosetta

Stone to break through seemingly insurmountable boundaries based on radical cultural or linguistic incommensurability.

In additional to generational transcendence, which notes the survival of ideas beyond their context of origin within an historical tradition, it is possible to locate nonabsolute transcendence in the contact between cultural traditions that can be understood as merely different from rather than superior to each other. Although each can be said to call into question the immanent self-sufficiency of the other, neither can claim universal, timeless validity. Someone within an immanent cultural frame can be credited with "native" knowledge and understanding that an alien "observer" lacks. What cultural anthropologists call an "emic" understanding means the tacit knowledge of an indigenous actor within a culture, who needs no road map to traverse the territory.[30] In contrast, an "etic" account is an external description by a social analyst or scientific observer, often employing more generic, crosscultural terms to make sense of what is not immediately meaningful to an alien gaze. We might say that the reversal of subject/object positions allows a mutual transcendence, which cannot claim universal or absolute validity, but is at least a check on the complacency of radical immanence and the fatalism of a priori incommensurability. Thus, a student of, say, ideas originating in Germany who comes from China may have insights denied a native informant and vice versa. Despite an imbalance in their hegemonic power, often backed up by power of a more material kind, the contact between cultures need not necessarily mean the domination of one over the other or the wholesale appropriation of the weaker by the stronger. It is also possible for a mutually beneficial interaction, which involves inclusion rather than exclusion, and at least some degree of reciprocity and self-critical learning through openness to otherness.[31]

To give the screw one more twist, there are times when the gravitational pull of contextual origins, rather than being blamed for undermining validity, can be credited with enabling a certain version of it. Traditionally called "standpoint theory" and defended by Marxists who argued for the privileged epistemological vantage point of the proletariat, it draws on the old argument developed by Giambattista Vico that "verum et factum convertuntur."[32] Those who make history are those who have privileged access to the truth of what they have made. Expressed in the vocabulary of "identity politics," "making" has often been superseded by the shared "experience" of those within an immanent frame as the source of a special insight lacked by those outside it. Being situated rather than hovering above the fray, "speaking as a . . ." allegedly confers an authority that is even denied a sympathetic outsider who speaks representatively "in the name of . . ."[33]

Now the issue becomes even more complicated. For as this last example shows, the relationship between genesis and validity is not necessarily adversarial. What might be called a dialectical relationship between the two terms is also possible, with truth claims actually more dependent on concrete embeddedness than on abstract detachment. Transcendence, rather than seeking its ground in an otherworldly realm accessible to faith or a generic human reason, can be located in worldly immanence itself, as, for example, in the claims made by "philosophers of life," such as Georg Simmel, that self-transcendence is the essence of life.[34] Nietzsche could thus both advocate a debunking, genealogical critique rather than a transcendental one, earning his reputation as one of the pioneers of a "hermeneutics of suspicion" rather than a "hermeneutics of recollected meaning,"[35] and yet at the same time champion radical self-overcoming and the willful positing of new values as the highest human goals.

Even scientific validity may also be grounded immanently, at least according to the phenomenology of Edmund Husserl. An early opponent of psychologism, Husserl nonetheless came to distrust what he saw as the objectivist Galilean tradition, which ignored the fact that scientists are subjects of lived experience before they are disinterested researchers. In his *Crisis of European Sciences and Transcendental Phenomenology* of 1936, he criticized positivist naturalism for failing to register the priority of the "lifeworld" over the procedures of the scientific method.[36] Whether or not his transcendental phenomenology successfully found in the intersubjective lifeworld a nonrelativist solution to the crisis is much debated.[37] But like Popper, he sought to rescue the validity of scientific knowledge from the relativistic implications of radical immanentism.[38] Those of Husserl's successors in the phenomenological movement who disdained any version of scientific epistemology, such as Martin Heidegger, tacitly relied on transcendental assumptions of their own for a similar purpose.[39]

There may even be a potential avenue to transcendence in perspectival "standpoint theory," as the Dutch sociologist Dick Pels has shrewdly noted.[40] The collectivity whose productive power or unique experience is taken to be the immanent source of epistemological validity is never as homogeneous or self-consciously reflective as it needs to be to serve as the uncontested ground of superior knowledge. As a result, there is an inevitable metonymic displacement in which certain privileged subgroups come to speak for the whole category. In Marxism, it is radical intellectuals or the vanguard party, who benefit from what Georg Lukács famously posited as access to the "ascribed class consciousness" of a working class that is not yet fully "for itself."[41] For women, to take another salient example, it is "feminists" who claim to speak for the gender as a whole, whose consciousness may have not yet been raised as much as it should be. Minority groups often experience struggles of different factions to represent their putatively collective consciousness or shared needs.[42]

There are, to be sure, attempts to bridge the gap between the larger community and the elite of enlightened spokespersons, for example, Gramsci's idea of "organic intellectuals" who emerge from the class whose interests they represent. But by and large they have been far less numerous than radicalized intellectuals from other classes who claim to know the "real" or "objective" interests of those they represent. Sometimes marginality within a group, drawing on alienation from conventional wisdom, is also assumed to enable special insight. But as Pels argues, "Marginalized standpoints do not suffice; they must be intellectualized, pass through theory, which evidently requires the guiding presence of the professionals of theory themselves." Ironically, the epistemological superiority earned by shared experience needs to be articulated through categories and with arguments that often come from theoretical discourses developed elsewhere. In the case of Marxism, for example, the impetus came from German idealist philosophy filtered through humanist materialism. Thus, Pels concludes, "consciousness is decisive, not situation or place. Knowledge, or critical thought, may in principle emancipate itself from all situational determination. It is this vicious circularity and voluntarism which ultimately turns standpoint theory inside out, and closely approximates the conventional transcendental view which it originally sets out to criticize."[43]

A more generous analysis of this dynamic, seeing the dialectic of immanence and transcendence as less a vicious circle than a virtuous spiral, has been offered by the third-generation Frankfurt School critical theorist Rainer Forst. Building on Habermas's theory of communicative rationality to claim that the essence of reason is giving and weighing justifications, he argues that "the question of whether the principle of reason has a transcendent (or transcendental), an abstract, or, on the contrary, a historical, context-specific character, is wrongly posed. The question of justification always arises in concrete contexts and equally points beyond them."[44] Rather than remaining trapped in the immanent frame out of which it emerges, passively reflecting the normative limits of its generative milieu, it can open up "an intensified reflective process that concerns not only the immanence of a context of justification, but is also able to subject the latter to general critical scrutiny.... Reason is at once the most immanent and the most transcendent faculty that human beings possess, and hence it is neither exclusively immanent nor exclusively transcendent."[45]

Another way to link transcendence positively with context involves the possible value added by the traveling of ideas from their context of origin to alien climes. Often, to be sure, the displacement or translation of ideas is lamented as a dilution or misreading of the original meaning, implying a loss rather than a gain. Think, for example, of the way native French commentators often condescendingly mock the caricature called "French Theory" in the Anglophone world. And yet, as Walter Benjamin pointed out in his celebrated account of "The Task of the Translator,"[46] intertextual enrichment can help overcome the limits of individual languages. In a comparable way, what we might call the truth potential of ideas may be enhanced by the ways in which hitherto unexpected dimensions of their meaning are revealed when they are creatively appropriated—even inadvertently "misread"—in new contexts.[47]

A comparable recursivity between context and transcendence, albeit in a different register, can be discerned when the relationship between works of art and their origins is considered. Most commenters would now resist the reductive idea that works of art, especially those that are considered "timeless," are mere confessional expressions of the biographies of their creators or emanations of the social classes out of which they arise. We use terms like "autonomy" or "aura" to distinguish genuine works that somehow transcend their conditions of production and continue to resonate for posterity, and others like "impersonality" or "disinterest" to draw lines between the work, which stands on its own, and the expressive intentionality of its progenitor. Objects that are "found" and then designated aesthetically meaningful are radically separated from their original utilitarian context or the intentions of their makers (although one might argue that they gain value only through the enunciative acts of those with the institutional power to designate them as such).

The ability of genuine works of art to transcend their contexts of reception has also been defended by those who devote great theoretical effort to distinguish them from the experiences they may generate in their beholders or their contexts of reception.[48] They are understood to be more than empty vessels to be filled by the interpretive communities that imbue them with meaning. For they contain an inexhaustible surplus that fuels their potential to stimulate new meaning in future receptions. Thus, we might say that the counterconcept to genesis in aesthetic terms is not validity, as it is with philosophical or scientific ideas, but rather inventive fecundity.[49] Or to put it in the terms of the philosopher of science Bruno Latour, works of art can be seen as "non-human actors," who exercise their agency well after their initial appearance and maintain it through a succession of interventions in subsequent history.[50]

But paradoxically, when it comes to the evaluation of unique creations in certain genres of art, most obviously the visual, there is nothing more important than their attribution to the hand of a master. Although the commodity value of such works may, of course, also ride on such judgments, what is relevant to our discussion is that their aesthetic status is largely dependent on questions of genesis, rather than understood as its antithesis. All the tools of forensic analysis are mobilized to determine the provenance of a work whose origins are in dispute, demonstrating that transcendent value can sometimes be dependent on genetic pedigree rather than on autonomous aesthetic judgment. Even in the case of aesthetic designators who turn found objects into "readymade" artwork, it matters who is doing the designating and by what authority they can do so legitimately.

Something similar, although on a collective scale, has influenced the ascribing of added luster to works that were once wrested from their "primitive" cultural context and given universal aesthetic value because of their formal qualities. That is, their "elevation" into generic works of art suitable for an art museum rather than an ethnographic one, which once seemed an enlightened gesture of broad-minded inclusion, has increasingly been called into question. Extracted from their original cultural milieu, often through violent imperialist appropriation, they are now understood to have been robbed of the function they once served as devotional or utilitarian objects.[51] As a result, acknowledging their genetic origin has paradoxically become a source of new value, rather than something to be overcome in the name of a universal aesthetic of formal beauty. Or more precisely, we have learned to value such works both for their formal qualities and for their expression of the once-denigrated cultures that produced them.

* * *

It would be easy to multiply other variations on the theme of genesis and validity, which has taken many different and often incongruent forms. But rather than turn this introduction into a full-blown treatise of its own, let me pivot to the more specific point I want to make: the practice of what is called "intellectual history" often explores with special acuity the tense relationships between context of origin and putative transcendent meaning in all of their motley variety.[52] In providing an arena for the retrospective staging of various iterations of the conflict and judiciously presenting the arguments on each side, it often clarifies the stakes involved, bringing into relief some of the complexities sketched above. Sharing with the more specialized histories of the arts a sensitivity to the dialectic of genesis and validity, it takes for its territory the widest range of cultural phenomena.

Unlike its cousin "cultural history,"[53] however, intellectual history often addresses the origins and development of allegedly "high" or esoteric ideas which can command respect and generate persuasive validity claims well past their "sell-by" date, while also tracing the trajectories of the figures who originated, defended, modified, and contested them. That is, a cultural historian studying, for example, the history of the restaurant in nineteenth-century France need not weigh in on the best way to cook coq au vin or another exploring the rise of ritual operas in Chinese popular culture is not compelled to evaluate their transcendent aesthetic value. They may well rest content with providing a "thick description," to borrow the anthropologist Clifford Geertz's familiar term, of the milieu in which they thrived, without being tempted to move from describing to judging.

But an intellectual historian who examines, say, the Davos Debate between Ernst Cassirer and Martin Heidegger or the unsettled origins of human rights theory may feel far more likely to opine on unresolved issues still troubling us today. Insofar as intellectuals are precisely those people, to borrow the felicitous definition of the sociologist of philosophy Randall Collins, "who produce de-contextualized ideas,"[54] scholars who study their history often feel dissatisfied with merely situating those ideas in their genetic contexts and entirely bracketing the question of their transcendent validity. By attending to what Dominick LaCapra has called the "worklike" qualities of texts rather than their mere "documentary" value, they are open to the ways in which they can continue to ramify and provoke well past their original historical moment.[55] Even when they promote the ideal of disinterested neutrality, intellectual historians often acknowledge their debts to the figures they study.[56] Because of the transferential relationship they often have with their subjects, whether positive or negative, they may find it hard to adopt a position of bland impartiality toward the ideas those subjects defended.[57] That is, to the extent that they also consider themselves intellectuals, the temptation to join the fray is often hard to resist.

Rarely, to be sure, are intellectual historians self-confident—or foolish—enough to hazard definitive answers to the questions that are raised by the figures they study.[58] For as Siegfried Kracauer famously put it with regard to the relationship between historical scholarship in general and the pretensions of metaphysics, intellectual historians are trained to focus only on "the last things before the last."[59] Many remain more comfortable with the institutions, lives, or generational experiences of intellectuals—the "social history of ideas"[60]—than the ideas themselves. Readers who want full-throated efforts to solve the ultimate mysteries—those transcendent "last things" historians usually refrain from addressing head-on—will be better advised to turn to theologians or philosophers, although in the end the results may be just as frustrating there as well.

But even if they resist the temptation to become self-assured participants in the discussions whose unfolding they narratively reconstruct, intellectual historians often find themselves entangled in questions of genesis and validity in reflecting on the practice of their own craft. To illustrate what I mean, let me pause to consider a recent effort by the distinguished Australian intellectual historian Ian Hunter to address "The Contest over Context in Intellectual History."[61] Because it draws on and criticizes several of my own essays included in this collection, it will also serve as a useful way to transition into a discussion of their relationship to the genesis/validity question. Hunter, who is a student of early modern European political theory, makes no bones about his attraction to the genetic rather than validity pole of the opposition. He is even at pains to show that the original context for the practice of intellectual historical contextualization is not the recent work of the so-called Cambridge School, associated with Quentin Skinner, John Pocock, John Dunn, and Richard Tuck, but rather seventeenth-century European ecclesiastical and constitutional disputes, which were situated in conflicts over religious practices and legal institutions. By drawing on documentary evidence of origins rather than arguing from abstract metaphysical principles, early modern contextualists critically debunked theological and juridical claims to transcendent value by means of empirical historical research and philological source critique. Hunter sees the ripening of this approach in the early nineteenth-century historiography of Leopold von Ranke, often dismissed for his allegedly naive positivism. Instead of being unreflectively objectivist, the contextualist tradition exemplified by Ranke, so

Hunter contends, was in fact self-reflective, pluralist, modest in its claims, and aware of its perspectival situatedness.

In his eagerness to defend contextualism, Hunter dismisses the charge that underlying genetic historical narratives lurks tacit and unexamined transcendental assumptions, which can take the form, as Hayden White in particular has argued, of a finite number of prefigural patterns of emplotment.[62] Tragedy, comedy, satire, romance, and irony are the abiding alternatives that White contends underpin all narratives, fictional and nonfictional alike. But for Hunter, prefigural formalism is merely a rhetorical version of Kantian transcendentalism.[63] No less problematic, he argues, is the adoption of Hegelian dialectics by nineteenth-century historians like Heinrich Leo to infuse the empirical, disinterested historiography of Ranke with metaphysical content. That is, rather than applying Kant's ahistorical schemes of transcendental validity or their rhetorical equivalents, Hegelian dialectics, as Hunter describes it, sought to reconcile historical facts and spiritual meaning, thus temporalizing the unitary metaphysical project that earlier pluralist contextualizations had undermined. But in fact, so he claims with an implicit nod to Michel Foucault, its adherents, then and today, merely represent a rival intellectual subculture struggling for hegemony in a field of competing alternatives.

Hunter's relentlessly contextualist attempt to read all anticontextualist efforts as merely tactical moves in a game of intellectual competition—whether couched in Kantian formalist or Hegelian dialectical terms—is not without its productive insights. As we will see when looking at Lukács's Hegelian Marxist classic *History and Class Consciousness* with its misplaced faith in a redemptive narrative of world history, the dialectical attempt to imbue historical contingency with transcendental meaning could indeed lead in some dubious directions.[64] But Hunter overplays his hand in several ways. First, he violates his own injunction always to contextualize ideas in their concrete circumstances by fashioning an early nineteenth-century German dispute between pluralist contextualization and dialectical transcendentalization into a template for "radically and permanently opposed intellectual cultures or comportments."[65] Ironically, in so doing he elevates the battle between Rankeans and Hegelians from its original genetic context into a perennial and irreconcilable opposition, turning a contest for cultural power in 1820s Prussia into the model for analogous conflicts in the Anglophone world almost two centuries later. Once the original context of generation is located, he implies, there is no need to pay attention to the disparate contexts of reception through which the template is refracted in new circumstances. Included in such contexts would be those that helped form the historian him- or herself, which are often bracketed by those who tacitly assume their view is from nowhere.⁶⁶ Rather than acknowledging the dialogic interaction of different contextual horizons, past and present, a kind of vulgar Foucaultian reduction of knowledge to little more than power serves as Hunter's own crypto-transcendental default assumption.

Second, eager to discredit all those he puts in the same transcendentalist pot, Hunter violates his own injunction against nonempirical historiography by attributing to all of them an underlying self-interested goal. He identifies it with the cultivation of the "higher moral selves" urged by German idealism.⁶⁷ Those who resist, for whatever reason, the relativist reductionism they fear will flow from the "genetic fallacy" arrogantly see themselves, Hunter charges, as members of "an academic clerisy with charismatic insight into a higher form of self and society."⁶⁸ Finally, by essentializing the alternative to radical contextualism and positing a putatively shared hidden agenda that underlies all of its manifestations, Hunter misses an opportunity to explore the much more nuanced stories that might be told about the ways intellectual historians have grappled with and continue to address the vexed relationships between genesis and validity, context and text, immanent frame and transcendent meaning.

* * *

How varied and heterogeneous the responses can be was made clear to me when I retrospectively canvassed my own attempts, often inchoate and indirect, to wrestle with the issue. It turns out that without consciously intending it, a substantial number of my efforts over the years addressed in one guise or another the tension between genesis and validity. These began more than four decades ago with a consideration of the consequences of the linguistic turn for intellectual history through an analysis of the debate between Hans-Georg Gadamer and Jürgen Habermas.⁶⁹ A subsequent consideration of some of the same issues appeared as "Two Cheers for Paraphrase: The Confessions of a Synoptic Intellectual Historian," published in 1986 in response to a deconstructionist critique of my prior work as an example of "synoptic content analysis."⁷⁰ Yet another aspect of the issue was addressed in an analysis of the conflict in the humanities between identifying ideas through proper names and redescribing them in more neutral generic terms, which sought to efface their genesis in the concrete life histories of their progenitors.⁷¹

Still other efforts dealt with the ambiguities of a purely textualist approach to intellectual history, the reaction to psychologism in modernist aesthetics, and the tension between avowedly national philosophical traditions and the normal claims of philosophy to transcend their genetic origins.[72] And my practical exercises in mapping out an intellectual "force field" or "constellation," derived from metaphors used by Benjamin and Adorno to designate "a juxtaposed rather than integrated cluster of changing elements that resist deduction to a common denominator, essential core, or generative first principle,"[73] also touched on the relationship between multiple contexts, including ones of reception, and the validity of ideas.

Each of these efforts has appeared in previous collections of my essays or individual books, and so does not warrant republication here. The more recent and still uncollected papers that are included address the issue of genesis and validity from a number of different vantage points, sometimes head-on, sometimes obliquely. The first, "Impudent Claims and Loathsome Questions: Intellectual History as Judgment of the Past,"[74] ruminates on a provocative remark from Theodor W. Adorno that challenges the condescending game of present critics who "appreciate" past thinkers like Hegel by trying to discern "what is living and what is dead" in their thought. "Impudent Claims and Loathsome Questions: Intellectual History as Judgment of the Past" turns on its head the widely held belief that we in the present can claim a higher validity for our ideas and condescendingly "understand" those of past generations by situating them in their historical situation and moment. Instead, it argues for treating our own standpoint, spatial and temporal, as itself a contingent historical context, which generates unexamined assumptions that often elude us. These might be fruitfully measured against the potentially transcendent alternatives presented by earlier thinkers. Doing so paradoxically helps us see the limits of both narcissistic presentism as the ground for absolute judgments and a relativizing contextualism of the past that resists scrutiny by anything outside its immanent borders. Drawing on Frank Ankersmit's idea of sublime historical experience—which will be more closely examined in a subsequent piece—the essay promotes the importance of opening ourselves to the radical alterity of a past that resists being "appreciated" or judged by present values, and in fact may fruitfully challenge them.

A very different question motivates the next entry, "Historical Explanation and the Event: Reflections on the Limits of Contextualization."[75] Its first half presents the arguments on both sides of the historical debate about contextualization, with attention to the strengths and weaknesses of each. The second half of the essay is devoted to the implications of the recent French discourse of "the event," which provides an alternative to genetic contextualism that is, *pace* Ian Hunter, anything but Hegelian in origin.[76] Rather than focusing on the transcendental prefigurations underlying narratives, in the manner of Hayden White, or on the textual mediations of past contexts, stressed by Dominick LaCapra, it looks at the ways in which unexpected "events" in history have interrupted the unfolding of developmental narratives. How, it asks, does "the new" break free from the constraints of the context out of which it arises? Drawing on the insights of the phenomenologist Claude Romano, who has written extensively on the idea of the event as an "advent" starting a new developmental chain, it resists the either/or that characterizes many considerations of the genesis/validity question. The time of an event is that of a future still to come, or perhaps what Ernst Bloch called "noncontemporaneity," a time both of "no longer" and "not yet." Like a child entering the world, events are almost all pure possibility and little, if any, actuality. Instead of reducing innovation and creativity to mere effects of their genetic ground, it is necessary to situate them in the potential futures they enable (although do not determine). Transcendence, understood in this case as radical change, is not folded back into a neatly coherent Hegelian fable of dialectical incorporation, but rather understood as the unexpected emergence of what is now possible against the gravitational pull of what is already actual.[77]

The next essay, "Intention and Irony: The Missed Encounter Between Hayden White and Quentin Skinner," turns to two of the most influential historians of our time.[78] Rather than casting them as antagonists in a straightforward contest between formalist transcendence and genetic contextualism, it explores the unexpected—and mutually enlightening—entanglement of their two positions. What brings about this outcome is the imbrication of their arguments about intentionality and irony. Skinner's stress has always been on recovering the illocutionary force of the speech acts of figures from the past, who intended their words to have a certain effect on a select audience in a specific context. White has understood that although irony is only one of a finite menu of possible prefigural emplotments underpinning the writing of history, it is, for good and for ill, the one that has dominated modern historiography. What links their two positions together is the fact that ironic narration, of whatever variety, requires a certain distinction between conscious intentions and unintended consequences. That is, historians in the present can view the past ironically, arguing with hindsight that outcomes often betray hopes, only if they assume they can gain access to the original intentions of the actors whose hopes have been dashed. Without Skinner's faith in the possibility of such access, an ironic attitude on the part of later historians would be meaningless.

Although not directly addressing the issue of genesis and validity, the essay has an implicit lesson for their relationship. It suggests that a mutual relativization of contexts—the one of the past actors, the other of the latter-day historians of their actions—may avoid a simplistic assumption of the total immanence of any singular period or culture, whether it be that of a past we are trying to recapture or a present whose framework we are trying to escape. There may be no transcendent point hovering above both periods in which absolute validity can be located, or at least not one to which we can honestly claim access. But insofar as each can in some way transcend the other, together they provide an antidote to the fantasy of self-sufficient immanence and cultural or temporal incommensurability. Or to put it in the anthropological terms we have already encountered, the interplay between emic and etic meaning, rendered ironic by the passage of historical time, provides a closer approximation of valid—or at least more complexly mediated—knowledge than either one by itself.

In the next essay, "Walter Benjamin and Isaiah Berlin: Modes of Jewish Intellectual Life in the 20th Century,"[79] the relationship between validity and genesis may seem only indirectly addressed. It focuses on the ways in which intellectual historians often deploy, sometimes consciously, sometimes not, metaphorical oppositions to epitomize the combination of substantive ideas, rhetorical styles, and personal life histories of the figures we treat. Frankly acknowledging the projection of the historian's categories onto intellectuals who were themselves rarely, if ever, aware of their representative character, the essay does not, however, assume that such metaphoric oppositions represent a finite repertoire of formal narrative prefigurations in the transcendentalizing manner of Hayden White. Instead, it considers a limited number of metaphoric oppositions—hedgehog/fox, jester/priest, husband/lover, parvenu/pariah, and producer/rentier—that can serve as heuristically suggestive ways of organizing our representations of past actors and their legacies. When we register the tacit effect such oppositions can have on the reception of ideas and intellectuals, we are tacitly conceding that the tension between genesis and validity does not always dominate our intercourse with the past. Or more precisely, we are acknowledging that even when intellectual historians do judge certain ideas as successfully transcending their context of origin and being still relevant today, our choices may well be refracted through tacit preferences for styles of thought and comportment rather than dependent on the unvarnished validity of the ideas themselves. That is, we need to pay attention not only to contexts of genesis but also to contexts of reception, including our own.

Fittingly, the next essay analyzes the work of Hans Blumenberg, the hybrid German philosopher/historian of ideas, who insisted on the history of metaphors—what he called "metaphorology"[80]—as no less important a theme for intellectual historians than the history of concepts. "Against Rigor: Hans Blumenberg on Freud and Arendt"[81] was occasioned by Blumenberg's posthumously published critique of what he saw as the absolute commitment to truth telling, the consequences be damned, in Freud's critique of Moses's promulgation of monotheism and Arendt's reaction to the Eichmann trial in Jerusalem.[82] The provocation of his essay is Blumenberg's chastisement of his protagonists for their alleged robbing the Jewish people of two of their most fundamental myths, or at least ones that made possible the Zionist project that had succeeded in the wake of the Holocaust. Although Blumenberg's characterization of the positions he criticizes, especially Arendt's, may be only partially persuasive, his argument against what he sees as an excessively rigorous insistence on truth-telling with no regard for consequences is very suggestive. But ironically, Blumenberg's claim that rhetoric, myth, and metaphor can never be swept aside in the name of dialectic, history, and literal prose is itself presented with transcendent assurance. Although answers change, he tells us, the perennial questions abide; although exhausted myths are debunked, new ones inevitably arise in their place; although we cannot ever translate "absolute metaphors" into straightforward concepts, we always need to create meaning to fill the void left behind by the absolute impenetrability of reality.

Blumenberg, it might be concluded, was as much of a seeker after fundamental truths as the figures whose rigorism he bemoans. And it is certainly hard to deny that his work, whose anthropological ambitions he willingly confesses,[83] rarely focuses on the concrete genetic circumstances—social, psychological, or political—that might account for the rise and fall of the ideas he discusses. New answers to perennial questions happen when the old ones lose their power to persuade, he argues, but the questions remain. Despite his disdain for the relativizing implications of contextualism, his own work, or at least his oddly vehement disdain for Freud's and Arendt's undercutting of allegedly foundational Jewish myths, itself cries out for some genetic explanation. The essay tentatively explores the circumstances that may have provoked Blumenberg to direct his ire against what he saw, correctly or not, as their misplaced insistence on telling the truth, no matter the consequences.

Blumenberg's metaphorology makes an appearance in the next essay, "Hey! What's the Big Idea? Ruminations on the Question of Scale in Intellectual History."[84] But its primary focus is on recent attempts by the intellectual historian David Armitage and others to restore respect for a transhistorical "history of ideas," which would trace the fortunes of "big ideas" over long periods of time.[85] Against the resistance of both contextualists, who stress the concrete circumstances in which ideas emerge and are deployed, and textualists, who resist the disembedding of ideas from the rhetorical and material vehicles of their expression, they emphasize the value of narrating the fortunes of ideas that transcend their origins and reappear in more than one textual form. Although the philosophical question of their "validity" or truth value cannot be answered by reference to their endurance, at least the possibility of "transcendence" is affirmed. Here that elusive term does not indicate eternal truth beyond an immanent frame, or radical events that puncture the historicist narrative, but rather the ability of ideas to survive and develop beyond the boundaries of their genetic context.

Such ideas, however, should not be understood to possess a constant essence in which the ambiguities of usage are suppressed nor as having a normative meaning that can be found in their etymological origins. Equally problematic is the assumption that their present meaning can be understood as the one to which they were inherently moving with some sort of teleological purpose. The history of "big ideas" follows the lead of the so-called history of concepts developed by Reinhart Koselleck and his colleagues, who focus on the inevitable ambiguities over time of the terms whose history is traced. As in the case of Blumenberg's metaphorological paradigms, there is a dialectic of continuity and discontinuity in the history of big ideas that prevents them from congealing into an essential or normative version, fixed like a dictionary definition. Instead, their interplay with other concepts in concrete semantic force fields means their meaning is always relational rather than stipulative.

The reservation that is expressed in the "Hey!" before the question "What's the big idea?" in the essay's title echoes an argument that was already broached in "Historical Explanation and the Event": there has to be some place for the unexpected emergence of new ideas, which can be understood as "advents" that cannot be smoothly folded into long-range histories, even nonteleological ones. Here Foucault's sensitivity to ruptures in historical continuity, which he understands in terms of Nietzsche's genealogical method, fits well with Koselleck's interest in "concepts of the future," which seed the ground for what is to come rather than merely shuffling the cards dealt by the past.

The event as a rupture in temporal continuity returns to prominence in the subsequent essay, "Fidelity to the Event? Lukács' *History and Class Consciousness* and the Russian Revolution."[86] Here the Hegelian imbuing of history with transcendent meaning, which Ian Hunter problematically attributes to all critiques of radical contextualism, does, in fact, accurately describe the alternative to relativist contextualization defended in *History and Class Consciousness*. Lukács's wager that something called "world history" would ultimately overcome the "antinomies of bourgeois thought" through the realization of a communist society without contradiction was an explicit attempt to immanentize validity in a redeemed future. And it certainly gave him warrant to believe that he belonged not to an academic clerisy but to a vanguard party with, to recall Hunter's phrase, "charismatic insight into a higher form of self and society."[87]

From what can called be "our" current vantage point—or rather points, because there is today no unified "we" that can retrospectively judge the past from a single point of view—Lukács's bet appears to have been lost. Because world history has not shown itself to be a salvific narrative—indeed not a coherent metanarrative of any kind—the essay concludes that the intellectual foundations of *History and Class Consciousness* have crumbled. It is for this reason that later Marxists such as Alain Badiou and Slavoj Žižek, who ruefully acknowledge that outcome, have attempted to turn 1917 into an "event" that ruptured the course of history rather than an episode in its triumphalist unfolding, an event to which the current revolutionary needs to be "faithful" despite everything. This final move, the essay concludes, relies on a secular version of the theological notion of a *figura*, which is no less problematic than the redemptive narration it seeks to replace.

The next essay deals not with the writing of historical narratives but rather the validity of photographic evidence, an issue which has increasingly troubled historians of the recent past. Growing out of my earlier interests in visuality and mendacity, "Can Photographs Lie? Reflections on a Perennial Anxiety"[88] introduces some unexpected turns in the dialectic of genesis and validity. Insofar as photographs—aside from those that are deliberately doctored or digitally manipulated—are normally understood to rely on the indexical trace of the objects or events they capture on film, they are conventionally assumed to be truthful representations of what they depict. Their validity, such as it is, derives not from their access to transcendent, immutable values with claims to universality, but rather to their faithful or "mimetic" representation of what was once present in front of the camera. Rather than timeless truths, these are moments—at times "decisive," if Henri Cartier-Bresson is right—plucked from the ongoing temporal flow and allowed to survive as reified images.

For a photograph to lie, however, normally requires a linguistic supplement, insofar as lies, as opposed to the deceptions of our senses that exist in nature, are speech acts involving a motivation to say what is not the case with the goal of deliberately misleading an interlocutor. Because of this nonvisual supplement, it is sometimes argued that photographs by themselves cannot lie. But if we take seriously the contexts in which they are produced and received, and then acknowledge the porosity of the boundary between the image as such and those enabling contexts—what Derrida called the interpenetration of the *ergon* and the *parergon*—we are left with the conclusion that photographs, understood in their full complexity, are indeed capable of a kind of mendacity.

The possible role of photographic images for historians is addressed from a very different perspective in the next essay, "Sublime Historical Experience, Real Presence, and Photography."[89] It examines Frank Ankersmit's plea for the elevation of a certain, albeit rare, experience that historians can have with the past through direct contact with its residues, an experience he calls sublime because it transcends conventional historical narratives and brackets questions of their intersubjective validation. It implicitly evokes theological notions of "real presence" in which the Eucharist is more than a symbolic or metaphoric representation of the body of Christ, but is somehow its miraculous incarnation. Like an "event" in the discourse discussed in previous essays, an interruption in normal temporal continuity, sublime historical experience resists both the genetic reduction of radical contextualization and the imposition in the present of a finite menu of narrative forms on the contingency of the past. Drawing on Georges Didi-Huberman's analysis in *Images in Spite of All* of four remarkable photographs taken surreptitiously by inmates in Auschwitz, the essay seeks to demonstrate the plausibility of Ankersmit's idiosyncratic argument. But it does so with the intention of widening the scope of "sublime historical experiences" to include traumatic events, rather than being restricted, as they are in Ankersmit's account, to ones that depend on a nostalgic longing for a lost past. It also questions his too-hasty dismissal of the ways in which historians try to validate the truth of their interpretations in favor of Heidegger's *aletheia* or truth as unconcealment.

Historians are not the only scholars who have to grapple with the dialectic of genesis and validity, context and transcendence. Sociologists, especially those who seek to make sense of modernity as a whole, face similar challenges. "The Heroism of Modern Life and the Sociology of Modernization: Durkheim, Weber, and Simmel" examines the efforts made by three pioneers of the discipline, Emile Durkheim, Max Weber, and Georg Simmel, to characterize the era in which they were living—and which in many respects remains our own.[90] The essay takes its cue from Foucault's idiosyncratic gloss on Baudelaire's notion of "the heroism of modern life" as the will to heroize the present, albeit ironically. Distinguishing between varieties of heroism, including Nietzsche's exceptional individuals and Hegel's world-historical figures, it argues that a certain ascetic self-distancing characterizes the heroic stance of the founding fathers of modern sociology, whose ironic reflexivity inoculates them against both resignation and the lure of easy remedies for modernity's shortcomings.

Here the issue of genesis and validity takes a somewhat unusual form. For all their insistence on the value-free, scientific credentials of their discipline, for all their aspirations to wrest order from contingency, sociologists cannot entirely escape the gravitational pull of the concrete contexts out of which they come. They may seek enduring patterns, formal regularities or relational constants amid the flux, or at least posit ideal types in Weber's sense of heuristic conceptualizations that can overcome the apparently random chaos of history, but they cannot entirely escape their own embeddedness in the dynamic world they seek to examine from afar. Their ironic reflexivity about their situation, however, can give them some transcendent distance from a merely affirmative relationship to the societies they seek to understand. Their heroism, such as it is, resides in their acceptance of this dual role as both outside and inside the societies they interpret, emic participants as well as etic observers.

The image of the individual sociologist heroically registering his or her own contextual situatedness may not, however, fully acknowledge the intersubjective constraints of the increasingly professional institution to which he or she belongs. The community of professional historians plays the same role in sharing responsibility for judging the validity claims of any representation of the past. The next essay, "Historical Truth and the Truthfulness of Historians" explores the implications of belonging to such a community for the perennial issue of discriminating true from false historical accounts.[91] It begins by pitting two extreme but ultimately untenable positions against each other: a naive realism that says history as post-facto narrative can somehow capture the past "as it actually was," and a no less simple-minded conventionalism that conflates historical and fictional narrative and fails to acknowledge the check on unfettered historical invention placed by the evidentiary record of the past and the stubborn effect it still has on the present.

Turning to three alternatives that acknowledge the impossibility of absolute certitude, but also the distinction between fictional and historical narrative, the essay examines what it calls "falsificationism," "the new experientialism," and "institutional justificationism." The first argues that historical narratives cannot be verified by showing that they "accurately" depict or represent the past, but that some can at least be falsified by measuring them against contradictory evidence. The second, already encountered in discussions of Ankersmit's work, brackets the question of truth or falsehood and focuses instead on the possibility of sublime historical experiences. The third turns to the community of historians offering truthfully defended justifications for their accounts and reaching conclusions, always tentative, about which to prefer.[92] In terms of the genesis/validity tension, it places whatever validation historical narratives might claim to have in the practice of such a community, whose intersubjective judgment is more meaningful than any putative fit between a narrative and the happenings in the past it tries to represent, interpret, and perhaps judge. Here the validity of historical accounts, such as it is, is not understood to transcend the genetic contexts out of which they emerge—the community of historians doing the research and writing about the past understood as itself such a context—but is dependent on their institutional protocols and moral commitment to truth-telling. Or rather, it is dependent on both them and the stubborn evidentiary residues of a past that never entirely disappears, at least in terms of its effects on the present and stubborn survival into the future.

The penultimate entry in the collection, "Theory and Philosophy: Antonyms in Our Semantic Field?,"[93] revisits my earlier essay "For Theory,"[94] which situated that concept in a field of its putative antonyms, such as practice, experience, and close reading. One antonym that I neglected was "philosophy," which has recently come into play as the main "other" of theory. Traditionally, what has been called philosophy has resisted its reduction to an expression of personal beliefs, communal worldviews, or social causes, preferring to identify its elusive goal with absolute knowledge or eternal values.

Or to put it differently, it has felt more comfortable residing in the nowhere of impersonal Mind rather than the various somewheres of different human minds. This resistance has meant, among other things, bracketing the mediating refractions of vernacular languages and searching for a neutral metalanguage or a universal symbolic code. What has recently come to be called "theory," in contrast, has taken on board many of the genetic arguments about the inevitable situatedness of ideas in contexts of power, desire, and cultural diversity. Refusing, however, to lament the relativistic implications of "psychologism," it has drawn much of its energy from the critique of unmarked Western, male, heteronormative assumptions underlying the transcendent claims of traditional philosophy.

The essay concludes, as do many of its predecessors, by refusing to come down firmly on the side of either genetic contextualism or transcendent validity. Instead, it urges an ongoing practice of mutual enrichment through receptive reflexivity about the value of each position. In other words, it betrays the characteristic hesitancy of intellectual history to speak authoritatively on "the last things" that more directly occupy many of the thinkers whose histories we attempt to write. What it offers is a less ambitious but still valuable perspective on the various ways in which the contest has been waged in different guises.

The final essay in the collection, previously unpublished, is "The Weaponization of Free Speech." It was prepared for a workshop at Dartmouth on "Truth, Power, and the Foundations of Democracy" convened in the summer of 2019 by David Plunkett and Russell Muirhead. Here the transcendent idea in question is the protection of uncensored free speech, which is often defended as an unimpeachable human right. For those who resist free speech purism, however, differing contexts or domains of application and the competing claims of potentially conflicting rights have often been marshaled to challenge the "absolutism" of the principle. The essay focuses instead on what it calls "teleological contexts," the larger purposes that are allegedly served by unimpeded speech. These include the objective quest for truth, the public expression of autonomous interiority, the exercise of intersubjective performativity, and the enrichment of cultural meaning. Because free speech is always in the service of an ulterior purpose, its alleged "weaponization" in the service of narrow political ends fails to acknowledge that it always has to be justified in terms of extrinsic teleological functions. In this case, genetic contexts, we might say with a nod to Aristotle, include final causes as well as efficient, formal, and material ones. Although free speech has become a principle that has apparently transcended all of its efficient genetic contexts, it is important to acknowledge that the purposes it is designed to serve can never be forgotten in any defense of its abiding value.

In conclusion, two lessons seem especially worth highlighting. The first is that it is possible to transcend genetic contexts without assuming the only alternative is the assertion of universal, absolute, timeless validity. That is, the synchronic contact between two different cultures with their own value systems and cognitive inclinations may allow members of each to see beyond the horizon of their specific milieu. The diachronic contact between past and present may also produce a similar result, with the arrow of transcendence pointing in both directions. Hans-Georg Gadamer's celebrated metaphor of a "fusion of horizons" may be too harmonistic a way to capture the critical potential in such contact, too positive a reconciliation of dialectical negations. But even when the dialectic is a negative one, there may well be a learning process that ensues. And in certain very different cases, the incursion of an unexpected "event" can serve as an "advent" that bursts the confines of any horizon, any immanent frame, and introduces the radically new into history.

The second lesson is that rather than always relativizing and parochializing ideas, attention to genetic context can sometimes bestow on them a certain expressive validation, albeit not necessarily absolute for all times and places. This can happen in two ways. First, it can arise from accepting the authority of experience, in which the legitimacy of an idea is taken to arise from the lives of those who espouse it or the culture out of which it comes. Understood in terms of historical method, this authority then enables the direct inheritors of a tradition to enter it from a sympathetic position denied those who approach it from the outside. Native speakers of a language can, it is argued, understand nuances of texts that are lost in translation or missed by those who come to them with imperfect mastery of a second language.

Taken to an extreme in what might be called a vulgar identity politics version of historical epistemology, this assumption can, however, lead to a simplistic faith in the inherent superiority of "speaking azza" against all outsiders who merely "speak for" others. It can ignore the metonymic identification of the group with its most self-conscious members, which can reintroduce a moment of theoretical transcendence, by stressing their "organic" roots in the community or class they represent. It can draw on a dubious elevation of the "authentic" insider over the allegedly inferior understanding of the alien outsider.[95] But when less self-righteously mobilized to acknowledge the value of emic know-how over etic observational knowledge, it can serve as a check on the imperialist imposition of categories from the outside, which places the ideas or values of one context over another.

The other way we have seen validity grounded in context concerns what might be called the restricted public sphere of credentialed researchers, whose judgment, however tentative and open to revision, provides the most persuasive standard for truth-telling about the past. When we say colloquially "History will judge," we are really saying that whatever authority historical judgments may plausibly earn is rooted in the protocols and institutions that bind together an intersubjective community capable of reasoning together.[96] Although such judgments are never absolute and always need to be defended against the weight of new evidence, different interpretative arguments, and evolving narrative vantage points, they are still grounded in the contentious community of historians who continue to weigh their merits. It is my hope, let me end this introduction by admitting, that this collection will add something to that ongoing conversation and stimulate the participants who follow to reach insights that will transcend my own.

CHAPTER 1

Impudent Claims and Loathsome Questions: Intellectual History as Judgment of the Past

On November 14, 1956, Theodor W. Adorno addressed a conference in Berlin on the 125th anniversary of Hegel's death. He began by decrying the genre that has come to be called an "appreciation" (*Würdigung*) in which the speaker sums up the lasting achievements of the figure celebrated. "It makes the impudent claim," Adorno charged, "that because one has the dubious good fortune to live later, and because one has a professional interest in the person one is to talk about, one can sovereignly assign the dead person his place, thereby in some sense elevating oneself above him. This arrogance echoes in the loathsome question of what in Kant, and now Hegel as well, has any meaning for the present—and even the so-called Hegel renaissance began half a century ago with a book by Benedetto Croce that undertook to distinguish between what was living and what was dead in Hegel." Proceeding in this fashion, Adorno went on, prevents us from asking the converse question: "what the present means in the face of Hegel.... All appreciations of Hegel fail from the start to capture the seriousness and cogency of Hegel's philosophy by practicing on him what he called, with appropriate disdain, a philosophy of perspectives."[1]

Whether or not one has to then judge the present specifically from Hegel's own super-perspective, that of the Absolute Spirit, is an issue I want to leave aside. What I would prefer to address instead is the challenge presented to intellectual history as a whole by Adorno's critique of the "impudent claim" to superiority by virtue of posterity and the "loathsome question" of the meaning of the past entirely "for us." Can we, in other words, avoid in this day and age of identity politics and freely acknowledged subject positions the pressure to adopt a historiography of finite, situated perspectives? Can we find a way out of the quicksand of what David Simpson calls "situatedness, or why we keep saying where we're coming from"?[2]

Narcissistic presentism is, of course, a perennial problem in all historical analysis, and in one form or another cannot be entirely avoided. That is, the questions we ask and the answers we tend to find persuasive cannot be disentangled from the exigencies of our present condition, assuming of course that there exists a collective "we" whose current state of mind influences these things in a uniform way. This is, needless to say, a very large assumption, but even if we challenge a transcendental notion of the current historical observer and rest content with a multiplicity of different present-day "we's," each bringing its own interests, assumptions, and needs to the table, the power of the present is hard to gainsay. The linguistic turn has made us all sensitive to the current tropological emplotments, as Hayden White has called them, that color our narratives of all history, intellectual or otherwise. And commentators like Dominick LaCapra have made us aware as well of the transferential projections that are inevitable impediments to an unmediated relation to the past. These involve, so it would seem, an inevitably moral dimension in our reconstruction of the past.

But are they so overpowering that we are utterly at their mercy in responding to and learning from that past? And are we inevitably forced to impose our standards of what is still relevant and alive in the thought we study, our values about what ideas are "merely historical" and what are of current and perhaps even future viability? Must we write "sovereign appreciations" in which we assign moral grades as well as acknowledgments of the vitality of the work we examine? These questions, which might be asked of all historical inquiry, are especially fraught for intellectual historians. As Peter Gordon has recently argued in his trenchant analysis of the Davos Debate between Ernst Cassirer and Martin Heidegger in 1931, there is a tacit tension between the contextual and transcendental impulses in the intellectual historian's recovery of past thought.[3] That is, we are torn between, on the one hand, understanding it as a symptom of or generated by or indirectly reflecting—the formula is always hard to pin down—something larger or more encompassing that we construe as its historical context and, on the other hand, finding in it perennial lessons, either inspirational or cautionary, as well as still plausible resources for addressing problems in the present. The two are not entirely at odds, but they do not always fit easily together.

Broadly speaking, the contextual impulse is accompanied by a tacit admission of the validity or plausibility or at least comprehensibility of ideas in their original context, which can imply a certain forgiveness if they fail to live up to later standards, either epistemological or normative. That is, contextualization and value relativism are often cozy bedfellows. Explaining and pardoning often, as we know, go together, at least if the explanation depends on a symptomatic reading of a larger context that limits individual responsibility. The historian eschews the role of judge or scold and tries to empathize as best as she might with the figures of a past era, whose horizons were more circumscribed than our own, or at least different from them.

The opposite impulse, valorizing the transcendental implications of ideas, generally betokens a willingness to risk seeing the present as superior to the past in terms of solving problems or learning moral lessons or tolerating differences. It can also be more open to looking for a pattern of ascent in history, reading the story that includes both of our points in time as a meaningful whole, a process of enlightenment or education or the accumulation of experiential wisdom. Sometimes this means a loss of false hopes and the rejection of utopian dreams rather than a faith in their realization, but it still involves privileging the present over the past.

Hegel, to come back to our point of departure, can at times be marshaled on the side of either position. That is, his insistence that the truth manifests itself least in some measure in all previous moments in the grand narrative of history prevents him from judging the past as entirely benighted and morally deficient. The temporalized theodicy in his attitude toward error and partiality means that he shares with contextualists a refusal to judge entirely by current standards, resisting the claim that enlightenment comes only late to those of us lucky enough to live in the present. But conversely, he is also willing to narrate that grand story in ways that infuse it with a transcendental meaning, allowing Minerva's owl the special wisdom of retrospection, avoiding the relativism that too insistent a contextualizing historicism would abet. Thus if world history can be seen as the world court, in the famous phrase from Schiller he adopted, we are the judge and jury, at least until we are replaced by another generation later on the bench.

Of late, there has been a manifest willingness to adopt that exalted role on the part of certain Anglo-American intellectual historians, who have reacted with scarcely disguised delight at the passing of a moment in cultural cum political fashion that we can roughly call Marxist deconstruction or left post-structuralism. Although loath to adopt anything so grandiose as a Hegelian narrative of rational dialectical development, they nonetheless share an identification with Minerva's feathered arbiter of the results as they see them. Most prominent among them are Tony Judt, Mark Lilla, and Richard Wolin. Identifying themselves with a version of Enlightenment liberalism that was itself on the defensive during the heyday of that fashion, they have taken their vengeance against a group of thinkers whose political judgments now seem more dubious than they did a generation ago and whose assault on the pieties of liberal bourgeois thought can be blamed for their political mistakes. In works like *Past Imperfect*, *The Reckless Mind*, and *The Seduction of Unreason*, they have charged that these intellectuals were shockingly irresponsible at best and tyrannophile dupes seduced by the lure of power at worst.[4] I don't want now to contest their readings or enter into an extended defense of the figures I have been drawn to most frequently in my own work. Many of the points they make are, in fact, worth taking seriously, at least by those who want to fashion a politics today that learns from past experiments. Rather, what I want to focus on is a larger issue: the assumption that historians are wise to pass such moral judgments on their subjects, allowing themselves to ask the "loathsome questions" and making the "impudent claims" Adorno so disliked in the arrogant "appreciations" of Hegel he tried to resist.

One way to address this question is to probe the status of experience in historical thinking, something I sought to do in my book on *Songs of Experience*.[5] After dealing with Dilthey and Collingwood and their ultimately unsuccessful attempts to conceptualize the primary task of the historian as re-experiencing or re-enacting the *Erlebnis* of actors in the past, I looked at the more recent debate between Joan Scott and John Toews over the implications of the linguistic turn for the question of experience. I finished with a short discussion of Frank Ankersmit's defense of what he calls, to cite the title of the book he was about to publish, "sublime historical experience."[6] Arguing against what he sees as the presentist linguistic transcendentalism of Hayden White and Richard Rorty, constructivists who privilege the current cultural context or the tropological imposition of the historian's own emplotments on a past that lies helpless and passive before his sovereign gaze, Ankersmit also wants to avoid the older and widely discredited objectivism that thinks it can access that past as it actually was. Instead, he seeks to liberate a notion of historical experience that is more akin to aesthetics than anything epistemological, one that inspired the great Dutch historian Johan Huizinga, the author of *The Waning of the Middle Ages*.

For Huizinga, reconstructive historical imagination in the present is complemented by what he calls an "historical sensation" of the past, which is not akin to the psychological re-experiencing, reliving, or reenacting of someone's past experience or thoughts. It is rather one of many variants of ecstasies, of an experience of truth that is given to the human being:

> the object of this sensation are not individual human beings, nor human lives or human thoughts insofar as these possess discernible contours. It can hardly be called an image what the mind forms here or undergoes. Insofar as it takes on any distinct form at all, this form remains composite and vague. . . . This contact with the past, which is accompanied by the absolute conviction of complete authenticity and truth, can be provoked by a line from a chronicle, by an engraving, a few sounds from an old song. It is not an element that the author writing in the past deliberately puts down in his work. It is "behind" and not "in" the book that the past has left us.[7]

For Ankersmit, Huizinga's somewhat inchoate idea of a sudden illumination of the past precipitated by an unexpected encounter with some trace or residue of radical otherness provides a model for historical experience that is neither dominated by the present nor entirely reducible to the recovery of a past experience that allows itself to be recaptured. It is more akin to that intimation of something there, but impossible to represent that the aesthetics of the sublime tries to capture or at least toward which it gestures. It resists domesticating and mastering the other it cannot fully represent by fully historicizing the residues in a comfortably smooth context that reduces them to exemplars or symptoms or instances of an era whose complexities and contradictions are suppressed. Nor, however, does it judge them by the standards of the present or see them as nothing but projections of current rhetorical or ideological needs. Instead, it pays heed to their mysterious effect on us as objects that produce new experiences rather than merely confirm the ones we already have had.

There is a lot more that can be said about Ankersmit's attempt to validate sublime historical experience and keep at bay the inevitable epistemological questions that cannot be entirely brushed aside by historians who want to evaluate the accounts we write after Huizinga's historical sensations have passed and we sit down to convey them to others in meaningful form. What his version of historical experience does allow us to understand, broadly speaking, is that the choice Peter Gordon poses between transcendental presentism and contextualizing historicism has to be supplemented by a third relationship to the past. That is, it alerts us to the possibility that we are located in a triangulated constellation with three poles: (1) the past as an englobing and perhaps coherent context that we can recapture and then employ to situate and make meaningful intellectual production that we may not find plausible by contemporary standards; (2) the present as the place where we are ourselves inevitably located and from which our judgments, implicit or explicit, flow, a present in which paradoxically we cannot avoid holding beliefs as if they were more than just expressions of our own limited horizons; and (3) perhaps most elusively, the experience of a radically incommensurable past that defies both reassuring contextualization in terms of an outdated coherent cultural whole, which we can comfortably reconstruct, and a no less easy dismissal according to current standards of truth or value that can be claimed to be superior to it. That is, it disrupts both the assumption that full narrative contextualization can be made of the past and that the present has the authority to judge the past rather than, as Adorno intimates in the case of Hegel, be judged by it. Such experiences, sublime or otherwise, are reminders that we come to history to be torn out of the complacency of the present, not to confirm our superiority by condescendingly assuming our ability to "appreciate," that is, judge it from our own perspective. In terms of intellectual history, this means opening ourselves to the possibility that even the most seemingly benighted errors of previous thinkers whose follies we think we have left behind may nonetheless still have something to teach us. Or more precisely, we may learn something from them, only if we learn how to open ourselves to the alterity of a past that resists domestication by either the powers of contextual historicism or transcendental moralizing.

CHAPTER 2

Historical Explanation and the Event: Reflections on the Limits of Contextualization

> Intellectuals are people who produce decontextualized ideas.
> —Randall Collins

For intellectual historians, no more powerful defense of the importance of contextual explanation has been launched than that mounted a generation ago by Quentin Skinner, J. G. A. Pocock, and their colleagues in the so-called Cambridge School of intellectual history.[1] Targeting the anachronistic presentism that encouraged historians to designate past thinkers precursors of later movements that were not yet in self-conscious existence, Skinner urged them to situate intellectuals and texts in their immediate contexts of generation and reception. Arguing against the fallacy of attributing a timeless essence to concepts or ideas that emerged only in particular historical circumstances, he warned against isolating even perennial keywords, such as those traced by Raymond Williams, from the changing discursive constellations in which they were situated.[2] Scorning the quest for a usable past that would be relevant to current concerns, he urged historians to honor the radical otherness of the past.

It was crucial, Skinner argued, to recover the original matrix of conventions and assumptions out of which a text emerged and into which it was inserted. The intention of the author could not be understood from the words in the text alone, what speech act theorists called their locutionary meaning, but could only be recovered when their illocutionary or performative force was also grasped. That is, texts were meant to *do* something, to have an effect on the world, not merely to describe it or express the ideas of their authors. They were communicative *acts* dependent on the conventions and usages of their day in order to be effective. They contained arguments meant to persuade, not merely propositions about the world or expressions of inner states of mind. Whether or not they achieved what they set out to do—their perlocutionary effect—was another question. But unless we appreciated what an author like, say, Hobbes or Locke had intended to accomplish with his intervention in the discourse of his time, we were in danger of missing the true historical meaning of his or her efforts. In other words, every text had to be understood finitely, but holistically, as a response to the unanswered or unsatisfactorily answered questions of the day, not as a contribution to an omnitemporal conversation outside of any historical context.

Although there may well be a surplus of meaning in a text beyond the author's intention—a point Skinner willingly granted[3]—the historically productive point of departure had to be the intentionality of the author understood as embedded in a particular force field of discursive relations. Radical contextualism, which has become such a bugaboo for philosophers anxious to avoid relativism and defend transcendental truths, was thus not a problem for historians dedicated to telling particular, contingent stories about the past.[4] Following the lead of anthropologists like Clifford Geertz with his celebrated exhortation to interpret the dense webs of relatively coherent meaning that we call culture, historians should set out to make sense of what might seem like isolated facts, events, actions, and ideas within the horizon of relations in which they were situated. The more saturated the context—the thicker the description, in the phrase that Geertz took from Max Weber and made famous—the richer the interpretive and explanatory payoff.

Although Skinner was by no means without his critics—and we will come to some of their objections in a moment—his general brief for contextualization as the historian's chief modus operandi has been widely influential, and not only among intellectual historians. Thus, to take a salient example, the social historian William Sewell, Jr., in his recent *Logics of History*, claims that historians must take seriously the heterogeneity of time, respecting the differences that separate one period from another, and adds: "Temporal heterogeneity also implies that understanding or explaining social practices requires *historical contextualization*. We cannot know what an act or utterance means and what its consequences might be without knowing the semantics, the technologies, the conventions—in brief, the logics—that characterize the world in which the action takes place. Historians tend to explain things not by subsuming them under a general or 'covering' law but by relating them to their context."[5] Or to take another typical example, John Lewis Gaddis writes in *The Landscape of History*, "Causes always have contexts, and to know the former we must understand the latter. Indeed I would go so far as to define the word 'context' as the dependency of sufficient causes upon necessary causes; or, in Bloch's terms, of the exceptional upon the general. For while context does not directly *cause* what happens, it can certainly determine consequences."[6]

But what it may mean to "relate" an idea, a practice, or an event to its context is by no means self-evident, nor is the claim that exceptions "depend" on general conditions. As a result, a number of cogent objections have been introduced to the overreliance on contextualization as the privileged method of historical inquiry, understood to extend beyond the sphere of intellectual history narrowly defined. First of all, the issue of how historians can reliably reconstruct the past context that will serve as the ultimate explanatory foundation of their narratives has been raised by those who argue that only through the textual residues of the past can we recover putative contexts.[7] The result, they point out, is an inevitable circularity between texts and contexts that prevents the latter from becoming the prior determining factor. In other words, we may not be able to understand a text or document without contextualizing it, but contexts are themselves preserved only in textual or documentary residues, even if we expand the latter to include nonlinguistic traces of the past. And those texts need to be interpreted in the present to establish the putative past context that will then be available to explain still other texts.

Because the interpretation of these texts and documents has to take place in the present, so runs a second objection, it will be necessary to employ theoretical tools or at least hermeneutic insights brought to the table by the contemporary historian. The documents that reveal contexts never simply speak for themselves without at least being questioned by their present readers. Benedetto Croce's oft-repeated dictum that "all history is contemporary history" implies that no past context is manifest without its current reconstruction, which is an active, not passive process. As Hayden White has noted, "Every contextualization requires, as a condition of its enablement as a representational or an explanatory strategy, a formalist component, which is to say, a theoretical model on the basis of which, first, to distinguish contexts from the entities inhabiting them; second, to generate hypotheses about the nature of the relations between the entities and the contexts thus distinguished; and third, to discriminate between radical, primary, and determining transformations of these relationships and what are only secondary, superficial, or local changes in them."[8] Skinner's use of the speech act theory of J. L. Austin and John Searle would be an example of the tacit formalism of which White speaks. It certainly wasn't in the vocabulary of the early modern figures whose illocutionary intentions he wants to recover.

Moreover, despite the exhortation to honor the historical uniqueness of the period we are studying, which as we've seen motivated Skinner's persuasive denunciation of precursoritis, the assumption that we can locate the proper explanatory context after the fact may also tacitly be at odds with the self-understanding of the participants at the time, a self-understanding that by definition lacks the perspective of the later historian. As the anthropologist Vincent Crapanzano has noted, "Whatever their objective claims, contextualizations are never neutral. They always have an imperative function; they tell us how the exchange they 'enclose' is to be read. They confirm, thereby, the theoretical underpinning of—the rationalizations for—such instructions."[9] Skinner, to be sure, has willingly conceded to his critics that "we inevitably approach the past in the light of contemporary paradigms and presuppositions, the influence of which may easily serve to mislead us at every turn." But as the word "mislead" suggests, he assumes there are ways to avoid those paradigms and presuppositions to gain access to the original intention of the authors he studies: "Such skepticism strikes me as unhelpfully hyperbolical, especially when we reflect that even animals are sometimes capable of recovering the intention with which people act."[10]

A still more telling criticism concerns the question of how to determine what the relevant context will be, if we acknowledge the impossibility of positing a single, homogeneous discursive whole in which texts might be situated. As Dominick LaCapra has warned, "Overcontextualization often occludes the problem of the very grounds on which to motivate a selection of pertinent contexts.... The farther back one goes in time, the less obvious the contexts informing discourse tend to become, and the more difficult it may be, at least in a technical, philological sense, to reconstruct them."[11] In other words, there is no reason to assume that the map of relevant contexts will look like a Russian matryoshka doll in which one is comfortably nested in the other. The passage from micro to macro contexts is by no means always very smooth. Instead, it might be more plausible to acknowledge competing and nonhierarchically ranged contexts of varying size and gravitational force, which produced an overdetermined effect irreducible to any one dominant contextual influence.[12]

Issues of scale are also hard to ignore. That is, is the most potent context something as global as a historical epoch or chronotope? Or is the proper level that of a language, a religion, a class, or a nation-state? Or do we have to look at more proximate contexts, say, the precise social, political, or educational institutions in which the historical actor was embedded, the generation to which he or she belonged, or the family out of which he or she emerged? Can we make sense of, say, Freud's invention of psychoanalysis in terms of his training in medicine and Darwinian biology, his background as an assimilated Jew, his anger at his unheroic father, his acquaintance with literary traditions of the unconscious, his disillusionment with liberal politics and the image of rational man on which it was based, his strange friendship with Wilhelm Fliess, or the crisis of the bourgeois nuclear family? All of these, and many more, have been adduced at one time or another to unlock the mystery of his creativity. Is there any way to assign their relative weight, or must we simply accept Freud's own notion of overdetermination and say they were all in one way or another at play? Or to put it differently, may there be a dynamic force field of contending contexts, both synchronic and diachronic, that never fully resolves itself into a single meaningful whole with a clear order of influence?[13] Indeed, the very assumption that there is a single, monolithic "text" to be contextualized falters when we acknowledge that it may itself vary according to the context(s) of its reception, which often alters its boundaries and even content.

Skinner himself may have prematurely foreclosed the issue by contending that however complex the notion of a context may be, "we can readily single out the most crucial element in it. This is the fact that all serious utterances are characteristically intended as acts of communication."[14] Such a restrictive definition, however, makes very difficult any broader contextualist explanation that tries to go beyond the conscious intentions of actors to communicate meaning, as, for example, one that takes seriously the concept of ideology. Ideology is, to be sure, a highly fraught concept with many difficulties of its own, but to the extent that it interprets historical actions and beliefs in terms of hidden motives—for example, a covert agenda of promoting self-interest in the guise of universalism or a defensive response to psychological strain—it opens up the question of how to explain ideas and actions that seem to lack self-evident rationality. Skinner borrows a principle from Max Weber to address this challenge: "Unless we begin by assuming the agent's rationality, we leave ourselves with no means of explaining his behavior, or even of seeing exactly what there is to explain about it, if it should happen that he is not acting rationally."[15] Of course, such a response opens up the question of which standard of rationality we are attributing to the past agent and which standard we are employing in judging his actions as irrational today. For surely there is no self-evident transcendental version of rationality that can be applied ahistorically and across cultures under all circumstances. Once again we are in danger of imposing present criteria on a past that cannot be approached by completely bracketing our own beliefs, experiences, assumptions, values, and prejudices.

Another troubling issue, which is raised by Skinner's suggestive adoption of speech act theory, concerns the issue of dialogical—or even pluralogical—rather than monological discursive interactions. It may not be sufficient to posit a one-directional illocutionary performance, situated in a constellation of conventions, as the basis of the recovery of an explanatory context. For there are always multidirectional interactions that produce the meanings that emerge, or impede the ones that fail to emerge, from an event or episode. That is, one intention is always in play with others, and actions always engage with other actions, prior and posterior, which can easily lead to unintended consequences.[16] The level of pragmatic utterance is never fully beholden to the deeper level of structural regularities, linguistic or cultural, that constrain but cannot fully determine it. Another way to describe the effect of this dialectic is to stress the agonistic, competitive quality of many speech acts that are not necessarily designed to bring about a consensus or a Gadamerian fusion of horizons. At its most extreme, the effect is the heteroglossia of which Bakhtin has made us so aware, a condition of multiple, competing voices that may well invade the consciousness of individual speakers, rendering their own subjectivities less than perfectly integral and dispersing their intentions. From the point of view of the later historian, the difficulty this raises is the instability of the unified context in which what is to be explained can be meaningfully placed. A dialogic, often agonistic context is one always already fractured, even if all participants are likely to be observing meta-level rules and conventions that limit the chaos and turn noise into some degree of successful communication.

Many of these criticisms will be familiar to those who have followed the debate over contextualization and its limits stimulated in large measure by the very impressive body of work generated by the Cambridge School. In most cases, they focus on difficulties faced by the contemporary historian in gaining access to the past and reflecting on the evidence that exists in the present: how to establish contexts if their residues are themselves in texts that need to be stabilized and interpreted; how to decide which contexts are pertinent and provide plausible explanations; how to articulate the relationship among the sometimes incompatible contexts that might be adduced to explain a text; how to acknowledge the theoretical underpinnings, explicit or not, of our reconstruction of the past; how to be sensitive to the dialogical and even heteroglossic nature of the contexts that we do decide are most important; how to balance a belief that actors in the past are rational with a fear that the standard of rationality is one that we impose upon them in the present, and so on.

There is, however, another vital consideration that brings us back to the actual historical moment when events, actions, and thoughts themselves occurred rather than lets us focus solely on the challenges faced by contemporary historical reconstructions of that moment. It involves what might be called the nature of the historical reality that contextualization purports to explain. For rather than assuming that all actions, texts, figures, or episodes in the past can be equally elucidated by embedding them in what we have seen William Sewell call the "logics" of their context of production, we might usefully distinguish, at least heuristically, between those that might be and those that might not. To help us understand the distinction, I want to turn to the complex discourse about the "event" in recent French thought, which has introduced some fundamental challenges to the assumption that what happens in history is either an exemplar of a deeper, abiding structure or an element in a meaningful narrative in which every moment can be understood as an episode in that narrative.

A number of leading thinkers in the wake of what came to be called "the events" of 1968 expressed dissatisfaction with the hegemony of structuralism in France, which in the field of history was most explicitly identified with the so-called Annales School. Instead, they began to revise their estimation of the value of the very *histoire évenémentielle* that Fernand Braudel, Lucien Febvre, and their colleagues at the *Annales* had seen as superficial and of little interest. Philosophers like Jean-François Lyotard, Gilles Deleuze, Jean-Luc Nancy, Jacques Derrida, Michel Foucault, and Alain Badiou developed extensive analyses of "the event," which often drew on the insights of earlier theorists like Kierkegaard, Benjamin, Schmitt, and Heidegger. This is not the place to spell out all the implications of their recovery of this vexed concept, a task I have tackled elsewhere.[17] Suffice it to say that their target was not only the recurrent patterns beneath the surface that the structuralists had sought but also the conventional emplotted stories valued by traditional historians, who by and large understood events, at least significant ones, as hinge moments in their coherent narratives. Although often they imbued the "events" they celebrated with an almost religious aura of importance—Kierkegaard's notion of the Absolute, Benjamin's idea of messianic "now time," and Heidegger's concept of an *Ereignis* were often among their inspirations—their ruminations have implications for the more prosaic issue of historical contextualization.

To understand those implications, I want to turn to a lesser-known French theorist who has recently written with great insight on the same theme but without the quasi-religious, metaphysical pathos of many of the others: Claude Romano. In *L'Événement et le monde* and *L'Événement et le temps*, the first published in 1998, the second a year later,[18] Romano provided a fine-grained phenomenological analysis of the event as opposed to a mere happening or occurrence. Developing what he calls an "evential hermeneutics," he argues that there is a link between "event" and "advent," which in French also invokes the future (*avenir*). Advent, moreover, must be understood in connection with the unforetold adventure that it spawns. Rather than instances of a static ontology, events cum advents are more like what Nietzsche called "lightning flashes," which are radical breaks in the status quo. They happen without intentionality or preparation, befalling us rather than being caused by us.

How do they relate to the larger context into which they are inserted, a context that Romano calls "inner-worldly"? "It is always within a world, embedded in a causal framework," he writes, "that an event is able to appear with its own meaning, interpreted in the light of other events that determine its own meaning." Derived from a welter of prior possibilities, its context can be understood as "a particular *unity of meaning* in light of which events become comprehensible in their mutual articulation, a horizon of meaning through which they are illuminated—that is, as a thoroughly hermeneutic structure."[19] That contextual structure is one of essential iterability, in which repetition rather than novelty prevails. Here he sounds very much in tune with the general program of the Cambridge School and other historical contextualists, and as such he may be vulnerable to the same objections we have encountered above.

But Romano then develops his argument in a very different direction. All events might seem to be comprehensible in terms of their enabling contexts, "were it not for events that radically upend their contexts and, far from being submitted to a horizon of prior meanings, are themselves the origin of meaning for any interpretation, in that they can be understood less from the world that precedes them than from the posterity to which they give rise." World-establishing rather than innerworldly, they are "an-archic" in the sense that they have no prior *archēs* determining their meaning or producing their occurrence. Although an event is not utterly free of antecedent causation, its "causes do not explain it, or rather, if they 'explain' it, what they give a reason for is *only ever* the fact and not the *event* in its evential sense."[20] For Romano, "evential" as opposed to mere "evental" in the normal use of the term means bringing a cargo of new possibilities with it, which provide novelty and openness to a process that otherwise would always reduce to repetition of the same. To give an obvious example, no matter how much Christians looked for prefigural anticipations in what they called the "Old Testament," the events described in the "New Testament" were radical ruptures that opened up a future that was very different from the past.

Rather, however, than being utterly omnitemporal and outside of history, as some celebrants of events, such as Kierkegaard, assume, they should be understood as inaugurating their own history, as advents that open up possible adventures in a future not yet determined. Unlike a historical fact, which can be neatly identified with a single date in a time line of comparable facts, events are "not so much inscribed *in* time, as they are what *opens* time or *temporalizes* it."[21] Rather than the present or the past, their temporality is that of a future still to be realized, a latency that may or may not become manifest, a meaning that is still deferred. Or to put it in the terms of the speech act theory introduced by Skinner, the perlocutionary effect of texts that qualify as cultural events is irreducible to the illocutionary intent of their authors. As Romano puts it, "An 'intended meaning' and a language must 'precede' an act of speech, which would be impossible without them. However, speech, like an *event*, is irreducible to its own 'conditions' and annuls them in arising."[22]

Although Romano does not develop it, there may also be another way that events open up possibilities, ironically for the past, not the future. In discussing the ways in which radical catastrophes challenge an evolutionary notion of historical development in which everything that happens is already prepared by what preceded it, Slavoj Žižek reverses the normal order of first possibilities and then choices. Instead, catastrophic events—and, one might argue just as easily, emancipatory or redemptive ones—may have the opposite effect in which a choice or act "retroactively opens up its own possibility: the idea that the emergence of a radically New retroactively changes the past—not the actual past, of course (we are not in the realm of science fiction or counter-factual narratives), but past possibilities, or to put it in more formal terms, the value of modal propositions about the past."[23]

Events, in addition, happen for Romano not to subjects, strictly speaking, but to "advenants." Whereas the concept of a subject generally implies an enduring identity beneath all the accidents that befall it, an "advenant" comes to be only in the very process of becoming that allows a new event to be in excess of what has already occurred. What happens to the advenant is existentially transformative because the event that occurs cannot be indifferently witnessed from the outside; instead, he or she is fully implicated in it: "To be implicated oneself in what happens (to us) is to be capable of *experience* in the most fundamental sense, which does not refer to a modality of theoretical knowledge understood as the way a subject and object face each other, but rather undergoing a passage from self to self, which is inseparable from a constitutive alteration."[24] The world produced by events is thus one from which a more or less unified subject may, to be sure, emerge, but it is not one that he or she, already integrated, can intend or create. And indeed, when such a subject does emerge, it means the return of innerworldly repetition, for "an *advenant* can only be characterized as a 'subjectivity' when he is no longer himself: an *advenant*. Subjectivity is precisely that posture where he holds himself back from the possibility of being touched and upended by any event whatsoever."[25]

The quintessential instance of an event is birth itself, which is never constituted by the one who is born but is always something that happens to it, when it is not yet a subject, not yet an identity, not yet autonomous. Although for others it may be an innerworldly fact actively intended by the parents who bring it about and capable of being witnessed as such, for the one born, it is always a heteronomous gift, an origin that is never self-produced, never without its impersonal character. As such, it is the template for all later experiences of real events, which ironically free the self from its subjection to the past, from being a mere "subject" with its connotation of subjection.

The alteration takes place not only in the advenant, whose experience of events is transformative, but also in the world itself. To the extent that an event is irreducible to its enabling context, intellectual or artistic events are also best grasped in terms of what they make possible rather than what makes them possible. According to Romano, a work of art "cannot be understood in its singularity except from the posterity to which it gives rise, the refashioning it brings about in the forms, themes, and techniques of a period. A work of art cannot be understood within the artistic context in which it is born, which it necessarily transcends if it is an original work."[26] Ironically, it can be understood from a contextual point of view only as "im-possible" in the sense that it is not merely the realization of the prior possibilities that already exist in the world; instead, it is the source of utterly new possibilities that may in turn be either realized or surpassed by new events.

Although he does not explicitly draw on their work, Romano is expanding on insights that go back at least as far as Kant and were developed in the twentieth century by thinkers as different as Ernst Bloch and Hannah Arendt. In his efforts to avoid the determinist implications of overly rationalist metaphysics, especially Spinoza's, and allow a space for human ethical choice—a battle he fought with great determination during the so-called pantheism debate of the late eighteenth century[27]—Kant had insisted that a causality of freedom can interrupt the mechanical causality of nature, bringing something new into the world. Bloch's utopian philosophy of hope was oriented toward the future, finding in the past prefigural traces of what had not yet come rather than origins to be repeated. The "novum," he argued, heralded something radically new that intervened in the mundane course of history. Arendt saw that intervention happening in the birth of every new human: "Every man, being created in the singular, is a new beginning by virtue of his birth; if Augustine had drawn the consequences of these speculations, he would have defined men, not, like the Greeks as mortals, but as 'natals,' and he would have defined the freedom of the Will not as the *liberum arbitrium*, the free choice between willing and nilling, but as the freedom of which Kant speaks in the *Critique of Pure Reason*."[28] Although events, as Romano describes them, are not deliberately willed, they nonetheless resist being absorbed by a prior explanatory context or tied to a causal chain. Nor are they determined by a telos like death, as Heidegger had assumed in stressing the importance of *Sein-zum-Tode* for *Dasein*.

For the historian, the upshot of all this is that for the class of extraordinary happenings that justify the label "event"—and it seems likely they are a small, if significant minority—contextual explanation, however we construe it, is never sufficient. As Romano puts it, "Understanding events is always apprehending them on a horizon of meaning that they have opened themselves, in that they are strictly nonunderstandable in the light of their explanatory context."²⁹ If this is true for events in general, it is perhaps more so for those we might call events in intellectual history. As Randall Collins writes in the opening words of the first chapter of his massive *Sociology of Philosophies*, cited as the epigraph of this paper: "Intellectuals are people who produce decontextualized ideas." And he continues, "These ideas are meant to be true or significant apart from any locality, and apart from anyone concretely putting them into practice.... Intellectual products are felt, at least by their creators and consumers, to belong to a realm which is particularly elevated.... We can recognize them as sacred objects in the strongest sense; they inhabit the same realm, make the same claims to ultimate reality, as religion."³⁰

This may seem an odd way to begin a thousand-page book on the sociology of intellectual change throughout the ages and across all cultures, and in fact Collins wants to show that chains of interaction rituals are the key to intellectual life, including creativity. But insofar as he alerts us to the ambitions of intellectuals to produce ideas that transcend their context of generation, he affirms the insight that we have derived from Romano: it may be insufficient to reduce those ideas to little more than a reshuffling of the cards dealt by any context. Of course, ambition and realization are not equivalent, and certainly the desire to produce radically new, decontextualized ideas is not always successfully realized. Events, as the French discourse that includes Romano freely acknowledges, are rare and not always easy to identify. To the extent that the vast majority of historical happenings are "innerwordly" in his sense of the term, little, if anything, is lost by treating most ideas in the ways that the Cambridge School insists we should: as comprehensible in their context of origin and immediate reception.

But for those ideas that may justifiably be called intellectual events, or for the rare figures who are intellectual legislators of their age, it may be wise to refrain from restricting our gaze to the contexts out of which they emerged. For as Nietzsche noted in *Beyond Good and Evil*, "The greatest events and thoughts (and the greatest thoughts are the greatest events) are comprehended most slowly. The generations which are their contemporaries do not experience, do not 'live through' them—they live alongside them."³¹ The historical meaning of a Machiavelli, a Locke, or a Hobbes may, *pace* Skinner, be inextricably tied to the posterity they generated and may continue to inspire. Insofar as the concept of posterity always implies an infinity of possible future instantiations, the contexts of their reception, those teleological rather than constitutive forces in their field of meaning, must be understood as a perpetually receding horizon.

Willing to talk of some ideas as "great" does not, however, mean that they are somehow eternal, omnitemporal, and outside of history, as some philosophers might assume. The alternative to contextualization is not necessarily transcendentalization. Such might be the implication of the covertly religious definition of an event as an interruption of the Absolute into ephemeral temporality. But if we adopt the more secular version articulated by Romano, we can realize that their time is that of a future still to come, or perhaps even better, a Blochian "noncontemporaneity" that is the time both of "no longer" and "not yet." Like any "natal" entering the world, they are almost all pure possibility and little, if any, actuality.

But as in the case of the advenant who turns into a settled subject, their adventure may come to an end, and they can be reabsorbed into a new context of reception that diminishes their power to change the world. Nothing, after all, is forever new. So there is a perennial role for extrinsic as well as intrinsic analysis, contextual as well as textual interpretation. Despite all of the questions raised above about the challenges of creating a plausible method of contextualization, it should also not be forgotten that the notion of a text is no less fraught with internal tensions and difficulties. Indeed, once we put the concept of "text" under pressure and sort out all the possible ways to treat them, it raises as many questions as "context."[32] In fact, as we have already noted, the two may not always be so easily separated. Thus, to take one example, based on a hasty reading of the now notorious sound bite that "there is nothing outside of a text," deconstruction is often taken to be a radically textualist method, but Derrida has also been called a "contextualist *par excellence*" because of his dissolution of texts in a boundless sea of intertextuality.[33]

This characterization comes from a recent book by F. R. Ankersmit called *Sublime Historical Experience*, which introduces some further considerations on contextualization. Implicitly tying together the two parts of my argument—the difficulties faced by the later historian establishing the pertinent context and the mixed reality of historical occurrences themselves, some innerworldly, others genuine events—it will help us reach a conclusion. As we have seen, Romano argues that the advenant as opposed to the subject is capable of a more fundamental experience in which genuine transformation can take place. According to Ankersmit, drawing on the ruminations of the distinguished Dutch historian of the late Middle Ages, Johan Huizinga, there is also a chance for the historian to have a comparable experience, which he calls sublime. It somehow gets us in touch with residues of the past in a more direct way than is normally the case. Such an experience is one that goes beyond the disinterested activity of subjects gazing at objects from afar, either spatially or temporally. As in the case of the advenant described by Romano, it is one in which the person is deeply and intimately implicated. "Context," Ankersmit writes, "is a term belonging to a world containing subjects and objects, and it loses its meaning and significance when there is only experience, as in the case in historical experience. And since historical experience is far from being meaningless, our conclusion must be that there *is* meaning without context. Historical experience gives us the fissures of sublimity in the web of meaning and context—and hence the authenticity of historical experience that Huizinga had so rightly and eloquently claimed for it."[34]

Ankersmit concedes that such sublime or authentic experiences enjoyed by the historian bypass the issue of valid knowledge about the past. It is not epistemological plausibility he is after, but rather the possibility of heightened intensity in our relations with the residues of the past. For many historians, of course, such a goal is not paramount; as disinterested subjects looking from afar at past objects, they continue to have cognitive intentions and hope to provide explanations of what happened in ways that respect the unbridgeable gap between then and now. But if we take seriously the claim made by Romano that a genuine event in the past only realizes itself in the possibilities it unleashes in an undetermined future and Nietzsche's argument that great ideas need a delay before their power is fully actualized, then such experiences may seem less implausible. Events in the strong sense posited by Romano and other recent French theorists are rare occurrences in the past. Sublime historical experiences are no less infrequent in the present. But when the two come together, no contextual explanation can contain their explosive power.

CHAPTER 3

Intention and Irony: The Missed Encounter Between Hayden White and Quentin Skinner

Arguably the most influential Anglophone philosophers/practitioners of history of the past forty years are Hayden White (b. 1928) and Quentin Skinner (b. 1940).[1] Both first made their marks with major works in the 1970s, White with *Metahistory: The Historical Imagination in Nineteenth-Century Europe* in 1973 and Skinner with his two-volume *Foundations of Modern Political Thought* in 1978.[2] Both have been inspired in one way or another by what has come to be called "the linguistic turn" in the human sciences.[3] Both have been drawn to the performative rather than representational functions of language, while nonetheless resisting the conclusion that the past is inherently a "text" to be read hermeneutically or deconstructively. Both have been attracted more to rhetoric than philosophy, especially as it was mobilized by early modern thinkers like Vico, in White's case, and Hobbes and Machiavelli, in Skinner's. Both have disdained the call to include history among the social sciences, preferring to stress instead its humanist affinities. And both continue to generate considerable controversy over what it means to write history in general and the history of ideas or concepts in particular.

And yet, to my knowledge, neither figure has spent any time reflecting on the implications of the other's work, nor has a sustained literature emerged that compares their legacies. As Kari Palonen notes, "Rather surprising is the lack of connection between Skinner and the rhetorical historiography practiced by Hayden White and Frank Ankersmit in particular."[4] There are, of course, obvious reasons for the mutual disregard. Their interest in linguistic theory has focused on very different aspects of that vast and incoherent human phenomenon we call language. In Skinner's case, it has been the later Wittgenstein's stress on language as use combined with the speech act theory associated with J. L. Austin and John Searle, whereas White has drawn more on the structuralist narratology of literary theorists like Kenneth Burke, Northrop Frye, and Roland Barthes.[5] As a result, Skinner's approach has been contextualist and historicist, while White in contrast is defiantly formalist—indeed, some would argue, more transcendental in his conclusions than genuinely historical.[6] And despite their common appreciation of the importance of rhetoric, Skinner interprets it largely in terms of the arts of persuasion, while White is fixated on the recurrent tropological and figural patterns that subtend any discursive act.

It is, however, primarily because of the very different centers of gravity in their understanding of the historical field that they seem incompatible, focusing on different levels of historical research and writing, or at least have talked past each other. For Skinner, the weightier force in that field is the actual historical moment the historian is trying to recreate and represent, the moment in which agents intervened intentionally to make something happen. Against attempts made to fix the proper meaning of a word for all time, Skinner follows Wittgenstein in stressing its use in specific forms of life or historical contexts. For White, who agrees that atemporal meanings are impossible to determine, it is nonetheless the present moment, or at least that of the post-facto historical representation of the past, that is most important, the moment in which "history" is a story told about the past, not actions or events that happened in it. As a result, whereas Skinner hopes to thwart the presentist inclination to see the past as the origin of a narrative whose telos is the current moment, White follows Croce in defending the idea that "all history is contemporary history," thus emphasizing the inevitable role of our pretheoretical, tropological, and ideological investments in shaping the narratives we fashion. In one of the few explicit contrasts between the two, Michael Roth characterizes their differences in the following terms: "White's analysis of the formal properties of the text is dependent neither on some notion of author's intention nor on an appeal to a context, nor even conventions, one knows about independently of the text. Thus White's attempt to articulate how a text achieves its effects is very far from, let's say, Quentin Skinner's efforts to get at what it *really does*."[7]

For Skinner, "what a text really does" is more often what its author intends it to do, what speech act theorists called the "illocutionary force" rather than the "perlocutionary effect" dimension of a speech act.[8] That is, it involves the intention expressed in saying or writing something more than its success in bringing about what is intended. Skinner is also careful to distinguish putative motives, which are psychological states antecedent to the actual production of the speech act, from the intentions embodied in it.[9] Rather than "intentions to do" something, they are "intentions in doing it." Against those who search for the meaning of texts outside of such authorial intentions, for example, New Critics who trust only the tale and never the teller, Skinner holds fast to the claim that without taking into account what authors intend in their verbal actions, the meaning of texts will escape us. He is careful, however, not to claim that meaning is reducible to nothing but authorial intention: "I see no impropriety in speaking of a work's having a meaning for me which the writer could not have intended. Nor does my thesis conflict with this possibility. I have been concerned only with the converse point that whatever the writer is *doing in* writing what he writes must be relevant to interpretation, and thus with the claim that *amongst* the interpreter's tasks must be the recovery of the writer's intentions *in* writing what he writes."[10]

How precisely the historian engages in that recovery is, to be sure, a challenging task. Skinner's suggestion is that we attend to the relevant matrix of conventions through which authors must express their intentions, allowing us to situate them in a polemical field of meaningful alternatives. Although more than mere rationalizations for the acquisition of power or influence, textual interventions are intended performatively to legitimate such goals. For historians to understand a speech act, written or otherwise, they have to be able to situate it against the backdrop of the prevailing conventional context of the time of its enunciation, and also understand the proximate audience for whom it was intended.

There may be difficulties, as many critics (myself among them) have argued, in establishing what exactly the relevant contexts might have been, or getting access to them without the intervention of textual evidence that needs to be interpreted in turn.[11] As in the case of situating ideas in the individual experiences of those who generate, defend, or disseminate them, we are faced with the challenging task of knowing how to define experience itself, as well as how to gain access to it in the case of historical figures long dead. We cannot easily bracket what words mean for us today before we try to establish what they may have meant for those who uttered them in the first place. And in addition, some of those who act in history, especially intellectuals, hope their deeds will reach a posterity that extends well beyond the immediate circle serving as their proximate audience.

It may, moreover, be useful, if we are self-conscious about what we are doing, to attempt what has become known as a "rational reconstruction" of the inherent logic of the arguments whose history we are tracing. This might involve, as it does in the work of Jürgen Habermas, a post-facto model of development based on the latent rules underlying the evolution of a tradition of thought.[12] Such a model can even be used as a normative standard against which deviations from the ideal might be measured.[13] Employed more modestly, it makes manifest and clarifies the underlying stakes involved in even the most rhetorically ambiguous texts. A variant of this approach can be found in the attempt of philosophers like Louis Althusser to write the history of political thought as a series of contradictions or aporias that propel later theorists to try to solve on a higher level the unresolved issues left by their predecessors, often leaving aporias of their own to stimulate posterity.[14] As Peter Steinberger has argued, "It is one thing to investigate, as Skinner does, the particular materials of a discursive community—of a 'language'—for the purposes of determining how particular terms are used and understood by members of that community. It is quite another to analyze a particular set of propositions with a view towards discovering and explicating their underlying argumentative structure."[15]

The result may move the balance of power away from the historical subjects to the writer of history, who is more interested in finding figures in carpets than listening to the hopes or dreams of the weavers. As James Clifford once candidly admitted, speaking of the related approach he called "discourse analysis," it is "always in a sense unfair to authors. It is interested not in what *they* have to say or feel as subjects, but is concerned merely with statements as related to other statements in a field."[16] In embracing this approach, intellectual historians become more like historians of philosophy trying to provide a genealogy for a current position than disinterested narrators of the past, and in so doing often turn proper names into tokens of intellectual arguments rather than references to once-living, three-dimensional individuals, whose biographies may complicate the pure implications of their ideas.[17]

As a result, Skinner's insight into the heuristic value of seeking to reveal intentions embedded in speech acts, understanding them as actions designed to produce an outcome in a field of competing forces that prevailed at the time of their enunciation, is still in many ways compelling, especially for intellectual historians who may be wary of the teleological threat in rational reconstructions. Its value becomes especially evident when we consider it in the light of Hayden White's tropological understanding of historical reconstruction. White's great provocation, still roiling the waters in which practicing historians attempt to swim, is to stress the inevitably figural dimension of all narratives, nonfictional as well as fictional. By showing that our explanations are unconsciously prefigured by a finite set of archetypical emplotments—he singles out tragedy, comedy, satire, and romance—and preconceptual tropes—in particular, metaphor, metonymy, synecdoche, and irony—White undermines any naive faith in the presentation of an account that was "wie es eigentlich gewesen." All history writing is thus in some sense metahistorical.

White's full taxonomic system, which also includes four types of argument (formism, organicism, mechanism, and contextualism) and four dominant ideologies (conservatism, radicalism, liberalism, and anarchism), has been subjected to considerable critical scrutiny and need not concern us now. What is more important to note for our own purposes is the special place of irony in his scheme. In *Metahistory*, he distinguished it from the other three tropes in several ways. Whereas they are "naive" in Schiller's sense of unreflective, irony is "sentimental" in its self-consciousness about its function as a mode of deliberate negation. Its basic rhetorical tactic is "catachresis," a misuse of language in which doubts are inspired about what is characterized or the language used to characterize it. "The aim of the Ironic statement," he writes, "is to affirm tacitly the negative of what is on the literal level affirmed positively, or the reverse. It presupposes that the reader or auditor knows, or is capable of recognizing the absurdity of the thing designated in the Metaphor, Metonymy, or Synecdoche used to give form to it."[18]

Irony, of course, has a long history and comes in many different forms, and there has been no dearth of attempts to unpack its multiple meanings, as well as to explore the ways in which it can work through wordplay, narrative devices, or implicit cues, such as tone of voice or body language. From a concise verbal performance congealed in a pun to the most sprawling cosmic reversal of fortune, irony usually involves some sort of contrast between two levels of meaning, often coded "apparent" and "real." The claim that it presupposes superior knowledge about what is real on the part of the reader or auditor originates in what is usually called its Socratic version.[19] Here ignorance is feigned by a mentor who possesses a truth that he hopes will ultimately be shared by all concerned. Thus in Plato's *Dialogues*, Socrates knows in advance the answers that he induces his interlocutors to reach by their own reasoning power, while all the time slyly pretending that he is ignorant of them. Appearance diverges from reality, but one party is aware of the divergence and the other, at least initially, is not. Like the noble lie defended by Plato, the ironic use of mendacity is understood as a necessary use of dubious means to achieve a positive end, a midwifery of deception in the service of enlightenment. Although sometimes reproached for his lying and distrusted for his negativity, the Socratic ironist, at least since Cicero, is normally exonerated because of the nobility of his motives. In Greek comedies, from which the term is taken, the figure of the *eirôn* is a dissembler who exposes and deflates the boasting *alazôn* (braggart) through a duplicitous self-portrayal as someone less clever than he actually is. The seemingly smart guy turns out to be really stupid and vice versa. Thus, it is morally acceptable to heap unearned, hypocritical praise on a braggart in order ultimately to cut him down to size, as it is justifiable to trick an innocent into learning a truth through his own reasoning power.

An alternative kind of irony, especially pertinent to historical narrative, is the dramatic variant that also pits superior knowledge against ignorance. Insofar as the reader of a Socratic dialogue is observing the conversation between a teacher and student, he or she is akin to the audience in a theater. In this case, it is a character in the drama who is unaware of the larger implications of his actions or the meaning of the story of which he is a part. The author of the play or novel allows the audience to share the superior knowledge that trumps the character's erroneous or at least limited grasp of those implications. In both tragedies—think of *Oedipus Rex* or *Othello*—and comedies—an early example is Aristophanes's *The Clouds* in which Socrates himself is made the butt of ironic mockery—narrative tension is created by the audience's awareness of a truth denied to the character, or at least often not revealed until the end of the story.

The relevance of dramatic irony for historical narratives is obvious, even more so than the Socratic variant because of its frequent exploitation of the gap between intentions and outcomes. Insofar as such narratives are post-facto reconstructions of a story that may achieve a meaningful closure not yet available to the actors in it, the knowledge of outcomes can provide ironic distance from the self-understanding of the protagonists. No account of a past war, for example, can fail to expose the illusions of at least one party to the conflict, the one on the losing side, and sometimes in fact both, if victory turns out to be pyrrhic. Insofar as history is often the accumulated result of unintended consequences of acts whose effects may well transcend the hopes and fears of those who wanted to influence their world, it is hard to narrate it without some irony. This is the case not only when positive expectations go awry—the First World War as the "war to end all wars" or a means to "make the world safe for democracy"—but also when catastrophes from one perspective produce positive outcomes from another, as, say, in the case of the fall of pagan Rome and the rise of medieval Christendom. Here posterity can claim superior knowledge, which transcends the limited horizons of those actors who were inevitably ignorant of the outcome.

Such superior knowledge, as in the case of Socratic irony, is grounded in the belief that although appearances may deceive, there is an accessible alternative that more accurately expresses the truth. As White notes, "Irony presupposes the occupation of a 'realistic' perspective on reality, from which a nonfigurative representation of the world of experience might be provided."[20] Or as he puts it with reference to Vico's use of the term, "Irony presupposes awareness of the distinction between truth and falsehood, of the possibility of misrepresenting reality in language, and of the difference between a literal and a figurative representation."[21] Often it is the perspective of temporal distance, allowing a clear-cut narrative pattern to emerge, that seems to make the difference. Thus in the case of historical irony, posterity is like an audience in a theater, which shares the knowledge of the larger truths that escape participants in the action, if not through the author's foreshadowing of the outcome, then through a direct experience of it at the conclusion of the story.

Or so it seems. For, as we know, "posterity" is itself a divided category, with neither a terminal point at which the story is definitively over[22] nor a universal consensus about what it means. And as White himself tells us, any pretense to a realistic perspective is challenged by an awareness of the tropological dimension of all narratives, which makes them inevitably one-sided and partial, thus opening the door for irony. Emplotting history from the point of view of those who are its losers as a tragedy can conflict with a comic emplotment of the same story, written from the perspective of the victors. The result is that one ironically undercuts the other, and neither can claim the position of the truth-knowing Socratic wise man or the sovereign author of a fiction, who has the certain knowledge by which to trump the incomplete or erroneous understanding of the actor. Adding to the potential for still more ironic uncertainty is the possibility that the audience may know *more* than the historian insofar as the latter is never the end point of the interpretative process. A bit like the unreliable narrator device employed by some novelists, the historian can only appear to occupy the place of the "one who knows" in Socratic irony, while in fact being only a moment in the unending process of competing, often conflicting readings of the story.

In this more radical variant of irony, which is sometimes called "paradoxical" or "unstable," the presupposition of a realistic position of superior post-facto truth is itself called into question. Ever since such Romantics as the Schlegel brothers in Germany lost confidence in the possibility of direct access to the reality of the world, irony expressed the ways in which the inevitable ambiguities of language prevented any simple distinction between appearance and reality or truth and falsehood.[23] Although paradoxical irony could give the subject a sense of freedom, elevated as he was above all determinations, it also could imply cognitive confusion and ethical indifference. White notes the result when he says irony "provides a linguistic paradigm of a mode of thought which is radically self-critical with respect not only to a given characterization of the world of experience but also to the very effort to capture adequately the truth of things in language."[24] In the hands of later masters of paradoxical irony such as Kierkegaard and Heine, the ground is forcefully undercut from any meaningful distinction between what is the case and what merely seems to be. Positivity never emerges from the abyssal structure of infinite negativity, although irrational commitment might be construed as an antidote to ironic indifference or cynical detachment.

Not surprisingly, devotees of linguistic undecidability, infinitely deferred meaning, and the limits of conceptual reasoning, such as contemporary deconstructionists, find paradoxical irony congenial to their way of thinking.[25] For Paul de Man, for example, irony is related to the rhetorical tropes of parabasis and anacoluthon in which narratives are always interrupted and syntax remains irreparably fractured. "Irony," he writes, "is the permanent parabasis of the allegory of tropes." As a result, it is questionable for historians to seek to overcome irony, for it is "very difficult to conceive of a historiography, a system of history, that would be sheltered from irony."[26] In fact, rather than wanting to overcome it or even write the story of its rise and fall, historians should recognize that irony is the very source of history itself. De Man's disciple Kevin Newmark goes so far as to say that "there can be no history of irony, because irony is the condition of possibility for history.... Irony, on occasion and by accident, is historical because it interrupts the reign of a formal causality that would otherwise be machinelike in its imperviousness to anything other than its own predetermined and crushing movement."[27]

Similarly, Richard Rorty found what he called a "liberal ironist" position conducive to the embrace of contingency and suspicion of final vocabularies in which words mean only one thing. Instead, irony was inherently "nominalist and historicist."[28] Rorty's historicism, as Frank Ankersmit has noted, gravitated more to the ironist than metaphorical moment in that tradition: "His outlook is closer to Burckhardt than to Ranke, so to speak. It would probably be more correct to say that both metaphor and irony have their job to perform in his thought but that he happens to subscribe to a theory of metaphor that robs it of its capacity to assert its rights against irony."[29]

For those, however, who hope for a way beyond such a transcendental assertion of ironic undecidability, the implications of the more radical version of paradoxical irony are problematic, leading at least potentially to quietism, nihilism, and moral indifference.[30] For all his provocative resistance to more traditional ways of writing history, Hayden White reveals himself to be profoundly uneasy with the domination of irony, especially in its more radical guise, over the other tropic emplotments he outlines. In his discussion of Jacob Burckhardt, whose historical realism he argues was written in a satiric mode, he notes with some dismay that the great Swiss historian's "ironic vision" led him to flee from acting in the world. In general, White observes,

> evidences of the crystallization of an Ironic language are the rise of skepticism in philosophy, of the sophistic in public speaking, and of the kind of argument that Plato called "eristic" in political discourse. Underlying this mode of speech is a recognition of the fractured nature of social being, of the duplicity and self-serving of politicians, of an egotism which governs all professions of interest in the common good, of naked power (*dratos*) ruling where law and morality (*ethos*) are being invoked to justify actions. Ironic language, as Hegel remarked later, is an expression of the "unhappy consciousness."[31]

White's discomfort with the nihilistic implications he saw in the more paradoxical variant of irony is palpable in his 1976 screed against poststructuralist criticism, "The Absurdist Moment in Contemporary Literary Theory." Here he specifically attacks what he calls Derrida's "favored trope . . . catachresis, the *ironic* trope par excellence. In his view, it is against the absurd imposition of meaning upon meaninglessness that all of the other tropes (metaphor, metonymy, and synecdoche) arise. And it is against the absurd impulse to endow the meaningless with meaning that Derrida's own antiphilosophizing takes shape."[32] Absurdism is, however, only the extreme outcome of what was called the "crisis of historicism" in the late nineteenth century, which White argues "plunged European historical thinking into the Ironic condition of mind" that "has continued to flourish as the dominant mode of professional historiography, as cultivated in the academy ever since."[33]

At the very end of *Metahistory*, White ruefully acknowledges that his own formalist, anti-realist analysis of the tropological prefiguration of historical narratives itself expresses the same ironic distancing from any naive claims to truth-telling about the past. With a certain desperation, he claims that once we acknowledge that irony is itself a function of tropological imposition on a past that lacks any inherent narrative shape, we are free to impose others at will. "If it can be shown," he writes, "that Irony is only one of a *number* of possible perspectives on history, each of which has its own good reasons for existence on a poetic and moral level of awareness, the Ironic attitude will have begun to be deprived of its status as the necessary perspective from which to view the historical process."[34] In the introduction to *The Tropics of Discourse*, he would advocate the same remedy: "Kant's distinctions among the emotions, the will and the reason are not very popular in this age, an age which has lost its belief in the will and represses its sense of the moral implications of the mode of rationality that it favors. But the moral implications of the human sciences will never be perceived until the faculty of the will is reinstated in theory."[35]

White's voluntarist solution—which allowed critics like Carlo Ginzburg to charge that he was channeling the extreme subjectivism of Giovanni Gentile, the fascist philosopher, via his early interest in Benedetto Croce and Carlo Antoni[36]—did not really lay to rest the nihilistic threat of paradoxical irony, as commentators were quick to note.[37] Merely to will an alternative, especially one that transcends the "sentimental" disillusioning reflexivity of irony and restores the robust "naiveté" of the other tropic emplotments, seemed highly dubious, a bit like consciously trying to will belief *ex nihilo* rather than simply being a prereflective believer. As Eva Domanska has pointed out, the crisis of historicism that led to the hegemony of the ironic attitude was itself a reflection of the decline of the sacred in modern European life, and its solution shares in the general difficulty of restoring faith to its previous cohesive status.[38] Negating negations—or in this case, ironizing irony—can produce a positive outcome only if you adopt a Hegelian comic narrative, which no one can plausibly derive from the hopelessly checkered historical record that has been left for us to interpret. Radical ironists from Kierkegaard to de Man have a case in refusing to fold it into a more capacious dialectical sublation of negation, even if the former scorned the Romantic lack of commitment.

But perhaps rather than trying to overcome irony entirely through an act of sheer will or dialectical *Aufhebung*, it might be better to entertain an alternative within the contested field of irony itself. As we have already noted, Socratic and dramatic irony are less threatening to historical narrative than the paradoxical or unstable variant that undermines any basis for judgment about which narratives are more plausible than others. Although White sometimes conflates the two indiscriminately, he implicitly invokes the distinction in several ways as a more effective solution to the menace of nihilistic relativism than his evocation of will. When he distinguishes between post-facto tropological emplotments and the manifold of past events, occurrences, actions, and so on that will be emplotted, he is tacitly drawing on a distinction that Kant would have appreciated between phenomenal appearances and noumenal essences, or at least between the past as it was and as it is later represented. Although like Kant, he denies the possibility of ever accessing the former without the mediation of the latter, he resists the implication that it is appearance all the way down. He also mobilizes at least the rhetoric of truth, which can be misrepresented (rather than just variously represented) when he argues that naive realism based on positivist notions of scientific objectivity is false and tropic emplotment of narratives is what in truth historians *qua* metahistorians really do. His own vantage point is one that tacitly assumes the possibility of a transcendent formalism of rhetorical strategies that can exhaust the repertoire of possible tropological devices available to make sense of the past. And when he expresses the hope that knowledge about the contingent quality of ironic narration, what he calls "the turning of the Ironic consciousness against Irony itself," will free us from the assumption that it is inevitable—an assumption he traces back with no hesitation to a transitional moment in late nineteenth-century European history—he is duplicating the Socratic strategy of using irony to bring about enlightenment, even if he expresses it in an untenable dialectical form.

The value of this approach is apparent only if we return now to Quentin Skinner's thoughts on recovering intentionality. The question of irony comes up, to be sure, only infrequently in Skinner's own work, and then largely in terms of the issue of interpreting the intentions of past actors whose speech acts may have been delivered ironically.[39] As in the case of speech acts in general, Skinner contends that it is not an issue of the meaning of the words used but rather of their illocutionary intent, what their authors were hoping to do through their utterances. Skinner maintains a certain optimism about the possibility of recovering the illocutionary force of even speech acts that were ironically delivered, and so he doesn't seem fazed by the objection that surface meanings may hide deeper ones. Skinner hasn't devoted as much attention to the issue of the prevalence of irony in the narrations of contemporary historians as has White. But he once did tell an interviewer for the *Times Literary Supplement* that writing a history of liberalism demonstrating the ways in which it steadily led to the decline of political participation would "embody the kind of irony that the greatest historians have always particularly relished. For it is surely ironic that the development of the Western democracies should have been accompanied by the atrophying of the ideal that the government of the people should be conducted by the people."[40]

Skinner's own passing thoughts on the role of irony in historical writing are less important for our argument, however, than his stress on the importance of recovering intentionality as the principal task of the historian. As any student of recent philosophical debates can well attest, there is no dearth of controversy over the issue of intention, with phenomenologists, speech act theorists, deconstructionists, and others struggling to arrive at a persuasive theory of its meaning and function in linguistic, ethical, and social terms. As the notorious "debate" between Derrida and John Searle in the 1970s demonstrated, the arguments often generated more heat than light. Skinner himself was at pains to align himself with those who resisted deconstruction's claim that it was impossible to know the intentions of others with any certitude: "If we insist, as Derrida does, on such an equation between establishing that something is the case and being able to demonstrate it 'for sure', then admittedly it follows that we can never hope to establish the intentions with which a text may have been written. But equally it follows that we can never hope to establish that life is not a dream.... The skeptic is insisting on far too stringent an account of what it means to have reasons for our beliefs."[41] Although this charge may be a tendentious interpretation of deconstruction—Derrida explicitly stressed, after all, that "the category of intention will not disappear; it will have its place, but from that place it will no longer be able to govern the entire scene and system of utterance"[42]—it serves to remind us of the value of at least trying to establish intentions as best we can.

It is, in fact, only if we can do so with at least some degree of confidence that the more moderate variant of irony, which doesn't descend into the paradoxes of infinite, destabilizing ironization, might be viable. That is, without the distinction between what actors thought they were doing, or at least what the illocutionary target of their speech acts were, we cannot assume a position of superior wisdom after the fact. To understand unintended consequences makes sense only if we can identify what the original intentions were. Although our own perspective is never definitive—there is always a chance it will itself be ironized by future narrators of more extended stories with different outcomes—we can at least benefit from the passage of time, which gives us a knowledge that is denied the actors themselves. In fact, it is only that passage that affords us whatever modicum of superior knowledge we might claim over those actors, who, after all, more directly experienced what we can only imperfectly recreate.[43]

What makes Skinner's understanding of intentionality particularly insightful is precisely his sensitivity to what the champions of paradoxical irony praise for undermining any intentionality that claims to be pure and self-sufficient, an intentionality that purports to locate meaning totally within the consciousness of the intending subject. That is, Skinner's stress on the matrix of necessary conventions in which acts take place allows us to get beyond the idea, as he puts it, that "every agent has a privileged access to his own intentions, as a way of 'closing the context' on the historical meaning of a text."[44] As such, it come very close to the deconstructionist emphasis on "iterability" as a necessary element of everything that seems unique and self-sufficient, a recognition that no speech act can be isolated from the possibility of it being a repeat of what preceded it and a foreshadowing of what follows. However singular and unique it may seem, every speech act achieves what meaning it may have only in the context of the conventions that allow it to be understandable by others.

The difference between Skinner's version of intentionality and the moderate kind of irony that it makes possible and the weaker notion of intentionality of the paradoxical ironists is, however, substantial. For whereas he sees the context as largely enabling the possible understanding of what is intended, both at the moment of initial enunciation and for later historical retrieval, the paradoxical ironists are attuned more to its disabling effects, undermining both communication at the time and accurate re-presentation later. It seems to me impossible to offer a knockdown argument on either side of the debate. That is, we certainly have many examples of the ambivalent meaning of language and obstacles to successful communication, which are only exacerbated with the passage of time. Whether or not you decry as a myth the metaphysics of presence that allegedly informs traditional philosophy, it certainly can never be found in historical inquiry, which can only register the inevitability of temporal absence and spatial displacement. The time of historians is always "out of joint," more "hauntological" than ontological, as Derrida would put it.[45] And so, no perfect re-experiencing of original intended meaning—or the context of conventions in which speech acts tried to do something through words—is ever possible. Nor indeed, if it were, would it be a sufficient explanation for subsequent historical developments, which involve the clash of intentions producing consequences no one desires.[46]

But whether this means we are doomed to the disabling paradoxical irony that so distressed Hayden White or can adopt with some degree of confidence a more Socratic or dramatic irony in which appearance and reality can be meaningfully distinguished is a different question. Certainly, practicing historians would be loath to abandon at least some privileged sense of knowing outcomes, even granting some are still provisional, better than the actors in medias res. Hindsight, we might say, provides the historian's equivalent of the Socratic or dramatic ironist's superior epistemological position of knowing what the actors did not know. In fact, it is precisely because of the ironic attitude in the more modest dramatic sense that we can honor Skinner's injunction to try to situate speech acts in their original illocutionary contexts and yet register the ways in which later periods may have transformed, distorted, or even betrayed those intentions.[47] Yes, John Locke may not have intended to be the father of a tradition that came to be called liberalism, and it would be anachronistic to pin that label on him, as if he were a self-conscious founding father. But if we take seriously the frequent role of unintended consequences in history, then it makes sense to understand that outcome in an ironic manner. And likewise, we can find in the seemingly very different methodological projects of Hayden White and Quentin Skinner a complementarity that neither would have intended and might still, if pressed, deny. Authors, after all, are not always the best judges of the historical meaning of their own ideas.

CHAPTER 4

Walter Benjamin and Isaiah Berlin: Modes of Jewish Intellectual Life in the Twentieth Century

If I may be permitted a little personal self-indulgence, let me begin by citing a letter I received in June 1973 from the distinguished European intellectual historian George Mosse, which served as the long-delayed stimulus for this essay. Mosse reported that he had just had dinner at the Jerusalem home of the celebrated scholar of Jewish mysticism Gershom Scholem, and he noted that he was sitting below Paul Klee's painting *Angelus Novus*, which had been bequeathed to Scholem by Walter Benjamin, although in the possession of Theodor Adorno until his death. And then as an intriguing afterthought, he added: "By the way, Sir Isiah [sic] Berlin was there too, and he knew Adorno but his opinion of him as a philosopher seems very low indeed. However, he found him amusing."[1]

Mosse, Scholem, Berlin, and, at least in spirit, Adorno and Benjamin all in one room on Abarbanel Street in Rehavia, the quarter of Jerusalem where so many other émigré Jewish intellectuals had settled! How to make sense of such an extraordinary assemblage? How, more to the point, to include *Sir* Isaiah, to use the title he had boasted since 1957 that Mosse felt obliged to employ, in this group portrait with other figures who were so far removed from a British knighthood? How in particular to find a way to think coherently about his intellectual career together with that of Walter Benjamin, the most removed of them all?

It may even be a surprise that Berlin, while never actually crossing paths with Benjamin, was only one degree of personal separation from him. But as this reported conversation testifies, more than one mediation tied them together. The first was their mutual friendship with Adorno. When Adorno went to Oxford as a guest of Merton College for several years in the mid-1930s, he had met Berlin, then a young philosopher at All Souls College. As Berlin later confided to an interviewer, "Although we made friends and talked about music and literature and many other subjects, I could not understand a word of [his] philosophical writings."[2] But enough of a bond developed for Berlin to visit Adorno in 1940 in New York en route to Moscow as a diplomatic envoy, an encounter Adorno thought worth reporting at length in a letter to his parents.[3] And a decade later, in a letter to Max Horkheimer, he described Berlin as "very intelligent" and praised his perfect command of German.[4] The second personal link between our two protagonists was forged through the friendship between Berlin and the host of the 1973 dinner party reported by Mosse, Gershom Scholem, whom Berlin met in 1934 on his first visit to Palestine and saw frequently thereafter, especially after the creation of the State of Israel.[5]

In neither case do we have hard and fast evidence that Benjamin was ever a topic of serious discussion between Adorno and Scholem, on one hand, and Berlin, on the other, although it is likely he was at least mentioned after he gained the fame that had eluded him during his lifetime. Berlin, to my knowledge, never treated Benjamin's thought in his voluminous writings, even if he once did allude in passing to his suicide to an interviewer.[6] If he found Adorno impenetrable, he surely would have been even less willing to tackle Benjamin's far more esoteric ideas. For his part, Benjamin, blissfully indifferent to British thought of any kind, is very unlikely to have found much sustenance in Berlin's own work, had he ever encountered it.

The two men did, to be sure, inhabit overlapping worlds and shared, as we've seen, a number of friends. And one has to acknowledge other similarities. Both were born into relatively comfortable, assimilated Jewish families, Benjamin in Berlin, Germany, in 1892 and Berlin in Riga, Latvia, in 1909. Both had happy childhoods often later serving as enclaves of remembered bliss. Both suffered the trauma of exile from totalitarian regimes, Berlin from the Soviet Union in 1921, Benjamin from Nazi Germany in 1933. Although quintessentially cosmopolitan, both stubbornly held onto their Jewish identities, even if what they derived from them was always unsettled and selective. Although Berlin came to be identified as an exemplary Russian Jew, the fact that he was from Riga, an old Hanseatic city outside the Pale of Settlement with a strong Baltic German tradition, and did not speak Yiddish as a child, meant that he was scarcely more of a typical *Ostjude* than Benjamin. Intellectually, they also had certain common inclinations. Both, for example, distrusted Hegel and other philosophers of history as a triumphalist narrative of progress, but were interested in Marx, albeit with very different evaluations of his worth. Both found counter-Enlightenment theorists of language like Hamann a welcome antidote to the naive optimism of positivist scientism but had no use for such twentieth-century descendants of his position as Martin Heidegger. And finally, both were intellectually omnivorous with an astonishing command not only of philosophy but also the arts, with Berlin favoring music and literature and Benjamin literature and the visual arts, including photography and the cinema.

And yet, as anyone who has spent time with their work and lives can quickly attest, Walter Benjamin and Isaiah Berlin represented two very different, even opposing types of twentieth-century Jewish intellectuals. Berlin himself acknowledged as much when he expressed in a letter to his friend Jean Floud, the British sociologist of education, his distaste for his counterparts from "the terrible twisted Mitteleuropa in which nothing is straight, simple, truthful, all human relations and all political attitudes are twisted into ghastly shapes by these awful casualties who, because they are crippled, recognize nothing pure and firm in the world."[7] He seems to have loathed in particular Benjamin's friend Hannah Arendt and had only dismissive things to say about Frankfurt School figures like Herbert Marcuse.[8] Symptomatically, when Berlin came to deliver his famous inaugural lecture as Chichele Professor of Government at Oxford in 1958 on "Two Concepts of Liberty," he ignored a comparable essay by Franz Neumann, Benjamin's erstwhile colleague at the Institute of Social Research, which had appeared five years before.[9]

In what follows, I want to speculate on how we might characterize the distinction between Berlin and Benjamin in ways that go beyond their explicit intellectual or political allegiances. Instead of belaboring the obvious differences between Benjamin the heterodox Marxist, believer in redemptive politics, and advocate of avant-garde art, and Berlin the pluralist liberal, antiutopian skeptic, and aesthetic realist, I want to step back and focus on what for want of a better term we can call the implicit styles of the intellectual lives they led and the different sensibilities they embodied, at least as they appear for posterity. I do so not with the intention of elevating one and denigrating the other, as both were formidable intellectuals worthy of our abiding attention, however much we may quarrel with some of their judgments. For many readers, Benjamin will seem clearly the more significant figure, not only in terms of the number of fields he has influenced but also because of the audacity of his imagination and the experimental daring of his writing. But the more cautious and moderate Berlin has also had his fair share of devotees, who continue to find inspiration in his work and recall with admiration his influential role in Anglo-American culture for several generations.[10] Symptomatic of the enduring high status of the two men is the steady stream of published volumes of their correspondences, which in both cases include letters to many of the most significant figures of their time.

Pitting Benjamin against Berlin as opposing ideal types in terms of metaphorically characterized styles may also have ramifying effects. It can suggest a set of tools to make sense of more than just their own individual careers and the tacit reasons why they have attracted different posthumous followings. Employing such instruments, of course, requires a full acknowledgment that typifications always reduce the complexity of a singular life, especially when the figures involved are in so many ways uniquely gifted and lived through such turbulent times. We should say of Berlin and Benjamin what Sartre famously said of Paul Valéry: "Valéry was a petit-bourgeois intellectual, of that there is no doubt. But not every petit-bourgeois intellectual is Paul Valéry."[11]

And yet, it is also important to remember that both Berlin and Benjamin employed such generic typifications in their own descriptions of other minds. For all the exquisite subtlety of their characterizations of individual people and ideas, their fine-grained responses to what Berlin called their "personal impressions" of people they met,[12] they also drew on general types to make larger points.[13] In Berlin's trenchant 1951 essay on Tolstoy, he famously borrowed the Greek poet Archilochus's distinction between hedgehogs and foxes, to differentiate between thinkers who know only one big thing from those who are open to the diversity and plurality of concrete reality.[14] Benjamin, for his part, talked about "the destructive character" and transfigured his friend Franz Hessel's "flâneur" into a modern urban heroic type. So they can hardly object if we seek to interpret their own lives as intellectuals in ideal typical terms.

Which binary ideal types work best to capture their distinct styles and sensibilities? Let me consider some of the obvious candidates before offering a few new alternatives. Perhaps the place to begin is with Berlin's own hedgehog/fox dichotomy, which has had so much traction over the years. It would, however, be questionable as a way to draw a distinction between him and

Benjamin. For, all things considered, both were more foxes than hedgehogs, open to too many competing intellectual currents to find a way to forge them into a single, obsessively repeated pattern. Although some might argue that Berlin's oft-repeated defense of pluralist liberalism and diversitarian values ironically places him in the hedgehog camp,[15] an essay by Robert Zaretsky concludes instead, and I think correctly, that "Berlin played with the foxes."[16] So not much help here.

What of the almost-as-influential opposition drawn by the Polish philosopher Leszek Kolakowski between "the priest" and "the jester"? "The priest," he writes, "is the guardian of the absolute; he sustains the cult of the final and the obvious as acknowledged by and contained in tradition. The jester is he who moves in good society without belonging to it; and treats it with impertinence; he who doubts all that appears self-evident." Carefully testing the limits of the accepted, seemingly playful in his taunting of authority, the intellectual as jester strives to "consider all the possible reasons for contradictory ideas. [His effort] is thus dialectical by nature—simply the attempt to change what is because it is. He is motivated not by a desire to be perverse but by a distrust of a stabilized system."[17]

Here too, although suggestive, the fit is not perfect. However much Berlin might be seen as a more establishment figure, mingling easily with the elite of his adopted country and supporting traditional British liberal values, he always opposed absolute and universal principles, challenged any catechism of final truths, and celebrated the lively clash of opinions. There was not much of the priestly in Berlin's makeup, which included a lively, often subversive sense of humor prized by all who knew him. As for Benjamin being a dialectical jester seeking to destabilize the hegemonic system, the characterization would seem more apt, except for the fact that jesters serve at courts, amusing the powers that be as much as they subtly challenge their authority. Jesters, in other words, work within institutions, whereas Benjamin remained resolutely apart from them. There is, moreover, precious little sardonic playfulness or savage wit in Benjamin,[18] no reveling in the role of a gadfly irritating the powers that be. For all his respect for figures like Karl Kraus, his own tone was always deadly serious, his mood more consistently melancholic than manic, his weapons not those of satire or mockery.

Do we fare any better with the dichotomy suggested by Hannah Arendt between "pariah" and "parvenu," a contrast she applied specifically to Jews, and in particular to the intellectuals among them? The dichotomy provides more nuance and punch than the simpler distinction between "outsider" and "insider," which has so often been employed to make a similar point.[19] It was Max Weber who had first borrowed the term "pariah" from the Indian caste system and applied it to the Jews, albeit not without certain controversy.[20] In a series of essays written in the 1940s, Arendt followed Bernard Lazare in reversing its negative valence to celebrate a "hidden tradition" of conscious Jewish rebels—her examples, in addition to Lazare himself, are Rahel Varnhagen, Heinrich Heine, Sholem Aleichem, Franz Kafka, and Charlie Chaplin—who turned their outcast status into fuel for critique.[21] Her editor, Ron Feldman, tacks Benjamin onto this list, an addition of which I think Arendt would have approved.[22]

There were, in fact, many moments in his life when Benjamin suffered more than just his people's generic fate as abjected pariahs. He lost the confidence of his family by refusing the safety of a normal bourgeois career. He failed to establish an alternative as an academic after a botched attempt at habilitation with his bafflingly obscure work on the *Origin of the German Trauerspiel*. He desperately sought, often in vain, publishing and other opportunities to support himself, especially during his seven long years of forced wandering after 1933. Following his early involvement in the German Youth Movement, ended by his bitter disappointment with its support for the First World War, he never found a settled political home. Rejecting both the Zionism urged on him by Scholem and Communism extolled by his friend Bertolt Brecht, he was a member of the "homeless left," whose melancholy he both decried and shared. Not surprisingly, he himself acknowledged his affinity to Heine, highly valued Kafka, and was a great fan of Chaplin's.[23]

Benjamin thus does represent in many ways what Arendt meant by a pariah, "À l'écart de tous les courants," as Adorno titled his final essay on him,[24] although his sheer talent and originality did earn him the respect of many who came to know him and his work. But can we then plausibly label Berlin an intellectual parvenu? There can be no question that rather than being marginalized and abjected, Berlin enjoyed a stellar career at the very pinnacle of British academic life; indeed, he became one of the most feted and admired public intellectuals of the twentieth century. Where Benjamin suffered failure after failure in his life—repeated unhappiness in love, professional rejection, the indignities of impoverishment and incarceration, and finally suicide at the age of forty-eight during a vain effort to escape from the Nazis—Berlin's good fortune was to enjoy a successful (if late) marriage, unparalleled clout in his profession, worldly prosperity, and an astonishing number of eminent and devoted friends. When he died in 1997 in the fullness of his years, his reputation was still very high, only to be burnished even more in the years since by the efforts of Henry Hardy to collect and publish the scattered writings of his long career.

Berlin was thus certainly no pariah, but can we plausibly call him a parvenu? If "parvenu" means someone who not only comes from an obscure background to achieve worldly success but also lacks the manners of the class to which he aspires and thus earns the contempt of those already safely ensconced in it, he clearly escapes the label. If you are an émigré who arrives early enough and with sufficient family means to attend posh public schools, are bright enough to shine at Oxford, and stay long enough to become president of a new Oxford college and the British Academy, as well as earning that aforementioned knighthood, you have pretty much avoided being resented by anyone as a late-coming arriviste. With one galling exception, Berlin was welcomed into any club he wished to join, and apparently he was a member of many.[25] As the extraordinary circle of friends he amassed during his long life attests—a record very different from Benjamin's brutal inclination to cut off old friends and keep the relationships he maintained in watertight compartments—and the generosity he bestowed on many who sought out his favor, he displayed none of the contempt for those left behind typical of the parvenu. Berlin seems to have genuinely earned the epitaph of a faithful student: "Few teachers will be as much loved and mourned as Isaiah."[26]

Moreover, Berlin himself explicitly distanced himself from one typical expression of the Jewish parvenu, who attempts to assimilate so fully that his ethnic identity is effaced. As Noel Annan remembered, "There was one public issue on which he left no one in doubt. Above all, Isaiah was a Jew, and never forgave those who forgot to conceal their anti-Semitism."[27] Ironically, this meant he had no patience for that cynical purchase of an "entry ticket" to European civilization infamously made by Heinrich Heine and Karl Marx. As his most recent biographer Ari Dubnow remarks, "Both Marx and Heine represented in Berlin's mind the type of Jew he did not want to become, because both aspired to an impossible state. They were *parvenus*, to use Hannah Arendt's language. The lesson Berlin drew from the stories was identical: total assimilation without self-abnegation was impossible, and one could not escape one's roots."[28] His Heine was not the critical pariah extolled by Arendt and Benjamin, but rather a compromised trimmer who sought acceptance at the price of his integrity. Whichever version of Heine we may prefer, the lesson is that for all his unmatched success and acceptance in the highest circles of power and prestige, it would be unfair to stigmatize Berlin as a parvenu. Arendt's dichotomy doesn't really capture what distinguished him from Benjamin.

Let us turn to several more promising alternatives, the first of which we owe to Susan Sontag's 1963 essay on Albert Camus. "Great writers," she suggests, "are either husbands or lovers. Some writers supply the solid virtues of a husband: reliability, intelligibility, generosity, decency. There are other writers in whom one prizes the gifts of a lover, gifts of temperament rather than moral goodness. Notoriously, women tolerate qualities in a lover—moodiness, selfishness, unreliability, brutality—they would never countenance in a husband, in return for excitement, an infusion of intense feeling." Camus, she argued, was "the ideal husband of modern literature," but rather than dismiss him as a result, she cautioned that "as in life, so in art both are necessary, husbands and lovers. It's a great pity when one is forced to choose between them."[29]

Here the metaphoric opposition works less in terms of the roles taken on by the intellectuals themselves than of the ways their audiences respond to them. Although one can find a certain corroboration in their actual biographies—Benjamin, unhappily married, had a weakness for successive love triangles that ended badly, while Berlin's romantic life was pretty uneventful until his successful marriage at the age of forty-six—there can be little doubt that it fits even better with the way posterity has fashioned each of them. Walter Benjamin has few rivals for the role as our quintessential intellectual lover. We thrill at the fact that he not only lived on the edge, contemptuous of bourgeois morality and conventional behavior, but he thought there as well.[30] Willing to entertain ideas that were extreme, often apparently incompatible, and at the fringes of the plausible, he expressed them in ways that were no less daring and unpredictable. Not only was he moody in personal terms, often oscillating between suicidal depression and euphoric mania, but his thought careened from one enthusiasm to another with theologically inspired fantasies of redemption mingling with surrealist yearnings for "profane illuminations" and Marxist calls for class struggle. Not only did he experiment on his own body with drugs that opened up new perceptual experiences and undermined whatever was left of his bourgeois selfhood, but he sought fresh ways of conveying whatever insights they may have provided to readers hungry for relief from conventional ideas and traditional ways of communicating them.[31] His suffering was for some a badge of distinction, as if somehow lovers gain value by sacrificing comfort and happiness in the service of their passion. Like a lover, he in turn demanded of his readers a certain blind obedience, rather than providing sober arguments to persuade them. In a sense, he was more a noetic than dianoetic thinker, drawing on intuitions of higher truths and searching for sparks of illumination in the debris of cultural ruins rather than patiently following inferential reasoning and soberly weighing evidence.

Not surprisingly, for those who are made uncomfortable by lovers, resistant to the siren call of their seductive lures, Benjamin has been a problematic figure. Thus, for example, Mark Lilla includes him in his dishonor roll of "reckless minds" and "philotyrants," warning that Benjamin was a "theologically inspired and politically unstable thinker, one whose messianic yearnings drew him dangerously near the flames of political passion that engulfed Europe for much of the last century."[32] Rather than lamenting the blindness to greatness that prevented his examiners at the University of Frankfurt from accepting Benjamin's *Habilitationschrift*, Lilla echoes their qualms, arguing that "Benjamin's notion of criticism as alchemy, his conviction that politics is a matter of apocalyptic nihilism, and his fascination with right-wing vitalism all came together in his major work of the Twenties."[33] Bemoaning his willingness to "flirt promiscuously" with both theology and materialism, Lilla concludes that Benjamin is one of those intellectuals who are "a riddle to themselves and to all who encounter them."[34]

Not surprisingly, Lilla finds a comforting alternative in Isaiah Berlin, citing with admiration the latter's "series of remarkably suggestive essays in intellectual history written in the postwar decades," which "made the most sophisticated case thus far for blaming the theory and practice of modern tyranny on the *philosophes*" because of their hostility to diversity and pluralism.[35] Although he goes on to balance Berlin's account with those of such historians as Jacob Talmon who blamed romantic irrationalism instead for later political sins, he concludes by damning the erotic impulse in intellectual life in general, the "love that induces madness, a blissful kind of madness we find hard to control, whether we are in love with another human being or with an idea."[36]

Isaiah Berlin may have been neither a hedgehog nor a priest, nor fairly accusable of being a parvenu, but he can, I think, be justifiably identified with Sontag's reliable, intelligible, generous, decent model of an intellectual "husband." Rather than indulging in exercises in ecstatic self-shattering, thus taking on himself the traumas of modern nomadic self-alienation, Berlin was ultimately at home in the world and in his own skin. In his youth, he was remembered as priggish, uneasy with sexuality, especially when it was deviant, and more an observer of life than a full participant.[37] He made an art of lively, urbane conversation, relished the conviviality of gossip and anecdote, and carried into his writing all the communicative virtues of a conversational style. As the secretary who had served him as president of Wolfson College recalled, Berlin was "even-tempered and reasonable. Rooted from childhood in the immense emotional security of being the only surviving offspring of adoring parents, he had a stable and hopeful nature, alight with humor and a sparkling joie de vivre. He seemed . . . to occupy a kind of Berlin bubble, a spaceship that flew happily about between Oxford and London, Jerusalem and Princeton, Paris and Milan, visiting the world's lecture theaters and opera houses."[38] For those like Lilla who think of self-control, the mastery of the irrational tyrant within us, as the responsible intellectual's first duty, intellectual husbands are clearly safer bets than their more dangerous and seductive rivals.

Conversely, for others who reckon domestic tranquility an overrated virtue, Berlin's innate moderation, excessive politeness, and refusal to challenge conventional wisdom bespeak intellectual flaccidity, moral fuzziness, and lack of political imagination. Thus, for example, Russell Jacoby, a staunch defender of utopian fantasy and the virtues of outsiderness, finds in Berlin an overly cautious waffler, unwilling to entertain anything that might roil the calm waters around him. His "truths teeter on the edge of truisms," Jacoby charges. "His ideas on pluralism and the dangers of utopianism partake of the basic Anglo-American mental household. . . . In political and intellectual worlds alike Berlin played it safe."[39] Rather than celebrating the agonistic, even potentially antagonistic implications of the clash of values or dwelling on the tragic consequences of incommensurable norms, he preferred to think in soothingly anodyne terms of complementarity and mutual toleration.

Another metaphoric opposition that may help define the difference between Benjamin and Berlin is suggested by Jacoby's further observation that "it is striking, even astonishing, that this much-honored, much-celebrated liberal political philosopher never risked a single sustained encounter with another twentieth-century thinker."[40] He did, to be sure, share his personal impressions of many contemporaries, often in the form of elegant elegies for the recently dead, and he grappled with an extraordinarily large number of earlier figures. But it is true that Berlin avoided tackling the thought of the major figures of his time, especially those from across the Channel. As a result, despite his towering reputation in the Anglo-American world, the impact he made on continental thought is very modest, although he may well have had a presence I cannot judge in Russian and Israeli intellectual life. As we have seen in the case of Adorno, Berlin often used the seemingly self-effacing ploy of confessing that he "couldn't understand a word" of a difficult thinker as a way to avoid grappling with their ideas, a semiserious excuse he had used with earlier philosophers like Hegel and would use for later ones like Heidegger. What jumps out here is Jacoby's observation that Berlin was averse to risk, unwilling to move beyond his comfort zone to open himself up to fresh and unsettling ideas. That is, to coin another dichotomy, he was less an intellectual gambler than a prudent investor who adeptly dealt in blue chip stocks of time-honored value.

Walter Benjamin, on the other hand, was a quintessential gambler, willing, as we have noted, to venture into enemy territory to acquire new ideas if he thought the journey were worth the risk. As Adorno once remarked, Benjamin explicitly identified with the figure of a gambler, "on which he brooded continually; thought renounces all semblance of the security of intellectual organization, renounces deduction, induction and conclusion, and delivers itself over to luck and the risk of betting on experience and striking something essential."[41] As it turns out, in his personal life, Benjamin was in fact an inveterate gambler in the literal sense of the term. Eiland and Jennings even report that he had a weakness for the gaming tables at places like Monaco, leading to the conjecture that his frequent pleas for money from his friends and relatives "were sometimes exaggerated so as to garner funds for gambling and women." But then they add that "for Benjamin, thinking itself is an existential wager arising from the recognition that truth is groundless and intentionless, and existence a 'baseless fabric.' The gaming table for him has ontological significance as an image of world play."[42] Much of Benjamin's work can be understood, in fact, as a desperate gamble against increasing odds that somehow he could preserve and help realize the redemptive dreams he thought were still alive in the debris of a world that was crashing down around him. Needless to say, his wager was disastrously unsuccessful, according to most standards of success. But by taking risks, at least some would argue, he left a legacy that might still somehow be potent in a future that was ready to receive it.

Berlin, in contrast, was a much more temperate investor, shrewd in securing his own status in the world and conveying the intellectual legacies of past thinkers. He invested in stocks that were safe—liberals or protoliberals like Herzen, Turgenev, Constant, Mill, Tocqueville—and when he did explore the ideas of more contrarian thinkers like Vico, Hamann, Herder, Sorel, or even de Maistre, he was careful to distinguish what was valuable in their thinking from what was dangerous. A collection of his essays was, to be sure, called *Against the Current*, which included his nuanced appreciation of the counter-Enlightenment tradition's debunking of the utopian pretensions of excessive Enlightenment rationalism. Berlin was, however, cautiously moderate in his consideration of their radical alternatives, so much so that Jacoby could mockingly title his earliest critique of Berlin—he has been a persistent critic over the years—"With the Current."[43]

Let me finish with one final candidate for a useful metaphoric opposition to distinguish our two protagonists, which is suggested by Benjamin's well-known 1934 essay "The Author as Producer." There is much going on in this provocative piece, which sought to define progressive art as following aesthetic rather than strictly political imperatives, or in Benjamin's words, "the tendency of a literary work can only be politically correct if it is also literarily correct."[44] Benjamin's main objective is to convince writers that they can make common cause with the proletariat only if they recognize that they too are producers who toil under conditions that are no less oppressive than those of other wage laborers in a capitalist economy. Rather than holding on to the old bourgeois myth of the creative genius, writers, indeed all intellectuals, have to recognize their shared lot with those who work with their hands. For Benjamin, the model artist who fit this description was Bertolt Brecht, whose epic theater turned dramatic works of art into dramatic laboratories in which disruptions of theatrical illusion involved the audience in a common productive project. In many ways, he relied on a technique that was so important in the film and radio of his day: montage, in which the smooth continuities of daily life were shattered by the use of defamiliarizing juxtapositions, which could result in the audience seeing the world in new ways.

Whether or not this description of the effect of Brecht's experimental dramas was only wishful thinking, Benjamin's essay alerts us to another potential metaphoric dichotomy, which is between the intellectual as producer and the intellectual as what we might call rentier. Whereas the former strives not to be a spectator but to intervene in the world, the latter lives off the productions of others, commentating rather than initiating, judging more than acting. Benjamin at least sought to be an active participant in the struggle for justice in his day, although it would be difficult to say that he ever succeeded in making common cause with flesh-and-blood proletarians. The performative effect of his often esoteric and elliptical writings was scarcely conducive to forging a united front between intellectual and manual laborers.

Although the category of rentier normally has a pejorative connotation in a society that makes a fetish of production, implying little more than parasitic indolence, in the realm of culture, it can have a more complex meaning. Thinking of Berlin in these terms helps us see how. It is well known that during the last years of the Second World War, he had a career crisis and gave up his hopes of becoming a practicing philosopher in favor of writing the history of ideas. The oft-told anecdote has him flying back from America to London on a long transatlantic flight in which he realized that the philosophy in which he had been trained was likely to be a dead end: "I gradually came to the conclusion," Berlin later recalled, "that I should prefer a field in which one could hope to know more at the end of one's life than when one had begun."[45]

Was this a tacit confession that his inability to produce new ideas meant Berlin had to settle for merely commenting on those of others, thus assuming the role of the sterile, unproductive rentier? Perhaps. But Mark Lilla makes a suggestive rejoinder to the assumption that it "was a step down the intellectual ladder." He observes that "it occurred to no one at the time that moving to the history of ideas might actually represent a step up. . . . Berlin never abandoned philosophy. . . . His instinct told him that you learn more about an idea *as an idea* when you know something about its genesis and understand why certain people found it compelling and were spurred to action by it. Then the real thinking begins."[46] In other words, there can be a constructive and even creative element in historical contextualization of given ideas, making sense of their complex origins, hidden debts, and unexpected receptions, that can rival that of pure theoretical contemplation, a conclusion that gives solace to denizens of my own corner of the scholarly universe.

There is, moreover, in Benjamin's own productive practice a suggestion of something similar. If, as we have seen him argue in the case of Brecht, the author as producer is really engaged in a kind of montage in which the unexpected juxtaposition of different given elements in a story produce defamiliarized insights, what Benjamin elsewhere called "profane illuminations," then there is a strongly derivative quality even in what intellectuals as producers do. That is, they often shuffle cards that have been dealt by others, something that Benjamin in his unfinished masterwork on the arcades of nineteenth-century Paris knew full well. It was, in fact, his utopian dream to write a book composed entirely of citations. Rather than glorifying the ideal of the creative genius, he damned it, as we have seen, as a bourgeois fantasy. The contrast between producer and rentier may thus not be as radical as it sounds, the main difference being the method of historicization involved. Berlin's kind of contextualization of ideas smacked, to be sure, of the unproblematized historicism that Benjamin with his more experimental methods decried, but both understood the impossibility of producing new ideas ex nihilo.

It would be possible to consider other contrasts, such as Jean Paulhan's distinction in *The Flowers of Tarbes*, between "rhetoricians," who follow conventional rules of language, and "terrorists," who demand they be subverted, or Max Weber's contrast between "emissary or ethical prophets" and "exemplary prophets," the former giving laws and conveying demands, the latter setting personal examples in the manner of the *imitatio Dei*.[47] There are, of course, also many singular metaphors—for example, Julien Benda's "clerks," Paul Nizan's "watchdogs," or Fritz Ringer's "mandarins"—that could easily generate binary oppositions through which we might contrast our two protagonists. But it is time to give Benjamin and Berlin a rest and consider the implications of the procedure itself. What, in conclusion, can we say of this little exercise in comparative metaphoric taxonomy or intellectual stylistics as a tool of historical analysis?

First, it might help us understand how more explicit categories, such as progressive and conservative, rationalist and empiricist, idealist and materialist, romantic and classical, may not fully account for the ways in which intellectuals can excite our interest and inflame our imagination. Conscious substantive labels, often adopted by intellectuals themselves, are insufficient to explain why posterity, indeed at times contemporaries, may treat them in unexpected ways. They fail to make sense of one of the most frequent but puzzling aspects of intellectual reception, the ardent adoption of ideas by one seemingly coherent camp that should find them anathema. Thus, for example, the recent left-wing romance of thinkers like Carl Schmitt, Martin Heidegger, and Ernst Jünger can't be explained just by looking at the ways in which their intellectual legacy might complement or enrich traditional progressive ideas. Instead, we have to understand their appeal on another level, as they can be seen as exemplifying the convention-defying, risk-taking "adventuresome hearts," to borrow the title of one of Jünger's books,[48] that cultural radicals of whatever stripe find irresistible. The transferential projection of our deeper needs, our penchant for living vicariously through heroes, or validating ourselves through scapegoating others, all may manifest themselves in the choices we may have trouble explaining in fully rational terms.

If we are drawn to "lovers" more than "husbands," it may not matter how implausible, inconsistent, or even dangerous their ideas might be. How else can we explain, for example, the current infatuation with Slavoj Žižek?

A second conclusion involves the often powerful effect a biography will have on our reception of the ideas of its subject. That is, we often conflate what we know of a life with the intellectual style of the author who led it, as explicitly urged by someone who has often benefited precisely from its effects, Friedrich Nietzsche, the "lonely genius" who knew that every philosophy is a personal confession. Benjamin's tragic and troubled existence lends a pathos to his thought that is hard to gainsay. Would he have attracted as much attention if he had successfully crossed the border from France to Spain, as did his traveling companions the day after he committed suicide? Would he have seemed as much a visitor from a lost world if he had ended up as Professor Benjamin reading blue book exams and writing letters of recommendation for his students at the New School? Can we likewise separate our appreciation—or disdain—for Berlin's *oeuvre* from the glittering life he led as the lion of Anglo-American establishment culture?

A third conclusion is suggested by the implicit gender implications not only of the "husband/lover" metaphor but also of others that tacitly draw on traditional roles. It is, for example, important to acknowledge the virtual absence of women as priests *or* jesters in at least traditional Western culture, and a "wife" may not always connote the same thing when she replaces "husband" as the antithesis of "lover." As a result, we may need a different taxonomy to do justice to figures like Rosa Luxemburg, Simone Weil, Hannah Arendt, or Susan Sontag herself. More precisely, we have to be careful not to transcendentalize what may themselves be historically variable categories that bring with them baggage, such as gender bias, of which we may not be immediately aware. After all, to call a female intellectual a fox is not as innocent as it may appear!

Fourth, as we've acknowledged on several occasions in our comparisons between Benjamin and Berlin, the metaphors are themselves inherently imperfect rubrics under which complex figures can be subsumed.[49] The imprecision is not, however, due only to the intrinsic differences between metaphors and concepts, the latter at least striving for subsumptive mastery of their individual exemplars, but also because history itself can undercut the power of their opposition. A powerful expression of this limitation appears at the end of Hannah Arendt's essay on "The Jew as Pariah: A Hidden Tradition," which appeared in the dreadful year of 1944. "Today," she grimly wrote, "the bottom has dropped out of the old ideology. The pariah Jew and the *parvenu* Jew are in the same boat, rowing desperately in the same angry sea. Both are branded with the same mark; both alike are outlaws."[50] Marriages, as we know, can dissolve, and husbands become lovers, investors can risk more than they can afford to lose and become gamblers, priests can play the fool and lose the authority of their role, and so on. Oppositions, in short, have to be treated as dialectical rather than binary, invasively haunting each other, historically evolving or even collapsing as conditions change. They are only useful if we acknowledge their limits as heuristic tools, helping us when they can to organize our responses to the infinite variety of a past that is never a fixed object simply to be observed from the distance of hindsight.

One final observation is in order, which concerns the status of European Jewish intellectuals as a historical phenomenon. As the 1944 citation from Arendt indicates, their very survival, no matter under which description, grew increasingly precarious during the Nazi era. What the Holocaust failed to accomplish, time and changed circumstances have worked to complete. That is, not only have the survivors of the worst horrors of "the Jewish Century," to adopt the ironic title of Yuri Slezkine's controversial book,[51] passed from history, but their descendants have by and large not been faced with the same existential choices and dire threats. Benjamin was moving from the fragile assimilation of his parents' generation to a renewed interest in Jewish theology, although not the observance of Jewish practice, while Berlin was diluting the residues of his family's religious commitment and practice while never repudiating his Jewish identity. But both were doing so in the face of a potent and sometimes deadly anti-Semitism that thankfully is no longer prevalent at least in the Western context. It has fallen to the lot of other groups to deal with the pariah/parvenu dilemma, the pressures of ethnic prejudice, the costs of assimilation and the potential alienation of elite from popular culture. Perhaps Jacques Derrida was the last major European Jewish intellectual—and he was, of course, himself actually born in colonial Algeria, not metropolitan France—who can claim the type of attention that a Benjamin or a Berlin once warranted. There will be, to be sure, other candidates for the roles that European Jewish intellectuals played with such brio. It is not the least of their legacy that they have left us such a rich repertoire of intellectual styles to serve as tools for making sense of not only the past but also the future life of the mind.

CHAPTER 5

Against Rigor: Blumenberg on Freud and Arendt

In his wrenching memoir of surviving Auschwitz, *If This Is a Man*, the Italian writer Primo Levi recalls a moment when he learned a bitter lesson about the vanity of seeking the meaning of his suffering: "Driven by thirst, I eyed a fine icicle outside the window, within reach of my hand. I opened the window and broke off the icicle, but at once a large, heavy guard prowling outside brutally snatched it away. '*Warum?*' I asked in my poor German. '*Hier ist kein warum*' (there is no why here), he replied, shoving me back inside."[1] The guard's chilling candor about the utter gratuity of his cruel gesture has become an emblematic moment in the unending struggle to explain, interpret, and represent the bafflingly savage rupture in civilization we have come to call "the Holocaust" or "the Shoah." It is the moment when all of our intellectual resources seem to fail us and we are confronted with the unyielding absurdity of actions and events that resist any attempt to provide a plausible answer to the questions of why they happened or what they signify. Like the icicle that melts in the guard's hand before it can slake Levi's thirst, reasons for the horror vanish into the air before they satisfy our yearning to find meaning in an indifferent universe bereft of it.[2]

It is as if Job in the Hebrew Bible is confronted not with an ineffable God but rather with God's Satanic opposite, who tortures him for reasons that he refuses to divulge.[3] The conventional rhetoric of tragedy, sacrifice, and martyrdom all reveal themselves to be woefully inadequate to characterize, let alone justify, the slaughter of so many innocents. Not surprisingly, for some survivors like Elie Wiesel in his searing fictionalized memoir *Night*, the consoling balm of religion could no longer provide comfort for an affliction that could find no conceivable justification. Although God may move in mysterious ways "his wonders to perform," he doesn't get a pass when it comes to performing unaccountable horrors. But for other survivors, precisely because it is the devil and not God whose unjust cruelty is inexplicable, the victim should never renounce the search for meaning and withdraw in the end, as does Job in the Bible, his seemingly hubristic demand for a reason for his suffering. Instead, they continue to press for an answer to "Warum?" For failing to do so, they fear, would be to grant a posthumous victory to the tormentors whose arrogant retort must not be allowed to serve as the last word.

For the intellectuals among those personally touched by the Holocaust, the imperative to deny that victory to the devil must have seemed especially overwhelming. Intellectuals, after all, are people defined by their need to explain and interpret the world, no matter how opaque it may appear, and then to justify their answers to others. To be in the midst of an unfolding catastrophe the likes of which even the long-suffering Jewish people could never have imagined must have compelled intellectuals identified, however tenuously, as Jews to explain or find deeper meaning in the cataclysmic events that menaced their existence. And inevitably, such unprecedented and unexpected horrors demanded all the imaginative resources at their command.

But what if the dogged quest for intelligibility might produce unintended consequences? If slaking one's thirst means ingesting an icicle of tainted water, is it perhaps better to accept that no "Warum" can be conclusively answered, to acknowledge that even if he were willing to do so, neither God nor the devil could provide a plausible explanation, let alone justification, for so dreadful an event? Refusing to concede this inability may, after all, lead to crediting false answers, with all of their attendant dangers. Or at least such was the worry that motivated one survivor of the Holocaust, the distinguished philosopher and historian of ideas Hans Blumenberg, to compose an impassioned reflection on the previous attempts made by two of the twentieth century's most prominent Jewish intellectuals, Sigmund Freud and Hannah Arendt, to answer Primo Levi's desperate question.

Unpublished in Blumenberg's lifetime, ostensibly because he feared it would offend his close friend, the philosopher Hans Jonas, *Rigorism of Truth*[4] was completed over a long period of intermittent rumination, which seems to have ended, according to the reckoning of the volume's German editor and Blumenberg's last assistant, Ahlrich Meyer, in the late 1980s. As the trail of notecards left in Blumenberg's voluminous *Nachlass* shows, he was already troubled by the implications of Freud's *Moses and Monotheism* (1939) as early as 1947, and he invoked it in *The Legitimacy of the Modern Age* a few years later as a cautionary example of the dubious practice of "working through" past circumstances as a cure for present ills.[5] Although Blumenberg had a marginal interest in Arendt's work before *Eichmann in Jerusalem*—they even had a brief correspondence and one unproductive meeting—it was apparently his reading of that volume in 1978, some fifteen years after its original publication, that stimulated Blumenberg to bring her together with the father of psychoanalysis.

Linking Freud and Arendt, as Blumenberg knew full well, was itself an audacious move, highly unusual in the voluminous literature on either of them, as was *a fortiori* the parallel he drew between Moses and Eichmann as the targets of their debunking. Arendt, after all, was never an admirer of psychoanalysis, even if she was awarded the Sigmund Freud Prize of the Deutsche Akademie für Sprache und Dichtung in 1969.[6] Their approaches to politics radically differed, with Arendt extolling its intrinsic virtues and Freud reducing it to allegedly deeper psychological causes.[7] Her classic work *The Origins of Totalitarianism* contains no insights from the psychoanalytic tradition, which set her apart from other exiles such as Erich Fromm, Wilhelm Reich, or Erik Erikson, who sought to interpret Nazism in terms of collective psychological pathologies. And yet, on the basic issue of relentlessly seeking the true causes of genocidal anti-Semitism no matter the consequences, so Blumenberg came to believe, Freud and Arendt were united.

Freud, it might be objected, died in 1939 in London, before the Holocaust's full fury was unleashed, in an exile forced on him by the annexation of his native Austria by the Nazis a year earlier. He was thus spared knowing the fate of his people, including his four sisters, one of whom died in Theresienstadt, the other three in Auschwitz. And yet, *Moses and Monotheism*, his controversial final book, was clearly written in the anticipatory shadow of the horrors to follow. It was, among many other things, an attempt to understand why the Jewish people were so often in their long history the target of hatred and bigotry. Rueful that his answer might be construed as blaming the victims, he nonetheless pointed to the very promulgation of Mosaic law, which, to make matters worse, he claimed was actually the work of a son of Egypt mistakenly understood to be a Jew and then killed by his people.

Tumbling the pantheon of pagan gods from their various pedestals, prohibiting idolatrous images, discrediting the tricks of magicians and their ilk, the Jews, Freud speculated, had turned the monotheistic message of that wayward Egyptian Moses into the elevation of spirituality—*Geistigkeit*—over the body and the senses.[8] In so doing, they unwittingly unleashed a seemingly never-ending struggle in human history between higher and lower, internal and external, paternal and maternal forces, a struggle responsible for both the glorious achievements of human culture and the smoldering resentment of its repressed victims, who mourned what they had lost in terms of more direct corporeal gratification. It was, Freud now tacitly acknowledged, not simply civilization *tout court* that brought with it discontents, but one specific civilization in particular that was grounded in the ethical rigor, sensual constraints, and rejection of matriarchal warmth that accompanied the triumph of Mosaic law.

But in a way, so Blumenberg argued, Freud had gone beyond merely exposing the resented costs of Jewish spirituality. For he also discredited the myth of Moses as the messenger of God, and in so doing he undermined Moses's foundational role as charismatic lawgiver for a people newly freed from bondage. That is, Freud had extended the rigorous spiritual logic of monotheistic lawgiving to discredit the very mythic figure who was its alleged source. Freud moreover knew that his scandalous debunking of the "legend of Moses," the acclaimed liberator of the Jewish people, combined with his exposure of the costs of renouncing the flesh in the service of spirit, risked being seen as a betrayal of solidarity with his fellow Jews at the moment of their greatest danger. In the very opening sentences of his book, he felt compelled to defend his decision in terms that Blumenberg would ponder with increasing disquiet: "To deny a people the man whom it praises as the greatest of its sons is not a deed to be undertaken lightheartedly—especially by one belonging to that people. No consideration, however, will move me to set aside truth in favor of supposed national interests."[9] In other words, Freud felt he had no choice but to follow the celebrated Latin imperative *Fiat justitia, et pereat mundus*,[10] albeit with truth substituted for justice.

This imperative, so Blumenberg claimed, likewise seized Hannah Arendt a generation later. She too was driven by an intransigent passion for the truth, the consequences be damned. Her "rigorism is very much like that of Sigmund Freud," he argued. "She believes in the truth—that is her truth, she can neither change nor prevent."[11] Also exiled by the Nazis but fortunate enough to survive well after their defeat, she often returned to the vexed question of how their regime, and that of their "totalitarian" counterparts, could have emerged in the heart of "civilized" Europe. Her most sustained confrontation with the specificity of the German case was in her response to the trial in Israel of the kidnapped Nazi official Adolf Eichmann, *Eichmann in Jerusalem:*

A Report on the Banality of Evil,[12] which generated a storm of criticism that has scarcely abated in the half century since it appeared.

Blumenberg shared many of the now-standard criticisms of her book: its problematic case against the "collaboration" of Jewish councils in the smooth running of the annihilation machinery, its dubious reduction of Eichmann to a thoughtless bureaucrat—or even feckless "clown"—rather than an ideologically committed Nazi, its disdain for the Zionist project in the service of a universalist internationalism, and its preference for charging Eichmann with a "crime against humanity" rather than a specific one against the Jewish people. But the most fundamental of Blumenberg's charges was against Arendt's alleged truth-telling absolutism, which was symptomatic of a moral rigidity as well: "Her book is a document of rigorism, the definition of which is the refusal to acknowledge an ultimate and inexorable dilemma in human action." As in the case of Freud, Blumenberg charged, her insistence on the truth despite everything, an insistence that bespeaks moral intransigence, produced lamentable consequences for the Jews. "As Freud took Moses the man from his people, so Hannah Arendt took Adolf Eichmann from the State of Israel. Some states are founded on their enemies."[13] In short, "a negative hero," as Arendt called Eichmann in one of her preparatory notes, was as necessary as a "positive hero" like Moses in the imaginary of a people striving for its full realization in the world. Both were mythic figures, one appearing when the Jewish people achieved its first political embodiment, the other when it reestablished it with the realization of the Zionist dream of a Jewish state.

In his careful annotations and the judicious afterword he prepared for the original German edition, Ahlrich Meyer addresses the plausibility of many of Blumenberg's specific charges and helps us see how the essay emerged from the voluminous card files left behind in his extensive *Nachlass*, a rich quarry still being mined for new publications more than two decades after his death. What I want to add here is some context for this little text by looking at Blumenberg's career as a whole, as well as casting a glance at his own relationship to the Holocaust and the challenge of its ineffability.

Hans Blumenberg (1920–1996) is certainly a less celebrated figure than either Freud or Arendt, but he has steadily earned a reputation as one of the towering presences in twentieth-century German thought, a unique combination of philosophical depth and historical erudition. The son of a Catholic father, a dealer in devotional objects, and a Jewish mother who had converted to Protestantism, he toyed with a career in the Church and spent a semester studying Catholic theology. But he was classified as a "half-Jew" by the Nazis, forced to suspend his education during the war and take shelter with the family of his future wife. In February 1945 he was interned in a labor camp of the Organization Todt in Zerbst in Saxony-Anhalt.[14] After the war he studied with Ludwig Landgrebe, a student of Edmund Husserl, in Kiel, and he later taught philosophy at universities in Hamburg, Giessen, and Bochum. His last and most extended position was in Münster, where he taught from 1970 to 1986, distant from the center of intellectual life in the Federal Republic. Whereas Freud and Arendt were quintessentially "public intellectuals,"[15] often commenting on the most pressing issues of the day, Blumenberg was the very model of a private scholar, not only eschewing pronouncements on current events but also disdaining the normal whirl of academic conferences, public lectures, and interviews, both in Germany and abroad. Although he was involved for a while with the research group Poetics and Hermeneutics, including leading postwar figures like Hans Robert Jauß, Wolfgang Iser, Jacob Taubes, Reinhart Koselleck, and Odo Marquard, he was essentially an intellectual lone wolf. Explaining his self-imposed isolation, he liked to say that he had to make up for the eight years of scholarly productivity he lost during the Nazi period.[16]

Blumenberg kept his distance as well from the political cacophony of the 1960s and 1970s, avoiding the controversies in which, for example, members of the Frankfurt School were so often embroiled. If he held strong political opinions, they were only indirectly expressed in his esoteric writings.[17] He founded no new school of thought with eager disciples spreading his gospel, and he was himself very hard to place in any tradition. Although his own forays into the history of metaphor—or more capaciously, "non-conceptuality"[18]—did find an appreciative if modest audience, they have not been as influential as the *Begriffsgeschichte* (history of concepts) developed by Koselleck, Otto Brunner, and Erich Rothacker.[19]

And yet, Blumenberg has earned enormous respect among serious students of Western thought from its inception in classical times to the present. His astonishing command of primary sources, it is widely acknowledged, was unmatched, while never supporting self-indulgent pedantry. His confident mastery of theological and scientific as well as philosophical traditions was unparalleled. In the 1980s the heroic translation by Robert M. Wallace in rapid succession of three of his earliest major books, *Legitimacy of the Modern Age*, *The Genesis of the Copernican World*, and *Work on Myth*, introduced the richness of his scholarship and the subtlety of his thinking to an

English-speaking public.[20] Despite their merciless demands on readers lacking his range of reference and the challenges of Blumenberg's often turgid prose, they stimulated novel ways of thinking about the most profound questions of the human condition, questions whose historically evolving answers Blumenberg skillfully traced. In particular, he offered new and arresting ways to make sense of the continuities and discontinuities between historical epochs, especially the transition from the Middle Ages to modernity, and the unending search for meaning in a world that consistently thwarts it. Against the reduction of ideas to their social functions as mere ideologies, he honored what might be called the substantive dignity of both concepts and their metaphorical counterparts, at least as honest answers to the challenges of an intractable reality.

Because Blumenberg was a critic of the claim made by Karl Löwith, Carl Schmitt, and others that the modern world was a pale, secularized version of what went before—a claim evident, for example, in the discourse of what has come to be called "political theology"[21]—he often came to be seen as a defender of modernity, even a champion of the Enlightenment project. If compared with the influential critique of modernity generated by, say, Martin Heidegger, from whom Blumenberg distanced himself throughout his career, his careful argument for modernity's inherent "legitimacy" certainly earned that reputation.[22] But if a defense, it was a nuanced one, without illusions about the capacity of reason and the scientific method to solve the perennial problems that have demanded answers since the dawn of human culture, thus overcoming the legacy of magic and myth. As Robert Pippen has pointed out, his was a modernity without a radical "disenchantment" of the type famously posited by Max Weber.[23]

Behind the intricate historical narratives spun out by Blumenberg was a fundamental belief in an essential human condition that owed a great deal to his training in Husserl's phenomenology and interest in the anthropology of Arnold Gehlen.[24] From Husserl, or more precisely the later Husserl who authored *The Crisis of European Sciences and Transcendental Phenomenology*, Blumenberg gained an awareness that the discursive world of concepts is rooted in a preconceptual, prereflective "lifeworld," the realm of everyday experience, in which the role of rhetoric in general and metaphor in particular is key. From Gehlen, he learned that our fecund cultural imagination allows humans to compensate as best they can for their lack of the biologically determined, instinctual preprogramming that orients other animals in the world.

In what is sometimes designated as his implicit "negative anthropology," Blumenberg contends that the recalcitrant opacity of the world, a world of irreducible contingency rather than necessity, presents never-ending challenges to fill the void left by previous failures to provide enduring answers to insoluble questions.[25] What he came to call the "absoluteness of reality"[26] means that the world can never be fully explained by human intellectual projections; it is always in excess of the most advanced interpretations of natural or social being. This is just as true, *pace* Freud, of the inner world of the subject as of the outer world of objects. It too stubbornly resists our best efforts to render it transparent.

But because that absolute reality is also one that relentlessly threatens our survival, we are compelled to find ways to cope and orient ourselves, both practically and theoretically, ways to domesticate and distance ourselves from the relentless indifference of the real. Escape from the world—the temptation of world-denying Gnosticism—is fruitless, although the temptation to do so always remains. Thus modernity, Blumenberg argued, could be understood as entailing "the second overcoming of Gnosticism," after the first attempt by the early Christians failed in the late Middle Ages.[27] Others in the future, he implied, would be likely, as the pragmatic struggle to replace ultimately unsuccessful cultural responses to the unforgiving "absoluteness of reality" would continue without resolution.[28] Despite the relief provided by technological antidotes to the indifference of "absolute reality"—Blumenberg was never inclined to disdain technology in the manner of, say, Heidegger—the precariousness of the human condition remained.

Because Blumenberg assumed that the deepest secrets of reality would always elude human attempts to reveal them, he concluded that there was more of a continuity between *mythos* and *logos* than a radical caesura.[29] Both were stratagems for managing the anxieties unleashed by the elusiveness of reality. Believers in a break between them usually advanced an exorbitant notion of reason—Blumenberg liked to call it "rigorous" with a nod to the early Husserl's dubious attempt to make phenomenology a "strenge Wissenschaft"— that sought clear and distinct ideas and unequivocally defined concepts. Blumenberg was by no means an enemy of logos, but he thought it wise to recognize as well the value of the more imprecise and flexible alternatives that the exponents of the rigorous view had so disdainfully rejected. For example, in rhetoric, which rationalists ever since Plato had scorned, Blumenberg saw an imperfect but still functional way to compensate for the "poverty of our instincts" and the limits of our intelligence. It is based on what he called, with a sly twist on Leibniz's famous formula, "the principle of insufficient reason (*principium rationis insufficientis*). It is the correlate of the anthropology of a creature who is deficient in essential respects." This is not, he emphasized, the same thing as an irrationalist's abdication of the need for justifications or giving reasons, just a recognition that the rules of logic and the scientific method do not exhaust the full repertoire of human attempts to make sense of their world. Indeed, rhetoric is "a form of rationality itself—a rational way of coming to terms with the provisionality of reason."[30] Sophistry was not the antithesis of reason but a more supple and effective form of it than its enemies had contended.

Metaphor in particular is a tool that humans, the *animal symbolicum*, have forged to cope with a world—both external and internal—they cannot fully understand or master. It seeks to replace something frightening and uncanny with something familiar and comforting, taking an indirect and often lengthy route to assuage the fears generated by the disorienting blockage of the more direct route provided by unthinking instinct. It inevitably retains a trace of the affect that generated it, in opposition to the development of rational concepts, which claim to transcend feeling.[31] Not only does it operate on the level of language, but it also functions in actions that substitute one thing for another. "If history teaches us anything at all," Blumenberg argued, "it is this, that without this capacity to use substitutes for actions not much would be left of mankind. The ritualized replacement of a human sacrifice by an animal sacrifice, which is still visible through the story of Abraham and Isaac, may have been a beginning. Christianity, through two millennia, has regarded it as quite understandable that the death of one can compensate for the mischief for which all are responsible."[32]

When such metaphoric displacements coalesce into full-fledged stories, myth emerges as a way to orient ourselves in a baffling world of natural forces beyond our control.[33] By anthropomorphizing those forces, giving them names and identifying them with personalities, mythic narratives served to allay fears, allowing humans to propitiate gods through sacrifices, rituals, and prayer. In particular, the myths of polytheism in which humanized gods struggle for power avoided the potential for dogmatic rigor that emerged with the monotheistic ideal of a transcendent and distant God—a conclusion, ironically, not so far from that reached by Freud in *Moses and Monotheism*, as Blumenberg had acknowledged in his earliest discussion of myth in 1968.[34] Even when myths are debunked, as inevitably they are, and lose their power to console us, they are not always replaced by rigorous scientific thinking or conceptual reason, for "demythicization is in large measure nothing more than remetaphorization."[35] And these new metaphors have the ability to become the foundation of new myths, as well as serve as the irreducible kernel of rational concepts. Moses, in other words, may have unleashed the spiritual revolution of monotheism and the law, which dethroned polytheistic mythic gods, but as the charismatic messenger of God, he was also the embodiment of a new myth. And although it was precisely Freud's great transgression to undermine Moses's mythic status as the founding father of the Jews in the name of disinterested science, he ironically set himself up as the mythic founder or primal father of psychoanalysis, a new attempt to break through the inherent opacity of "absolute reality."

Blumenberg's ruminations on the enduring function of myth, which have earned him a comparison with Giambattista Vico, place him somewhere on a spectrum between Nietzsche, who urged that it replace logos, and Cassirer, who hoped for the opposite.[36] Inevitably, they have generated considerable controversy. Not only have defenders of monotheism, such as Jacob Taubes, been troubled by the relativizing moral implications of polytheism, but other commentators have also wondered how Blumenberg could ignore the political costs of mythmaking so soon after the disaster of Nazism.[37] Although it has transpired since the original publication of *Work on Myth* in 1979 that he had left out a final chapter that did touch on the Nazi case, at least in an oblique way,[38] he never really confronted head-on the dangers of mythic thinking in the political realm.

All the more surprising, therefore, is his critique of the debunking of myth in Freud and Arendt. For it appears to be motivated by an unexpected allegiance to the Zionist project of a Jewish homeland, based on the belief in the unique destiny of the Jewish people challenged by Freud and the persistent threat of radically evil anti-Semitism undermined by Arendt. Blumenberg's Jewish identity, such as it was, appears to have been derived as much from Nazi racial categorizations as from anything more deeply felt. Rarely if ever included in discussions of Jewish philosophers, he doesn't seem to have drawn much sustenance from explicitly Jewish cultural traditions.[39] He contributed nothing of note to postwar debates about "working through" the Nazi past or Germany's responsibility to compensate the survivors of its crimes. Nor did he weigh in publicly on the touchy subject of the Israeli/Palestinian conflict.[40] Significantly, in his last letter he stressed his intellectual debts to the early training he had received in Catholic theology.[41]

And yet, in the notes rescued from his *Nachlass*, we find several brief but clearly heartfelt ruminations on the challenges of being Jewish in a hostile world. In one, he speculates that anti-Semitism has engendered two basic responses, which he calls "the cloven consciousness of Jewry": anarchic opposition to and resentment of the dominant social order, on the one hand, and self-abnegation, on the other. Ironically, the latter can be redescribed in the Freudian terms he so vigorously resisted as "identification with the aggressor."[42] Blumenberg may perhaps have recognized it as a temptation to which he had himself succumbed. And if so, in now bemoaning Freud's and Arendt's alleged demolitions of a necessary myth for the Jewish people in the name of disinterested intellectual rigor, was he trying indirectly to distance himself from Jewish self-abnegation? And if he were, did he fully succeed?

A clue might be found in another notecard in his file, titled "Ambiguity without Comprehension,"[43] in which he recalls an episode during the war in which Thomas Mann reflected on the reactions to Hitler he encountered at a party at the Frankfurt School philosopher Max Horkheimer's house in Pacific Palisades. Mann was apparently uncomfortable with what he saw as their inflated sense of the Nazis' importance. "These Jews have a sense of Hitler's greatness," he confessed, "that I cannot bear." Noting that Mann's reaction anticipated Arendt's dismissive characterization of Eichmann two decades later in Jerusalem as a "buffoon of pathetic insignificance," Blumenberg contrasted it with the need of Horkheimer's friends—"these open or disguised Hegelians"—to find deep meanings in the events unfolding before them, even a manifestation of "the cunning of reason." Blumenberg, however, confessed that he identified with Mann, not Horkheimer: "No, he too, to whom this was unbearable, was right." Blumenberg, in short, sided not with the Jewish detractors of a demonic Hitler, desperately trying to address the unanswered "Warum?" posed by Nazism, but with the gentiles who were unable to share their full sense of Hitler's monstrosity and who resisted fishing for deeper answers, at least on the level of rational explanations.[44]

Such a choice suggests his own struggle to come to grips with both his own conflicted identity and the challenge of explaining Nazism and the Holocaust—or accepting that they can't be satisfactorily explained. For in siding with Mann, and explicitly linking his position with Arendt's, he was admitting that from an objective point of view—one, in other words, that sidestepped the pragmatic implications of the positions taken—she was actually right in denying the demonic monstrosity of Eichmann. Her argument about the "banality of evil" was thus problematic not because it trivialized what required a deeper explanation, but rather because it eroded the function that myth played in the founding of a Jewish state. When he got around to directly addressing Arendt's argument in *Rigorism of Truth*, Blumenberg more explicitly embraced the pragmatic necessity of myth as an alternative to both deep explanations and impotent skepticism. That is, he applied his general lesson in *Work on Myth* that the impenetrable "absolutism of reality," and *a fortiori* a reality where one can boast "hier ist kein Warum," needs some sort of myth to console and orient those who are beset by it.

However, in so doing Blumenberg, it has to be noted, unwittingly subjected Arendt herself to a certain mythic reconstruction as the latter-day Platonic defender of truth at all costs and a moral rigorist, a deontologist with no sympathy for the consequentialist implications of her actions. For in building his image of her, Blumenberg ignored the fact that Arendt was herself deeply suspicious of the fetish of truth, at least when it came to politics, explicitly claiming that the assumption of a single correct view of the world contradicted the pluralism and contest of opinions necessary for freedom in the political sphere. Although the shoe fashioned by Blumenberg may have fit Freud, who often did seek to pierce the fabric of self-delusions and the armor of defense mechanisms to uncover occluded truths, it was far less comfortable in the case of Arendt.[45] In an essay written after the controversy over *Eichmann in Jerusalem*, Arendt directly addressed the wisdom of *Fiat justitia, et pereat mundus* and its correlate *Fiat veritas, et pereat mundus*.[46] Although skeptical of the former, she acknowledged that the latter was worth heeding, at least in general, for "the sacrifice of truth for the survival of the world would be more futile than the sacrifice of any other principle or virtue."[47] But, and this was a point Blumenberg missed, when it came to the specifically political realm, the lesson was different. Whether in what she called its "factual" or "rational" guise, truth-telling was inherently antipolitical, for "seen from the viewpoint of politics, truth has a despotic character. . . . The modes of thought and communication that deal with truth, if seem from the political perspective, are necessarily domineering; they don't take into account other people's opinions, and taking these into account is the hallmark of all strictly political thinking."[48] Although never specifically sanctioning myth as an antidote to the dubious imperative to tell the truth no matter the cost, she understood the virtues of rhetoric, metaphor, and even mendacity, at least when it came to politics.[49]

It was thus problematic to associate her, as did Blumenberg, with a Platonic hostility to Sophistic rhetoric. In a posthumously published essay on

Socrates, originally written in the 1950s, Arendt explicitly condemned Plato's elevation of truth over *doxa* (opinion) as inherently hostile to politics.[50] The world of politics, moreover, is the world of appearances, not essences. In general, Arendt defended the importance of phenomenal reality, the reality of surfaces rather than depths, including the deeper psychological interiority posited by Freud. As she put it in *The Life of the Mind*, "Our habitual standards of judgment, so firmly rooted in metaphysical assumptions and prejudices—according to which the essential lies beneath the surface and the surface is 'superficial'—are wrong.... Our common conviction that what is inside ourselves our 'inner life,' is more relevant to what we 'are' than what appears on the outside is an illusion."[51] Later in that work, moreover, she approvingly drew on Blumenberg's metaphorology in a longer argument against Plato that stressed the inevitability of metaphors in metaphysical language, many of which are based on the body and produce unintended consequences.[52]

Blumenberg was also on unsteady ground in characterizing her as a moral rigorist, a deontological thinker in the absolutist mold of Kant. In fact, her essay celebrating Lessing's sacrifice of truth to the value of friendship explicitly argues that "the inhumanity of Kant's moral philosophy is undeniable. And this is so because the categorical imperative is postulated as absolute, and in its absoluteness introduces into the interhuman realm—which by its nature consists of relationships—something that runs counter to its fundamental relativity."[53] In *Eichmann in Jerusalem*, she mulled over Eichmann's startling defense, which on the surface seemed outrageous, that he was observing Kant's categorical imperative. Although admitting that in most respects the defense was dubious, she nonetheless concluded, "There is not the slightest doubt that in one respect Eichmann did indeed follow Kant's precepts: a law was a law, there could be no exceptions."[54]

Still, on the larger issue raised by his essay, Blumenberg was right to include Arendt along with Freud as a theorist who could not rest content with the cynical answer "Hier ist kein warum," when it came to explaining the centuries of anti-Semitism that culminated in the Holocaust. *Eichmann in Jerusalem*, for all its flaws, can be understood as an attempt, to cite the Finnish political theorist Tuija Parvikko, to resist the conventional wisdom that tends to "absolutize and depoliticize the Holocaust by claiming that it was an indecipherable and incomparable phenomenon" in which the victims were denied their role "as active contributors to their own history."[55]

It was, of course, that latter claim regarding Jewish complicity in their own destruction that most rankled, as it seemed to be a case of not only blaming the victim but also insisting on the truth no matter the consequences.⁵⁶ Blumenberg was, as we have noted, deeply suspicious of the ideal of truth-telling at all costs, or indeed the faith that truth can ever finally be established. As he put it in one of the notecards in his *Nachlass*, ironically titled "The Power of Truth": "Among the intimate convictions of European history is that the truth will triumph. That is as little self-evident as can be, considering what measure of description and polemic was deployed in order to represent and warn against rhetorical distractions up to the possibilities of demagogy."⁵⁷

And yet, the hope that the truth will triumph is so powerful that we can see it operating in the case of Blumenberg himself. For ironically, he was no less of a compulsive truth-teller than his two targets, no less reluctant than they to risk the world's doom in the name of intellectual honesty. Tacitly echoing Freud's confession at the beginning of *Moses and Monotheism*, Blumenberg tells us in *Rigorism of Truth* that he was "prepared to court indignation" but could not draw back from his inflammatory comparison, even if he were "aghast by the deep-rooted similarities" he discerned in Freud's and Arendt's most controversial works.⁵⁸ Moreover, despite his suspicion of exorbitant rationalism and defense of the enduring role of mythos even after the emergence of logos, he nonetheless rejected their binary status as mutually exclusive. Thus he could promote an "ology" of metaphors and himself eschewed presenting his thoughts in an aesthetic form rather than in a traditional scholarly fashion. For all his hostility to ahistorical Platonic universalism, the never-ending challenges of the human condition posited by his negative anthropology have even earned him the label of an "immanent Platonist," uncomfortable with a radically historicist denial of any constants in history.⁵⁹

But it was perhaps most in his treatment of myth itself that Blumenberg showed his unexpected affinity to his two targets in *Rigorism of Truth*. That is, contrary to other recent exponents of mythic thought, such as Joseph Campbell or Mircea Eliade, he did not claim that myths represented eternal wisdom or enduring archetypes of the human mind.⁶⁰ His own stance was that of someone investigating its functions from afar, a cultural anthropologist of a tribe to which he didn't fully belong, a metatheorist of both mythos and logos in their pure forms. He was, more precisely put, a forgiving analyst of myth from the outside, but a more ambivalent critic of reason from within. Thus, when he accused Freud and Arendt of robbing the Jewish people of their enabling myths, it is not at all clear he ever believed in them himself. There is very little evidence, in fact, that he shared the Zionist dream of a Jewish homeland, at least one to which he was personally drawn.⁶¹ Nor, as his concluding remark in the notecard devoted to Mann and Horkheimer shows, did he really believe that Eichmann was actually a nonbanal "negative hero," whose symbolic role was crucial in justifying the existence of the new state.

If anything, by his very act of exposing that role as grounded in myth rather than reality, and arguing that the pragmatic function of myth was necessary as a way for humans to cope with the contingent "absoluteness of reality," Blumenberg revealed that he too could not rest content with mythical consolations for both the general "hier ist kein warum" of "absolute reality" and the specific lack of a justification for the Holocaust. Although he eschewed deontological rigorism, he showed himself to be an ethical consequentialist, fully aware of the practical implications of beliefs whose compelling power he did not himself feel. For all his fury at the damaging effects of compulsive truth-telling, for all his pessimism about conceptual precision replacing metaphoric play, for all his insistence that logos cannot emerge from the shadow of mythos, Blumenberg reveals himself in the end to be one of those insistent intellectuals *malgré lui*, Jewish, half-Jewish, or otherwise, who cannot entirely relinquish the need to seek a nonmythic answer to Primo Levi's desperate question: "Warum?"

CHAPTER 6

"Hey! What's the Big Idea?": Ruminations on the Question of Scale in Intellectual History

Students of recent trends in historiography will likely hear in the familiar phrase in this essay's title an echo of a widely discussed manifesto by the Harvard historian David Armitage in 2012 titled "What's the Big Idea? Intellectual History and the *Longue Durée*."[1] It made a spirited case for the revival of a long-range history of ideas traversing centuries, even millennia. Those more conversant with the history of American popular culture may, however, find the inclusion of the interjection preceding the question a reminder of something very different: the frequency with which it once voiced exasperation and annoyance in response to a provocation, real or imagined. It was, in fact, an incessantly uttered catchphrase employed in precisely this way during the first half of the last century by, among others, the cartoon character Donald Duck, the real comedian Bert Lahr, and the Three Stooges, who hovered halfway between cartoon and reality.[2] It is useful to recall the way they all employed the little "Hey!" before addressing the question that followed it to register the fact that there has often seemed something obnoxious about the very concept of a "big idea," a trace of pretension and arrogance that has worked to annoy more than enlighten those on whom it is foisted.

Attempts to trace the fate of "big ideas" over long periods of time by intellectual historians have in fact often been met with a collective "Hey!" expressing the skeptical dismay of their colleagues. Suspicion has been generated not only when the idea is itself overly abstract and general, but also when attempts are made to fashion a coherent narrative of its history over many centuries, that *longue durée* that so entranced Fernand Braudel and his colleagues in the Annales School back in the mid-twentieth century.³ The reaction to the first danger was already voiced in 1900 by Georg Simmel in his explanation of what he called "the tragedy of human concept formation" in *The Philosophy of Money*, a tragedy that "lies in the fact that the higher concept, which through its breadth embraces a growing number of details, must count upon increasing loss of content. Money is the perfect practical counterpart of such a higher category, namely a form of being whose qualities are generality and lack of content; a form of being that endows these qualities with real power and whose relation to all the contrary qualities of the objects transacted and to their psychological constellations can be equally interpreted as service and domination."⁴ Here the anxiety is that higher concepts—which at this point in our argument we can equate with "big ideas"—hover too far above the messiness of the lifeworld, with all its contrary impulses, nuanced ambiguities, and metaphoric displacements. The grander the idea, so Simmel noted, the less likely it is to attend to the qualitative distinctions of the particulars it commensurates. Like money, it has the potential not only to provide a useful service but also to dominate the concrete actions subsumed under its general rule. Reminiscent of the nominalist critique of real universals during the Middle Ages—although Simmel's sociology stressed relationality and interaction and eschewed methodological individualism—this skepticism about "big ideas" was as much philosophical as it was historical.

The second worry, often directed at the Annales School, was unleashed by the search for enduring structural regularities at the deep level of historical continuity. Their programmatic indifference to discrete events and the complexities of individual texts underwrote a search for general *mentalités* in the realm of culture, which many critics found too sweeping to do justice to the finer distinctions that make intellectual history more than an imprecise and impressionist account of the *Geist* of a particular *Zeit*. As Armitage himself concedes, "Big history, in all of its guises, has been inhospitable to the questions of meaning and intention so central to intellectual history."⁵ In fact, insofar as it has relied on either biologistic or economistic explanations for long-term trends, it has minimized the role of ideas in history *tout court*.

Tellingly, resistance to the history of "big ideas" has come from defenders of both contextualist and textualist approaches to the field. The former stress the embeddedness of ideas in relevant matrices of generation, dissemination, and reception, the local and finite contexts that ground ideas that otherwise would float too freely in an imagined ethereal *Geist*. History of ideas, they often argue, should become intellectual history—which implies, among other things, the history of actual intellectuals—in the sense that it deals with flesh-and-blood thinkers, whose social position, psychological makeup, and intended audiences need to be considered in any thick description of the ideas they generate, promulgate, or criticize. To be understood historically, knowledge has to be intertwined with power, ideas with the material vehicles of their propagation and transmission. Excessive prolepsis in which a teleological narrative rides roughshod over the uniqueness of each local context, understood both spatially and temporally with its own set of problems and particular vocabulary, should be avoided.

For the textualists who have taken seriously the lessons of the "linguistic turn" in the humanities, the medium in which ideas are generated and through which they are transmitted means that close attention has to be paid to the refracting power of language.[6] Texts have to be treated as unbounded sites of unresolved contestation rather than closed, organic "works" reflecting congealed authorial intention and expressing consistent and coherent ideas. They should be understood as nodal points in intertextual webs that transcend any one work, individual *oeuvre*, or univocal intention. Because of the rhetorical complexities of texts and their inevitable immersion in an ever-changing sea of other texts, it is problematic to isolate their conceptual core, hoping to shuck off their linguistic husks to reveal their substantive kernel,[7] and make them amenable to essentializing synopsis and paraphrastic reduction.

Nonetheless, despite all of these reservations, intellectual historians of late, Armitage correctly observes, have increasingly been willing to employ what he calls a telescopic rather than microscopic gaze to produce "transtemporal" histories that range beyond the boundaries of period or epoch and follow ideas through many different local contexts. Among his examples are works by Charles Taylor, Jerrold Siegel, Darrin McMahon, Lorraine Daston and Peter Galison, Sophia Rosenfeld, Rainer Forst, James Kloppenberg, Andrew Fitzmaurice, Richard Bourke, and Armitage himself. He even contends that comparable efforts can be found by Cambridge School intellectual historians known as fierce defenders of strong contextualization, such as Quentin Skinner, Richard Tuck, and John Pocock.[8]

Also included on Armitage's list is my own *Songs of Experience: Modern American and European Variations on a Universal Theme*. Published in 2006, this book was, in fact, not the first nor the last of my efforts to track "big ideas" over an extended period of time. *Marxism and Totality* (1985) followed "the adventures of a concept" called "totality" through the history of twentieth-century Western Marxism. *Downcast Eyes* (1993) traced the denigration of visual primacy or "ocularcentrism" by French intellectuals from Henri Bergson to Luce Irigaray, Michel Foucault, Jacques Derrida, Jean-François Lyotard, and Emmanuel Levinas. *The Virtues of Mendacity* (2010) examined attitudes toward lying in politics from Plato to Hannah Arendt, and in so doing discriminated among variations of the concept of "the political." And *Reason after Its Eclipse* (2016) followed the fortunes of rationality from the Greeks through the first generation of the Frankfurt School and Jürgen Habermas. Without consciously intending it, my own inclination as an intellectual historian has almost always been to practice what Armitage preaches as a refreshing alternative to business as usual.

I do not want, however, to present a self-indulgent *apologia pro vita mea*, or even return to the issues raised by the method of synoptic content analysis and the virtues of paraphrastic reduction, which I've tried to explore elsewhere.[9] Instead, I would like to ruminate on the possible reasons a tension has existed between the search for a history of big ideas over long periods of time and the inevitable "Hey!" that it seems to induce in its skeptical critics. In so doing, I want to focus on three main issues: the nature of the beast whose long-term history is being tracked, understood variously as ideas, concepts, and metaphors; the relationship of "big ideas" to the various contexts in which they are more or less embedded, and the more general question of the passage from macro and micro levels of narrative analysis, which applies to more than just intellectual history. In my conclusion, I will return to the larger implications of the interjection "Hey!" so often prefacing the question "What's the big idea?"

Already in the classic and now much maligned "history of ideas" tradition inaugurated by Arthur Lovejoy and his colleagues at the Johns Hopkins University almost a century ago, there was acute awareness that the idea of an "idea" was itself highly unstable. In fact, Lovejoy's protégé George Boas began his programmatic essay "What Is the History of Ideas?" by acknowledging that "few words are as ambiguous as the word 'idea.' By latest count it had twenty-five meanings." Although one might consider this an advantage insofar as it creates a rich opportunity for exploring semantic play, in the same essay Boas explicitly disagreed: "It is clear that before one can write a history of an idea one must disentangle it from all the ambiguities that it has acquired in the course of time. One must expect to find it appearing in contexts that vary from age to age."[10]

But, his critics quickly wondered, can one produce this disambiguation for the idea of "idea" itself? Boas, in fact, spared himself the effort in this particular essay, but when it came to contributing the entry on "Idea" to the *Dictionary of the History of Ideas* a few years later, he made an attempt that was more inductive than deductive. Beginning by noting the etymology of the word in the Greek verbs for "to see" and "to know," he observed that "the notion that ideas can be apprehended by a kind of vision or intuition, by looking and seeing them, has never been lost in Occidental philosophy, for knowing as a kind of insight, illumination, revelation, has almost always been retained." But significantly, after tracing its fortunes based on the assumption that it could be understood as identical from Plato to the neo-Kantians, he then ruefully acknowledged in conclusion that Hans Vaihinger, the late nineteenth-century neo-Kantian philosopher of "as if," had used the word in a totally different way. For him, "ideas" were fictions that orient humans in the world and not "guideposts to impersonal truth completely detached from human desires, forming the matrix of reality." Boas could only finish his essay by throwing up his hands, lamenting that "seldom has the history of an idea manifested such a reversal of meaning."[11]

By and large, the attempt by classical historians of ideas to bring order into the semantic chaos they encountered was only rarely successful. Implicitly rejecting the identification of ideas with visually clear objects of conscious mental intuition and scorning coherent systems or "isms" with all their vagueness and complexity, Lovejoy turned his attention to what he called "unit-ideas." These were more basic building blocks of thought, which lurked beneath the visible surface as "implicit or incompletely explicit *assumptions*, or more or less *unconscious mental habits*, operating in the thought of an individual or generation."[12] His greatest example was "the great chain of Being," whose fortunes he traced with formidable erudition from Plato to the Romantics. Unlike Boas, who asserted that there was little profit in probing unconscious motivations because "ideas, after all, exist on the conscious level and their history has to stay on that level,"[13] Lovejoy fully acknowledged the affective power of what he dubbed "metaphysical pathos," the ability of an idea, "like the words of a poem, [to] awaken through their associations, and through a sort of empathy which they engender, a congenial mood or tone of feeling on the part of the philosopher of his reader."[14] The most telling example was the "metaphysical pathos of obscurity" that enhanced the reception of certain philosophies—he singled out those of Schelling, Hegel, and Bergson—by imbuing them with a mysterious pseudo-profundity that resisted straightforward clarification and easy paraphrase.

Even on the basis of these sketchy and inadequate remarks, we can see that the classical history of ideas was itself conflicted about the meaning of the immaterial object whose history it sought to trace. It acknowledged the connotative as well as denotative dimension of ideas, admitted their often unconscious affective valence, and recognized their frequent imbrication with images and metaphors. Lovejoy and his colleagues also conceded that in addition to their cognitive function, ideas could have rhetorical force and win over—or alienate—potential adherents by more than their logical cogency. Ideas, moreover, could manifest themselves outside of their primary textual form, as shown by the variety of different landscape garden styles, often identified with specific national characters, whose deeper meanings were noted by Lovejoy.[15]

But even with all of these qualifications, the main impulse behind the Lovejoyan approach was to isolate manifest ideas or latent unit-ideas from their social, psychological, and material contexts of origin and reception and seek to capture their core meaning, a meaning that endured over time despite the vicissitudes of their development. Their integral unity was captured in the metaphor Lovejoy often used to describe that development as a "life-history."[16] Although they could also form new combinations with other unit-ideas—one commentator compared them to "randy chemical elements in an unstable soup"[17]—they somehow remained coherent with their integrity intact over large periods of time. Thus, despite some recent suggestions that classical history of ideas might be due for a renewal,[18] Armitage is adamant that the "big ideas" whose *longue durée* he wants us to trace are something very different. "No intellectual historian," he writes, "would now use Lovejoy's creaking metaphors of 'unit-ideas' as chemical elements, nor would they assume that the biography of an idea could be written as if it had a quasi-biological continuity and identity through time, along with a lifecycle longer than that of any mortal human subject."[19]

A more promising approach, now enjoying considerable popularity, was promoted by the so-called conceptual history (*Begriffsgeschichte*) launched in Germany by Erich Rothacker, Otto Brunner, and most notably Reinhart Koselleck in the 1960s.[20] Arguing for the "desubstantialization" of concepts, they took to heart Nietzsche's celebrated warning that "only that which has no history is definable"[21] and Wittgenstein's insight—anticipated in the definitional practices of the *Oxford English Dictionary* in the nineteenth century—that the meaning(s) of a word can be found in its various uses over time. The Cartesian preference for "clear and distinct" ideas in the mind was not only problematic philosophically but, *pace* Boas, also a misleading model for intellectual history. Concepts, in fact, could be contrasted with commonplace words precisely in terms of their resistance to essentializing definitions. As Koselleck put it, "A concept must remain ambiguous in order to be a concept. The concept is bound to a word, but is at the same time more than a word. . . . A word presents potentialities for meaning; a concept unites within itself a plenitude of meaning. Hence a concept can possess clarity but must be ambiguous."[22] Even when neologisms are consciously minted with one intended meaning, they have the capacity to escape the intentions of their coiners and accrue different, even contradictory meanings over time. Thus it is wrong to assume the priority of etymology, in which the alleged original meaning, often in a classical language such as Greek or Latin, is privileged over its later "dilutions" or "corruptions." Nor is it correct to understand the meaning of a concept teleologically in which current meanings are the "right" ones with earlier ones being considered more or less prescient precursors.

A history of concepts is thus inherently "big" in the sense that it involves a class of richly polysemic terms that have accumulated a welter of disparate meanings that were often very different from their current acceptations. Rather than assuming simple iterability over time, in which recurrent motifs transcend individual contexts, it urges us to follow the musical model of themes and developing variations, without, of course, necessarily adopting the practice of tonal recapitulation fundamental to classical Western music. But insofar as all of those developing meanings can still be clustered under the umbrella of the concept—or "grasped" by it, as the etymology of the German *Begriff* in the verb *begreifen* suggests[23]—there is at least some rough commensurability that ties them together. Although not based on the policing of lexical boundaries via normative definitions, concepts appear to operate through the logic of subsumption or at least the seeking of a common denominator underlying different usages.

An alternative method called "metaphorology," developed in the shadow of *Begriffsgeschichte* by Hans Blumenberg, argued for a more analogical or paradigmatic approach in which figurative language resists translation into conceptual abstractions.[24] Although Blumenberg shared the conceptual historian's resistance to essentializing definitions, he focused on the role of what he called the "nonconceptual," including myths, anecdotes, and rhetorical tropes, as recurring figures worthy of the historian's attention.[25] "Absolute metaphors," he argued, were foundational and irreducible elements of even the most austere philosophical discourse and ought not to be seen as merely inchoate anticipations of clear and distinct concepts. Although conceptual history should not be replaced wholesale by metaphorology, it could be supplemented by it in valuable ways. Thus, for example, the history of "light as a metaphor of truth,"[26] one of Blumenberg's earliest metaphorological exercises, revealed the recurrent and often hidden image underpinning a fundamental concept of Western thought.[27] It was what we might call a "big metaphor," which persisted over many centuries and was operative in many different cultures. It was, as we've noted, still evident in Boas's definition of "idea" in the mid-twentieth century.

The power of Blumenberg's approach was evident in an audacious essay he wrote in 1976 on Simmel's *Philosophy of Money*, which revisited the remarks I cited above about the tragedy of the concept.[28] Understanding money in Simmel not as the antonym of "life" but rather as a metaphor for it, Blumenberg argued that both reveal an immanent and unending dynamic between "rigidification and liquidity, form and dissolution, hoarding and squandering, institution and freedom, levelling out and individuality."[29] The key to their analogical status lay in their shared enactment of the dialectic of subjectification and objectification. That is, money, by providing a neutral, objective medium available for subjective choices about how it will be spent, choices expressing the desires and values of the spender, is like formally unconstrained "life" in its opening up of a range of undetermined possibilities. Despite its apparent enabling of the quantifiable commensuration of human relations, it is therefore ultimately in the service of human freedom. Rather than a principle of conservation, in which exchange creates nothing new, it allows the pursuit of subjective happiness on the basis of individual values.

Blumenberg's arresting reading of *The Philosophy of Money* cannot be adequately addressed here, but by alerting us to the unexpected analogy between money and life in Simmel, he forces us also to reconsider the nature of the other analogical relationship posited by the German sociologist between the concept and money as its "practical counterpart." That is, the comparison enables us to appreciate that in addition to the subsumptive, commensurating, abstracting force of conceptualization, there is also a potential for free play in the ways in which concepts dialectically interact with what exceeds them. Or to put it in Simmel's terms, the role played by big ideas in relation to the particulars they subsume "can be equally interpreted as service and domination." They can accommodate both unity and diversity rather than making us choose one over the other.[30]

Conceptual history and metaphorology thus avoid some of the vulnerable assumptions of traditional history of ideas, which seeks to still semantic ambiguity. Additional assistance comes from the insight, shared by among others the Cambridge School contextualists, that no concept or metaphor ever exists in a vacuum, isolated from the dynamic force field of counterconcepts and competing, or at least alternative, metaphors in which it is situated at particular moments in its history. The symbolic import of a metaphor can alter with its positioning in a constellation of other metaphors, and synonyms can, in fact, even turn into antonyms. No history of the concept of "community," for example, can ignore how it came to be pitted against "society" in sociological discourse from at least the time of Ferdinand Tönnies, nor could a comparable account of the fortunes of "culture" fail to understand its tense relationship with "civilization," at least in German thought from the eighteenth century on, as well as with "nature." Words that once expressed contrary ideas can coalesce into a new composite package, for example, "liberal" and "democrat," which were at odds in the nineteenth century, now happily cohabit in the familiar formula "liberal democracy." Although using the same word, terms of art in different discourses can come to mean very different things; think, for example, of "rationalization" in the vocabularies of Max Weber and Sigmund Freud.

Some words in one language that seem to have a unified meaning reveal their latent tensions when it is registered that they translate into different words in other languages, a salient example being the way in which the English "experience" can be rendered by the contrasting German terms *Erfahrung* and *Erlebnis*.[31] Conversely, some words seem to gain richness of meaning when they embrace distinct terms that another language keeps apart, for example, *Geist* as both "spirit" and "mind" in English or *Seele* as both "soul" and "psyche." It is even possible, *mirabile dictu*, for the same word to be pitted against itself in languages where gendered articles matter, as can be observed in the distinction recent French theorists make between "le politique" and "la politique," the former implying an ontological and the latter a more empirical version of politics.[32] Nor can a powerful metaphor like "ground," which has done so much work in philosophical discourse, be understood without seeing its relationship to "foundation," "soil," "bottom," or "earth," all of which can serve as metaphors carrying heavy loads of alternative connotations.[33]

When Cambridge School intellectual historians such as Pocock talk of the "languages" of political theory—also variously called "vocabularies," "rhetorics," or "idioms"—they alert us to the ways in which ideas truly become "big" only when they are embedded in ever-shifting discursive fields that imbue them with special meanings and rhetorical force.[34] As Skinner has noted in his critique of Raymond Williams's lexicon of "keywords," one must take into account "the strongly holistic implications of the fact that, when a word changes its meaning, it also changes its relationship to an entire vocabulary."[35] Without the need to be card-carrying Hegelians, historians of ideas can be sensitive to the negations, contradictions, and sublations that make those discourses dynamic constellations of meaning that coalesce and fragment over time. Indeed, one of the ways in which an idea can be accounted "big," or a simple term earn the honorific title of "keyword," is precisely its survival in new semantic contexts, in which it often also carries the traces of sedimented meanings, some more manifest than others, from its placement in previous constellations.

Situating ideas or concepts in their discursive contexts opens the larger question of how other contexts—institutional, biographical, political, social—need to be taken into account in writing the history of big ideas. Armitage addresses it by arguing that instead of treating ideas as the heroic, self-contained protagonists of a traditional historical narrative, it would be better to attempt a "history *in* ideas" based on "serial contextualism," understanding ideas as "focal points of arguments shaped and debated episodically across time with a conscious—or at least a provable connection—with both earlier and later instances of such struggles."[36] This approach would allow us to take on board the crucial speech act distinction developed by John Austin and John Searle and stressed by Cambridge School contextualists between a term's locutionary and illocutionary, or constative and performative, dimensions, the latter often dependent on the work its users intend to do in respect to specific audiences (or the unintended consequences they provoke).[37]

Being sensitive to this distinction may, however, prevent us from the wholesale adoption of one tool of the current turn toward "big" ideas, which is touted by Armitage: drawing on an "N-gram" model to measure the progress (or regress) of an idea or keyword over time based on the statistical findings allowed by database searching of massive numbers of texts over long periods. The value of such tools for the nascent field of digital humanities, to be sure, should not be dismissed out of hand. In their tracking of the varying frequency of words, phrases, tropes, and the like, they provide suggestive information about large-scale patterns of usage, allowing us to gauge the waxing or waning popularity of terms and compare them with others in their semantic field. Based on what the literary critic Franco Moretti has puckishly called "distant reading," they can relieve the intellectual historian of the need to focus on the complexities of allegedly representative texts—whose canonical aura may be more a function of posterior than current judgment—by mapping or graphing the larger patterns of which they are a part.[38] Such a "macroanalysis" of ideas, concepts, metaphors, tropes, genres, styles, or whatever else is amenable to statistical retrieval can help expand the purview of humanist study beyond the usual suspects.[39] It can also, if Moretti and his fellow digital enthusiasts are right, suggest structural explanations of unintended trends, disseminations, and differentiations (or in his vocabulary, "morphological trees" revealing evolutionary survival and extinction) rather than depend on hermeneutic interpretations of meaning, intended or otherwise, in individual texts.

It cannot, however, register the often latent metaphoric play in concepts that is stressed by Blumenberg, which helps undermine their substantialization. Nor can it turn the specific, local use of an idea, concept, or metaphor into a mere example of a larger, secular trend, which is amenable to structural explanation from, as it were, the outside. That is, there is no easy passage from micro- to macroanalysis, especially when the former requires hermeneutic tools and sensitivity to illocutionary contexts, which are factored out by the latter. Intellectual historians, to be sure, rarely emulate the close readings of literary critics, who are more rigorously trained in the formalist techniques of the new criticism and narratology. But some have followed Dominick LaCapra's exhortation to regard texts as "worklike" in their dialogic solicitation of new meanings rather than as transparent "documents" revealing intended old ones,[40] and in so doing avoid reducing them to mere instances of a large-scale pattern revealed in a data bank. They have also adopted a self-consciously discordant focal practice, moving from what film critics call "establishing shots" to "close-ups," a metaphor already suggested by Siegfried Kracauer in his still very useful rumination on the parallels between making films and writing history in *History: The Last Things Before the Last*.[41] They have understood the need to oscillate between scales of analysis, relying on whatever gauge tools are most appropriate for the questions they pose.

Why, then, we might wonder in conclusion, might it still be prudent to acknowledge the uneasy and indignant "Hey!" that so often prefaces the question "What's the big idea?" Among its many possible justifications, let me single out two that may make us pause before unequivocally welcoming the return of long-range, large-scale intellectual history, even with the refinements suggested above. Whereas Braudel may be the muse inspiring Armitage's enthusiasm for the *longue durée*, it is Michel Foucault who helps us see the limitations in its adoption. Much has been written about Foucault's idiosyncratic approach to history—some indeed have even questioned if he was really doing history at all—and the differences in his own "archaeological" and "genealogical" methods.[42] But when it came to mainstream history of ideas, it is at least clear that he had trenchant reservations. In *The Archaeology of Knowledge*, he dismissively characterized it as "an uncertain object, with badly drawn frontiers, methods borrowed from here and there, and an approach lacking in rigor and stability ... the discipline of beginnings and ends, the description of obscure continuities and returns, the reconstitution of developments in the linear form of history."[43]

Foucault's archaeological alternative, to be sure, may not have itself been fully convincing. Few historians, after all, have honored his call to shift their attention entirely from ideas, representations, thoughts, and images to the rule-bound discursive practices subtending them. Nor have they shared his disdain for authors and their *oeuvres*, and his rejection of interpretation and the search for meaning in favor of the enunciative function of "statements." But what has been called the "nominalist" impulse in his historical writing has produced two caveats worth taking seriously.[44] Stressing dispersion rather than unity and contingency rather than necessity, he raised justifiable doubts about the coherence of long-range narratives, which smoothed over ruptures and discontinuities in favor of "genesis, continuity, totalization."[45] Any history of "big ideas," he warned, has to be sensitive to the ways in which the apparent persistence of an idea or concept or metaphor doesn't necessarily betoken survival—or even development—of essential meaning or function. As Boas acknowledged with chagrin in the case of Hans Vaihinger, reversals of meaning may occur in ways that undermine the long-range narrative being fashioned by historians who are blind to the frequency of rupture in the discursive force field in which the seemingly same term may be located. Even the conceptual historians' Nietzschean wariness about definitional mortification may not do justice to the radical breaks that undercut any meaningful continuity. Metanarratives of coherent development or evolution are no less hazardous in intellectual history than they are in other variants of historical storytelling.

No less important is the second lesson bequeathed by Foucault, who shared with a number of other recent French thinkers a great deal of interest in singular "events" as unexpected and disruptive incursions in a developmental pattern or emplotted narrative.[46] The always vexed issue of innovation, the new idea that emerges without being fully prepared in advance by a context, even one that becomes apparent after the fact, cannot be easily resolved. Rather than focusing on what is objectively possible in any situation, following an infinite regress of influences, it is sometimes more productive to wonder at the realization of what seemed virtually impossible at the time and cannot be reduced, even in retrospect, to the conditions that prepared it.

Conceptual historians have, to be sure, sometimes acknowledged the sudden emergence of what Koselleck called "concepts of the future,"[47] which do not reflect the context of their genesis but rather seed the ground for a potential practical realization at a time to come. As a result, one commentator has even been able to compare Koselleck's work with that of Foucault, because of their shared interest in "the rupture of conceptual meaning, the transformations that take place in intention when a term is uttered in different contexts, and the different conceptual content of given terms across time."[48] But ironically, it is precisely because *Begriffsgeschichte* rarely arouses the indignation generated by the "history of ideas" that one of its limits is revealed. For the "Hey!" so often preceding queries about big ideas may well signal an element of shock and surprise at the interruption of a settled way of thinking stimulated only by what we call "ideas." Indeed, at times the very word can performatively solicit that outcome, which is absent in our response to what seems in so many other ways to be its synonym, the word "concept." No one, after all, ever says "Hey! What's the big concept?" Despite all of its baggage, it may well therefore be worth sticking to the old notion of a "history of ideas," if at the same time we remain sensitive to the justifiable "hey" that it so often arouses. Only then will we fully appreciate that the biggest ideas are the ones that can trouble our complacency, transcend our parochial horizons, and astonish us with the audacity of their insolent ambition.

CHAPTER 7

Fidelity to the Event? Lukács's *History and Class Consciousness* and the Russian Revolution

To read Georg Lukács's magnum opus *History and Class Consciousness* a century after the revolution whose still-ramifying implications it sought to explain and whose goals it hoped to foster is, alas, an unbearable experience. This was not always the case. When I first wrote about it in *Marxism and Totality* in 1984, I could describe it with admiration as "the charter document of Hegelian Marxism," "a milestone in Marxist theory," and "one of those rare synthetic visions that launch a new paradigm or problematic in thought, in this case Western Marxism."[1] Praise no less hyperbolic continues to infuse later accounts by commentators such as Slavoj Žižek, who wrote the postface to the translation in 2000 of Lukács's newly discovered defense of the book, titled "Tailism and the Dialectic." "*History and Class Consciousness* (1923)," Žižek could still gush, "is one of the few authentic events in the history of Marxism."[2]

Such enthusiasm reflected not only appreciation for the ingenuity and rigor of the book's arguments but also admiration for the evident passion of its author, whose abrupt and unexpected conversion to Marxism in early December 1918 was taken by virtually all who knew him as akin to a Kierkegaardian leap of faith.[3] Determined to move from contemplation to action, realizing as best he could the unity of theory and praxis extolled by Marx, Lukács wrote the eight essays that comprised the book—in fact, he heavily rewrote the first two—while involved in the thick of revolutionary politics in Central Europe. The highpoint of his activism—and actual political power—came when he served as deputy people's commissar for education and culture in the turbulent 133 days of the Hungarian Soviet Republic led by Bela Kun from March 21 to August 1, 1919. In addition to fostering radical cultural reforms, he also acted as political commissar attached to one of the army battalions of the Communists, and he did not shy away from enacting violent revolutionary justice when he thought it warranted. When the Hungarian Revolution faltered, Lukács went underground for two months before fleeing into exile in Vienna, where he finished the final essays in *History and Class Consciousness*.

As is often the case with recent converts, the intensity of Lukács's belief produced a maximalist zealotry—he later called it the "idealism and utopianism of my revolutionary messianism"[4]—that soon earned him Lenin's chastisement for ultraleftist infantilism.[5] He accepted the rebuke as valid, unlike his response to many others that were to rain down on him in the years to come, despite his invariable willingness to acquiesce in public. *History and Class Consciousness* is in part a record of his struggle to square the impatience and intensity of his revolutionary commitment with the pragmatic realism displayed by Lenin during the Russian Revolution, which had avoided the dire fate of its hapless Hungarian clone. What made the book seem such a breathtaking achievement was its intricate interweaving of theoretical issues with practical ones, its heady mixture of German idealism, historical materialism, and advanced sociological theory with factional disputes in the socialist movement, culminating in a full-throated defense of the organizational virtues of the vanguard party. There can, in fact, be few if any comparable exercises in ongoing theoretical clarification written by someone deeply engaged in life-or-death political activity, involving not only factional battles in the Hungarian Communist Party but also in the political drama unfolding in Moscow and the Comintern. Rather than a unified, post-facto account of a past event, the book itself records the changing responses of a participant-observer as the event itself was occurring.

Accordingly, *History and Class Consciousness* was immediately recognized as a book with explosive implications, providing ammunition both for critics and defenders of the Communist movement supported so fervently by its author. It earned added luster with the recovery a few years later of Marx's early manuscripts with their focus on the question of alienation, which seemed to confirm the remarkable analysis of reification developed in the book's longest and most original essay. When Lenin's wartime *Philosophical Notebooks* were discovered and then published in 1929–1930, still further credit accrued to Lukács for having intuited the importance of Hegel for Lenin's understanding of dialectics. And yet, the book was soon under severe attack by the guardians of dialectical materialist orthodoxy, then being established as the ideological counterpart to the Stalinization of the party in the Soviet Union and elsewhere. The story of how *History and Class Consciousness* drew swift condemnation from official Soviet ideologues, while inadvertently inspiring the heterodox tradition that later came to be called Western Marxism despite its author's desire to hold fast to Marxist orthodoxy, has often been told.[6] Lukacs's own defenses and self-criticisms—most notably the text called "Tailism and the Dialectic" unpublished in his lifetime and his 1967 preface to the new edition that was allowed to appear in that year—complicate the story still further by raising questions about the extent to which he remained faithful, and for how long, to its central arguments.

The debate over precisely what those arguments were also continues today, reignited by new readers hopeful that *History and Class Consciousness* can still inspire radical politics in the twenty-first century, and paradoxically stoked by the fears of the authoritarian government now ruling Hungary that they might be right.[7] Many interpretative issues remain unresolved. Were there still traces of Lukács's earlier "romantic anti-capitalism" "abstract utopianism," and "infantile leftism" in some of the essays? Or had he already embraced the neo-Hegelian "realism" that emerged full-blown in his 1926 essay on Moses Hess and the so-called Blum Theses two years later, which some have seen as preparing his reluctant capitulation to the Stalinization of the Communist movement? Did he successfully expunge the Fichtean subjectivism infusing his postconversion activism, or were there still residues of it in his characterization of the interventionist role of the vanguard party? Did he really find a successful way to overcome the antinomies of bourgeois thought epitomized by Kantian dualism by identifying with the totalizing gaze and practical activism he attributed to the proletariat? Did his bold critique of the dialectics of nature in Engels and Second International orthodox Marxism mean an excessively idealist distinction between spirit and matter? Did he instead provide a still materialist way to characterize the relationship between history and nature, while avoiding the domination of the latter that some critics saw in his excessive elevation of the subject? Did his critique of scientistic "vulgar Marxism" and the hypertrophy of technological rationality emerge from a romantic disdain for science and technology *tout court*, or just his understanding of their complicity with capitalist rationality? Did he satisfactorily explain the radical transformation of the working class from the worst victims of capitalist reification and commodity fetishism into their most self-consciously intransigent opponents, or in Hegelian terms, from a subject-in-itself to a subject-for-itself? Did his stress on the vital role of political organization in that transformation lead him, despite all his protestations to the contrary, to validate a party that was no longer really organically embedded in the class it sought to lead, a conclusion enabled by the waning importance of the mediating link of workers' councils—also known as soviets—in his analysis?

These and a host of other questions have been chewed over incessantly in the very substantial commentary devoted to *History and Class Consciousness*, and they are obviously not going to be resolved in the compass of one short essay. What I would like to do instead is focus on just three issues in particular, which I hope will explain why, as I suggested at the outset, returning to the book now is such a painful experience. The first involves the assumptions it makes about the historical process and the specific conjuncture in which it was written. The second examines the crucial category of "objective possibility," which Lukács borrowed from one of his teachers, Max Weber, and used to distinguish his position from the passive spontaneism of his "tailist" opponents, on the one hand, and the putschist adventurism of his erstwhile "infantile leftist" comrades, on the other. The final issue concerns the implications of the category of "fidelity to the Event," an attitude toward the Bolshevik Revolution that latter-day Leninists like Alain Badiou and Slavoj Žižek have ascribed to Lukács and claimed is a template for uncompromising radicalism today.

It is no accident, although not often remarked, that the title of *History and Class Consciousness* gives pride of place to the importance of history, as Lukács's investment in it, both as a methodological imperative and an actual process, was profound. The former meant he was opposed to any attempt to confuse Marx's "historical materialism" with an ontologically dubious dialectics of nature, a charge he leveled with great audacity against no less a socialist icon than Friedrich Engels.[8] Nor, he argued, should historical materialism be understood as a conventional social science, like sociology, with its search for objective regularities comparable to those observed in nature, which he soon criticized in Nicolai Bukharin and Karl August Wittfogel.[9] It was reminiscent instead, as the literary critic Fredric Jameson later emphasized, of the meaningful narratives fashioned by the great realist novelists of the nineteenth century, whom Lukács always celebrated in opposition to their naturalist and modernist competitors.[10] These narratives were, to be sure, aesthetically contrived carpets with figures hidden in them, stories, that is, with protagonists, turning points, and meaningful conclusions, all of which may well be absent in the flow of nonfictional historical occurrences, where contingency and overdetermination so often defeats attempts to discern intelligibility. But Lukács was confident that the carpet did indeed have a figure that was not merely imposed by aesthetic fiat.

Understanding historical method as more like a narrative art rather than a social science was not only necessary for theoretical purposes but also for Lukács had practical implications. Hegel and Marx had been right to argue that philosophical contradictions, such as the antinomies Kant had mistakenly thought were eternal, could not be resolved by purely intellectual means, but only by their future overcoming in the social relations of real human beings. Historical consciousness in methodological terms thus meant more than the contemplative stance of an observer of the past, no longer with a personal stake in the outcome of struggles long since concluded. Instead, it meant realizing that the observer was also a participant, embedded in a still-unfolding historical story, and that the present with all of its uncertainties and possibilities was part of an ongoing narrative that would extend into the future. The Marxist demand to unify theory and practice meant that historically self-conscious theory informed and was in turn informed by history-creating action. "The historical knowledge of the proletariat begins with knowledge of the present, with the self-knowledge of its own social situation and with the elucidation of its necessity (i.e., its genesis)."[11]

But as active participants in the historical process, Lukács insisted that we—or at least the potential universal class that was the proletariat and its spokesmen—are able to act in such a way that future history can be fashioned differently from the past. In fact, as Vico had understood when he famously argued that *verum et factum convertuntur* (truth and making are convertible), even past history is accessible to us because humans have made it, albeit inadvertently, and can fathom its meaning from within, whereas our knowledge of the natural world, a world of already existing laws and processes, can only be of objects from the outside. Thinking historically is thus a necessary antidote to the reification that naturalizes bourgeois social relations and the antinomies of bourgeois thought, which appear to be expressions of an unchangeable "second nature." Recalling the past origins of present pseudo-natural relations is crucial, for, as Horkheimer and Adorno would later put it, "all reification is forgetting."[12] But although necessary, recollection alone is insufficient, because only action to destroy the existing institutions and practices of bourgeois society will make possible meaningful de-reification, understood as the consciously intended, collectively subjective determination of the social world.[13]

Lukács's belief in the methodological cum practical importance of thinking historically was so strong that he opened his book by provocatively asserting that even if all of Marx's conclusions about actual occurrences were proved wrong, the approach itself would still survive. Orthodox Marxism, he insisted, "does not imply the uncritical acceptance of the results of Marx's investigations. It is not the 'belief' in this or that thesis, nor the exegesis of a 'sacred' book. On the contrary, orthodoxy refers exclusively to *method*."[14] Ultimately, however, the proof of the method's validity would be practical; indeed, it was a method that was never contemplative or disengaged. If it could inspire and guide the struggle of the proletariat to assume the role Marx had assigned it, in a phrase Lukács soon came to abjure for being overly idealist, as "the subject and object" of history, it would then show itself to have been correct. Significantly this appeal to future historical validation would continue to inform his 1967 preface to the new edition of *History and Class Consciousness*, which ended by pleading ignorance about the "fruitful results" produced by the book, whose merits Lukács refrained from assessing because it would "raise a whole complex of questions whose resolution I may be allowed to leave to the judgment of history."[15]

It has been more than fifty years since Lukács invoked that judgment, and so it might be tempting now to venture a verdict. But even if some might claim it is still premature, we should, I want to argue, question the underlying premise that allowed Lukács to invoke something called "history" in the first place to judge the validity of a method or the practices it fostered. Its origins go back at least to Friedrich Schiller's famous claim in his poem "Resignation" of 1786 that "Die Weltgeschichte ist das Weltgericht" (world history is the world court), which was repeated and given wider currency by Hegel in his *Philosophy of Right*.[16] A secularized version of the Christian idea of the Last Judgment, this celebrated aphorism transferred the awesome power of God's final justice to either a fantasized posterity possessing the wisdom of hindsight or the raw survival of the fittest in a contest where success is the only criterion of value. It denies the transcendental, ahistorical power of ethical norms in favor of posthumous validation at some uncertain time in a future yet to be fashioned.

As all students of Lukács's sudden conversion to Marxism know, it was over this very alternative that he himself agonized in the period when he made his leap of faith, moving dramatically from one to the other. Just before he jumped, he wrote an essay titled "Bolshevism as a Moral Problem," which sided with transcendental moral norms. Rejecting the assumption that ultimate good can come from the employment of evil means, he warned that there was "an insoluble moral dilemma in the foundations of the Bolshevik position."[17] But then shortly after his conversion, he dramatically reversed himself in an essay titled "Tactics and Ethics," which argued instead that "the decisive criterion of socialist tactics" is "the philosophy of history," and that "all means by which this historico-philosophical process is raised to the conscious and real level are to be considered valid."[18] The logic of historical validation was directed against not only abstract moral imperatives but also the political norm of democratic will-formation and the legal norm of abstract formalism. The willingness to violate them in the name of ultimate historical vindication—reminiscent, some might argue, of the Jewish Sabbatian idea of "redemption through sin" famously elaborated by Gershom Scholem[19]—was to become a mainstay of revolutionary apologetics. It was, for example, still operative in Maurice Merleau-Ponty's 1947 *Humanism and Terror*, which justified the Soviet purge trials of the 1930s by arguing that "bourgeois justice adopts the past as its precedent; revolutionary justice adopts the future. It judges in the name of Truth that the Revolution is about to make true; its proceedings are part of a *praxis* which may well be motivated but transcends any particular motive.... The Moscow Trials only make sense between revolutionaries; that is to say between men who are convinced they are *making history*."[20] Because no one can have absolutely "clean hands," Merleau-Ponty contended, the ultimate test of even the most violent actions will be their efficacy in enabling an improved future to supersede the current debased order.

Setting aside the question of how one is to compare superior and inferior orders without implicitly ahistorical criteria, the crucial point for our consideration of the role of history in *History and Class Consciousness* (and texts like *Humanism and Terror*, which owe so much to its example) is the more basic assumption that history can be written in the manner of a realist novel told by an omniscient narrator, as an intelligible narrative concluding with an act of judgment by an imputed posterity that can share a unified perspective on what preceded it. In addition to his stress on the historical nature of Marx's method, Lukács embraced with no hesitation the metanarrative of *Weltgeschichte* it had adopted. That is, he understood history as a collective story of humankind's progress through various stages of development, culminating for the moment in capitalism, whose terminal crisis was imminent. The critical category of "totality," which rather than the primacy of the economy Lukács saw as the hallmark of Marx's method, was thus applicable not only to the social whole existing at the time but also to history as a meaningful story, or in the terms I adopted in *Marxism and Totality*, as a "longitudinal" as well as "latitudinal" reality.[21]

It was, moreover, a story with an emerging protagonist, a nascent "subject," understood in collective rather than individual terms, who was in the process of awakening from the slumber engendered by capitalist reification and assuming its prophesized role as the self-conscious maker of the history of the future. Whether or not that subject somehow was latent in history from the beginning or emerged only as the concrete negation of Capital, which had become the abstract pseudo-subject of bourgeois society, has been a frequent bone of contention among readers of *History and Class Consciousness*.[22] What is, however, indisputable is that Lukács assigned to history, understood as a longitudinal totality, a crucial capacity of its own, which he described in these terms: "The totality of history is itself a real historical power—even though one that has not hitherto become conscious and has therefore gone unrecognized—a power which is not to be separated from the reality (and hence the knowledge) of the individual facts without at the same time annulling their reality and their factual existence. It is the real, ultimate ground of their reality and their factual existence and hence also of their knowability even as individual facts."[23]

Lukács, to be sure, vigorously disputed the erroneous conclusion often drawn from the Marxist metanarrative of history as "a real historical power" that the transition from one stage to another was inevitable, as the crisis of capitalism played itself out and the workers' movement came into its inheritance. His admiration for Lenin's vanguard party was rooted in its disdain for the dominant Second International strategy of patient passivity, in which conditions were left to ripen by themselves into a terminal crisis that would somehow open the door for socialism. Rather than an economistic reliance on the contradictions of capitalism automatically leading to collapse and the birth of a new order, Marxists should recognize that although capitalism was characterized by the primacy of the economy and thus would run aground when the contradictions between the mode of production and relations of production reached the point of no return, its socialist successor could only be achieved by practical activity on the political and cultural levels as well. Even Rosa Luxemburg, who had been so critical of the overly cautious orthodox leadership of the Second International, had succumbed in her critique of the Bolsheviks to a dubious faith in the spontaneous revolutionary fervor of the working class based on what Lukács damned as an "overestimation of *the organic character* of the course of history."[24] Because history was characterized by uneven and irregular development, Lukács argued there was a need to seize opportunities and act boldly when they were presented rather than wait patiently for all stars to be aligned.

Seeking to overcome the undialectical either/or of passive, economistic determinism and putschist, utopian adventurism, Lukács drew on a theoretical category developed by his mentor Max Weber, that of "objective possibility."[25] For the neo-Kantian Weber it was a counterfactual concept allowing the historical sociologist to recover possible alternative outcomes for past events, and speculate retrospectively about their probability of success. In contrast, Lukács, indebted to Hegel rather than Kant, gave "objective possibility" ontological weight as more than just a heuristic device employed in disinterested social scientific inquiry. Instead, it achieved what realist novels did by employing what literary critics have called "side-shadowing," the technique of avoiding the fatalistic implications of unilinear foreshadowing by presenting a field of still-possible outcomes as the narrative plays out.[26]

Not only did sensitivity to "objective possibilities" mean realistically assessing structural possibilities at any one historical conjuncture, but it also suggested that class consciousness could be understood in more than merely subjective terms. In a sentence written entirely in italics, Lukács insisted in *History and Class Consciousness* that "*the objective theory of class consciousness is the theory of its objective possibility.*"[27] Lucien Goldmann, one of Lukács's most insightful followers, glossed "objective possibility" as "the external situation of a class which limits its field of possibility with regard to thought and action. The mental structures of a class also circumscribe its theoretico-practical field of possibility. The objective possibility of a class determines its possible consciousness and inversely, according to Lukács. The two are inseparable."[28] Fredric Jameson concurred: "The epistemological 'priority' of 'proletarian consciousness,' as a class or collective phenomenon, has to do with the *conditions of possibility* of new thinking inherent in this particular class position."[29]

It was faith in the ontological validity of objective possibility that underlay what is perhaps the most audacious argument in *History and Class Consciousness*, which provided a sophisticated theoretical warrant for the Leninist Party, the theory of "imputed" or "ascribed" class consciousness. Of a piece with his suspicion of surface appearances, unmediated abstractions, and empirical "facts" in favor of the deeper trends coursing through the concrete, complexly mediated totality revealed by the historical materialist method, Lukács's imputation of latent revolutionary consciousness to a class that was still only inchoately aware of it allowed him to answer the charge that the Leninist Party was importing it to the proletariat entirely from the outside. It also gave him warrant for hope that what was objectively latent would soon become subjectively manifest through the praxis of a class already "in-itself" that was on the threshold of achieving its potential as a class "for-itself."

Crucial to this hope was the confidence that the narrative of history was legible, at least from the standpoint of its makers, and that the proper method would give the theorist aligned with the potentially universal class access to its probable—albeit never guaranteed—future course. Failing to understand this premise misled commentators like John Rees in his introduction to the English translation of "Tailism and the Dialectic" to argue that Lukács was merely doing what people normally do when they disdain someone's false consciousness about their true needs or interests. "We 'impute' a consciousness to them," Rees writes, "based on an appreciation of what we think they would see their interests to be if they were to look at the situation in a wider framework."[30] Rather, however, than this subjective interpretation of one person allegedly knowing the "true interests" of someone better than he or she does, Lukács's argument was that objective social processes unleashed by the crisis of capitalism were the real source of the theorist's imputation or ascription.

Although never explicitly drawing on it, the opposition between empirical and ascribed class consciousness, it might be argued, relied on some of the same assumptions that had informed the medieval notion of the king's two bodies, famously elaborated a generation later by the historian Ernst Kantorowicz.[31] Drawing on the religious distinction between the mystical and natural body of Christ, one eternal, the other mortal, medieval notions of monarchy contrasted the sacred institution of kingship with the human, sometimes all-too-human embodiment of it. For Lukács, there was an ideal proletariat, whose revolutionary consciousness and role as subject-object of history were objectively possible, and an empirical proletariat, whose actual consciousness and political engagement were not—or at least not yet—up to the level of their ideal counterpart. The crucial standpoint from which knowledge of history might be said to flow was thus the ideal rather than empirical working class. Although the hope remained that empirical and ideal levels would ultimately converge, the task of bridging them in the still-imperfect world of the present necessitated the mediating role of the party, which somehow had the ability to attain a higher consciousness without, however, losing its connection with the still-immature masses. Wrestling with precisely what such a mediation might mean in the last essay of *History and Class Consciousness*, by which time his earlier faith in the workers' councils had collapsed, Lukács once again resorted to the historical metanarrative underlying his entire argument: "The growth of proletarian class consciousness (i.e. the growth of the proletarian revolution) and that of the Communist Party are indeed one and the same process—seen from a world-historical perspective. Therefore in everyday praxis they condition each other in the most intimate way. *But despite this their concrete growth does not appear as one and the same process. Indeed there is not even a consistent parallel.* . . . The Communist Party is an *autonomous form* of proletarian class consciousness serving the interests of the revolution."[32]

The premise that there was such a thing as "world history," whose "perspective" could somehow be shared with the workers by the party and its theoreticians, allowed Lukács, as we have noted, to believe that the antinomies of bourgeois thought, including the tension between ethical norms and practical imperatives, were in the process of being overcome historically. It was the same assumption that gave him the warrant to believe that "objective possibilities" were ontological truths in the real world rather than merely heuristic devices to make sense of the completed past. It was the same conviction that allowed him to dismiss the recalcitrant "facts" of the world of mere appearances as insufficient evidence to falsify the historical materialist method that defines "orthodox Marxism." And it was the same unquestioned belief that allowed Lukács to envision the ultimate integration of the autonomous form of proletarian class consciousness that was the vanguard party with the actual class consciousness of a fully militant mass movement able to de-reify the world and fashion it anew in socialist terms.

If we pause for a moment to reflect on the foundational role something called "history," as Lukács saw it, played in his narrative of revolutionary struggle, it is not difficult to see why reading *History and Class Consciousness* almost a century later is so unbearable. "The totality of history is itself a real historical power," he tells us. Viewed from a "world-historical perspective," he argues, the party and the masses are one. "The historical knowledge of the proletariat begins with knowledge of the present," knowledge, he claims, that can uncover "objective possibilities" able to guide revolutionary praxis. Whether or not the arguments of *History and Class Consciousness* will be validated, he concludes, must be left to "the judgment of history."

Although it may well have been plausible in the years immediately after the Russian Revolution to imbue an unfolding narrative called "history" with all of these characteristics and wager on its moving in the right direction, however unevenly with backward steps as well as forward, and even still possible to wager on it against longer odds in the era of the New Left, a century later it is increasingly difficult.[33] Remembering Chou En-lai's famous response to Richard Nixon's question about the impact of the French Revolution—"it's too early to say"—we might want to cut Lukács some slack and postpone any final reckoning. But instead, we should abandon the idea that such a conclusive final judgment is even possible. For the real issue is the plausibility of turning lived history, however we choose to emplot it, into a unified story, whose outcome can ever be confidently weighed by an imagined posterity able to render a singular judgment. How legitimate is it, we should ask, to impose the ruling assumptions of realist fiction on the interpretation of actual history, which may well lack heroic protagonists, meaningful plots, and cadential conclusions? Already in 1979, Jean-François Lyotard famously defined postmodernity as "incredulity towards metanarratives."[34] Although the category of the postmodern has itself lost its allure, Lyotard's point is ironically hammered home by that very fact. That is, we now know there is no straightforward succession story from modernity to what allegedly comes after it. Nor can we easily go back to the universalist modernization theory that served for a while as the anti-Marxist version of "world historical" development.[35] And the fatuous claims about the "end of history" made by triumphalist liberals after the fall of Communism have also proven false.

What has, in fact, survived Lyotard's overblown proclamation of the arrival of a postmodern epoch is his insight into the increasing implausibility of treating world history as a coherent, meaningful narrative, let alone one that has a potential subject in the process of emerging into its own as the conscious maker of an emancipated future. Instead of the Russian Revolution serving as a model for those that would follow, which still seemed likely to Lukács even as he reflected on the failure of the Hungarian experiment, the regime it created survived for only seventy-four years, having lost its emancipatory potential far earlier. Nor can it be said that, despite whatever else it might have served as a vanguard, the Leninist Party hastened the de-reification of social relations and the birth of a universal subject and object of history.

In addition, even if capitalism has certainly not overcome its many flaws, it is no longer plausible to affix the temporal modifier "late" to it and claim to be on the threshold of its terminal crisis. Instead, it keeps on showing its resiliency as a system that is never quite late enough. Nor have its victims, such as they are, been able to keep up the momentum of their outrage and maintain confidence in being the harbingers of a new order. Instead of starry-eyed young people around the world willing to risk all in the cause of socialist ideals, as they did, say, during the Spanish Civil War, their twenty-first-century avatars seem more likely to join a jihadist movement designed to restore a religious theocracy that would have seemed repugnant, for all their messianic yearnings, to Lukács and his generation. On a more proximate timescale, the Age of Obama, which began with the audacity of hope, was succeeded by the Age of Trump, in which America will be made "great" again by undermining all of the progressive achievements of the past century. There may seem, in short, lots of "objective possibilities" that one might impute to the present, but none of them looks remotely like the ones discerned by the recent Marxist convert and recovering infantile leftist Georg Lukács in 1923.

In 1988 Fredric Jameson may have still been able to call *History and Class Consciousness* an "unfinished project" and stubbornly endorse Lukács's belief that the mark of reified bourgeois consciousness was precisely its helpless embrace of contingency and chance, in which "events that are meaningful socially or historically turn incomprehensible, absurd or meaningless faces to individuals who can henceforth only ratify their bewilderment with the names of accident or of well-nigh natural convulsion and upheaval."[36] But today, the putative standpoint of the collective class whose shared experience somehow allows it to discern beneath the chaos and fragmentation a deeper meaning seems more tenuous than ever.

It is thus not difficult to see why some of Lukács's most recent celebrants have resorted to Badiou's category of "fidelity to the event" to defend his—and in some cases, their—stubborn faith in the promise of 1917, despite all that has happened in the interim. Unwavering faith is, of course, often seen as a sign of a religious mentality, and there has been no shortage of attempts, ranging from René Fülöp-Miller's *Mind and Face of Bolshevism* in 1926 to Yuri Slezkine's *The House of Government* ninety-one years later, to characterize the Bolshevik appeal in these terms.[37] In Lukács's case, the comparison is almost too easy. He explicitly understood his "leap of faith" to be an embrace of a Kierkegaardian absolute in defiance of conventional ethical norms, and he characterized it in the immediate aftermath of the revolution as a frankly "messianic" gamble. To quote his biographer Arpad Kadarky, "Lukács rationalized his conversion [to Bolshevism] by quoting Kierkegaard's saying that sacrificing one's life for a cause is always an irrational act. 'To believe,' said Lukács, 'means that man consciously assumes an irrational attitude toward his own self.' . . . As if to symbolize his new life, Lukács moved out of the family villa and joined his sect of 'Franciscan' communists in the Soviet House. . . . In the Soviet House, Lukács and his sect discoursed on Jesus, St. Francis, and the Old Testament prophets as if they were their close friends."[38] A number of commentators, among them Michel Löwy and Anson Rabinbach, have convincingly situated him in the larger context of apocalyptic and redemptive enthusiasm engendered by the war and its aftermath, which included other Marxist theoreticians such as Ernst Bloch, Walter Benjamin, and Leo Lowenthal.[39] Although Lukács sought to distance himself from the still-smoldering messianism acknowledged in their work, in particular that of Bloch, it is not clear he was fully successful.[40]

In most cases, of course, the claim that revolutionary fervor is a poorly disguised semblance of religious fanaticism is aimed at diminishing its originality and robbing it of any legitimacy. This, however, is a tedious game I would prefer not to play. The complex defense of the "legitimacy of the modern age" by Hans Blumenberg against debunking secularization theorists such as Karl Löwith and Carl Schmitt is, I would argue, applicable in this case as well.[41] That is, rather than a simplistic reduction of later secular forms of belief to watered-down versions of earlier religious ones, in which the noun "theology" always trumps the adjective "political," it would be more fruitful to treat both religious and secular modes of thought as imperfect attempts in different idioms to address perennially exigent but unanswered questions. So rather than focus on the issue of fidelity with its implication of displaced religious piety, I want to conclude this essay by looking instead at the category of the Event and see if it accords with Lukács's interpretation of the Russian Revolution as expressed in *History and Class Consciousness*.

In his postface to "Tailism and the Dialectic," Žižek celebrates what he calls Lukács's "art of *Augenblick*," which he defines as "the moment when, briefly, there is an opening for an *act* to intervene in a situation" and argues that it "is unexpectedly close to what, today, Alain Badiou endeavors to formulate as the Event: an intervention that cannot be accounted for in the terms of its pre-existing 'objective conditions.'"[42] The category of "Event" has in fact enjoyed a remarkable upsurge of interest in recent years, especially among French theorists who still live off the experience of the 1968 *événements* and their unexpected disruption of conventional republican politics.[43] Lyotard, Foucault, Derrida, and Deleuze joined Badiou in celebrating the "Event" as an ineffable break in the normal flow of occurrences, a singular explosion that resists contextual explanation, upsets the equilibrium of the system, and escapes the constraints of historical determination. A caesura in the continuum of empty time, it signals what the Greeks called a kairos in the flow of chronos or the Christian descent of the sacred into the profane world exemplified by the Incarnation and evident in miracles that suspend the laws of nature. More than just a punctual break, the Event occurs in a complex pluritemporality that disrupts the flow of forward-moving time by reviving earlier moments of thwarted desire and anticipating later realizations of utopian hopes. The Event is thus, as Claude Romano has made clear, also an "advent" of something new, the beginning of an adventure that may spawn something radically different from the present order.[44] Whether or not it is the product of a willed decision—Badiou and Žižek speak grandiloquently of it resulting from "the act"—or just comes unbeckoned like a lightning flash, it is a tear in the fabric of coherently emplotted, narratively meaningful history. Although, of course, conventional historical narratives, just like realist novels, routinely include surprises and unanticipated interruptions in the evolutionary development of plots, Events in this maximalist sense are more radical, ungrounded ruptures that call into question the larger stories that try to contain them.[45] As such, they often are experienced as traumatic or emancipatory, but never as business as usual.

Inevitably, however, Events show themselves to be ephemeral, fragile, and susceptible to recuperation, as the tear repairs itself and the bracket closes.[46] And so it was in the case of the revolution whose emancipatory energy was already being blunted while Lukács was fashioning the essays that make up *History and Class Consciousness*. As George Lichtheim once sardonically commented, with the French experience in mind, "if it has been said of the early Christians that they awaited the coming of the Savior and instead got the Church, it may be said of the French proletariat that it expected the Revolution and instead got the Communist party."[47] "Fidelity to the Event" for those keeping the flame burning resists this outcome by refusing to capitulate opportunistically to the Thermidorian restoration that marked both the establishment of the official Church and the Stalinization of the party. Ironically, rather than insisting on the utter singularity of the Event, it holds out hope for its repetition at a later date, as a second coming in which the suffering of the first will be redeemed.[48]

Did this mantle fit on the shoulders of Lukács when he wrote *History and Class Consciousness*? When he underwent his self-critical reconciliation with the party in the mid-1920s, signaled by his decision to leave unpublished his last-ditch attempt to defend that book against his "tailist" critics, it had clearly waned. Indeed, by the mid-1930s he was explicitly endorsing the Thermidorian character of Stalin's regime against Trotsky's denunciation of it.[49] But in the fast-moving years when *History and Class Consciousness* was written, he steadfastly scorned those who fell back fatalistically on a belief in the ripening of conditions that would inexorably produce system change without decisive action. Although he sought to distance himself from the taint of Fichte's subjective idealism, there was a palpable residue of the latter's impatience with facts in the name of the deed underlying his belief that the normative totality of the future was in the process of being made by the proletariat as the metasubject of history.[50] As he could still put it in the concluding paragraph of his 1924 little book on Lenin, "Leninism represents a hitherto unprecedented degree of concrete, unschematic, unmechanistic, purely praxis-oriented thought. To preserve *this* is the task of the Leninist."[51]

And yet, at the same time, Lukács also struggled to exorcise the remnants of his infantile ultraleftism, by rejecting imprudent actions oblivious to the "objective possibilities" that had to exist before those actions had a chance to succeed. Getting the balance right was, alas, not easy, and the differing formulae he adopted over the years, both while writing *History and Class Consciousness* and in his subsequent career, testify to the frustration of his ongoing efforts to do so. But what has to be acknowledged is that all throughout that career, he maintained that confidence in the ultimate justification of those efforts in something called "history," indeed "world history," that we have identified in so many places in *History and Class Consciousness*. "The totality of history," he tells us, "is a real historical power." There is a "judgment of history" that will decide if the ruthless acts of the revolutionary can be absolved of their immoral taint. The superior knowledge of the proletariat and their spokesmen is grounded in their awareness that they are the makers of history and will come to know what they have made. There is a "world-historical perspective" that can be shared with those who can somehow understand the "objective possibilities" that lie before them. Tellingly, the same recourse to the coherence of a metahistorical narrative is still apparent in a remark he made in *Lenin* about the meaning of an isolated event, which cannot be called "either a victory or a defeat; only in relation to the totality of socio-historic development can it be termed either one or the other of these in a world-historical sense."[52]

In other words, not having had the opportunity to read Badiou, Žižek, or other recent celebrants of ineffable Events as the antithesis of "socio-historic development," Lukács did not understand them as kairotic interruptions in the flow of historical chronos. Straining to reconcile antinomies through a dialectical reading of history in which theory and practice were mutually reinforcing, he believed that vanguard parties were only one step ahead of the masses they led, and that objective possibilities really did exist for both the terminal crisis of capitalism and the emergence of revolutionary self-consciousness in a proletariat ready to assume its historical role. Although he sought to avoid a smooth, "organic" notion of historical progress, which we have seen him fault in Luxemburg, he still believed that despite all its dialectical reversals and uneven lurches forward, history as a whole could be understood as an intelligible story, indeed one with normative implications. In short, heavily invested in a historical meta-narrative that soon began losing its plausibility, Lukács bet on an outcome that a century later is farther away from realization than ever. Rather than analogous to a realist novel with heroic protagonists and a narrative arc, history as we now experience it seems more and more like a random congeries of contingent happenings that refuse to congeal into a meaningful plot, let alone one with emancipatory implications.

It is, I would argue in conclusion, a mark of just how far we have come that *History and Class Consciousness* can now be defended only in terms of a dogged—and dogmatic—fidelity to an Event, whose nature is precisely the antithesis of that faith in History that underlay Lukács's wager on the intelligibility of the story that led to 1917, as well as its redemptive denouement in the future. What makes reading *History and Class Consciousness* so unbearable today is the sober realization that when faith in History, in particular its future trajectory, wanes, we are left with little but pious recitations of formulae that can sustain only the most devout of believers. Witness the recent attempt to defend the continuing relevance of Leninism by Žižek, who defends the Chinese Cultural Revolution in these terms:

> If we read it as a part of historical reality (Being), we can easily submit it to a "dialectical" analysis which perceives the final outcome of a historical process as its "truth." . . . If, however, we analyze it as an Event, an enactment of the eternal Idea of egalitar-

ian Justice, then the ultimate factual result of the Cultural Revolution, its catastrophic failure and then reversal into the capitalist dynamic, does not exhaust the real of the Cultural Revolution: the eternal Idea of the Cultural Revolution survives its defeat in sociohistorical reality; it continues to lead a spectral life as the ghost of a failed utopia which returns to haunt future generations, patiently awaiting its future resurrection.[53]

For those of us unable to believe in ghosts or their ultimate resurrection, sociohistorical reality is, alas, all there is, and no amount of patience for an apocalyptic revenant will help us deal with its daunting challenges. Although we too are denied the vantage point of an ultimate judgment and must therefore concede that future redemptive Events, despite everything, may still be possible, the sorry history of the past century—told from virtually any perspective—makes it necessary for us to look far more carefully than Lukács did after 1917 before we leap into the unknown.

CHAPTER 8

Can Photographs Lie? Reflections on a Perennial Anxiety

On Thursday, March 4, 2015, the *New York Times* reported an embarrassing turn of events in the field of professional photography: the revocation of the World Press Photo contest's first prize, which had been awarded a short time earlier to the Italian photographer Giovanni Troilo. He had won for a series of ten images called "The Dark Heart of Europe" about the city of Charleroi in Belgium. The controversy over his prize focused on one photo in particular in which, to quote the *Times* article, "Mr. Troilo had photographed his cousin having sex with a woman in the back of a car, using a remote-control flash to illuminate the steamy back seat. By putting a flash in the car, critics had said, Mr. Troilo effectively staged the photo, violating the rules of the contest. The photographer disagreed." Troilo's offense, in other words, had occurred prior to the taking of his photograph, violating a prohibition on staging an allegedly documentary image, which was defined as "something that would not have happened without the photographer's involvement." Before their rescinding the first prize, the article also noted, jurors for the World Press Photo prize had already "disqualified 20 percent of the photos that made the contest's final rounds because they had been digitally manipulated by photographers who added or subtracted key elements of the images in postprocessing, violating the rules of photographic integrity."[1]

In short, the jury for the prize, pressured by critics who insisted that definitions were binding and rules were meant to be followed, reaffirmed the time-honored distinction between photographs deliberately intended as artifacts or even works of art—where presumably staging, postproduction manipulation, and something called "the rules of photographic integrity" would *not* be at issue—and photographs claiming to be accurate records of real events occurring contingently in the world, where they clearly would. Well, maybe not so clearly, as the original jury award had been premised, the *Times* article revealed, on the assumption that Troilo's photograph "could be seen as documentary photography or portraiture, where such use of a flash is considered acceptable." What seems to have convinced it to rethink its judgment was less the flash in the car than the caption that had accompanied the image, which read "locals know of parking lots popular for sexual liaisons." By not signaling he was one of the locals in the know, the photographer had deceptively elided his complicity in what was being photographed. Troilo later protested that he had never meant the photo to be taken as showing a couple caught unawares *in flagrante delicto*, because he had solicited the prior cooperation of his cousin (although he neglects to mention whether or not the other party in the car was asked for hers). His aim was to "show voyeurism through voyeurism. The camera becomes active; it becomes the sense of shame."[2]

Whatever the precise merits of this particular case or the plausibility of Troilo's cryptic explanation, it is worth rehashing because it reminds us that the controversy over photographic mendacity, fueled by anxiety about what Tom Gunning calls the "truth claims" of photographs as trustworthy representations of what they record, continues to rage.[3] And perhaps not coincidentally, it seems to be intensifying at the very same time that "photography matters as art as never before," to cite the title of Michael Fried's recent celebration of such contemporary photographers as Jeff Wall, Cindy Sherman, Hiroshi Sugimoto, Philip-Lorca diCorcia, Thomas Demand, Rineke Dijkstra, the Bechers, Thomas Struth, Andreas Gursky, Thomas Ruff, and Candida Höfer.[4] That is, there seems to be emerging, at least conceptually, a more categorically rigid distinction between photographs that claim to be truthful, having what we might call evidential weight and providing impersonal testimony about real events, and photographs that willingly bracket truth claims to align themselves with other more self-consciously creative image-making practices, such as painting, which normally privilege imagination and control over mimesis and serendipity.

One way to understand these sharpened categorizations is to see them as reactions to the anxieties unleashed by the digital revolution in photography that began around 1990.[5] There has, of course, been a great deal of ink spilled—or rather pixels generated—over the implications of digitalization, in particular on the widely debated role of so-called indexicality in the truth claims of photographs.[6] Without the physical trace of the light rays bouncing off objects in the world and being registered chemically on photographic film, so it was feared, iconic verisimilitude would not be enough to verify the truth claims of images. Indeed, some even talked melodramatically of the resulting "death of photography." Whether there was a radical break between analog and digital techniques, one with ontological significance, or merely a technological enhancement of methods of doctoring images that were there ever since the first double-exposure "spirit" photos of the nineteenth century, is, however, still being debated, if perhaps without the apocalyptic dread infusing many of the original responses to digitalization.

My own inclination, for what it is worth, is to side with those who hold that Photoshop has not really undermined our still-potent faith in photography's ability to represent the world with fidelity, even if we are a smidgeon less confident that it is always being scrupulously maintained. Airbrushing, after all, long antedated what is now called the "rasterization" of pixels on our computers. Significantly, as many observers have noted, we do not ban digital images from our passports or driver's licenses, but consider them trustworthy, if not always very flattering, portraits of their holders, capable of identifying them with just as much accuracy as analog images or even indexical fingerprints. When we hold them up to the immigration officer or highway patrolman, he or she still can recognize us in the face on the page. Whatever the technological changes may imply, the institutional support for believing in photographic veracity remains pretty much in place. Moreover, as W. J. T. Mitchell has pointed out in his discussion of the Abu Ghraib torture photographs, digital images carry with them invisible metadata, which allows the expert to know the precise date and time the picture was taken and with which camera.[7] This information provides evidence within the image—or more precisely, the image file—that is normally archived outside it, if at all, and thus potentially increases our confidence in its veracity or in our ability to detect lies told about it.[8]

From the very beginning of the medium's invention, such confidence has, to be sure, always drawn on a certain suspension of disbelief. The world, after all, doesn't appear to our sense of sight in two dimensions or in geometric frames, say three inches by five, or in black and white rather than color, or frozen in time rather than almost always in motion. Nor does it depend on a supporting medium such as photographic paper or a computer screen, whose material presence can never be entirely effaced. Nor does it withhold information about the actual spatial location of objects, producing instead what philosophers, referring to photographs, call "spatially agnostic informants."[9] Photographs, chemically or digitally enabled, are, in other words, re-presentations of an experienced world with a difference, always mimetically imperfect, always nonidentical with the objects or events they capture for later contemplation. Even when they allow us to experience new visual phenomena—or better, old ones in new ways—through arrested motion or enlargement, giving us access to what Walter Benjamin famously called the "optical unconscious," photographs do so by revealing their secrets to the camera eye first and the human one second.[10] For these reasons, their tacit truth claims require a translation process, in which they signify or represent, to borrow C. S. Peirce's familiar trichotomy, via a mixture of iconic and indexical signs with the occasional symbolic supplement. However much they may resemble what they depict, they are not equivalent to it.[11] However much they may be said to escape coding and present the world directly, *pace* commentators like the early Roland Barthes,[12] they are dependent on extratechnological conventions that establish their verisimilitude, those "rules of photographic integrity" cited by the judges in the World Press Photo contest. Although these conventions and mediations may be construed as ways to maintain perceptual contact with the world rather than simply distort it, as some commentators have insisted,[13] they nonetheless trouble the naive notion of accurate recording of what is photographed.

Or if one prefers to think in very different terms about the idea of truth itself, although defenders of the truth claims of photography may invoke the rhetoric of truth based on the adequate correspondence of an image in the mind's eye to the object it represents, the Scholastic idea of *adequatio rei et intellectus*, photographs may draw their power instead on an alternative view of truth. That is, they may abet the disclosure or unconcealment of a world hitherto unseen, or truth in Heidegger's sense of *aletheia*. As such, they may share a certain revelatory capacity with works of visual art, which also do more than merely report or reflect the world as it has always already been seen. Even if we may not be convinced by the Heideggerian account of truth as disclosure, it alerts us to the possibility that the simple opposition between artistic and photojournalist practices of photography may be problematic.

It is for all these reasons that the resistance to photography's aesthetic pretensions in the name of accurate, documentary realism—or at least resistance to the creative moment in the objective recording of an undoctored truth—has always had something implausible about it. However automatic the recording device, however much contingency may sneak into the finished result against the intention of the photographer, however much the world discloses itself in unexpected ways, there is also always some choice made in the point, click, and crop moment that brings a particular image into existence. In other words, the camera eye is itself a function, at least in part, of the intervention of the photographer. Even such a staunch defender of the truth claims of photography as the contemporary critic John Roberts builds his case by acknowledging that "the photodocument is a critically *ostensive* medium, it points at and picks out things because the photographer judges these things to be worth attending."[14] There is thus a certain continuity between prephotographic staging defined as "something that would not have happened without the photographer's involvement" and his or her decision to take the picture at a particular moment from a particular angle in a particular light. If you are skilled enough, to borrow Henri Cartier-Bresson's famous phrase, it will be the "decisive moment," capturing something extraordinary, even revelatory. But even if you are not, the resulting representation is still never of the world as it actually is.

Although often celebrated by those who want to include photography with painting among the visual fine arts, this disparity can also lead to dismay over the ideological potential in photographic practice when it is seen to abet an unwanted and deceptive aestheticization. Take, for example, the case of Walter Benjamin. In his celebrated 1931 essay "Little History of Photography," where Benjamin coined the term "optical unconscious," he approvingly cited the warning of the Russian-born photographer Sasha Stone that "photography-as-art is a very dangerous field." Benjamin's prime example was the much-lauded album by the Neue Sachlichkeit photographer Albert Raenger-Patsch, *Die Welt ist Schön*: "The creative in photography is its capitulation to fashion. *The world is beautiful*—that is its watchword. In it is unmasked the posture of a photography that can endow any soup can with cosmic significance but cannot grasp a single one of the human connections in which it exists, even when this photography's most dream-laden subjects are a forerunner more of its salability than of any knowledge it might produce."[15] What Benjamin, in other words, feared was the capacity of the photographer to prettify the reified world of commodities, imbuing the surface appearances of modern life with an aura of aesthetic value without, however, penetrating to the dialectical relations beneath them that were the deeper truth of that world. Or as he put it when he returned to Raenger-Patsch's work in his essay "The Author as Producer," "it has succeeded in transforming even abject poverty, by recording it in a fashionably perfected manner, into an object of enjoyment."[16] In contrast, he invoked the images of vacated city streets by Eugène Atget, which had been rightly compared with crime scenes, and posed the rhetorical questions: "But isn't every square of our cities a crime scene? Every passer-by a culprit? Isn't the task of the photographer—descendent of the augurs and haruspices—to reveal guilt and to point out the guilty in his pictures?"[17]

Benjamin's distinction between deceptive and aestheticized appearances and the truer and more brutal realities beneath them depended on a dialectical notion of reality that located truth in occluded contradictions rather than superficial harmonies. Anticipating Guy Debord's critique of the "society of the spectacle," he lamented the visual equivalent of commodity fetishism in which the underlying human sources, both in terms of productive labor and the suffering of unjust compensation for it, were forgotten. What he elsewhere damned as the "aestheticization of politics" was also at work, *mutatis mutandis*, in the duplicitous beautification of a world whose deeper ugliness—and the guilt of the system that produced it—remained hidden. For Benjamin, such images were mendacious, even if they involved no preproduction staging or postproduction doctoring.

What, however, distinguished his position from contemporary defenders of a realistic photojournalism that seeks to distinguish itself as radically as possible from art photography—or a somewhat tendentious versions of it[18]—is the alternative he defended against the Neue Sachlichkeit beautification of the world. He may have invoked Sasha Stone's warning against "photography-as-art," but he admired Stone's own work, which owed a great deal to the constructivist aesthetics of the journal *G*, whose leaders included Moholy-Nagy, El Lissitsky, and Mies van der Rohe. Benjamin, in fact, considered the photomontage that Stone did for the book jacket of his own *One-Way Street* in 1928 "one of the most effective covers ever."[19] In his "Little History of Photography," he also cited Brecht's claim that "the reification of human relations—the factory, say—means that they are no longer explicit. So something must in fact be *built up*, something artificial, posed." And then he added, "We must credit the Surrealists with having trained the pioneers of such photographic construction."[20] In other words, for Benjamin, the possibility of overcoming photographic mendacity based on conventional notions of harmonious formal beauty lay in the ability to harness other aesthetic innovations to counteract the reifications of a world whose deeper workings could not be revealed in allegedly "objective" images that stayed on the surface. Here, we might say, the spear that had caused the wound—aestheticization as mere beautification—could be wielded once again to cure it—aestheticization as constructivist juxtaposition and defamiliarization. That latter, however, is not based predominantly on the creative imagination of the artist, who conjures up images *ex nihilo*, but rather his or her manipulation and combination of fragments of images and sometimes texts that existed before. In other words, however much photomontages were the product of a *monteur*, an inspired assembler, they were also still based on the semiautomatic process of photography itself and the re-constellation of the visual readymades that resulted. It was an activity, we might say with a nod to Heidegger, that could disclose a truth hitherto occluded, albeit one that was the truth of historical materialism, not existential phenomenology. Along with the revelation of the "optical unconscious" through techniques like enlargement and fast shutter speed, constructivist juxtapositions could break through the crust of conventional seeing and allow us to gaze at the world with fresh eyes.

Whether photographic truth is advanced by the abjection of the aesthetic, broadly understood as any deliberate staging of a scene, as the jurors for the World Press Photo think, or by its proper employment for critical constructivist purposes, as Benjamin had believed, what is clear is that those who seek it are convinced of the danger that certain photographs can be mendacious, providing a false, ideologically nefarious view of the world. Alerting naive viewers to the "lies of photography," to cite the title of an 1899 French newspaper article exposing composite images of alleged political allies during the Dreyfus Affair, is, in fact, frequently advocated by those who worry how easy it is to be taken in by their implicit truth claims.[21]

But what, I want to ask, does it mean to say that a photograph can actually lie? Is it the image itself that intentionally deceives, or is it something else that is added to it that is responsible? Is a photograph that lies merely one that lacks the qualities that allow others to make convincing claims to be truthful, or does it actively have to do something more? To address these questions, we have to pause with the issue of what constitutes a lie in the first place, an issue that inevitably moves us away from images to language. Although there are, of course, many different ways in which linguistic questions can be approached, let me invoke only two, speech act theory and deconstruction, with a quick nod to Michel Foucault's thoughts on the subject as well. Pseudologists or students of mendacity indebted to the first tradition tell us that, strictly speaking, a lie is a speech act with four distinct components, and it has both constative and performative qualities. The first component is the liar's conscious but unexpressed knowledge of the truth or what he or she thinks is true. For example, I look outside the window and know it is a sunny day and not raining. The second is the liar's utterance, verbally or in writing, of an assertion that is the contrary of or at least at variance with what the speaker knows or thinks is the truth. This is the locutionary or constative aspect of the speech act, a statement about either objective or subjective reality. I say, "It is not sunny, it is raining." The third is the liar's illocutionary intention to deceive the listener or reader into believing that such an assertion is indeed true, although the speaker knows or thinks he or she knows otherwise. I intend you to believe falsely that it is raining, even though I know or at least believe it is not. A corollary of this intention is to convince the listener that the speaker is trustworthy, or at least to rely on the listener's unreflective assumption that the speaker indeed is. In other words, I also want you to believe or continue to assume that I am a truth-teller and not a liar. And fourth and finally, if the lie is what can be called a "felicitous" speech act, its perlocutionary effect is indeed to persuade the listener or reader that what is not the case actually is. You fall for my intended deception and now think it is indeed raining, and are thus conned into buying one of the umbrellas I have for sale.

It is important to note the difference between a simple error articulated without an intention to deceive and a lie. In the Middle Ages, for example, honest men and women would have said that the sun went around the earth. Although what they believed was wrong, they were not mendacious or untrustworthy. Ironically, one can intend to mislead and yet tell the truth, if one's belief in what is the case is itself flawed. In other words, one has to distinguish clearly between the truth and error, however we define them, and the truthfulness or mendacity of a speaker, whose intentions are more important than the veracity of his or her assertions.

There is also a crucial difference between unconscious deception—say, a chameleon changing its color automatically to fit into a new environment—and a conscious decision to lie by a responsible agent. Deception happens all the time in nature, especially when it comes to the dance of death between predators and prey or the competition for sexual partners, but there are no lies involved in the sense we have described above. As Jacques Lacan notes in *Écrits*, "An animal does not pretend to pretend. He does not make tracks whose deception lies in the fact that they will be taken as false, while being in fact true ones, that is, that indicate his true trail. Nor does an animal cover up its tracks, which would be tantamount to making itself the subject of the signifier." Pretense or deception in nature is not dependent on any kind of signifier, Lacan argues, because it is not situated in the general order of signification that is language. He calls this order of signification another locus from the dyadic interaction of predator and prey, "the locus of the Other, the Other witness, the witness Other than any of the partners."[22] The Other (*le grand Autre*) is not something constituted empirically through the use of language, not a norm imposed by language, but is rather the transcendental condition out of which language emerges, the presupposition of truth-telling that underlies all speech acts. As a result, there is always an asymmetry between truth-telling and lying, the latter being parasitic on the former. Whereas falsehood is an unjustified truth claim, telling the truth is not an unjustified lie, but rather a justified assertion of the truth. Significantly, there is a verb "to lie," which suggests an agent who acts on his or her own initiative, whereas there is no verb "to truth," because the premise of telling the truth is hardwired into language as such as its transcendental *a priori*, at least when it involves assertions.[23]

What is sometimes called human self-deception, in which one part of the self allegedly knows what is true but hides it from another, may be understood as a hybrid case, as it combines elements of intentional lying with unintentional deception. Or because it rarely involves speech acts, it may be something outside of the problematic of lying entirely, perhaps better understood in terms of the psychoanalytic concept of denial.[24] But however we consider such anomalous cases, by and large the distinction between natural deception without a speech act and human lying through one is worth maintaining.

Finally, we should also understand that lies have an important temporal ambiguity built into them. They involve constative assertions about the current or past state of the world or the actual beliefs and the intentions of the speaker. When they are false promises, they are current assertions about future actions, which they now pretend they will carry out at some later time. But the performative intention of all lies is entirely future-oriented, that is, to produce in the listener or reader a false understanding, a misleading belief in what is or was not the case (or when it comes to false promises, a mistaken belief in what will, in fact, not be the case in the future). All lies, we might say, are based on the imagination of what is not now the case, performatively making a new future reality, or at least a new belief about it. It is for this reason that Hannah Arendt could audaciously contend that there was a critical link between lying and political action, for both were based on imagining a possible change in the status quo and a different future.[25]

With those clarifications behind us, it may seem that we can now return to the question of photographic mendacity. To help answer it, however, we have to widen our lens a bit to consider, if briefly, the larger question of the issue of truth and lying in visual experience in general. Here we may find some inspiration in the work of two stalwarts of twentieth-century French theory, Jacques Derrida and Michel Foucault. A number of years ago in a remarkable book called *The Truth in Painting*, Derrida pondered the implications of Cézanne's promise in a letter of 1905 to his friend Emile Bernard: "I owe you the truth in painting and I will tell it to you." Examining what he called the painter's *"speech act* promising perhaps a *painting act,"* Derrida noted that Cézanne "promises that he will *say* the truth in painting."[26] In exploring the implications of that promise, Derrida first examined the assumption that paintings or other artwork were self-sufficient entities unto themselves, disinterested enclaves walled off from the external world and capable of expressing their own internal truth. Deconstructing the distinction between *ergon* and *parergon*, a work based on the capturing of creative *energia* and the frame around it, he showed instead that the boundary between them was always permeable. What seemed an extraneous, ornamental excrescence like columns in front of buildings, the pedestal under a statue, or the garment draped over it inevitably intruded on the objects themselves, undermining the integrity of allegedly autonomous and autotelic work of art. Examining, then, the alternative claim that the truth of a painting could be found outside it in terms of representative fidelity to the object mimetically depicted, he looked carefully at the dispute between Heidegger and the American art historian Meyer Schapiro over the alleged model for Van Gogh's painting *Old Shoes with Lacings*. Schapiro had claimed that they were the artist's own unlaced shoes, Heidegger that they were those of a peasant, but Derrida said that the dispute could not be definitively resolved on the evidence each provided. The implication he drew was that the truth of a painting could not also be derived externally through reference to the accuracy of its representation. He finished by looking at paintings that contained snippets of writing on the canvas, in particular the work of Valerio Adami, which he denied could be read with confidence in either mimetic, semiotic, or formal terms. The upshot of these explorations was the conclusion that radical undecidability thwarted all attempts to find the truth in painting promised by Cézanne to his friend.

In this book, Derrida did not address the specific question of whether paintings, if they can't, *pace* Cézanne, tell the truth, can instead be accused of lying. The question of mendacity, however, was treated in one of his later essays titled "History of the Lie: Prolegomena," which appeared in the collection *Without Alibi* in 2002, and it is from this piece that we can perhaps infer his possible answer.[27] In it, he stressed the performative quality of the lie, "which is not a fact or a state; it is an *intentional* act, a lying. There is not *the* lie, but rather this saying or this meaning-to-say that is called lying." In addition to stressing the importance of the action over the deed, he also insisted on "the irreducibly ethical dimension of the lie, where the *phenomenon* of the lie as such is intrinsically foreign to the problem of knowledge, the truth, the true and the false."[28] The liar betrays the trust of the person he or she seeks to mislead, in particular the trust in sincerity on which normal assertions in communicative interaction depend.

A similar stress on the ethical, intersubjective dimension of lying as the breaking of trust between people characterized Michel Foucault's ruminations on the ancient Greek notion of *parrhesia*, which he defined as "a verbal activity in which a speaker expresses his personal relationship to truth, and risks his life because he recognizes that truth-telling as a duty to improve or help other people (as well as himself)."[29] Foucault's interest in the verbal performance of the truth-teller, based on his or her sincerity, is relevant to the question we are addressing because he pitted it against a more modern notion of epistemological validity based on the testimony of the eyes. In an earlier essay, whose arguments I won't rehearse now, I sought to explore the implications of Foucault's thoughts on truth and visuality.[30] It concluded that however much he may have favored certain ocular practices over others—for example, the decomposed calligrams of a René Magritte over the traditional Cartesian perspectivalism of mimetic representation—he never supported the ideal of "truth-showing" or visual *parrhesia* as an antidote to sinister practices such as the surveillance of the panopticon.

There are several lessons that might be drawn from Derrida's and Foucault's analyses of the complex relationship between visuality in general and truth-telling, which bear on the question of photographic mendacity. One is the distinction between lying as a speech act—*telling* a lie, parasitic on the act of *telling* the truth—and an image, whether a painting or photograph, which *shows* something, either in the world or in the imagination (or a mixture of both), but cannot *say* or *tell* it. Thus photos lack crucial dimensions of the speech act of lying outlined above, in particular prior consciousness of the truth and the intention of saying otherwise to fool a second party. Although nonverbal images can, of course, have illocutionary intentions once their conventional codes are established—think of a skull and crossbones on a bottle of poison, warning you not to drink it, or a red light at a crossroads—by themselves they are mute, a condition shared by photographs. If there is a transcendental *a priori* for visual experience—and philosophers like Kant have argued there is in spatial intuitions—it is not *"le grand Autre"* of language in Lacan's sense of the term. The implication of all this is captured in Tom Gunning's observation in his insightful essay "What's the Point of an Index?, or, Faking Photographs": "The apparatus, in itself can neither lie, nor tell the truth. Bereft of language, a photograph relies on people to say things about it or for it."[31]

A second plausible lesson to draw concerns the intersubjective and ethical dimension of lying. There is nothing in the taking of a photograph per se that is inherently intersubjective, let alone involves an ethical relation between subjects. I can take a picture of my big toe for my own private admiration and never show it to another human being. There are, to be sure, many photographs that do involve interactions between subjects, and elaborate protocols have emerged concerning the implicit contract that ties the photographer with the photographed, one that often has legal ramifications in terms of ownership of the resulting image. And if Ariella Azoulay is right in her controversial study of *The Civil Contract of Photography*, the contract can have profound political and human rights implications as well.[32]

To return to the offending photograph by Giovanni Troilo, which cost him his World Press Photo prize, was such a civil contract betrayed in the case of his cousin's unwitting partner in the staging of their illuminated lovemaking in that steamy back seat in Chaleroi, Belgium? The answer to that question may well be yes, at least in the terms set by the contest, but it is not clear that the reason has anything to do with the mendacity of the image, which simply recorded what the flash revealed. One can even claim that by using a flash, the photographer enabled a sharper image of the event he wanted to capture, and in this sense made possible a "truer" effect—or more precisely, a greater claim to verisimilitude—than if it had been in the shadows. So, although the photo was disqualified because the event it depicted was staged rather than merely captured, the image itself was innocent of any lying in the sense we have been developing.

The upshot of all of these considerations would seem to be that claiming photos can lie is based on a category mistake, a confusion of the logics of figurality and discursivity, of showing and telling. Their temporality is inherently past-oriented, magically preserving an ephemeral moment that no longer is, whereas lies, as we have argued, are future-oriented, seeking to change the status quo rather than merely record it. They are, moreover, only contingently intersubjective, whereas a lie—the ambiguous case of self-deception aside—is essentially so. If photos deceive, and we know of course that they can, perhaps it is best to group them with the unintentional, nonlinguistically mediated deception of the natural world rather than with the human—all too human—speech act we call lying.

And yet before we too hastily adopt this conclusion, it may be worth returning to one of the arguments we have encountered in Derrida's exploration of Cézanne's promise to show his friend the truth in painting. In his discussion of the distinction between *ergon* and *parergon*, you will recall, Derrida challenged the ideal of aesthetic immanence, the claim that works of art are organic wholes with clear boundaries separating them from extrinsic contexts of production and reception. Instead, he argued that the supplement of the frame always inhabits the interiority of the work, which cannot achieve its effect of self-sufficiency without it. An aesthetics of pure form, seeking to abject materiality, or pit poesis against mimesis, is always haunted by what it banishes. The self-pleasuring of a work, its "auto-affection," is never complete: "The most irreducible heteroaffection," Derrida writes, "inhabits—intrinsically—the most closed autoaffection."[33] Or to put it in more temporal terms, the reified solidity of the *ergon* cannot contain for very long the *energia* that went into its production and that is unleashed by its reception, in the same way that Marx argued that the fetishized commodity cannot entirely obliterate the memory of the labor that went into its production and the use to which it will be put.

If we extrapolate from this argument about paintings and other works of art to photographs, it suggests that however isolated the image may seem from its discursive context, however "bereft of language" the photo may appear to be, it is nonetheless not entirely immune from contamination—or enrichment—by its enabling contexts of generation and reception, which include discursive moments. When we take seriously the congealed intentionality in a photograph, which, as we noted earlier, extends beyond conscious staging of the scene or postproduction manipulation to include the choice in deciding to take it at a specific moment and aim in a certain direction, we can say that the finished image, however self-contained it may seem, is always haunted by the process that produced it. Appearing in more than just the added caption or the post-facto written interpretation of the image, discursive interruption of the pure figurality of the image already occurs in the residual impact of previous photographs and the ways in which they have been integrated into discursive circuits of meaning. Tom Gunning comes close to acknowledging this integration when he follows his statement about the apparatus's inability to lie or tell the truth with the acknowledgment that "historically and institutionally, in order to tell the truth, the photograph must be subjected to a series of discourses, become, in effect, the supporting evidence for a statement. . . . In order to speak the truth the photograph must be integrated into a statement, subjected to complex rules of discourse—legal, rhetorical, even scientific."[34]

Drawing on Derrida's argument about the *ergon* and *parergon*, we might push this argument a little further to say that the subjection of the image to a discursive context is not something that happens *after* it has come into the world as a mute object, something that is tacked on from the outside, but rather has *always already* happened in the constitution of the image itself. As in the study of movies in which discrete "films" are best understood as permeated by the forces that constitute "cinema" as an englobing institution, involving production, distribution, reception, preservation, and intermediality, the seemingly isolated image that we call a photograph cannot be entirely extracted from the mediations of the larger context we call photography.

In fact, the very term "photography," introduced to replace the earlier "photogenic drawing" and promoted by William Henry Fox Talbot in *The Pencil of Nature* (1844), may also alert us to the entanglement of the figural and the discursive. As Hagi Kenaan has recently noted in an insightful essay on the role of shadows in the origins of photographic images, the neologism includes "the Greek *graphein* with its double-sense meaning of drawing and writing. The term *photography* thus introduces a certain ambivalence into nature's pencil, which now operates between drawing and writing, between visual depiction and the codified signs of a language." He then adds that the new process of image making enabled the "ability to see the shadow as a code and, consequently, to create a new visually uprooted image whose self-sufficiency is no longer indebted to vision."[35]

It is perhaps for these reasons that the truth claims of photography are never reducible to a simple indexical trace of the real, the automatic registering of an object or event through a chemical or digital process. As we've seen in the case of Benjamin with his pitting of one tacitly aesthetic practice against another, photomontage versus the beautification of reified surfaces, truth can be understood as a dialectical construct, not a passive recording of the world as it appears. Pure disclosure or unhiddenness, *pace* Heidegger with his notion of *aletheia*, needs a helping hand. Not surprisingly, we find Benjamin advocating the conscious imbrication of figurality and discursivity, when he writes, "What we require of the photographer is the ability to give his picture the caption that wrenches it from the modish commerce and gives it a revolutionary useful value."[36]

The contemporary critic John Roberts, sharing the same militant political agenda as Benjamin, contends that the truth claim of photography is not based on its direct, unmediated showing of something in the world, but rather the shock it gives to our normal, unreflective experience of sight, the violation of our conventional way of looking. It is what he calls its "indirect or secondary ostension," based on "an undeclared secondary meaning" that is "essential to the social and discursive claims of photography."[37] The act of disruption, even one that may violate the privacy of the subject photographed, is what overcomes the soothing aesthetic effect that Benjamin so disliked in his critique of Neue Sachlichkeit superficial beauty. It has a future-oriented intention in unsettling the visual status quo. There is an affective truth in photography, which Roberts identifies with "*its unrivaled capacity to reveal the fact that what we see is not convergent with what we know to be true, and therefore that what we know about what we see we are unable to freely assimilate—there is a fundamental gap between representation and truth.*"[38]

The implication of these challenges to what we might call the mimetic ideology of the photograph's truth showing for our own question of the photograph's ability to lie is clear. If photographs are necessarily embedded in the larger institutions and practices of "photography" and those institutions and practices have an inevitably discursive moment, we can understand them as the contested sites of figurality and discursivity, which are intertwined, although not collapsible one into the other. If photography's truth claims are more than just a function of the unintended, indexical moment in the process of recording but also depend on discursive assumptions, and if lying is parasitic on truthfulness, as we have seen it is in linguistic terms, then it may well be the case that mendacity can also be discerned even in the mute world of the photographic image. As the philosopher Arthur Danto once put it when discussing the practice of photographing people unaware, "Cameras do not lie, but photographers do."[39] What in fact makes the hybrid practice we call taking a photograph so richly overdetermined is its ability to show and tell at the same time, sometimes with parallel implications and sometimes not.

It is ironically because the "rules of photographic integrity," to cite the normative procedural standards invoked by the jury for the World Press Photo contest, are never really observed in their pure state that we can meaningfully speak of the ability of photographs to be truthful, and also to lie. And to compound the irony, such lying may result from reinforcing the naturalization of a world of reifications that reflect a social reality that needs to be disrupted, even violated, to reveal a potential for an alternative that may have a better claim to the truth. Or to give the screw one more twist, if Arendt is right about the link between lying and resisting the status quo, it too may under certain circumstances have a critical function, pointing to a future truth denied in the present world. Maybe Giovanni Troilo, not despite but because of his staging, deserves his prize after all.[40]

CHAPTER 9

Sublime Historical Experience, Real Presence, and Photography

I have always accounted it a great good fortune to have been one of the first responders to Frank Ankersmit's boldly original advocacy of what he called "sublime historical experience." By chance, both of us were grappling with the vexed concept of experience and its vicissitudes at the same time in the early years of this century and were able to begin a fruitful dialogue whose beneficial results found their ways into books we both published in 2005.[1] We exchanged chapters and I served as a reader of his manuscript for Stanford University Press, on which I drew liberally—still citing the title he later abandoned, *Historical Experience: The Embrace of Romeo and Juliet*—in my chapter on concepts of historical experience, whose other main protagonists were Wilhelm Dilthey, R. G. Collingwood, and Joan Scott. I did my best to summarize the gist of his argument, which ambitiously sought to go beyond both the correspondence theory of Dilthey and Collingwood, with their notions of present reexperiencing or reenacting of the experiences of past actors, on the one hand, and Scott's post-structuralist disdain for experience *tout court*, on the other. Although I was troubled by Ankersmit's defiant avoidance of epistemological questions about the truth value of accounts of sublime historical experiences in favor of their aesthetic justification,[2] and not clear how one might turn an individual historian's experience—which he conceded was a rare and ineffable event—into a warrant for a new narrative or representation of the past that might be judged by the community of historians, I found the concept itself intriguing.

A good part of the reason was its resonance with an extraordinary encounter I myself had once had with the past that was now illuminated by

Ankersmit's analysis of sublime historical experiences. I had described it in some detail in an essay published in 1995 titled "The Manacles of Gavrilo Princip."[3] During a visit to the Nazi concentration camp in Theresienstadt the previous year, I had come unexpectedly upon the prison cell where the teenaged assassin of the archduke Franz Ferdinand had rotted away until his death in 1918, a few months before the end of the horrific war precipitated by his violent deed. Holding the rusted chains that had bound the miserable boy to the floor of his cage, I was shaken out of the melancholy Holocaust narrative I had been following as I made my way through the camp. It was, I later recalled, "as if suddenly in the pages of *Middlemarch* someone had surreptitiously introduced a chapter, say, from *The Charterhouse of Parma*." Included in my Holocaust narrative had been a mournful rumination on the truncated life of the poet, playwright, and puppet maker Petr Kein, a young man with whom I clearly identified and one of whose puppets was on view in the museum at the camp. "How," I wondered, "could I reconcile my admiring reverie for the gifted hands of an innocent young puppeteer with the shock I felt in the 'presence' of the manacled hands of an infamous assassin?"[4]

My answer was to muse on the entanglement of the Holocaust with the violence unleashed by the First World War and the still-unfolding catastrophe in the Balkans following the breakup of Yugoslavia, which involved new variants of the ethnic cleansing that had reached its height in the Nazi extermination of the Jews. I was thus led to ponder the Holocaust's inextricability, however much one might want to protest its ineffable uniqueness, in the tangled web of horrors discharged along with an assassin's bullet and still being spun eighty years later. Despite the dangers of "relativization" or "normalization," it was wrong, I concluded, to transfigure the Holocaust into a quasi-metaphysical eruption of the demonic into the turbulent flow of historical occurrences. Even the imperative "never again" made sense only if one implicitly recognized that it, or something very much like it, could indeed happen more than once.

Such were my attempts to make sense of the unanticipated material reminder of the First World War in one of the most disturbing sites of the Second. What I could not realize at the time, however, was that in many ways my encounter with the manacles of Gavrilo Princip could profitably be understood in the terms Ankersmit was to develop in *Sublime Historical Experience*. Perhaps his most daring move in that work was defending an intense encounter with a past that refused not only to be explained in causal terms but also to be interpreted as meaningful. Certain powerful experiences in the present of past realities, he argued, defy attempts to narrate or represent them in intelligible terms. They cannot be domesticated, *pace* Hayden White, by locating them in stories guided by prefigural tropes of emplotment. They thwart all efforts, *pace* Quentin Skinner, to reduce them to interventions in a particular historical context available for present reconstruction. Their sublimity lies precisely, as such celebrated students of the sublime as Burke and Kant had argued, in their resistance to representation or explanation, their being beyond the capacity of mere language to redescribe them in communicable terms. Fittingly, my essay on the visit to Theresienstadt ended with a recollection of my inarticulate reaction to the experience of holding Princip's manacles: "The impulse that overwhelmed me was to shake them as furiously as I could, while impotently hurling at the ghost of the boy who once filled them the earthy epithet that the inmates of Theresienstadt would have understood all too well: 'Schmuck!!!'"[5]

My sputtering, visceral fury at Princip's ghost fit well with Ankersmit's claim that some experiences of the past have an emotional effect unmediated by prior historiography, maybe even unfiltered through traditional categories of the understanding. Rather than based on the disinterested impartiality abetted by visual distance, they partake of the immediacy of haptic interaction, in which we grasp with our own hands a material residue—say, the rusted chains in a prison cell—that has survived from the past. They come to us, moreover, unbidden and unprovoked by the questions we put to the past or the hypotheses about it that we put to the test by carefully weighing evidence. Akin to Bergson's "involuntary memory," which Walter Benjamin had linked to the unassimilated residues of trauma, such an experience, Ankersmit wrote, "suddenly presents itself like a meteoric invasion by the past into the present. Everything surrounding us in the present is pushed aside and the whole of the world is reduced to just ourselves in this specific memory—where the memory sees us, so to say, and we see only *it*." If such an experience has any truth value, it is that of a revelatory truth akin to Heidegger's *aletheia*, based on passive receptivity rather than active interrogation. It is what Huizinga seems to have sought: "A truth that arises from a quasi-mystic union with the world that no longer allows itself to be enchanted by the abstractions that we all so unproblematically use. It is a mysticism that does not put us at a distance from reality but that brings us to its very heart."[6] Rather than a subjective encounter with an external object, this experience is one where the subject loses any constitutive power, perhaps even its sense of individual autonomy, and is overwhelmed by the power of the emotion.

The very distinction between subject and object falters, and what is left is experience without a strong notion of the subject who has it. Ankersmit, while stepping back from embracing mystical irrationalism, nonetheless argued that "historical experience pulls the faces of past and present together in a short but ecstatic kiss."[7]

Although there was nothing very romantic in my Theresienstadt visit, let alone a whiff of mystical union with the world, I did experience the emotional power of what I had called in my essay "the 'presence' of the manacled hands of an infamous assassin." In so doing, I unwittingly anticipated a key term of the discourse of sublime historical experience, albeit one perhaps more explicitly foregrounded in the work of Ankersmit's two most important allies in its elaboration: Hans Ulrich Gumbrecht and Eelco Runia.[8] All of them stress the importance of the powerful presence of what Runia called a "stowaway" from the past. For Ankersmit, more precisely, it is a combination of absence and presence that defines sublime historical experience: the absence of the mediating representational, explanatory, contextual, narrative frame and the presence of a direct "sensation"—the term is taken from Huizinga—of a past that intrudes on our consciousness.

One possible precedent for this elevated version of a past that manifests itself ontologically in the here and now is the Christian doctrine of "real presence," the transubstantiation of the body and blood of crucified Jesus in the Eucharist.[9] As historians have long understood, a certain slippage might occur from an explicitly divine presence to a more secular one, one in which belief in the literal identity of the Holy Eucharist and Christ could somehow be transferred, at least in part, to other semisacred figures. A salient example was the medieval doctrine of the king's two bodies, one comparable to the eternal *corpus mysticum* of Christ, the other to his mortal, creaturely counterpart.[10] A later manifestation of this miraculous transformation appeared, so the historian Louis Marin contended, in the portrait of Louis XIV on coins and medals during the early modern period. "The king is only truly king, that is, monarch," he writes, "in images. They are his *real presence*. A belief in the effectiveness and operativeness of *his* iconic signs is obligatory, or else the monarch is emptied of all his substance through lack of transubstantiation, and only simulacrum is left."[11] The king's body is at once sacramental, symbolic, and historical, as his physical presence is transfigured into the real presence of an image that is more than a mere resemblance or likeness. Although theologians were often careful to distinguish ontological identity in the Eucharist from both the sacred aura of icons and the representational imitation of mere images, some of the magic associated with the former can wander into the latter.

The further transformation of such devotional images, religious or political, with sacramental potency into art objects with only aesthetic value, traced by Hans Beltung in his *Likeness and Presence*, is a fundamental element in the familiar narrative of modernization as secularization.[12] Whatever aura of holiness may still cling to such disputed residues of an earlier era as the Shroud of Turin, the modern world by and large lost faith in the magic of an icon as a direct imprint of divinity, an *archeiropoietos* not made by the hands of men, quintessentially present in the image on the handkerchief of Saint Veronica that wiped the face of Jesus on his way to the Cross.

Or rather one might better say that the religious sanction for such beliefs has waned, but perhaps something of their power abides, even in avowedly secular thinkers like Ankersmit. In what follows, I want to consider the ways in which sublime historical experience, as Ankersmit has described it, may draw on its power in considering the role of photographs in producing such experiences. That role has, in fact, been acknowledged by both Runia and Ankersmit. In the former's *Moved by the Past*, the photographs introduced by W. G. Sebald in his novel *Austerlitz* are said to "function as fistulae or holes in which the past discharges the present. . . . Sebald's illustrations are a kind of 'leak' in time through which 'presence' wells up from the past into the present."[13] In *Sublime Historical Experience*, Ankersmit cites approvingly Walter Benjamin's appreciation of the photographs of late nineteenth-century Paris by Eugène Atget: "Benjamin's argument is that the openness or indeterminacy that is the heart and the essence of the present is, somehow, preserved in the photograph, so that the photograph effects in us a conviction of being momentarily contemporaneous with the scene depicted by the photograph." And then he adds that Benjamin praised Atget for preserving the reality of the past, which was almost like a fossil, "because of the absence of any traces of human activity . . . as if we succeed in reaching the past through some time-indifferent layer that is typically devoid of all time-bound human projects and planning." Such images, empty of human warmth, are also void of deep meanings, all surface and no depth, providing the experience of what Benjamin memorably called "the scene of the crime." Pivoting to a discussion of Benjamin's analysis of the disinterested gaze of the flâneur, Ankersmit then adds that "the eye operates here like the sense of touch—the eye then firmly resists the tendency so natural to it of searching for truths behind how the world appears to us."[14]

Such an analysis of the power of photography, Ankersmit notes in a footnote, recalls Roland Barthes's famous distinction between the *studium* of a photographic image and its *punctum*, on which Runia also draws.[15] The former depends on an intelligible context of meaning in which the photograph can be comfortably inserted, for example, a narrative in which it functions like an episode in an emplotted story, indeed perhaps as what Henri Cartier-Bresson once famously called the "decisive moment" of that story.[16] The *studium* is dependent on a shared cultural code, which allows the viewer to interpret its meaning. The emotions it arouses are moderate, restrained, docile, more on the order of mere "liking" than the passionate intensity of "loving." It is on the side of convention and artistic "good taste." In contrast, Barthes's photographic *punctum* exceeds conventional coding, producing a powerful emotional charge that is unique to the individual beholder. It rudely and unexpectedly punctuates the flow of narrative coherence, and it feels more like a physical puncture wound than a serene viewing at a distance. Like a traumatic experience, it resists the easy closure in a reassuring world of coherent meaning that is promised by the *studium*. As Ulrich Baer has argued in *Spectral Evidence*, his penetrating Barthesian analysis of the photography of trauma, "photographs are unsettling. Some images bypass painstaking attempts at contextualization and deliver, straight up and apparently across the gulf of time between viewer and photographically mummified past, a potent illusion of the real."[17]

Much more can be said about the implications of Barthes's distinction, but it is clear that it helps us understand what Ankersmit is getting at in his advocacy of sublime historical experiences, those unusually intense, emotionally laden encounters with the past that refuse, like the *punctums* of photographs, to be contained in conventional explanatory or hermeneutic frames. The potential relevance of photography, however, goes beyond the general arguments of Barthes, which can be shown if we turn now to a particularly vexed debate sparked in 2001 by the publication of a catalog for an exhibition in Paris called *Mémoire de camps: Photographies des camps de concentration et d'extermination nazis*, which included four remarkable photographs taken in Auschwitz of the actual extermination. The essay accompanying the catalog was written by the distinguished theorist and historian of photography Georges Didi-Huberman. It was almost immediately met with outrage in the pages of *Les temps modernes* in two articles by Gérard Wajcman and Elisabeth Pagnoux, who were in accord with the passionate denunciations of visual representation of the Holocaust famously made by Claude Lanzmann, the director of the acclaimed documentary film *Shoah* and the editor of *Les temps modernes*.[18] Didi-Huberman published his long rebuttal two years later in a book translated in 2008 into English as *Images in Spite of All: Four Photographs from Auschwitz*.[19]

The images in question are unique in several respects, which make them more than typical examples of photographs serving as documentary evidence of the past. They demonstrate instead the power some may have to serve as secularized manifestations of "real presence" that produce sublime experiences of the past. Unlike the some forty thousand images of Auschwitz produced by the Nazis themselves, perversely determined as they were to record their deeds for posterity, they were surreptitiously taken by *Sonderkommandos*, Jewish prisoners selected by their captors to help in the murder of their fellow inmates.[20] In 1944 the Polish Resistance, hoping to acquire a record of the killings, smuggled in a camera in the false bottom of a bucket. Two images were taken by a Greek Jew named Alex—we don't have his last name—from within a damaged and nonfunctioning gas chamber within Crematorium V; two others were blurred snapshots taken outside the crematorium, possibly as the photographer walked quietly away. The camera was then placed back in the bucket, and the film put in a tube of toothpaste, which found its way with an accompanying note explaining its origin and content to the Resistance. In the four images, we glimpse what appears to be the cremation of gassed bodies and women being herded to the gas chambers.

Cropped and formatted, these images had been made public before and had served as iconic documentary illustrations of the Holocaust. But Didi-Huberman insisted in his introduction to the exhibition that they were more valuable in their raw, undoctored state, with large swathes of black and their off-center, blurred awkwardness retained. "The cropping of these pictures was no doubt believed to preserve the *document* (the visible result, the distinct information)," he wrote. "But instead, their phenomenology was removed, everything that made them an *event* (a process, a job, physical contact)."[21] Although their power was magnified by their juxtaposition in a modest montage, their physical integrity was vital to their lasting value. For what was not visible in the images was no less telling than what was. As gestures of defiance, they were more than just records of what was preserved on the film itself, mere shards of a much larger and more complex annihilating machine. They were also the surviving remnants of the courageous acts by the *Sonderkommandos* whose lives were on the precipice of extinction, producing images "in spite of all."

The scorn heaped on Didi-Huberman in *Les temps modernes* was fueled in part by the anti-ocularcentric discourse that has been so influential in modern French thought, which I attempted to trace in *Downcast Eyes*.[22] The distrust of images as inferior to verbal testimony is palpable in Lanzmann's cinematic practice, and informs the critiques of Didi-Huberman as well. But their authors also made three more focused objections. First, they charged that Didi-Huberman had succumbed to a religious fetishization of the image as a kind of holy relic, which was inherently Christian in origin. Second, they claimed that he had fed the perverse voyeuristic impulses of contemporary culture, thus contributing to an unethical pornography of violence or "*jouissance* in horror."[23] Third, they accused him of a more general violation of the healthy taboo against trying to imagine the unimaginable, to make visible what was outside of any illustration or representation. All such images, railed his accusers, are lies because they can only capture a miniscule part of the whole, which can never be shown in its entirety. Instead, as Lanzmann had demonstrated in *Shoah*, the testimony of witnesses is far more potent in preserving the memory of the Holocaust. "I have always said," Lanzmann argued, "that archival images are images without imagination. They petrify thought and kill any power of evocation. It is much more worthwhile to do what I did, an immense work of development, of creation of the memory of an event."[24]

Didi-Huberman's long and spirited response marshaled many different arguments, drawing on everything from the status of the historical archive to the use of montage in cinema, and invoking a range of theorists from Lacan and Bataille to Benjamin and Kracauer. The points he made that are relevant to the larger question we are posing of the value of sublime historical experience are as follows. Against the charge of fetishism, taking the part for the whole, Didi-Huberman challenged the assumption that any account, based on written sources, testimonies, or images, can ever claim total recall. It is thus wrong to conclude that because the photograph is a mere fragment, incapable of showing the whole, it shows nothing at all. Words, after all, also suffer from the same inadequacy when it comes to describing and interpreting historical events, *a fortiori* one as immense and ineffable as the Holocaust. Archives never perfectly reflect the events whose traces they preserve, but themselves have ideological biases and inevitable lacunae that require techniques of montage and cross-checking to allow the historian to reconstruct the past. Testimonies are no less partial, falling far short of the absoluteness assumed by Lanzmann and his disciples.

Nor it is it correct, Didi-Huberman continued, to assume that all images are similar, thus assimilating victims and victimizers into one seamless spectacle for a distant voyeur to contemplate aesthetically. The four images in question are in fact at odds with the thousands of others taken by the perpetrators: "They are a *historical symptom* capable of disrupting, and reconfiguring, the relation habitually maintained by the historian of images with his or her own objects of study. In this extreme case, therefore, there is something that questions our own seeing and our own knowing." Against attempts to narrate or depict the Holocaust as a fully intelligible story, they provide an experience of a very different kind, one that functions to call into question received wisdom. They force us, Didi-Huberman writes, "to distinguish, in the immense corpus of images of the camps, between that which *veils* and that which *tears*. That which holds the image in its consensual rule (where nobody really looks) and that which swells the image toward its tearing exception (where everyone suddenly feels looked at)." Such "tear-images" produce a sense of vertigo in the current observer, who is not comforted by seeing what is expected: "These images will never be reassuring *images of oneself*; they will always remain *images of the Other*, harrowing, tearing images as such, but their very otherness demands that we approach them. . . . *Identity is altered*: for an instant, the looking subject, however firm he is in the exercise of observation, loses all spatial and temporal certainty."[25] Veil-images, in contrast, are the true fetishes insofar as the latter, according to Lacan, produce screen images or "shield-images," which can anaesthetize the viewer and obscure rather than reveal the truth.

The four images taken clandestinely by the *Sonderkommandos* are best understood, in terms Sartre developed, not as objects or representations but as past actions that are there for our present quasi-observation.[26] That is, they allow us to observe now the earlier actions of the photographers, whose defiant courage unsettles the received wisdom about the passivity of Holocaust victims. *Pace* post-structuralist critics of the indexicality of the photographic image—the enduring physical trace of a past event famously contrasted by C. S. Peirce with a photograph's iconic and symbolic meanings—they provide access in the present to the actions that brought them into being. "The four images of Birkenau," Didi-Huberman writes, "are precious to us only because they offer *the image of the human in spite of it all*, the resistance by means of the image—a scrap of film—to the destruction of the human, which is documented nonetheless."[27] As such, they can be compared with the survival of texts whose performative power exceeds their mere descriptive function, texts that made something happen in the world. Or better put, texts that still have the potential to do so even after the passage of time.

It is precisely this ambiguity—at once the presence of the act of resistance and the absence of those who perished after taking it—that distinguishes the images Didi-Huberman is defending against the claim that images are either all or nothing. He calls them "lacuna-images," which he defines as a *"trace-image* and a *disappearance image* at the same time. Something remains that is not the thing, but a scrap of its resemblance. Something—very little, a film—remains of a process of annihilation: that something, therefore, bears witness to a disappearance while simultaneously resisting it, since it becomes the opportunity of its possible remembrance. It is neither full presence, nor absolute absence."[28]

How does this analysis, we now have to ask, comport with Ankersmit's description of sublime historical experience? Clearly, it shares with it a sense of the ways in which traces of the past, visual objects as well as texts, can become powerfully alive in the present, traces that somehow bypass the filters of language and representation to perform something on later viewers. It is also sensitive to the ability of those traces to subvert received explanatory and hermeneutic grids, punctuating—and puncturing—narratives that imbue the past with a comforting, but illusory, coherence. And it shares with it a faith that they get us "in touch," following the haptic logic of indexicality, with a past that has a palpable presence in the here and now, even as they register what is irreparably different about that past. They are survivors, like the stowaways extolled by Runia, offering a sliver of hope for the future.

But what of Didi-Huberman's impassioned resistance to the charge that he is trafficking in relics, which depend on a fetishistic Christian notion of redemption? How does this fit with the suspicion that there is a residue of the theological notion of "real presence" in Ankersmit's idea of sublime historical experience? Didi-Huberman was, in fact, at pains in his rebuttal to stress the Jewish rather than Christian origins of his defense of the four images from Auschwitz. Citing Franz Rosenzweig's *Star of Redemption*, Gershom Scholem's studies of Jewish messianism, Walter Benjamin's theses on history, and the critical realist film aesthetics of Siegfried Kracauer, he argued that "the Jewish notion of redemption (*ge'ulah*) forms a harsh contrast to the notion—a Christian notion, then a Hegelian one, even a Marxist one—of historical salvation. It is a response to the condition of *exile*, but a response guided by an 'absolute pessimism' as regards history and its progress." Neither reawakening the dead nor consoling us for their loss, the image, in this reading, is redemptive "only in precious moments of its disappearance; it expresses the tearing of the veil *in spite of all*, in spite of the immediate re-veiling of everything in that which Benjamin would call the 'desolation of the past.'"[29]

Does this argument imply an important distinction between Ankersmit's sublime historical experience and Didi-Huberman's defense of "images in spite of everything"? The two thinkers do, it must be admitted, differ in their reactions to the meaning of the Holocaust. Without in any way minimizing its horror, Ankersmit explicitly denies its exemplary status as the type of traumatic wound that sublime historical experience seeks to overcome. Against Dominick LaCapra's contention that the unendurable collective pain it caused produced such a rupture, he contends that "what is typical of trauma is precisely an *in*capacity to suffer or to assimilate the traumatic experience into one's life history. What comes into being with trauma is not so much an openness to suffering but a certain *numbness*." One way to interpret this distinction is to say that because the pain and suffering of the Holocaust remain so palpable and the wound still not healed, it has not really fostered the radical dissociation from the lost past that generates the yearning for its recovery. Its effects are still too disturbing for it to have passed into the kind of collective amnesia that subconsciously wants to be overcome. Indeed, Ankersmit argues, "what Hitler and his henchmen left to posterity is something that should be avoided forever and ever and that could under no circumstances be a legitimate part of our present and our future."[30] Unlike the lost feudal, agrarian society supplanted by the modern industrial world, the waning of the Renaissance, or the *ancien régime* left behind in the wake of the French Revolution, it is still very much part of who we are, at least as an absolute cautionary limit.[31] In an interview with Frode Molven conducted shortly after the book appeared, Ankersmit also argued that whereas individuals suffered traumatic loss, "when you look at it from the perspective of European civilization, we didn't *loose* [sic] that with the concentration camps, which were very dear to us. On the contrary, we were very happy when it was over."[32] What these awkwardly translated sentences suggest is that our relief at the end of Nazism confirmed our continuity with the humanist tradition of the West, rather than signaling its demise, and therefore cannot count as stimuli to sublime historical experiences.

For those experiences to occur, Ankersmit claims, the past must break away entirely from the present, a process that does merit the adjective "traumatic"[33] to describe its effect on the mind of historians who register its impact. It is necessary that "a former identity is discarded ruthlessly, although with the greatest pain, and transformed into the cold heart of a new identity. In a civilization's later life these discarded identities will remain only as an absence—much in the way that a scar may be the only visible reminder of an amputated limb." They achieve a kind of quasi-mythical status, which puts them "beyond the reach of even the most sustained and desperate attempts at historicization. They must be situated in a domain that is outside a civilization's historical time. They possess the highest dignity: They are a civilization's historical sublime."[34]

Coming at the very end of *Sublime Historical Experience*, prior to a short epilogue on Rousseau and Hölderlin, these sentences alert us to the stakes involved for Ankersmit in our rare experiences of such residues of the lost past. They give credence to the characterization offered by Anton Froeyman in his comparison of Ankersmit and Runia: "Ankersmit describes both historical experience and historical sensation as conscious states of mind, as a longing towards the past as a lost paradise, comparable to nostalgia. The past itself seems attractive, but the experience of distance, of not being able to bring it back, arouses a historical experience. In Runia's account, however, there is no conscious longing for the past. On the contrary, the past is too terrible and chaotic to represent, and it forces itself upon us and makes us behave in a certain way, outside of our control."[35]

If it is nostalgia, an emotion that seems consonant with the conservative political sympathies often attributed to Ankersmit,[36] it is nostalgia of a certain kind. In an interview conducted in 2007, he distinguished between the type that tries to efface the difference between present and past, and its sublime historical counterpart where "one is permanently and painfully aware of this distance . . . and the whole drift of nostalgia is the always unsuccessful attempt to overcome this distance. This is the kind of nostalgia that I would primarily associate with historical experience: historical experience is the experience of the distance between, or the difference between past and present."[37] In his book, Ankersmit goes so far as to say that the lost object mourned by sublime experience is not that of a real past, which we never could have really owned, but is rather a myth. "First it is a *myth*, in the sense that we did not lose anything that we had ever possessed. Second, it *is* a myth, in the sense that myths are those parts of nature we grant the honor of being part of our history."[38] In other words, history as something that is part of our own story has been turned into an alien object that we know to be outside of ourselves, and yet for which we still pine, if in vain.

Ankersmit's longing for an unrecoverable past is evidenced in *Sublime Historical Experience* inter alia by his extensive threnody for the rococo ornamentation he had adored as a child. In addition to its aesthetic value and role in the story of ornamentation, he writes, "It represents and expresses for me, a world of moods and feelings. A world of moods and feelings having its deepest resonance in myself.... Moods and feelings define the place where the transition from past to present (and vice versa) will preferably be enacted." What it evokes for him, Ankersmit confesses, is nothing less than "the Enlightenment's optimism and its conviction that the sciences would make us the victors of the natural world," providing a "cure from boredom and the feelings of estrangement from reality."[39]

Two troubling questions arise from this turn in Ankersmit's argument. The first concerns the uncertain transition from a very personal encounter with the past, one that is moving enough to stimulate these kinds of powerful feelings in him, to a more collective response. Ankersmit fully understands that his nostalgia for rococo is idiosyncratic and rooted in his childhood experiences with illness, boredom, and the fascination he seems to have developed for decorations in his parents' bedroom. But if sublime historical experiences depend on such individual circumstances, it is hard to see them coming to emblematize an entire culture's sense of irretrievable loss. Ankersmit often, in fact, stresses the communal nature of the loss that is experienced, and yet his personal examples inadvertently undercut that assumption.

Second, the issue of what is communally mourned from that lost world has to address the inevitable objection that a differential, perhaps even internally contested, collective attitude accompanied the loss when it occurred and likely survives in our own contrasting responses to it. Take, for example, the nefarious legend of the "lost cause" of the defeated Confederate States of America, which fed white supremacist nostalgia for generations afterward, but was deeply repellent for emancipated slaves and their descendants. The alleged heroic defense of antebellum southern values was for those oppressed by them anything but sublime, and contact with the physical residues of that past—flags, uniforms, restored plantations, and the like—evoked very different feelings, similar, in fact, to those Ankersmit ascribes to all of us in the wake of the Holocaust. If the latter is prohibited from evoking sublime historical experiences because we do not want it to return, the same is the case for the antebellum South, at least for those who resist the white supremacist narrative of its heroic, if vain nobility. I can imagine comparable resistance to the charms of rococo design by those who would identify it primarily with aristocratic opulence and frivolity. The loss of the old world may have been traumatic for some, but surely liberating for others.

How fatal are these conclusions to Ankersmit's defense of sublime historical experience? As suggested by the resonance I felt it had for making sense of my own encounter with the manacles of Gavrilo Princip, as well as for the four images from Auschwitz discussed by Didi-Huberman, I don't think they are all that damaging. The connection between the experience Ankersmit describes and mourning for a world whose loss is lamented rather than celebrated is, I would argue, external to the description of the experience itself. That is, what serves like the punctum in a photograph, resisting absorption into a comforting narrative or representational frame, can come in many different forms. The power of the past to move us in the present is not dependent on its being felt as the bemoaned loss of something as total as a mourned civilization from a different era. Sublimity, after all, can entail terror as well as awe, and be accompanied by feelings of astonishment that overcome the beholder. It is often connected with violence and destruction on a scale that dwarfs the individual imagination, something that certainly characterizes any belated encounter with the Holocaust.

It is here that the relevance of photographic residues of the past, or at least some of them, comes, as it were, into focus.[40] As Ankersmit himself notes in his evocation of Barthes's distinction between the *studium* and *punctum* of photographs, the latter disrupts the coded, intelligible, narrative potential of the former. It does not provide a smooth continuum of memory in which past and present are made whole, but rather operates as what psychoanalysts call a "part object" unleashing desire for what cannot be restored or repaired. An accidental, contingent effect unintended by the photographer, it exceeds hermeneutic attempts to defuse its inexplicable emotional charge. Barthes understands its power as more metonymic than metaphoric, gesturing toward what he calls "a subtle *beyond*—as if the image launched desire beyond what it permits us to see."[41] Significantly, it is not desire for a blissful future, for it is resolutely directed toward the past. But it does not function in the manner of a Proustian madeleine, which restores the lost past in a consoling reverie of reconciliation and healing. Instead, it produces an intensified awareness of the irretrievability of the past and the trauma of a loss that cannot be made up, as well as a shudder of recognition that we too are destined to die and be left behind.

As such, historical photographs can be likened to the unexpected "events" so much the focus of recent theoretical discussion, unprepared or anticipated interruptions in the normal course of things that defy contextualization and refuse to be integrated into developmental narratives.[42] Such events can, to be sure, be understood as prefiguring a return, as in the case of the Incarnation of Jesus, which for believing Christians is the incursion of kairotic time into the flow of chronos and anticipates a parousia at its end. The doctrine of Real Presence, which we speculated was a possible way to make sense of sublime historical experience, might be understood as positing the Eucharist as a placeholder for that second coming, a kind of promissory note for believers that the Redeemer would return. Here Presence subtly changes into presentiment. Although Ankersmit would doubtless resist the reduction of his theory to a secularized version of this theological premise, his nostalgic yearning for a lost past, which finds momentary relief in the historical sensations of what remains of it, may suggest a possible similarity.

And yet, it is important to register that Ankersmit also acknowledges the impossibility of this quest. In fact, in certain of his moods, when he is not romantically musing about mystical unions or ecstatic kisses, we might even say that he comes close to that specifically Jewish version of redemption invoked by Didi-Huberman, which expresses an "absolute pessimism" about such a restoration. Because of his rueful acknowledgment of the "dissociated" quality of the moments of sublime recognition that cannot be historicized, defeating attempts to explain, interpret, or judge them epistemologically, he allows us to expand their range. More than mythic ciphers of a lamented "world we have lost," they also can get us in touch with the demonic residues of a radical evil that make a mockery of any complacent historical narrative of progress or development. They remind us, in short, that the love between Romeo and Juliet was not only a challenge to the stifling mores of their day, but also the inadvertent cause of their shared catastrophe.

CHAPTER 10

The Heroism of Modern Life and the Sociology of Modernization: Durkheim, Weber, and Simmel

> ANDREA: Unhappy is the land that breeds no hero.
> GALILEO: No, Andrea: Unhappy is the land that needs a hero.
> —Bertolt Brecht, *Life of Galileo* (1938), Scene 12, p. 115

Among the plethora of efforts to define modernity, Michel Foucault's attempt in an essay answering the question "What Is Enlightenment?," which was famously posed by the eighteenth-century German *Aufklärer*, is particularly suggestive.[1] Modernity, he argued, is neither a temporal period nor adherence to a set of progressive beliefs and practices; it is instead an attitude, "the attitude that makes it possible to grasp the 'heroic' aspect of the present moment. Modernity is not a phenomenon of sensitivity to the fleeting present; it is the will to 'heroize' the present."[2] Here Charles Baudelaire's seminal essays, "The Salon of 1846: On the Heroism of Modern Life" and "The Painter of Modern Life" (1863), which celebrated the illustrator Constantin Guys's depiction of the unsettled, turbulent world of the modern city, served Foucault as a recipe for a more general response to "modernity" in all of its motley variety.[3]

What makes that response a heroization is the unflinching affirmation of our world as inherently superior to what preceded it. No nostalgia for a lamented past, no pining for a world of lost traditions or shattered communities, no fantasies of a golden age from which we have fallen. "Il faut être absolument moderne!," to cite the famous injunction of Arthur Rimbaud. It takes, however, a measure of courage to live in the modern world, a world without the comforting illusion of settled norms, prescribed practices, and unquestioned authorities. Impelled by no inherent telos, modernity is a constant flux of transformations, a maelstrom of destruction and creation, in which we can rely on no one but ourselves to provide any purpose, order, or stability. It is a world of opportunity and self-fashioning, as well as risk and danger, a world in which the horizon of past experience, as Reinhart Koselleck noted, is no longer capable of orienting our expectations about the future.[4] It thus demands a constant exercise of heroism, as Baudelaire already noted in the mid-nineteenth century, to cope with the shocks and assaults of life in a fast lane going to an unknown destination, whose speed limit always seems to be increasing at an accelerating rate.

And yet, if Foucault is right, the heroization of the present, and by extension our self-image as heroes courageously responding to its demands, must be understood ironically.[5] Or rather, the modern attitude is always already itself ironical about what it heroically celebrates.[6] As Foucault notes, "For the attitude of modernity, the high value of the present is indissociable from a desperate eagerness to imagine it, to imagine it otherwise than it is, and to transform it not by destroying it but by grasping it in what it is."[7] That is, the present for the modern attitude is always understood as a transition to something other than it is, potentially—although not necessarily—better, a way station to a different future. Thus the rhetoric of "modernization" as a conscious project that understands itself as an endless task of emancipating our species from what Kant, answering the question about the meaning of the Enlightenment, called our "self-incurred immaturity," a condition we are always in the incompletable process of leaving behind.[8]

Rather, in other words, than complacently heroizing the present as an accomplished end state, the modern attitude acknowledges both its necessity and its insufficiency. We are living, it tacitly concedes, not in a fully realized modern age, but only in an age of unending modernization. Not only, as Bruno Latour provocatively put it, have we never been modern, but on some level we know we never will be.[9] We realize that the uncompleted "project of modernity," to borrow Jürgen Habermas's formulation, will remain indefinitely open-ended, and so "modernity" is precisely not a condition or state of being, but an ongoing process without closure. To cite Foucault again, "The attitude of modernity does not treat the passing moment as sacred in order to try to maintain or perpetuate it. It certainly does not involve harvesting it as a fleeting and interesting curiosity." Rather than passively spectatorial, the modern attitude is active, "an exercise in which extreme attention to what is real is confronted with the practice of a liberty that simultaneously respects this reality and violates it."[10]

In addition to the ironic heroization of a transient present that knows we are perpetually en route, but never quite there, modernity has also adopted an increasingly ironic attitude toward many of its substantive self-understandings. Thus, to cite obvious examples, belief in the scientific method, the virtues of technological innovation, and the superiority of reason to its various "others" have all been subjected to serious doubt. What following Horkheimer and Adorno has come to be recognized as the ambiguous "dialectic of enlightenment" has spread to virtually all variants of the project of modernity.[11] The origins of that project in a Western culture whose motives in "civilizing" the rest of the world have seemed, to put it mildly, less than pure have been invoked to undermine virtually all of its claims to emancipation. Or to be more precise, those claims have been subjected to rigorous reflection about their often contradictory implications, allowing a more nuanced judgment about their costs and benefits. Indeed, it is sometimes argued that a main characteristic of modernity, or at least "late" modernity, is precisely its ambivalent reflexivity, its willingness to step back from its earlier unproblematized commitments and aspirations and take on board the lessons learned from its unexpected negative consequences. What for a while was called "postmodernity," prematurely suggesting that modernism had in fact somehow ended, is now widely acknowledged as little more than a moment of heightened reflexivity that was a fold within modernity itself.

In fact, if Walter Benjamin is right in an earlier invocation of Baudelaire's consideration of the heroism of modern life, self-critical doubt about the project of modernity was already evident in the nineteenth-century poet's inconclusive search for a type to play the role of the modern hero, who could somehow exhibit the noble traits of a classical character in contemporary garb. After noting that for both Honoré de Balzac and Baudelaire, "the hero is the true subject of modernism" because "it takes a heroic constitution to live modernism," Benjamin observed that while for the novelist the *commis voyageur* (traveling salesman) is the modern version of the ancient gladiator, for the poet instead the proletarian is the current incarnation of the ancient fencing slave. But then Benjamin quickly admitted that there were many other candidates for the role of the modern hero in Baudelaire's eyes: the artist, the ragpicker, the flâneur, the apache, the dandy, the lesbian, the conspirator, even the suicide, whose self-destruction may well have been "the only heroic act that had remained for the *multitudes maladives* [sickly multitudes] of the cities in reactionary times." In fact, as shown by the threadbare and inauthentic heroism of that imposter emperor, Napoleon III, so devastatingly mocked by Marx and Hugo, it is not easy to play the hero convincingly in the modern world. Indeed, according to Benjamin, Baudelaire himself knew this all too well: "Because he did not have any convictions, he assumed ever new forms himself. *Flâneur*, apache, dandy and ragpicker were so many roles to him. For the modern hero is no hero; he acts heroes. Heroic modernism turns out to be a tragedy in which the hero's part is available."[12]

Whereas Foucault read Baudelaire in a cautiously optimistic mood—the heroism of modern life is a "practice of a liberty" that actively violates the present, while nonetheless not trying to escape it—the more saturnine Benjamin understood that the poet's quest for a new constellation of the eternal values of antiquity with the flux of modernity would likely be in vain. Both recognized, however, that the smooth flow of progress assumed by liberal historicists is the antithesis of a genuinely modern heroism, which appreciates that time is out of joint and that the "now" is more than a moment in an inexorable evolutionary drive upward toward enlightenment, however it might be defined. Both Foucault and Benjamin knew, in other words, that heroizing the present, although necessary, can only be attempted in an ironic mode. For even when you try to write it as a tragedy, there is no obvious candidate to play the role of tragic hero.[13]

* * *

What are we to make of the provocative claim that modernity can best be understood as the heroization of the present, a claim first introduced by Baudelaire and then given an ironic twist by Benjamin and Foucault?[14] Can it be reconciled—and this is really the primary question I want to address—with more mainstream explanations offered by the leading sociologists of modernization, Emile Durkheim, Max Weber, and Georg Simmel? "The heroism of modern life," as we know, has become a frequent trope in cultural studies—symptomatically, two recent books and one film on the great visual artists Daumier, Eakins, and Manet borrow it for their subtitles[15]—and cultural critics such as Marshall Berman have been characterized as its contemporary diagnosticians.[16] But does it comport with more systematic and ambitious sociological attempts to differentiate modernity from what preceded it, attempts that went beyond the brilliant but underdeveloped insights of a Baudelaire?[17]

Before tackling that question head-on, we must acknowledge the importance of two very modern different attitudes toward heroism, which were anything but ironic and, as we will argue, had little resonance among sociologists. They were narrated instead in what might be called romantic and comic modes. In the former, the historical field is understood to be a chaos of contingency in which only the will of the great man, who is engaged in an endless romantic quest, might fashion meaning, however fleeting, from the flux. As Hayden White puts it in his analysis of metahistorical romance, "The appearance of a hero represents a 'victory' of 'human Free-will over Necessity.' . . . The "Chaos of Being" [is] the situation the heroic individual faces as a field to be dominated, if only temporarily and in the full knowledge of the ultimate victory this 'Chaos' will enjoy over the man who seeks to dominate it."[18]

Heroism in a romantic key can be found in what Eric Bentley, writing in the middle of the Second World War, dubbed "heroic vitalism."[19] He discerned it in such figures as Thomas Carlyle, Friedrich Nietzsche, Richard Wagner, Oswald Spengler, Stefan George, and D. H. Lawrence, all of whom reviled the mechanization of modern life, the mediocrity of political democracy, and the banality of mass culture. Here the founding premise, as Carlyle put it in his 1840 lectures *On Heroes, Hero-Worship, and the Heroic in History*, was that "Universal History, the history of what man has accomplished in the world, is at bottom the History of the Great Men who have worked there."[20] Focusing on six categories of heroes—divinities, prophets, poets, priests, men of letters, and kings—Carlyle advocated the return of an unapologetically worshipful, that is, religious, attitude toward them in an age that he lamented "denies the existence of great men; denies the desirableness of great men."[21] As Nietzsche likewise proclaimed in his *Untimely Meditations*, "the goal of humanity lies in its highest specimens,"[22] whose striving against all odds produced an endless quest for greatness. Such heroes exhibited a "pathos of distance" from common men, whose ignoble status could not be remedied through resentful efforts to revenge themselves on their betters.[23] An ideology of "heroic realism" was kept alive in the writings of such twentieth-century glorifiers of the technological sublime as Ernst Jünger, whose armored warriors were impervious to pain, both suffered and inflicted.[24] Its residues were still evident as late as Freud's last work *Moses and*

Monotheism, in which he criticized history based entirely on impersonal forces, and concluded "we will keep, therefore, a place for the 'great man' in the chain, or rather in the network of determining causes."[25]

The defense of those highest specimens could, however, also be based on very different premises from the ones motivating the elitist irrationalists identified by Bentley, who wrote in an essentially romantic mode in which the infinite quest was an end in itself. They could instead be read as playing a role in a more comic narrative, in the sense of leading to a happy ending, in which all contradictions come to be harmoniously reconciled. Here Hegel was the main exemplar. He not only pondered the role of the hero in such Greek tragedies as *Antigone* but also celebrated the important role of "world-historical" figures like Napoleon in his own day. From the subjective point of view, such heroes were best understood as tragic figures, who achieved little satisfaction or happiness in their own lives. But from the objective point of view of history as a whole, they performed necessary functions in an ultimately triumphal story, a story, that is, of comic resolution justifying their personal sacrifices.

When it came to the contemporary distrust of heroes, Hegel famously noted that "no hero is a hero to his valet, but that is not because heroes are not heroes, it is because valets are valets."[26] The deeper meaning of this celebrated observation has been recently glossed by the Brazilian philosopher Vladimir Safatle, who writes, "What this witticism gestures at is a certain problem of perspective: a viewpoint (such as the valet's) that erases the notion of historical subject reduces sequences of events to the lesser condition of collections of random occurrences, which is to say, to occurrences bereft of history. . . . What the sneering chamber valet fails to grasp is how one's interests lose their particularistic traits once they become integral to the unfolding of historical processes."[27] That is, for Hegel, the hero is not merely a powerful and inspirational figure; he is also the vehicle through which Reason enters the seeming contingency of history, the means by which manifest disorder reveals itself as latent order. The valet is too shortsighted to grasp what is happening beyond his ken.

It was, however, against both the romantic, irrationalist worship of saviors, individual or collective, in the heroic vitalist tradition and the comic Hegelian celebration of great men as the vehicles of Reason in history that we have to understand the ironic heroization of modern life defended by Baudelaire, Benjamin, and Foucault. They distrusted both the elevated rhetoric of salvation via sacrifice and the faith in history as a quest, successful or otherwise, for redemption, whether rational or not. Instead, they acknowledged that the world had been irrevocably disenchanted and that the course of history could not be accounted a narrative of reason's increasing emergence amid the flux of contingency. And yet, although they focused new attention on the little rather than the great man, they did not adopt wholesale the cynicism of the valet, who denied all claims to heroism as fraudulent in the modern world. For their irony, if we follow Foucault's formulation, was not directed at heroization per se, but rather at modernity's endless quest to realize its romantic hopes or achieve a state of harmonious, "comic" reconciliation. For despite everything, it was still possible for some individuals to confront the challenges of unredeemed modern life heroically without vain hopes or resigned despair.

Was there, to turn finally to the main subject of this exercise, a comparable attitude expressed in the work of the founding fathers of modern sociology? Despite the occasional exception, such as Werner Sombart, who thought he belonged to a nation of heroes,[28] sociology is usually identified with the debunking perspective of the valet, who looks behind the facade of his master's pretensions to reveal the latent forces and embedded structures that really affect society. Although one of its founding fathers, August Comte, did include a roster of secular heroes of progress to replace the discredited Christian saints in his Religion of Humanity, sociologists with less exalted goals tended to stress impersonal processes instead. Herbert Spencer, for example, railed against Carlyle's "great man" theory of history in his 1860 *Study of Sociology*: "You must admit that the genesis of a great man depends on the long series of complex influences which has produced the race in which he appears, and the social state into which that race has slowly grown.... Before he can remake his society, his society must make him."[29] Although Spencer still believed in the idea of progress of the species, he did not think humanity's "highest specimens" were necessary to bring it about.

By the time of Durkheim (1857–1917), Weber (1864–1920), and Simmel (1858–1918), sociologists were also growing far more skeptical of progress, at least as an evolutionary necessity, and the collective subjects who were its putative agents.[30] Instead, they had grown increasingly sensitive to the challenges of a modernity whose costs seemed as great as its benefits. Even when they worked within a broad framework of narrative change, allowing them to understand modernity as a meaningful rupture with what preceded it, they resisted a triumphalist account, which glossed over the multiple discontents fostered by the change.[31] The rhetoric of crisis or even decline often accompanied their account of the transition away from the comparatively settled, inert, and integrated world modernity had irrevocably left behind.

But when they attempted to identify the source of that crisis and explain modernity's discontents, they infrequently pondered the decline of heroism in a direct way. This indifference was most evident in the case of Durkheim, who excoriated the corrosive power of excessive individualism, which had become a disturbing "cult" in the modern world, in favor of the maintenance of social solidarity. In methodological terms, this meant resisting the reduction of "social facts" to the level of the psychological or the whole of society to its component parts.[32] For Durkheim, society was ontologically sui generis, prior to and distinct from the individuals within it, who were wrongly thought to have constituted it by an act of contractual consent.[33] The structural forces that enabled social action were, he argued, more fundamental than the agency of the actors themselves.[34] Nor could a heroic metasubject be construed as the genetic origin of the social totality. For Durkheim, man was *homo duplex*, a conflicted being whose egoistic desires and interests are in tension with cognitive and moral imperatives internalized from their society as a whole. Thus, even extraordinary individuals were subjected to the "external constraint" exercised by social facts, which were collective representations that can be examined as if they were objective "things" in the world. As such, they could be subjected to a rigorous scientific analysis, fulfilling the hopes of Comtean positivism.

Against the Nietzschean ideal of heroic supermen who posited and followed their own individual morality, Durkheim was concerned with the recovery of a robust moral community, which he feared was undermined by the rampant individualism of modernity. Indeed, he thought that the science of sociology would provide a means to that end. What he famously bemoaned as anomie, a pathological erosion of the norms that bind a society together sometimes leading to suicide,[35] could only be countered by the restoration of institutions, such as the family or corporation, that might foster the meaningful cohesion and unalienated sense of belonging that no individual hero—even one inspiring a rejuvenated nation-state—could provide. Similar premises underlay his thoughts on politics. Appalled by *soi-disant* political heroes like General Georges Boulanger, whose coup to overthrow the Third Republic ended in a fiasco in 1889, Durkheim remained a staunch supporter of solidaristic republican values throughout his career.[36] Although there was, in fact, a hypermasculinist, antirepublican cult of heroism in France before World War I, which sought to counter the alleged decadence of the times through a revitalization of the military ideal and the cultivation of competitive sports, Durkheim was not tempted by its regressive solutions to the ills of the modern world.[37] Nor did he succumb to the cult of vitalist *élan* spawned by the writings of Henri Bergson.

Even when it came to religion, whose "elementary" or primitive forms Durkheim explored late in his career, heroic founding figures played a very minor role. Although there were, he conceded in his discussion of the religious lives of Australian aboriginals, what he called "civilizing heroes," their function was entirely symbolic: "The fabulous beings whom we call by this name are really simple ancestors to whom mythology has attributed an eminent place in the history of the tribe, and whom it has, for this reason, set above the others." They are often simulacra of a great god, who is an ancestral spirit given a special place in a totemic system and who is cast in turn in the image of individual souls. But these "are only the form taken by the impersonal forces which we found at the basis of totemism, as they individualize themselves in the human body."[38] Whatever the source of Durkheim's understanding of the sacred as a category rooted in the collective consciousness of society—sometimes it is attributed to his nostalgia for the concretely embodied, organic Jewish community out of which he had come[39]—it was prior to the utilitarian pursuit of individual self-interests or the hedonistic satisfaction of appetitive desires. Its role, moreover, was still central in even the allegedly secularized society of the present.[40] For Durkheim, who has been rightly called a "symbolic realist," the internalization of moral norms created an internal moral environment, which was the source of even the apparently spontaneous actions of a genius.[41] Insofar as rituals and shared behavioral patterns are prior to conscious beliefs, heroes are the effects of collective effervescence and not its causes.

Thus, although it might be possible to see some residues of Baudelaire's symptomology of modernity in Durkheim's description of anomie or interest in the issue of suicide,[42] it would be difficult to attribute to him any notion of individual heroism as an antidote to it. The sociological tradition inspired by Durkheim and institutionalized in the university system of France after his death retained a strong disdain for the priority of the individual over society, and was accordingly uninterested in whatever residues of heroism might be active in the modern world.[43] Despite the occasional desperate appeal to self-sacrificial heroism by the outlier "sacred sociologists" who gathered around the Collège de sociologie in the 1930s, French sociology resisted even an ironic valorization of the "heroism of modern life."[44]

But can the same be said of his two great German counterparts, Weber and Simmel?[45] In contrast to Durkheim, both came to sociology filtered through German historicism's validation of the unique individual, and thus they resisted the Frenchman's insistence on the sui generis quality of constraining "social facts" understood objectively from the outside. However much they sought to understand the regularities of social life in the spirit of scientific disinterest, they still pitted what the neo-Kantian Heinrich Rickert famously called the "idiographic" against the "nomothetic" impulse in historical and social analysis. Weber's celebrated reliance on "ideal types" as heuristic devices drew on an ontology that was more nominalist than realist when it came to the general patterns of social life. Although resisting what he saw as Simmel's problematic effacing of the boundary between psychology and sociology, Weber stressed social action and its motivations rather than focusing, as had Durkheim, on the level of constraining structures. Moreover, unlike Durkheim, neither Simmel nor Weber entertained much hope for the restoration of collectively binding meaning via the expedient of restored corporative institutions (or what another founding father of sociology, Ferdinand Tönnies, had famously called "community" [*Gemeinschaft*] as opposed to "society" [*Gesellschaft*]). Despite their enthusiasm for the German cause in the First World War, they were reluctant to follow Sombart in applying the category of "hero" to their own nation and contrasting it with so-called merchant nations on the enemy side.[46]

When it came to heroic individuals, Weber and Simmel were more ambivalent than their French counterpart, and traces of the heroic vitalism of *Lebensphilosophie* can be found at points in their work. Admiring Nietzsche's diagnosis of the crisis of meaning in modernity, both Weber and Simmel were deeply impressed by his validation of the nobility of character and distrust of egalitarian leveling.[47] Weber's celebrated concept of "personality" (*Persönlichkeit*) resonated with Nietzsche's disdain for the impersonality and functionality of modern existence, in which a yawning gap had opened between inner life and external role, subjective feelings and objective norms.[48] Responding to the imperative of what Weber understood as a secularized version of the Calvinist "calling" (*Beruf*), which evoked an ascetic constraint disdained by Nietzsche in his Dionysian moods, meant more than internalizing conventional social norms.[49] At a time of value relativism, it required choosing one's own ethical code, even worldview, and having the fortitude to live by it. It involved maintaining a dignified inner life rather than succumbing to base interests, needs, or desires, the motivations ascribed to men by the utilitarian tradition. It demanded a "pathos of distance," to cite Nietzsche's *Genealogy of Morals*, that was especially valuable in a political leader.[50]

In his wide-ranging ruminations on comparative religions, Weber in fact fully acknowledged the seminal role of heroes in founding many traditions.[51] It is indirectly evident, for example, in the lessons of an "ethical prophet," who provides a code of moral conduct that demands to be rigorously followed. In a letter of 1907 expressing his cautiously respectful view of Freudian psychoanalysis, Weber specifically referred to a "heroic" ethic, "which imposes on men demands of principle to which they are generally *not* able to do justice, except at the high points of their lives, but which serve as signposts pointing the way for man's endless *striving*."[52] Even more directly, he argued, religious heroism is manifested in an "exemplary prophet," one who enjoins his followers to imitate his virtuous example. In such cases, discrete instances of heroic behavior can congeal into a characterological essence, as "formal sanctification by the good works shown in external actions is supplanted by the value of the total personality pattern, which in the Spartan example would be an habitual temper of heroism." Such heroism can be evident in the inspirational courage of a warrior, who enacts righteous justice on the foes of God, but also in the loving mercy of a follower of a God whose measure of justice is ineffable to mere humans: "Unconditional forgiveness, unconditional charity, unconditional love even of enemies, unconditional suffering of injustice without requiting evil by force—these products of a mystically conditioned acosmism of love indeed constituted demands for religious heroism."[53]

Religious heroism appeared most explicitly in Weber's celebrated concept of charisma, which, although often compared to Durkheim's idea of the sacred, stressed with Nietzsche the importance of unique individuals rather than cultural symbols or ritual practices.[54] An enormous amount of interpretive energy has been exercised in explicating the origins, meaning, and implications of this seminal idea, whose applicability Weber extended well beyond the religious sphere, but only a few points can be made here.[55] First, Weber, who prided himself on being a value-neutral social scientist, introduced charisma as an ideal type to characterize one of three major forms of "imperative coordination," or legitimate authority, that generated voluntary submission to a social order.[56] The other two were "traditional" and "rational-legal" authority. He was careful to note that "it will be applied to a certain quality of an individual personality by virtue of which he is set apart from ordinary men and treated as endowed with supernatural, superhuman, or at least specifically exceptional powers of qualities. These are such as are not accessible to the ordinary person, but are regarded as of divine origin or as exemplary, and on the basis of them the individual concerned is treated as a leader."[57] By carefully noting that a charismatic leader functions as such only so far as those who follow him believe that he—and the pronoun is apt, as women are never among his examples—has certain gifts, Weber was distancing himself from the assumption that such a leader possesses intrinsically heroic qualities. He notes that the "gift of grace" attributed to the charismatic leader works only so long as he delivers what his followers expect of him; if not, the magic fades and the leader's feet of clay crumble. Charisma, in other words, is a relational concept based on intersubjective recognition, not inherent worth, an ascribed role in a traditional hierarchy, or a bureaucratic office.

Weber wore his disinterested "scientific" hat in spelling out all of its various forms—in addition to religious prophets and magicians, he includes political leaders, military heroes, gang leaders, and all who demonstrate the "rule of genius" as opposed to socially defined status—as well as its ability to be "routinized" in institutions that outlive its original moment, such as the Catholic Church.[58] He took pains to stress that false prophets, demagogic politicians, shamans, and "berserkers" must also be included in the category, for "sociological analysis, which must abstain from value judgments, will treat all of these on the same level as the men, who according to conventional judgments, are the 'greatest' heroes, prophets, and saviors."[59]

Second, Weber saw charismatic leadership as a rare phenomenon in the modern world, a world increasingly accepting only rational-legal authority, buttressed by bureaucratic organization, and spiritually disenchanted. Instrumental rationality, privileging efficiency and formal regularity, has undermined the rule-bending power of a leader who could proclaim, as often had Jesus, "It is written, but I say unto you." Because it comes unprepared and its tenure is uncertain, charismatic appeal, in fact, rarely exists in its pure form for very long, even if its aftereffects can linger in the new routinized order that solidifies after its brief disruptive moment. It does, to be sure, always have the potential—and here Weber was acknowledging that his ideal types were normally mixed in practice—to enhance the authority of those whose legitimacy was primarily derived from traditional or rational-legal sources.

More purely charismatic authority, Weber did concede in one of his heroic vitalist moods, was still possible as an enlivening intervention in the prevailing order, an unexpected disruption of the everyday life that somehow can start something new in the world. But whether Weber, despite his efforts to mask his own emotional, political, and moral investments behind a facade of scientific value neutrality, covertly yearned for its emergence as a deliverance from what he famously described as the "iron cage" of bureaucratic rationalization is much in dispute.[60] In the last years before his death in 1920, so a number of commentators have argued, Weber did indeed flirt with the idea of such a solution to the impoverished life he lamented in modernity. "The extreme rationalization of the modern world," writes Harry Liebersohn, "set the stage for extreme heroism. Those who really wished to prove their personal charisma had to test it in an impersonal world: the scholar in the modern factory of learning, the politician amid the bureaucratic machine."[61] According to Wolfgang Mommsen, Weber, disillusioned by the failures of liberalism but not willing to scorn the masses, yearned for a Caesarist "plebiscitarian leader-democracy" to break the stalemate of modern politics.[62] This sympathy may well have found its logical conclusion in the antinormative "decisionism" of Carl Schmitt and been realized historically in a form Weber would never have embraced thirteen years after his death in 1920.[63]

On a more specifically cultural, or more precisely aesthetic, level, Weber's ambivalent attitude toward the lure of heroism has often been inferred from his complicated relationship with the poet Stefan George, the leader of an antimodern, aristocratic cult in the years before World War I.[64] Weber was introduced to the George-Kreis by Friedrich Gundolf in 1910 and deeply admired the charismatic poet's verse, which he saw as harnessing the formalist rigor of asceticism in the service of ecstatic transformation. But he soon became disillusioned with the snobbish elitism and political posturing of George's circle, differing, for example, over the justification of women's emancipation—George's homoeroticism was infused with explicit misogyny—as well as over "the meaning of heroism, which George considered insufficiently physical in the modern age and Weber, insufficiently intellectual."[65] Because its members foolishly mistook their cult for a genuinely revolutionary movement, the circle around George seems to have disabused Weber of his heroic vitalist belief, always tenuous, that charismatic leadership could really save the modern world. By the time he delivered his celebrated lectures on "Politics as Vocation" and "Science as Vocation" shortly before his death in 1920, Weber was drawn increasingly to a noncharismatic politics, based more on an "ethics of responsibility" than an "ethics of ultimate ends," even if the former might reach a limit with a *mature* man" who felt the imperative to stand by his convictions.[66]

The revolutionary events at the end of the war also dampened any belief Weber might have had in charismatic heroes, and he grew increasingly estranged from friends like the Hungarian Marxist Georg Lukács, who embraced the revolutionary heroism of Lenin.[67] And yet, even in the famous final paragraph of his great lecture on the political vocation, in which he introduced the poignant metaphor of politics as "the strong and slow boring of hard boards," Weber could still acknowledge that attaining the possibility for someone with a political "calling" sometimes meant reaching for the impossible: "But to do that a man must be a leader, and not only a leader but a hero as well, in a very sober sense of the word. And even those who are neither leaders nor heroes must arm themselves with that steadfastness of heart which can brave even the crumbling of all hopes. This is necessary right now, or else men will not be able to attain even that which is possible today."[68]

For a man, such as Weber himself, whose vocation was that of a scientist, however, even a sober heroism was less important than acknowledging that "the fate of our times is characterized by rationalization and intellectualization, and, above all, by the 'disenchantment of the world.'" For those too weak to bear this disillusionment, there was always the option of making an "intellectual sacrifice" and retreating into the bosom of the Church, which was more laudable than the academic prophecy that sought to use the lecture hall as a platform for demagoguery. But for those with the integrity to face the end of the age of heroes, there was only one course: "We shall set to work and meet the 'demands of the day,' in human relations as well as in our vocation. This, however, is plain and simple, if each finds and obeys the demon who holds the fibers of his very life."[69] It was sober sentiments like these that allowed many in the Weimar Republic to see Weber as an anti-utopian realist, a "heroic skeptic" who was right for "an age of iron."[70]

How did Simmel comprehend the role of heroes in the modern world? He was, it seems, often more tempted by Nietzsche's heroic vitalist defense of heroism than Weber, and he was far less suspicious of the cultic pretensions or antifeminism of Stefan George.[71] He specifically embraced the virtue of distinction (*Vornehmheit*), which he had praised as Nietzsche's ideal in his study *Schopenhauer and Nietzsche*, as an antidote to the homogenizing pressures of modern life.[72] Identifying it with an inner quality of character that transcended deeds in the world, it suggested an aristocratic state of being, an autonomous bearing, that was very different from the bourgeois stress on deeds in the world. Against what he saw as the "Roman" or Enlightenment version of egalitarian, quantitative individualism, he favored a "German" or Romantic alternative that stressed qualitative difference instead.[73] "For Nietzsche," Simmel approvingly wrote, "it is the qualitative *being* of the personality which marks the stage that the development of mankind has reached; it is the highest exemplars of a given time that carry humanity beyond its past. Thus Nietzsche overcame the limitations of merely social existence, as well as the valuation of man in terms of his sheer effects."[74] But unlike Weber, he never seems to have been tempted by the role such "highest exemplars" might play as political leaders. Nor did he theorize charisma as a relationally grounded mode of legitimate authority, even if for a while he was caught up in the enthusiasm for the war effort in 1914.

When it came to the mass society of modernity, Simmel contended that it was a new phenomenon "made up, not of the total individualities of its members, but only of those fragments of each of them in which he coincides with all others. These fragments, therefore, can be nothing but the lowest and most primitive."[75] Echoing Hegel's gloss on the relationship between heroes and valets, Simmel blamed the latter for not tendering the respect owed to the former, failing to display the "inner compulsion which tells one to keep at a distance and which does not disappear even in intimate relations with him. The only type for whom such distance does not exist is the individual who has no organ for perceiving significance. For this reason, the 'valet' knows no such sphere of distance; for him there is no 'hero'; but this is due not to the *hero*, but to the valet."[76]

But lacking Hegel's faith in the ultimate rationality of history, Simmel resisted casting the hero in the role of world-historical agent of that rationalization and disdaining the ignoble valet for failing to appreciate his larger function. "However true it may be that the valet does not understand the hero because he cannot rise to his height," he wrote, "it is equally true that the hero does not understand the valet because he cannot lower himself to his subordinate level."[77] Because of Simmel's relativist perspectivism, which abjured Durkheim's objectivist stance and belief in observable "social facts," and his scorn for the disinterested scientific rigor sought by Weber, it is difficult, in fact, to define a conclusive position on the question of heroism or much else in modern life.[78] Although initially attracted to Spencer's scientific theory of evolutionary social differentiation, Simmel went through a neo-Kantian phase and ultimately embraced the *lebensphilosophische* stress on the ineffable qualities of a "life" that defied subsumption into conceptual categories or long-term historical patterns. As much a philosopher and aesthetician as a sociologist, Simmel was a self-defined formalist, interested in the abiding interactions of social life, the web or labyrinth of interrelated connections in which fragmented personal experience took place, rather than their historical development over time or their coalescence into a coherent community above the shifting social relations between and among individual selves. Even the metacategory of "society," which was so crucial for sociologists such as Durkheim, Simmel found wanting.[79]

Simmel's increasing attraction to vitalism did not, however, lead him to embrace the heroic variety emplotted in a romantic mode described by Eric Bentley. As a shrewd phenomenologist of the modern experience, a micrological analyst of the endless differentiations of everyday life, he in fact earned the plaudits of those who see him as developing the insights of Baudelaire so valued by later thinkers like Benjamin and Foucault.[80] Steeped in the aestheticism that Weber only knew from the outside and a gifted interpreter of the fleeting, surface manifestations of modern culture, Simmel wrote extensively about the arts and adopted a method that often invited comparison with the impressionist painters of his era. When he wrote about economic themes—as he did in his magisterial *Philosophy of Money*—it was more in terms of their effects on personal experience than in those of historically discrete modes of production or the rise of capitalist industrialization; value, he insisted, was a subjective, not an objective category, and the exchange value of a commodity was more important than the labor congealed in it.[81] Simmel was an acute diagnostician of the interaction of technological innovations, epitomized by the emergence of electricity as a radical new source of energy in the lives of urban dwellers, and the emotional stresses of those subjected to them, producing the epidemic of "neurasthenia" suffered by many in the modern world.[82] Even for those who escaped its pathological consequences, Simmel argued in his most influential essay "The Metropolis and Mental Life" that "the psychological basis of the metropolitan type of individuality consists in the *intensification of nervous stimulation* which results from the swift and uninterrupted change of outer and inner stimuli."[83] As a reaction to overstimulation, the typical attitude of the modern urban dweller was one of blasé indifference and cautious, self-protective reserve, providing the beleaguered individual space to enable some exercise of personal freedom. His dispassionate "cool conduct" may have preserved a certain interpersonal distance, but it did not provide that "pathos" of elevation of mankind's "highest exemplars" over the herd extolled by Nietzsche.[84]

Where, if anywhere, we might ask, was the ironic heroism in Simmel's analysis of modern life? One obvious place to look for an answer would be his invocation of the model of tragedy to characterize enduring aspects of modern life. In his essay "The Individual's Superiority over the Mass," Simmel introduced the term "the sociological tragedy," defined as the tension between people understood as distinct individuals, where they might become figures of distinction and refinement, and people in their role as members of the "folk" or "mass," where they are reduced to their "lower and primitively more sensuous levels." Exposure to collective pressures, Simmel lamented, "corrupts the character. It pulls the individual away from his individuality and down to a level with all and sundry."[85] That is, heroes are turned into valets when they make common cause with the masses. This was a sociological tragedy because it prevented men of distinction from assuming leading public roles.

Simmel's even more influential notion of the "tragedy of culture," which he developed in a series of essays that culminated in "The Conflict of Modern Culture," written shortly before his death in 1920, pointed to the unbridgeable gap between the act of subjective creation and the objective world of enduring prior creations. This type of tragedy resulted from the ineluctable conflict between dynamic, creative life and the reified "spiritual" forms that it left behind, forms that could only confront the creative subject as external constraints.[86] Although a cultural constant, the gap seems to have widened in the modern world. According to Simmel, "the real cultural malaise of modern man is the result of this discrepancy between the objective substance of culture, both concrete and abstract, on the one hand, and, on the other, the subjective culture of individuals who feel this objective culture to be something alien, which does violence to them and with which they cannot keep pace."[87] Attempts to reassert the dominance of life, whether in philosophy with pragmatism, art with expressionism, or religion with mysticism, were doomed to fail, for no one was able to reconcile life and forms, subjective and objective culture.

The tragedies of society and culture are ongoing, indeed accelerating dramas in the modern world, and Simmel had no faith in a future comic resolution to their tensions. A romantic quest to do so, extolled by heroic vitalists, was thus not worth pursuing. What for our purposes is perhaps even more important, these tragedies lack what might be called a tragic hero, whose courageous if vain quest for redemption is thwarted by fate. Even the outsider figures extolled by Baudelaire—prostitutes, artists, ragpickers, flâneurs, dandies, lesbians, apaches, conspirators, suicides—are unable for Simmel to play this heroic role, which, it will be recalled, Benjamin had said was still "available" to be filled in the poet's lifetime. As one commentator has noted, "While sharing Baudelaire's emphasis on the fragment and the micrological, Simmel's modernity departs radically from Baudelaire through grounding modernity in the metanarrative of irreconcilable tragedy of culture, its failure to generate unity in the face of commodity fetishism and reification."[88]

Whereas Simmel's student and friend Georg Lukács came to believe the conflict between form and life was only a feature of bourgeois society and not culture in general, and was thus able to identify a class hero—the proletariat—as the means to overcome it, Simmel himself never did.[89] The noble personalities he valued for their Nietzschean *Vornehmheit* and pathos of distance were inner émigrés from the modern world without the will or means to transform it. The distinction between healthy objectification and pathological reification, which allowed Marxists like Lukács to believe the latter could be overcome through the overthrow of capitalism, was not for him a meaningful alternative. As Jürgen Habermas was to put it, "He detached the pathologies unveiled in the modern lifestyle from their historical connections and attributed them to the tendency, embedded with the process of life, towards the estrangement between the soul and its forms. A strangeness that is so deeply rooted in metaphysics robs the diagnosis of the times the power and courage of political-practical conclusions."[90]

But there was still in Simmel, in the final analysis, a glimmer of the ironic heroism that Foucault had discerned in Baudelaire's response to modern life, and one that ties him to the attitude we have already noted in Durkheim's cool observation of "social facts" from the outside and Weber's ruminations on science as a vocation. In "The Salon of 1846," Baudelaire had identified the black frock coat of the dandies of his day as the "outer skin of the modern hero" and called it "the inevitable uniform of our suffering age, carrying on its very shoulders, black and narrow, the mark of perpetual mourning." And then he added, "A uniform livery of grief is a proof of equality."[91] Foucault understood the implications of this insight, which he said was as much a mode of relationship with the self as with the present moment: "The deliberate attitude of modernity is tied to an indispensable asceticism."[92]

Although Foucault went on to say that Baudelaire understood this asceticism to be the special preserve of artists alone, with no place in society or politics, it may well be that it found a place as well in modern sociology, at least in the variety inspired by the founding fathers we have examined. As David Frisby has noted, Simmel's project was like Baudelaire's painter of modern life because they shared a certain mode of experiencing the present, a mode involving ascetic self-distancing: "Its presentation carries with it a necessary confrontation with the reflexivity of his analysis since the mode of accounting for *modernité* also belongs to the modernist tradition itself."[93] That is, the heroic ironization of the present extends as well to the sociologist's own attitude toward modern society. And as such, it also extends to the modern self, including that of the sociologist. For all of Weber's ambivalent attraction to charismatic authority, he too, as we have seen, interpreted the calling of the scientist, a calling that echoed the Calvinist tradition of ascetic constraint, as one of ironic distancing.[94] As one observer has noted, the "heroic renunciation" of the Puritans who espoused the "Protestant ethic" may well have been the ideal model for Weber's man of science.[95]

This insight leaves us with an unexpected conclusion. The hero of modern life, it turns out, may not be that romantic man of action on an infinite quest for whom the heroic vitalists so passionately yearned, nor the comic world-historical leader who is an agent of historical reason, as Hegel had hoped. He—or she—may be instead the ascetic, distant observer of a rapidly unfolding tragedy, who only has ironic reflexivity to ward off the lure of false solutions to intractable problems that remain, alas, far easier to acknowledge than to solve. *Pace* the latter-day devotees of Marx's eleventh *Thesis on Feuerbach*, the hero of modern life may well be the one who soberly interprets the world rather than tries rashly, and, alas, vainly, to change it.

CHAPTER 11

Historical Truth and the Truthfulness of Historians

The question of history's relationship to truth, always a challenge to answer, seems especially fraught in this era of "fake news," "alternative facts," and the erosion of established media gatekeepers. Traditionally, it has been addressed either ontologically—the possibility of eternal verities appearing amid the flux of historical change—or epistemologically—the veracity of our accounts of the past. Whereas some philosophers and theologians still ponder the former, few working historians have been concerned with the alleged relationship between ontological truth, however it might be construed, and historical occurrence.[1] They have remained content instead with understanding their subject matter, to cite the subtitle of Siegfried Kracauer's insightful ruminations on history, as merely "the last things before the last,"[2] at least one step removed from anything pretending to be absolute in metaphysical terms.[3]

Ever since what has been called the "scientific revolution" in the practice of writing about the past, a slow and uneven process of professionalization that made of history a proper scholarly "discipline," working historians have focused on truth as an effect of valid cognition, plausible inference, logical reasoning, or warranted assertion, rather than speculative metaphysics.[4] History, they insist, cannot depend on authority or memory, but must instead be a critical, always open-ended process of discovery. Using the methodological tools developed by archaeologists, paleographers, diplomatists, archivists, and statisticians, practicing historians have sought to separate historical knowledge from myths, legends, and fables by refining their techniques of retrieval and subjecting the results to various tests of plausibility and authenticity.⁵ Anachronisms—the term itself was invented in the seventeenth century⁶—were challenged, and residues of material culture, such as inscriptions, coins, or architectural ruins, were examined to supplement the written word. What are sometimes called the "disciplines of erudition,"⁷ devoted to the rigorous examination of the formal properties of texts or images beyond the content they convey, enrich the repertoire of forensic instruments in the toolbox of professional scholars of the past.⁸

History's "scientific revolution" has, however, been dogged by increased concern about the truth claims—often expressed in terms of "objectivity"—it has generated.⁹ What allows us to claim our knowledge about the past is both plausible and reliable? How do we ascertain the convincing evidence on which to justify our accounts? By what criteria do we deem some documents more accurate, some artifacts more authentic, and some accounts more persuasive than others, and who has the authority to judge? Can accounts of the past be verified, or only falsified, and what counts as conclusive for either outcome? How do we build compelling narrative reconstructions from the evidence deemed reliable and authentic?

All of these questions assume an inherent distinction between the two dominant meanings, at least in English, of the word "history": first, as the events, occurrences, or actions that happened in the past (*res gestae* or "things done"), and second, as the representation, narrative, or account of those happenings (*historia rerum gestarum* or "the story of things done") in the present. "History" thus signifies, for epistemologists of historical knowledge, both an object of inquiry and a subjective discourse or narrative about that object. As such, it raises issues similar to those raised by other self-described scientific methods based on the binary distinction between subjects and objects. But it differs from them in the inevitable absence, indeed the irretrievable loss, of the past object it seeks to "re-present" in the present.¹⁰

Two Extreme Alternatives

The Positivist or Hyperrealist Fallacy

At each end of the spectrum of possible answers to the epistemological questions raised by the distinction between the dual meanings of "history" are two extreme positions that are equally untenable. The first, which can be called "naive positivism" or "hyperrealism," claims that history, understood as a narrative or a discourse, can accurately and adequately represent history, understood as significant past occurrences, events, and actions. It is often emblematized, with little regard for the complexities of his actual practice, by the great nineteenth-century German historian Leopold von Ranke's imperative to write history "wie es eigentlich gewesen" ("as it actually happened").[11] Here the historian's craft, based on what Ranke called his "pure love of truth,"[12] is understood essentially as a "science"—or at least *Wissenschaft* in the German sense of a rigorous scholarly discipline—that can skillfully sift through reliable evidence to present an accurate, unbiased, and complete representation of the past, or at least of those aspects of it deemed significant. Aping the visual model of cognitive distance favored by modern science and drawing on the metaphor of a nondistorting mirror,[13] it privileges an ideal observer identified with "posterity," which extends beyond any concrete subject situated at a particular vantage point at a particular moment in time. It elevates disinterested observing over evaluative judging, which it rhetorically signals by the adoption of an impersonal and omniscient narrative voice, in which the historian's deictic particulars—his or her temporal and spatial locations—are suppressed. Honoring the alleged authority of "primary sources" often gathered as "documents" in institutional "archives," it understands historical research as an essentially empirical enterprise based on uncovering "facts" or describing "events" unfiltered through a theoretical or ideological lens.[14] Historical truth for those who hold this position is essentially the same as it is for those who believe with Thomas Aquinas that "veritas est adaequatio intellectus et rei," truth is a correspondence between the object of inquiry and a mental representation of or linguistic statement about it.[15]

Correspondence theories of truth may be defended in sophisticated ways by contemporary philosophers,[16] but they rarely inform serious discussions of historical epistemology. Although the advances made since the historical "scientific revolution" in evaluating the reliability of sources are widely appreciated, little, if any, confidence remains in the ability of even the most rigorous methods to produce an objective and accurate representation of the past "as it actually was," even on the level of seemingly granular events. The majority of historians and philosophers of history alike have awakened from the "noble dream" of objectivity, the motto ironically adopted by Peter Novick to characterize the American historical profession's quest for disinterested and accurate representations of the past.[17]

There are many reasons the quest was abandoned, but I want to foreground only three. The first is the radical asymmetry between history as the totality of all that happened in "the past" and history as an inevitably finite and selective representation of "what happened." Even if totality as a goal is abandoned, the assumption that "significance" can replace it as a norm is problematic because of the inevitable quarrel over what is meaningful, both for those who lived through it and those who attempt to recount it. Although in many other respects unlike individual or collective memory, history as post-facto representation shares with them an inevitable and, I would argue, salutary dependence on the involuntary forgetting of the vast majority of past actions, events, experiences, and occurrences that might serve as grist for its mill.[18] Rather than full anamnestic recall, in which everything of possible significance in the past is available for later recapitulation, history as a representative discourse ironically depends on the limits of memory and the fickleness of preservation. For without the drastic selection and condensation of what is worthy of being recalled and recorded, as well as the limited, often chance survival of a small portion of possible remnants of the past, no finite historical narrative could be fashioned. Although historians do, of course, often seek to reverse the malign effects that can also flow from undeserved oblivion, seeking to hear the voices of those previously silenced, they concede that the vast majority of past occurrences remain shrouded in the proverbial mists of time.

As a result of this radical asymmetry, no plausible notion of historical truth can aspire to what is demanded of witnesses in a court of law sworn to tell "the truth, the whole truth, and nothing but the truth."[19] For there can be no simple adequation between subjective knowledge—even understood as the cumulative knowledge contained in all the history books ever written—and an impossible object that is the entire "past as such."[20] Put differently, there can never be a satisfactorily replete, fully saturated "context" in which to situate "texts" or "documents," the latter understood in the broadest sense as evidentiary traces left by the past, because the boundary of such a context would ultimately have to encompass all of the past at any one moment as well as an infinite temporal regress with no access to an ultimate ur-cause (cosmogenic theories of the Big Bang notwithstanding). The historian's frames are always limiting devices, necessarily if sometimes arbitrarily employed to blunt the threat of infinite explanatory or narrative regression. What was once present and its post-facto re-presentation are thus inherently distinct in terms of scale and plenitude, making any simplistic notion of accuracy as a perfect isomorphic fit between the two nonsensical.

There is, moreover, no inductive transfer from microhistory, focusing on the atomic level of past occurrences that may seem less open to contestation, to macrohistory, seeking large-scale patterns. No cumulative aggregation of isolated facts, even assuming their reliability, can produce synthetic generalizations. There is a leap in kind, not merely in degree, from a chronicle or annal, which records events or actions that occur in a periodically ordered time line, and a more ambitious history, which imbues them with meaning, seeks their causes and effects, and presents them in stories with beginnings, middles, and ends. The universe of historical narrative is inherently heterogeneous, with multiple levels that defy easy passage from one to another.[21] There is no smooth transition from a discrete event to, say, the precise dating of a historical period, which is only a matter of retrospective interpretation. Nor can there be, *pace* advocates of "world history," a coherent synthesis of local histories, however we define their boundaries, and the general narrative of universal history, the totalized story of the species as a whole.[22] However much we may try to fill in the gaps, search for uncovered records, or listen to hitherto unheard voices, the overwhelming majority of "what happened," history as *res gestae*, is lost forever. And thankfully so, as Tristram Shandy realized when he tried in vain to write his autobiography as fully and faithfully as possible in Laurence Sterne's famous eighteenth-century novel.[23]

A second salient reason for the implausibility of naive positivist historiography is, paradoxically, the opposite asymmetry. That is, rather than the vastness and infinite complexity of a past that exceeds our capacity to recall or record it, we who are doing the recording have a much richer sense of the later outcomes of events and actions than those who experienced them directly in their own lives. The benefit of hindsight means that our histories are not written by recovering "what actually happened" *when* it was happening but inevitably draw on the additional knowledge of what happened next, a knowledge that was impossible at the time. Although historians are often implored to avoid presentism and block out the intervening history in assessing the past, it is impossible to suspend entirely our own *situation* and restore the innocence of outcomes enjoyed by those from that past. We know the unintended consequences unavailable to the actors themselves and can experience an ironic distance from intentions gone astray that they could not.[24] We can periodize the past in terms of epochs, whose outlines are never known by those whose lives fall within them (think, for example, of the absurdity of a twelfth-century serf aware that he was living in "the Middle Ages"). However much historians are exhorted to be sensitive to the multiple possibilities in a still-unfolding story—"side-shadowing," in the current jargon, rather than "foreshadowing" the future[25]—we cannot willfully bracket the knowledge of which possibilities were actualized and which not, which became factual and which remained counterfactual.

A final reason the naive positivist or hyperrealist position is unconvincing emerges from a consideration of the subject who composes the stories of *historia rerum gestarum*. The putative "object" construed by defenders of objectivity is the mirror image of the putative "subject" of knowledge, whose certainty is assured by assigning it a transcendental position "thrown under" (the etymological Latin origin of the word "subject") all acts of cognition.[26] But not only are no narrators really omniscient, they are also never perfectly neutral, objective, and disinterested, never entirely unaffected by what Freud would have called their emotionally driven "transferential" investments in the past.[27] "Posterity" is a fictional, disembedded, tacitly singular placeholder for an always contested, always dynamic field of different perspectives, which defy integration into a singular transcendental point of view.[28] Although they may not map neatly onto discrete "subject positions" in a social or cultural field, they are also never entirely above them, able to observe with the proverbial eye of a bird, such as Minerva's famous owl, let alone that of an omniscient God-like posterity able to render a last judgment.

To complicate matters still further, if we historicize the actual subjects who write historical narrations, taking into account the ways in which the end points of their narratives inexorably extend into an uncertain future, it is highly unlikely that any one representation, however definitive it may now seem, will survive the new evidence or interpretative tools that are still to be discovered. We are, in short, always in the middle of a story whose conclusion is yet to come, for as Chou En-lai allegedly said when asked his opinion of the impact of the French Revolution, "It is too early to tell."[29] Because of all these reasons, and others that might be adduced, there can never be a fully adequate correspondence between "history" in its two distinct meanings, as what happened and our representations of it.

The Constructivist Fallacy

Because the naive positivist and hyperrealist faith in objective, scientific history has been undermined by these and other qualms, some commentators have been led to deny any veridical relationship between the past and its subsequent representations. Recalling Cicero's claim that written history is an "opus oratorium"[30] (rhetorical work), "constructivists"—or "hyperrelativists," as their critics sometimes call them[31]—question the very distinction between fact and fiction. Having come to prominence in the heyday of "postmodernism," they apply the lessons of the "linguistic turn" in the humanities during the last third of the twentieth century.[32] Constructivists argue it is representations all the way down, for there is no access to the past unmediated through present interpretive reconstructions and implicit criteria of value.[33] If Ranke's "wie es eigentlich gewesen" became the emblem of the naive realist position, the Italian idealist philosopher Benedetto Croce's assertion that "all history is contemporary history" often plays a comparable role for radical constructivists, who tip the balance between "history" as what happened in the past and "history" as the representation of those happenings in the present entirely in the latter direction.[34] Even isolated "facts," they contend, should be understood as "events under description," which like truth claims in general, are linguistic through and through.[35]

If there is any "truth" in historical reconstructions, constructivists argued, it is thus more "made" than "matched," "discovered," or "found." Historical narratives are always dependent on what Roland Barthes called "reality effects," creating an illusion of objectivity based on various rhetorical devices working to conceal the subjective intervention of the author. "Historical discourse," so Barthes charged, "is a fake performative discourse in which the apparent constative (descriptive) is in fact only the signifier of the speech-act as an act of authority."[36] The narratives fashioned by historians, Hayden White added, always follow latent conventional patterns or "tropes," with tragedy, comedy, satire, romance, and irony as the most frequent exemplars. Beneath the temporal flow of the storytelling are always structural regularities that endure no matter how unique the recounted events may seem. Also drawing on such standard figural devices as metaphor, metonymy, and synecdoche, historical narratives can never mimetically correspond to their putatively real object, even when the latter is not understood as the infinite past, but as any finite fragment of it. All history (as *historia rerum gestarum*) is thus really what White calls "metahistory," dependent on linguistic conventions that shape every post-facto narrative, intentionally or not.[37]

There are, constructivists also insist, radical incommensurabilities between time as it is experienced and time as it is narratively recounted, as we say, "after the fact." The time of the told is never the time of the telling. The former is lived essentially in the present tense, even while including what phenomenologists like Edmund Husserl called the retention of the past and protention of the future,[38] while the latter is written in the preterite (or as it is sometimes called, aorist) tense, which signifies a completed action, no longer open to an indefinite future. Whereas life moves forward in chronological order, narration is often far less linear, with regressions and anticipations shaping the story as it is told. Rather than emulating the inexorable march of time, historians often flash forward or backward, leaping ahead proleptically to foreshadow outcomes or circling back to recount origins. Every written reconstruction, moreover, also contains significant differences in the pace of storytelling, so that fifty pages can be spent on one day followed by only two on the next ten years.

In addition, what narratologists following Gerard Genette call "focalization" means that all stories are necessarily told from a specific perspective.[39] A narrative where all the information presented reflects the subjectivity of a particular character is "internally focalized." "External focalization," in contrast, is more like a camera eye, which sees the action from a discrete position outside the subjective views of any of the actors. The point of view assumed by an omniscient narrator is called "zero focalization." Whichever focalization is chosen, other points of view are necessarily excluded or at least marginalized; even attempts to include different voices—for example, Saul Friedlander's acclaimed history of the Holocaust, which allows us to hear from both victims and perpetrators[40]—necessarily selects some and excludes others. The result is thus additive, not synthetic. Nor does the use of free indirect style or "the middle voice" conflating the narrator's perspective with that of a character, as in many realist novels, produce a genuinely totalized account.[41] The putative point of view of "posterity" should therefore be understood only as an imaginary overcoming of the concrete particularization of focalized narration, or more precisely, a displacement forward of zero focalization. The historian's active imagination—whose importance had already been stressed by philosophers like R. G. Collingwood even before the "linguistic turn"[42]—always plays a key role in any story told about the past. The implied meaning of the word "source" suggests it serves as a stimulus to a post-facto representation, rather than as an inert trace of a past occurrence. Instead of an objective "science," history as a discourse may well be better understood as an "art."[43]

As in the case of the unnuanced realist pole of the spectrum, however, the constructivist alternative has also been vigorously disputed. Its critics worry that, absent a strong referential imperative, the unfettered imagination can become a bit too active and sanction a dangerous attitude of "anything goes." A slippery slope, they fear, leads to the utter conflation of fictional narratives, peopled by invented characters engaging in invented acts, with the recorded deeds of their historical counterparts, who really existed and left traces of their actions that cannot be ignored. The most compelling test case, on which much of the debate has focused, has been the Holocaust, whose outrageous denial by latter-day anti-Semites shows the dangers of effacing that distinction.[44]

While conceding that all representational narratives depend to some extent on rhetorical techniques, the critics of constructivism distinguish between those that draw on the evidentiary fruits of "scientific" retrieval and those that are free to create *ex nihilo*. Disdaining the "linguistic transcendentalism" of anticorrespondence theorists who bracket the world outside of language as entirely unknowable, they claim that however much language may mediate our interaction with a world beyond our consciousness, it does not spin it entirely out of whole cloth. Infants, after all, interact with the world prior to the acquisition of language, and we never entirely lose our ability to respond directly to sensual stimuli (feeling pain, for example, without having to say "ouch"). Constructivists, they charge, have succumbed to a pan-fictionalist fantasy that forgets the critical distinction, made at least since Sir Philip Sydney's sixteenth-century "Defense of Poesy," between a narrator, such as a historian, who asserts truth claims that can be validated, and a poet—or fiction writer in general—who "nothing affirms, and therefore never lieth."[45] Although realist fiction, *pace* Barthes, may draw heavily on "reality effects" in its use of thick descriptions and references to conventionally accepted "real historical events," it does so with an explicit acknowledgment that the language game it plays is not that of referential assertion.[46] In historical narratives, in contrast, the world, including residues of the world of the past, pushes back against our fantasies about it. Although "facts" are always linguistically mediated—"events under description"—they are also derived from the disclosure of the world to our experience, which can be what Husserl called "pre-predicative," prior to language.[47]

Critics of radical constructivism also revisit the familiar contrast between chronicle or annal and history, but now in order to stress the importance of the former. That is, without an uninflected, banal, routine recording of events when they occurred arranged on a mechanically articulated time line, there can be no later imaginative emplotment of the past as a meaningful story. There is, they also point out, an important parallel between historical knowledge of the distant past and that of our own personal pasts whose practical effects cannot be ignored in our present lives. As the philosopher of history David Carr has put it, "Just as I cannot pretend to have added salt and expect the soufflé to turn out well, so I cannot pretend to a talent or capacity I never had and then expect to put it to use. Many of our plans go awry (and stories have to be rewritten) because we make mistakes about the past, about what happened and what we have done. The past *does* constrain us; it does have a fixedness that allows reinterpretation only up to certain limits."[48] If, moreover, there are levels in a heterogeneous historical universe and the historian cannot move in an upward direction by inductively generalizing from micro- to macrohistory, it is also wrong to move effortlessly down the ladder and conclude that the active narrative imagination that "makes" the most synthetic level also guides the primary researcher's encounter with the evidentiary record. Some of the resistance of isolated "facts" to the imposition of more general narrative meaning is expressed rhetorically in what has been called the "laminated" character of historical prose itself when it includes direct citations from original sources in its narrative reconstructions, which are unmediated residues of the past that stubbornly check the historian's full imaginative sovereignty over the story he or she is telling.[49]

It is this tension between levels and voices that allows the writing of history to become a "learning process" rather than a mere chaos of different narratives, randomly replacing one another with no advance in knowledge. While such learning is never perfectly linear and there are often regressions, the telos of the advancement of knowledge is hardwired into the modern historical enterprise. Although not as inexorably cumulative as normal science (Thomas Kuhn's paradigm shifts aside), the expansion and refinement of historical knowledge can benefit from the discovery of new evidence, greater temporal perspective, and the collective vetting of competing accounts.

Three Plausible Alternatives

As a result, rather than the two untenable extremes of radical positivism and radical constructivism, the most interesting epistemological questions involve the intertwining of residues of the past with its present reconstruction, which allow us, despite everything, to retain a heuristic model or regulative ideal of historical truth asymptotically approached over time. Three suggestive responses to those questions can be characterized as falsificationism, the new experientialism, and institutional justificationism. Each helps us navigate the treacherous waters between the Scylla of naive realism and the Charybdis of radical constructivism, without, however, allowing us to reach the dry land of certitude at the end of the voyage.

Falsificationism

Wary of ever establishing a single, verifiable version of historical truth, but reluctant to efface the distinction between history and fiction, falsificationists have stressed the value of exposing and rejecting untrue accounts, dubious facts, inauthentic documents, and the like. As the French historian and philosopher Michel de Certeau put it, "Western historiography struggles against fiction. . . .Not that it appeals to the truth; never has the historian pretended to do that! Rather, with his apparatus for the critical reading of documents, the scholar effaces errors from the 'fables' of the past. The territory that he occupies is acquired through a diagnosis of the false."[50] The procedures of falsification are most effective in combating deliberate fabrications, such as forged documents or doctored photographs, often introduced for ideological reasons, which are very different from honest errors or fictions that explicitly identify themselves as such. Like forensic investigators in criminal cases, falsificationists employ the methodological tools honed by the scientific revolution in historical research and the "disciplines of erudition" devoted to the authentication of sources, textual or otherwise.[51]

Deliberate fabrications or forgeries are, to be sure, relatively rare, and so the more pressing issue is how honorably fashioned accounts can also be falsified. In the philosophy of scientific reasoning, the criterion of falsifiability is most often identified with the attempts of Karl Popper, a critic of the positivist faith in inductive verification, to demarcate legitimate science from pseudoscience in terms of the former's ability to be falsified experimentally.[52] Even before being evaluated, claims to scientific authenticity must be formulated so that every conjecture made in the context of discovery is open to refutation in the context of justification. Every hypothesis in a theory must be refutable to warrant the honorific title of "science." To avoid the threat of both relativism and dogmatism—Popper's favorite examples of the latter were Marxism and psychoanalysis—it is necessary to formulate statements about the world that can be discredited by counterexamples (e.g., the generalization "all swans are white" by the discovery of a black swan). In such a way, the desired end of objective truth, which Popper never denied was the telos of science, could be more and more closely approximated, if never fully reached.

Although Popper's antiverificationist model of scientific method helped undermine naive positivism, his own demarcation criteria, based on the power of observation to contradict a false scientific claim, were subjected to widespread criticism by rival philosophers of science such as Imre Lakatos, Thomas Kuhn, and Paul Feyerabend. Whether his criteria were ever applicable to the discipline of history is even more problematic, as Popper himself targeted only what he called, in an idiosyncratic defiance of normal usage, "historicism."[53] By this he meant the assertion of dubious historical laws that would allow the prediction of the future. Despite a vain search for so-called covering laws in history by philosophers like Carl Hempel in the 1940s and 1950s,[54] actual historical accounts have rarely been vulnerable to Popper's falsification criteria. The singularity of narratives and the centrality of meaning in them—meaning being a category Popper, in a polemic with Wittgenstein, had banished from scientific epistemology[55]—makes it difficult to subsume them under even a nonverificationist scientific model. Moreover, if one takes seriously the discontinuity between the heterogeneous levels of the historical universe, an anomalous "fact" on a microhistorical level cannot easily refute a macrohistorical generalization. There is nothing comparable to the *experimentum crucis* of natural science, at least as Popper understood it, that would definitively falsify a large-scale historical narrative or complicated causal explanation. Indeed, the explosive expansion of the historical archive makes it virtually impossible to avoid a certain arbitrariness in the selection of which pieces of factual evidence to apply to which narratives.

The New Experientialism

If Popperian falsificationism failed to provide conclusive answers to the challenge of truth in history, some commentators, equally unhappy with the radical constructivist alternative encouraged by the "linguistic turn," have been tempted to bypass epistemological and rhetorical questions entirely and return instead to what may appear to be a more ontological version of historical truth. This is the stratagem apparently adopted by a group of theorists—sometimes called the "new romanticists,"[56] although "new experientialists" is more accurate—who focus on the question of "historical experience," but redefined in an unexpected way.[57]

Rejecting the empathetic "re-experiencing" of the original experience of the actors of previous generations, promoted in the nineteenth century by Wilhelm Dilthey as the most fruitful way of revealing the meaning of the past, the "new experientalists" have turned to a more direct communion with the past in the present, which their leading exponents Eelco Runia and Frank Ankersmit respectively call "presence" and "sublime experience."[58] The epistemological objectivism of the positivists and the linguistic idealism of the constructivists are both based, they claim, on a dubious dualism between present subject and past object. Instead, they prefer the metaphor of proximate touch and immediate contact to that of distancing perspectival sight or rhetorical imposition to describe an experience of history prior to the very split between subject and object.

Rather than explaining events causally or offering a meaningful interpretation of the past through narrative emplotment, the "new experientialists" extol present experiences that seem to overcome temporal distance and make the past alive now, rather than merely empathetically duplicating the putative experience of past actors. Inspired by the great Dutch historian Johan Huizinga's notion of "historical sensation"[59]—an epiphany manifest in rare but life-altering encounters with the past, unfiltered by conceptual mediations or interpretative prefigurations—they celebrate fissures "in the temporal order so that the past and the present are momentarily united in a way that is familiar to all of us in the experience of déjà vu."[60] Jacob Burckhardt's account of his first visit to the church of Santa Croce in Florence, which magically brought the Renaissance to life, is one example.[61] Neither scientific history with its penchant for causal explanations of past events nor historical narration imbued with rhetorically inflected meaning drawing on implicit tropes can contain and normalize such disruptive and illuminating experiences.

Are the "new experientialists" returning from an epistemological to an ontological approach to the question of history and truth, one in which prepredicative experience gets us in direct touch with the presence of the past? Ankersmit concedes that what he seeks is "closer to moods and feelings than to knowledge; like them it is ontological rather than epistemological; and sublime experience is to be defined in terms of what you *are* rather than in terms of what knowledge you *have*."[62] Runia, for his part, stresses the role of noninterpretative metonymy rather than metaphor as the master trope of historical experience, and he contends that it "wants us to believe that it imparts one 'meaning'—the truth—that this 'meaning' lies right at the surface, and that this one 'meaning' is all that it conveys."[63] Such an antirepresentational agenda may seem even reminiscent of the Christian doctrine of "real presence" in which the body and blood of Christ is substantially, not merely symbolically, present in the Eucharist.[64]

But it would be wrong to draw too hasty a conclusion about the actual return of an emphatic, ontological concept of truth in history. For Ankersmit explicitly declares his radical indifference to the question of truth, understood ontologically as well as epistemologically. In a passage in *Sublime Historical Experience* set entirely in italics, he writes: "*Sublime experience is sovereign master in its own territory and no longer subject to the epistemological legislation of truth (as experience is in its more trivial form that we know as the scientific experiment). It therefore makes no sense to ask for 'the truth of (sublime) experience' or for what might or should (in)validate historical experience.*"[65] And while Runia may contend that the metonymic transfer of presence—in which parts stand for the whole—as opposed to the metaphoric transfer of meaning—in which analogous comparisons convey sense—is in the service of something called the truth, he nonetheless acknowledges that "metonymy is the trope of *dissimulation*."[66] That is, although metonymic representation may seek to give the impression of being prior to the split between subject and object, history as experienced and history as written, it in fact fails to achieve it. Whatever attraction we may feel for the presence of a sublime historical experience—and its defenders do make suggestive arguments for its virtues, which cannot be addressed now—it gives us little, if any, help with the issue of truth and history. Although situated in the contested territory between the positivist and constructivist extremes, it survives the turbulence by hunkering down and refusing to be drawn into the crossfire. But the relationship between truth and history remains a vexed issue, which, despite what may seem the disdain of Ankersmit and Runia, continues to exercise anyone who conducts research into and writes the story of the past.

Institutional Justificationism

Does the alternative that I've called "institutional justificationism" provide a more plausible solution? Traceable to the pragmatist C. S. Peirce's ideal notion of a credentialed scientific community of inquiry, which has come to be called a "community of the competent,"⁶⁷ it displaces the question of the truth about the past to that of the truthfulness of the historian in the present. More precisely, "institutional justificationism" replaces a concern with the truth of our accounts of the past with a focus on the integrity of historians, the sincerity of their claims, openness to counterarguments, and adherence to standards of evidentiary authenticity. Although acknowledging that truthfulness is normally accounted a virtue for individuals, "institutional justificationism" emphasizes the pressures to produce it dialogically and institutionally. "Institutional justificationism" defines historians collectively as a loosely integrated, professionally credentialed community engaged in a collaborative, critically vetted enterprise with no final resting place, no unified "posterity" at the end of the day, no last judgment that ever comes. The community's members operate only with an "as if" concept of truth, which provides an underlying asymptotic telos for their endeavors, but which they know is always unreachable.

The importance of the intersubjective assessment of historical accounts was already clear to Collingwood, who contrasted fictional narratives with their historical counterparts, even though both were based on an active imagination. In addition to their explicitly bracketing truth claims, fictions were distinguished from historical narratives, Collingwood argued, by the possibility of repeating the intellectual labor that produced the latter. Although certainty can be elusive, we can at least form an educated opinion about the plausibility of an earlier historian's narrative "by doing his work over again for ourselves, that is, by reconsidering the evidence upon which his picture is based and, exercising upon this evidence our own historical imagination, finding that we are led to the same result."⁶⁸ No one, in other words, would think of judging the truth content of, say, *War and Peace*, by duplicating Tolstoy's authorship and rewriting his novel; but many historians have found cause to rewrite the account of many of the same events written by Armand-Augustin-Louis Caulaincourt in *With Napoleon in Russia*.⁶⁹ Although there is no definitive final account, the process of frequently revisiting earlier ones fuels the ongoing effort to reach some sort of rough consensus about which assertions are warranted and which not. While eschewing the ideal of an absolutely definitive history that makes further revision unnecessary, it understands the cumulative impact of multiple perspectives on the "same" historical events or developments.

The value of this distinction between fictional and historical narratives becomes even clearer if we reconsider the rhetorical moment in the construction of all narratives invoked by Hayden White. He stresses its importance to highlight the latent structural logic of our stories according to a finite number of conventional patterns or figural tropes. But rhetoric, *pace* White, can mean more than tropology or structural poetics; it can also signify the figures of speech through which intersubjective dialogue takes place.[70] That is, rhetoric understood as a normal part of everyday speech alerts us to the communicative function of language, which can involve persuasion rather than demagogic mystification or authoritarian imposition. Whereas White's focus on rhetoric meant recognizing formal structures latent within texts, its communicative counterpart alerts us to the dimension of manifest interactions between or among speakers.

As Jürgen Habermas argues in his defense of the public sphere, universal pragmatics, and communicative rationality, there is at least a potential for consensus based on the better argument and the most compelling evidence, following procedures that take seriously the resistance of that evidence to dubious interpretations.[71] The justificatory exchange of reasons, including those couched in metaphorical or metonymical terms, in a discursive community extending over time characterizes the modern discipline of history, with its professional credentialing and vetting procedures enabling responsible evaluation. Rather than being reduced to the pseudo-reasoning damned by Plato as sophistic, rhetoric can be employed to persuade, not seduce. It can support what the analytic philosopher Michael Dummett calls a "justificationist" rather than verificationist or falsificationist approach to the unending quest for truth, which maintains a realist attitude toward the object of inquiry, but knows that such an object is accessible, if at all, only through intersubjective argumentation always open to future revision.[72] For Dummett propositions are not like "arrows" that we aim at a target called reality (which may well be so far away that we can never know if we actually hit it), but rather tools we use according to rules or moves in a language game. We can still talk of "truth" if we avoid understanding it in the terms of an arrow hitting its target, because there is no ultimate standard by which we can measure our efforts, no transcendent observer able to judge our success. Even Ankersmit, returning to the question of cognitive veracity after *Sublime Historical Experience*, acknowledges that "historical truth is firmly attached to the practice and rationality of historical discussion. . . . Disciplinary truth is not in need of philosophical explanation—unless the philosopher has the pretension to be better informed about historical writing than historians themselves."[73]

It would, of course, be easy to belittle the actual functioning of this community of justification, showing its departures from an ideal Habermasian model of undistorted communication. It can be mocked as another case of liberal delusion about the free market of ideas or of unwarranted faith in Peirce's meritocratic standard of recognized "competence."[74] The process of professionalization, it is often charged, can exclude those who are deemed beyond the pale: uncredentialed amateurs, autodidacts, and what have come to be called "barefoot historians," whose unvetted work appears in unauthorized venues, which have proliferated mightily with the growth of the Internet. Rather than a single "community of competence," there can be several, driven by incommensurable interests or values that impede unbiased communication. In short, all the familiar arguments made by Michel Foucault about the inextricable entanglement of knowledge and power in discrete "regimes of truth" can be marshaled to cast doubt on the naive conclusion that historians in the collective are able to do any better than any single historian in avoiding the dangers of relativism and dogmatism.[75] Such reservations are, it must be admitted, worth taking seriously.

But there may well also be a positive lesson in how these qualms have been taken on board by historians, insofar as doing so has created an awareness on a metalevel of the ways institutions, including the ones in which historians are more or less embedded, have histories of their own, which themselves are open to intersubjective critiques that can influence subsequent practices.[76] That is, historians can take seriously voices from outside the guild, relentlessly weed out deliberate falsifiers of evidence, and become self-consciously aware of the rhetorical dimension of the narratives they write and the standards of competence they employ. Despite their differences, some productive discursive exchange can occur between communities that may appear to be grounded in utterly incommensurable assumptions. Historians, in short, can learn reflexively from the history of historiography with all of its vicissitudes. Putting it in terms that resonate with the new experientialism, we can say that historians' most valuable experiences may not be sublime quasi-ontological encounters with the "presence" of the past, but rather their entrance into and engagement with the ongoing metacommunity of historians, past, present and future, which is a regulative ideal of their craft.

Although such a community always falls short of its ideal norm, it can install in those who enter it the imperative to be vigilant about its limitations and shortcomings. This means acquiring a reflexive appreciation of the value of truthfulness, even if historians know they can never reach a final truth, and embracing the process of pluralist argumentation about their always tentative conclusions, which will never reach a perfect consensus. Perhaps most telling of all, becoming sensitive to the importance of the collective obligation to be truthful, even in the face of doubts about reaching ultimate truth, forces them to realize that their enterprise is not only epistemological and rhetorical but also inherently moral in character. This is not to suggest, I hasten to add, that historians should set themselves up as moral judges of past actors, measuring their deeds by contemporary standards of behavior. It means instead that they should feel duty-bound to do all they can to avoid imposing their own prejudices and interests on the people who came before them, acknowledging the otherness of historical actors even as they try to empathize with their struggles and dilemmas. If it didn't sound so old-fashioned, we might call this a code of honor tacitly underlying membership in the guild, where the truthfulness of the telling is valued over the truth of the told.

Perhaps no less importantly, sensitivity to the importance of truthfulness without illusions about the truth of our accounts of the past also means historians are morally obliged to honor the protocols and master the practices of the professional community they join, however imperfectly those standards may be observed in reality. As Bernard Williams contends in *Truth and Truthfulness*, "While we must demand that interpretations of the past should tell us the truth, in the sense that they should not lie or mislead, what we need them for is not to tell us something called 'the truth about the past.' We need them to be truthful, and to make sense of the past—to us."[77] That is, in addition to their obligation to the people who have preceded us to tell their stories as honestly, fairly, and judiciously as possible, historians also owe to their present and future audiences the example of their vigilant efforts to do so. For they too, after all, will come to depend on later historians to tell their own stories with comparable integrity.

Conclusion

The truth of history, understood in either ontological or epistemological terms, may forever elude us. But, I would argue in conclusion, it is crucial to maintain an abiding commitment to the truthfulness of historians—or, more precisely, to that of historians as an intersubjective community of fallible scholars who honor the imperative to justify their accounts. This means being truthful about our motives, truthful about the validity of the evidence as best we can judge it, and truthful in our willingness to accept the better counterargument and the force of new evidence. For without that commitment to truthfulness, we have no way of preventing the triumph of "fake news" and "alternative facts," or surviving the threat posed by Orwell's ominous warning in *1984*: "Who controls the past controls the future. Who controls the present controls the past."[78]

CHAPTER 12

Theory and Philosophy: Antonyms in Our Semantic Field?

In 1996 the sociological journal *Theory and Society* devoted a special issue to "Theory and Theoreticians." My contribution, titled "For Theory,"[1] was intended as an homage to the late Alvin Gouldner, the radical social theorist, self-described "outlaw Marxist," and founding editor of the journal, whose many books included one called *For Sociology*.[2] The essay was also dedicated to the memory of Bill Readings, a gifted literary theorist inspired in particular by Jean-François Lyotard, and a participant in the seminar I had led at the School of Criticism and Theory a decade earlier. Best known for his unflinching critique of what he called "the university in ruins," Bill had lost his life at the age of thirty-four in an airplane crash only a short time before. He was, as I called him in my dedication, a "theorist *extraordinaire*."

During the mid-1990s, as all of these various evocations of the word suggest, something called "theory" could still be said to cast its spell in the Anglo-American academic world, and literacy in the competing schools that vied for influence remained a ticket to relevance—and career advancement—in the humanities and, at least to some extent, the social sciences. Although Gouldner and Readings drew on very different traditions, they could be linked together as advocates of the value of theoretical self-consciousness in their respective disciplines. But as indicated by the elegiac tone of my essay, it was also clear that the ascent of theory had stalled. The worst days of the so-called theory wars had ended, it is true, with a precarious cease-fire allowing various schools to coexist uneasily. However, as is inevitable as wars drag on and the casualties mount, a growing backlash had developed among those who objected to the hegemony of theory in whatever guise. Indeed, as early as 1982, warnings had been sounded by neopragmatist literary critics impatient with attempts to impose a general interpretative framework—any general framework—on the reading of specific texts.[3]

It was in response to the increasing momentum of what the deconstructionist literary critic Paul de Man had already identified in 1986 as "the resistance to theory"[4] that I had felt there was a need to make a case "for theory" in general, rather than trying to defend one or another of its versions, such as the Frankfurt School's Critical Theory whose legacy I had previously explored. For as I noted in the essay, "theory" as such had been turned into an emotionally laden, generic signifier of uncertain meaning, and stigmatized by many of its critics as little more than "a game of mastery, tainted by its association with the evils of transcendentalism, foundationalism, essentialism, and the vain search for a meta-language."[5]

In the years since my defense appeared, the erosion of enthusiasm for theory has only accelerated. By 2001, even stalwarts of deconstruction like Herman Rappaport could characterize the spectacle of woeful misunderstandings and dubious applications as "the theory mess."[6] The antitheoretical wave may also have had a generational dimension, as people who came of intellectual age after theory's heyday identified it with an older cohort of scholars blocking their career path. Tellingly, so Nicholas Dames argued, the rise and fall of theory could be traced as well outside of the academy in the recent history of the American novel. Novelists who emerged during the 1970s and 1980s, such as Thomas Pynchon, Don DeLillo, or David Foster Wallace, were supplanted by others who returned to more traditional forms of psychological realism. Perhaps the shift was emblematized in a key episode in Jonathan Franzen's 2001 novel *The Corrections,*

> in which Chip Lambert, former holder of an "assistant professorship in Textual Artifacts," teacher of "Consuming Narratives," lecturer on phallic anxiety in Tudor drama, and casualty of a drug-fueled affair with an undergraduate, heads repeatedly to the Strand Bookstore to sell his large, costly collection of Theory. It is a miniature triumph of realist notation at its most aggressive. Starting with his Marxist theorists, whose collective sticker price of $3,900 is knocked down to $65, Chip works his way through "his feminists, his formalists, his structuralists, his poststructuralists, his Freudians, and his queers" to raise money for expensive dinners to impress a new girlfriend. Reduced at the end to "his beloved

cultural historians," Chip "piled his Foucault and Greenblatt and hooks and Poovey into shopping bags and sold them all for $115."[7]

The crash in the economic market for theory in this satirical anecdote exemplifies its decline as a cultural force, which is assumed to reflect the exposure of its intellectual bankruptcy.

Such an account, however, neglects to acknowledge the reasons "theory" had enjoyed its heyday in the first place, turning it instead into little more than a faddish ploy in the struggle for intellectual power and prestige. Nor does it ponder the ways in which despite fading from fashion, it may still have much to teach us. "For Theory" had been an attempt to address some of its virtues, which almost a quarter century later I think still merit consideration. Accepting the semantic play of the term, I refused to legislate a normative meaning, which would have inevitably excluded certain usages from the discussion. Nor did I seek to restore its innocence against a welter of charges such as those listed above, which in fact were plausible complaints against only one of theory's versions. Instead, I situated the term in a force field of its alleged "others," sometimes outright antonyms, which I hoped would reveal the stakes involved in resisting it in the name of an allegedly more compelling alternative.

Seven in all came to mind, although there was clearly room for more. The first focused on the particular, qualitatively distinct object that was thought to be essentialized by the homogenizing force of generalizing concepts and *a fortiori* by higher-level theories. The next five focused less on the dominated object of theoretical subsumption than on the subjects doing the theorizing, who might interact in different ways with whatever objects, material or textual, they encounter. Here the alternatives included, with all of their various meanings, the terms "practice" and "experience," sometimes understood as uniquely individual or intersubjective, but invariably contrasted as "concrete" against the alleged "abstraction" of theory.[8] Two other modes of subjective encounters with objects were identified with "narration" and the hermeneutic arts of "reading," "looking," and hearing," understood as heightened modes of apprehending and interpreting individual texts, artifacts, and performances. The final "other" of theory faced in the opposite direction from the objects of theoretical inquiry, and went back before individual interpretative approaches. It was located instead in the community of theoreticians, where questions of power and the institutions of validation prevailed, and the contexts of theorizing were even more important than the theories they generated.

This is not the place to rehearse all of the nuances of the denotative and connotative play between theory and this heteroclite field of its "others" traced in "For Theory." Nor do I want to criticize once again their implicit claims to be immanently self-sufficient in their own right rather than in constructive tension with theoretically informed reflections on their premises and limitations. Instead, I want to direct attention to an important term in the dynamic semantic force field of "theory" that the essay failed to address. The term in question may seem an odd choice, as it has more often served as a synonym than an antonym in the history of its relations with "theory," and often suffered the same fate in the struggle with its alleged opposing terms.[9] Or at least the potential tension between them was rarely articulated until the resistance to a generic notion of theory emerged full-blown in the last decades of the twentieth century. The term in question is "philosophy." Although they are often understood to be overlapping terms, or one has been nested in the other in a hierarchy of abstractions, mounting tensions between the two terms began to emerge as "theory" went increasingly on the defensive.

One can, to be sure, still find relatively anodyne distinctions between them, such as this one from a 2016 entry in an online dictionary: "Philosophy is basically the study of the fundamental nature of knowledge, reality, and existence. Theory is a supposition or a system of ideas that is intended to explain something. This is the key difference between philosophy and theory."[10] Sometimes philosophy has functioned as the master concept and been divided into theoretical and practical realms, a distinction traced all the way back to Aristotle's division between natural and moral philosophy and continuing with Kant's first two *Critiques*. At other times, a mutually beneficial complementarity has been posited between philosophy and theory, when the former is understood to deal with timeless questions and the latter with the historical or social conditions that hamper or enable the realization of philosophical ideals.[11]

No sustained consideration of the semantic force field between philosophy and theory should ignore these kinds of positive, even reinforcing interactions. But what concerns us here is the sharpening of tensions that developed between them in the last decades of the previous century, and which continue today. With all of their accumulated baggage, they have come to occupy very different positions in our denotative and connotative discursive universe. What may seem only semantic distinction has reflected in part institutional and substantive changes. For a long time, philosophy, especially as it evolved in the Anglo-American professional sphere, shed many of its traditional preoccupations, abandoning its sovereign role as arbiter of other fields for the mastery of a finite set of what appeared to many as increasingly abstruse and even irrelevant problems. Its voluntary contraction created a vacuum, slowly filled by what became known as theory and flourished in other academic departments, such as English, comparative literature, and cultural studies. Areas of inquiry that had been forcefully abjected clamored for a new hearing, for example, aesthetics, which grew increasingly marginalized in Anglo-American departments of philosophy.[12]

At first, a tacit division of labor, sometimes expressed by a simplistic geographical distinction between continental and Anglo-American philosophy, prevailed, but the truce did not last forever. It is not easy to pinpoint a moment when the split first manifested itself for all to see, but perhaps the bitter public squabble between Jacques Derrida and John Searle, which began in 1977 and never seemed to end, would serve as well as any.[13] At around the same time, the much-discussed disillusionment with traditional philosophy experienced by Richard Rorty, who turned to cultural and literary critical alternatives and switched academic departments, showed that the challenges could come from within the citadel of Anglo-American philosophy as well as outside it.[14] Although the so-called linguistic turn had been absorbed by participants in both camps—Derrida and Searle butted heads, among other things, over the implications of Austin's speech act theory— what constituted its lessons differed dramatically. In time, a bright line began to separate the two, which is still operative, as typified, for example, by the charged rhetoric employed in Brian Leiter's blog post of June 10, 2018, where he disclosed the now infamous letter in support of accused sexual harasser—and outspoken champion of deconstruction—Avital Ronell. According to Leiter, "the signatory list reads like a 'who's who' of 'theory' (as they call bad philosophy in literature departments)."[15]

This snarky put-down neatly encapsulates several of the sources and symptoms of the gap between theory and philosophy. For guardians of philosophical purity like Leiter, "theory" lacks any qualities of its own but is simply a "bad" version of philosophy. Not conducted in its proper space, firmly located in academic philosophy departments, it can be accused of transgressing borders and poaching on someone else's territory. Because entry into that territory is restricted to those with professional training and credentialing, the invaders can be condescendingly dismissed as amateurs, who lack the rigor and discipline of those allowed entrance by the border police.

Because they so often come from literature departments, the intruders bring with them an inability to distinguish clearly between philosophical argumentation and literary language, between the quest for certainty and consensus about meaning, on the one hand, and the appreciation of polysemic ambiguity, metaphoric richness, and the figural over the literal, on the other.

Even Leiter's reference to the letters' signatories as a "who's who" of theory is telling. It points to the importance of the personalities involved in the world of "theory" rather than the mere force of their ideas. Insofar as the writers on Ronell's behalf did, in fact, try to deflect the accusations made against her by appealing to her international reputation and were clearly trying to draw on their own substantial cultural capital, the insinuation was not without merit. But there was a larger assumption on which it rested: the longstanding philosophical rejection of what has become known as "psychologism," tacitly expressed by Kant at the end of the eighteenth century and then more explicitly by Edmund Husserl and Gottlob Frege at the end of the nineteenth.[16] The epithet "psychologism" served to discredit a variety of attempts to understand philosophical arguments as expressions of anything beyond the logical, inferential validity of the arguments themselves.[17] An eternal and disembedded notion of Mind was detached from the finite minds—and *a fortiori* of the fleshly bodies—of the actual people who were doing the arguing, whether they were understood as psychologically unique individuals, representatives of social types, or expressing the *Geist* of a specific *Zeit*. Most avidly evoked in the case of logic, which defied attempts to relativize its conclusions by grounding them in a time or place, the critique of psychologism also found its way into more recent defenses of "the culture of critical discourse" or the modern "public sphere," where the better argument allegedly trumps the authority or status of those in the debate.[18] Against those like Nietzsche or Foucault, its exponents defied any attempt to entangle questions of knowledge or truth with those of power.

The struggle to protect philosophy from the threat of psychologistic reduction, and the accompanying relativization of its claims, has, of course, a long history, which can be traced at least as far back as Plato's disdain for the Sophists. In modern philosophy perhaps the most influential response to its threat came from Kant's distinction between the transcendental mind necessary for all human cognition and the individual minds of the psychologically and culturally distinct people doing the cognizing. Among modernist artists and the critics who interpreted their work, psychologistic reduction was also for a long time anathema, as the integrity of the work was praised over its extrinsic sources, understood sociologically as well as psychologically, and isolated from its reception history.[19] In both cases, "the genetic fallacy," a term coined in 1934 by Morris Raphael Cohen and Ernest Nagel in their *Introduction to Logic and Scientific Method*,[20] was denounced for reducing an idea's validity to its genesis, conflating the "context of discovery" with the "context of justification," or an artwork to the life and times of its creator.

The rise of theory, in contrast, opened the door to the defiant embrace of psychologism in one form or another, thus effacing the boundary between objective arguments and those who make them, and raising, most explicitly by Michel Foucault and his followers, the question of knowledge's relationship with power. Reversing the tendency of philosophy to purify itself of the remainders of what it had abjected in its struggle to professionalize, theory in some of its manifestations even embraced the alleged "pollution" and "contamination" that mocked such efforts. Certain of its exponents explicitly focused attention on the process and effects of abjection itself, understood largely in psychoanalytic and anthropological terms, which Julia Kristeva in particular had first explored in 1980 with an eye to gender issues in *Powers of Horror*.[21]

Often accompanying this defiance of philosophy's policed borders came an increased attention paid to rhetoric, which complicated the straightforward presentation of ideas by drawing attention to the linguistic vehicle of reasoning rather than to the reasons themselves.[22] Attending to the complex role of rhetoric, understood both in terms of nonlogical techniques of persuasion and tropological mechanisms in texts, undercut the effort of philosophers to abolish ambiguity and opacity from their analyses of ideas in their own right. Although not all devotees of theory, especially in the social sciences, abandoned a model of systematic coherence based on the rigorous definition of terms and the application of discursive logic, after the linguistic turn, many theorists in such fields as sociology, anthropology, history, and political science became increasingly sensitive to the refraction of their ideas through the rhetoric of their expression. Whereas in the nineteenth century, philosophy often had to defend itself against the claims of natural science to solve many of the problems it traditionally addressed, in the more recent contest with theory, the flank exposed to rhetorical challenges has been where most of the heat has been generated.[23]

A salient manifestation of the struggle involved the question of cultural uniqueness, often reflected in different languages, as an obstacle to realizing philosophy's traditional yearning for universal truths.[24] "Why is theory foreign?" asked Bill Readings, with specific reference to the Anglo-American penchant for labelling post-structuralism as "French theory."[25] His answer pointed to the privilege often given in English departments to native "readers" of texts, who possessed hermeneutic skills that theorists—and their theories—from abroad could allegedly only envy. Anglo-American philosophers, to be sure, rarely relied on their putative command of the nuances of vernacular languages to counter the threat of "foreign" theory, but their tacit faith in the possibility of achieving a view from nowhere served the same purpose. Theorists, in contrast, confronted more squarely the refractions of concrete languages—including their own—in all but the most abstract of intellectual endeavors (i.e., mathematics and logic) than did most conventional philosophers. Without positing the inherent incommensurability of languages, they also raised important questions about the ways in which translation can thwart the goal of perfect communicability. Although philosophers have been sensitive to the challenges of translation, the influence of sedimented etymological origins, and the ways language use determines meanings, they have sometimes been tempted by the dream of a neutral metalanguage in which the ambiguities and obscurities of natural languages have been overcome. Typically, philosophers stress the importance of definitional uniformity, stipulating common usages, whereas theorists—and here they are often inspired by philosophers outside the mainstream, such as Nietzsche or Adorno—work with the different, sometimes even contradictory meanings that terms have accumulated in their long histories rather than trying to standardize them.[26]

However much it may have been violated in practice, modern philosophy since Descartes has valued clear and distinct ideas, stipulated definitions, and the process of discursive clarification. Although some philosophers, and here Nietzsche and Adorno might easily be joined by Hegel and Heidegger, have explicitly distanced themselves from the Cartesian exaltation of clarity, philosophical training in the Anglo-American tradition favors the careful parsing of arguments and exploration of their ultimate premises. Drawing on its sensitivity to metaphoric resonances and stress on the embeddedness of mind in the body, theorists have instead discerned in the valorization of clarity an unexamined ocularcentric prejudice that underpins much modern Western thought.[27]

Challenging Cartesian ocularcentrism and the telos of increasing clarification often accompanied resistance to the triumphalist narrative of modern philosophy as a progressive shedding of outmoded problems. It is not by chance that the ascent of theory and the backlash against it roughly matched the rise and fall of "postmodernism" as a term of art introduced to question the modernization story that underlay a certain image of philosophical progress that relegated such previously central preoccupations as metaphysics to an earlier age. Nor is it an accident that the origins of "theory" have been traced by some commentators to premodern, medieval ways of dialectical thinking, revived by modern outliers like Hegel.[28] The unexpected openness by some theorists to theological arguments, which were increasingly marginalized by mainstream philosophy during the nineteenth century, undermined the linear secularization narrative that enabled the development of professional philosophy as beholden to reason rather than revelation. As in other instances, boundaries—in this case between the sacred and the profane—were violated by theory and upheld by philosophy. Or to put it in other terms, the dianoetic method of philosophy—carefully considering reasoned arguments on all sides of a question before coming to a conclusion—was challenged by the openness to noetic intuitions, or even revelations, that allowed theorists to suspend normal procedures of discursive validation. Although there was certainly a deflationary impulse in certain theoretical quarters—Rorty would perhaps be the most salient example—where the putative "death of philosophy"[29] was greeted with glee, in others, ontotheological questions that once seemed obsolete enjoyed a renaissance of interest.

Other dimensions of the putative opposition between theory and philosophy might be adduced, but what I would prefer to do in conclusion is stress the insufficiency of each in isolation and the constructive outcome of maintaining a negative dialectic between them. A positive integration, to be sure, may be difficult. Indeed, one commentator, John MacCumber, has argued that even civil dialogue is unlikely:

> For theoreticians, to argue "rationally" with philosophers would be to give up in advance. For philosophers, to use reason against theoreticians would be to expose themselves, not to arguments but to questions, and even to mockery—as John Searle found out most spectacularly. So, instead of a debate, we get clashes in which the theoreticians indulge in mordant badinage, while the philosophers take refuge in stony silence. The Searle/Derrida encounter is only one of these. It and its like, I am afraid, generally resemble nothing so much as the penultimate scene of "Monty Python and the Holy Grail," in which John Cleese, playing a Frenchman, prances about on Castle Doune while hurling recondite insults at Graham Chapman's utterly flummoxed King Arthur.[30]

At the height of the "theory wars," even rival factions in the theory camp were often at each other's throats, and mockery, mordant badinage, and stony silence were sometimes the only ways in which communication occurred, if it can be said to have occurred at all.

But now that the dust has more or less settled, as it has for the once-raging battle between modernism and postmodernism, it may well be time to take stock and learn lessons from each approach. Or to put it differently, a certain well-deserved humility on the part of stalwarts of both camps would allow each to benefit from the insights of their opponents, as well as admitting the limits of their own positions. We have learned that "theory" and "philosophy" are not always synonymous terms and can occupy different territories in the landscape of contemporary thought. But even when they fight over the same turf, they are not inherently antonymic with the victory of one entailing the vanquishing of the other.

Like those "others" of theory examined in "For Theory," philosophy can learn from theoretical reflexivity about its constructed boundaries, unexamined assumptions, and entanglement with what it has tried so hard to abject: rhetoric, cultural difference, the body, gender, even the residues of theology. It can engage more openly with the larger questions it abandoned when it contracted into an overly professionalized discipline facing inward. It can moderate its hostility to psychologism in its various forms and overcome its fear that any attention paid to genesis necessarily undermines the claims of validity. It can reenter some of the territory it relinquished when it retreated into a disciplinary citadel, without trying to reconquer it and establish unchallenged sovereignty, and learn from neighboring disciplines rather than resisting pollution by them.[31]

"Theory" for its part can take on board objections raised by defenders of professional philosophy, who refuse the putative opposition of arguments and questions, but see them instead as intrinsically intertwined. Insofar as "theory" has itself been able to "travel,"[32] it can admit that it too often transcends its genetic contexts, linguistic as well as cultural, and shares with philosophy an impulse toward universalization or at least escape from its provincial origins. It can resist the debunking tendency to reduce validity entirely to genesis in the service of relentless unmasking, and moderate its inclination to practice a hermeneutics solely of suspicion.[33] Rather than decrying the traditional philosophical quest for normative and epistemological foundations as naive, it can acknowledge the crypto-normativity and tacit truth claims that fuel its own critical energies. Rather than aggressively asserting its capacity to be a universal solvent of all that resists its sway, it can rest content with a weaker version that humbly acknowledges its own limits.[34] And it can face more directly the imperative to justify rather than merely assume or assert its underlying premises, even as it continues to put pressure on the grounds and protocols of justification itself.

In short, rather than continuing to treat the tension between theory and philosophy as a latter-day version of the "contest of the faculties," in which one has to emerge as a winner at the expense of the other, it may be healthier to grapple with their dialectical interaction—call it negative if you want to resist too harmonizing a telos—that draws on the strengths of one to counter the weaknesses of the other. It may be Pollyannaish to hope for a full cessation of hostilities, but the effort to move beyond the conflict is worth pursuing—at least, in theory.

CHAPTER 13

The Weaponization of Free Speech

In our increasingly topsy-turvy political climate, one of the most bizarre developments has been the apparent embrace of free-speech fundamentalism by the alt-right and its defenders. Alleging that censorship has prevented controversial conservative speakers from reaching audiences, especially on college campuses and the social media that have hesitantly begun to deny them platforms, they charge liberals, so long committed to defending the First Amendment, with hypocrisy. Pushing back against what they stigmatize as "politically correct" attempts to limit "hate speech," they seize the mantle of nonconformist victims of a tyrannous majority. Intensifying their longstanding claim that the media is biased to the left, they increasingly focus on a comparable stifling of real dissent in academia, where it pretends to flourish. They mockingly note, for example, that having once given birth to a "free speech movement," the University of California, Berkeley now hesitates before providing platforms to provocateurs like Milo Yiannopoulos and Ben Shapiro, allegedly to protect them against the violent objections of Antifa hecklers. Although it is not likely that the Koch brothers will now become major donors to the ACLU, conservative stalwarts like Jordan Peterson have started media sites—his is called Thinkspot—to promote the dissemination of ideas they claim are censored by the mainstream media.[1] The role reversal perhaps reached a climax when Donald Trump signed an executive order in March 2019 proclaiming that public universities will have federal funds withheld if they attempt to regulate speech on their campuses.

It would, of course, be easy to decry this campaign as an exercise in blatant cynicism designed to make the world safe for obnoxious and dangerous ideas espoused by insincere "victims" who wouldn't hesitate for a moment to suppress others they disliked were the megaphone on the other mouth. Nor has it been difficult to note that what the First Amendment prohibits is the government—or more precisely, Congress—passing laws "abridging the freedom of speech, or of the press," not privately owned social media platforms or universities (even ones publicly funded) limiting it when it threatens other rights or the safety of the audience. Academic freedom, it is often pointed out, is not the same as freedom of speech, and the research and pedagogical functions of institutions of higher learning demand certain protocols of discrimination between good and bad ideas and discretionary access to the floor of a lecture or seminar. Journal submissions, moreover, are vetted, chairs of meetings recognize who gets to ask a question, and lectures are not free-for-all shouting matches. Credentialed experts, while not granted automatic immunity from making mistakes, have earned their privileged status.[2]

All of this has been extensively treated by serious scholars of the law and litigated in courts for a very long time, and I am not sure I have anything of note to add to the discussion. What I would like to do instead in this essay is focus on the charge directed against the alt-right of "weaponizing" freedom of speech, using it as a cudgel to beat the left. Although coined earlier, the term seems to have been given widespread currency in 2018 by Supreme Court Justice Elena Kagan.[3] In addition to its connotation of violent force rather than persuasion,[4] "weaponization" implies that there is a more normal state of affairs in which free speech stands on its own and is not an instrument for some ulterior motive. Understood absolutely, as befitting an inalienable and inviolable "human right," unregulated speech is honored as an end in itself. Replaying the age-old debate between deontological and consequentialist moral theorists, absolutists adopt the language of abstract principle against concrete efficacy.

Although historically identified more with the liberal left, where it was classically defended by Supreme Court Justice Hugo L. Black,[5] absolutism has now been adopted by the right, which was far less eager to employ it when, say, defending "national security" during the Cold War or protesting flag burning, pornography, and public obscenity. It is not surprising to find such a reversal denounced by liberals as hypocritically instrumental, despite its lofty appeal to abstract principle. As in the case of conservative critiques of affirmative action by newly pious egalitarians who denounced it as "reverse discrimination," it reeks of bad faith. But at the same time, many of the same liberals, who once were staunch supporters of free speech absolutism, also have also found themselves vulnerable to the charge of hypocrisy or at least inconsistency when they recycle antiliberal critiques of "repressive tolerance" made by such radical leftists as Herbert Marcuse in the 1960s in their accounting of the costs of unregulated speech.[6]

Observing these ironic reversals, I want to argue, suggests that absolutists, whatever their political inclinations, have failed to acknowledge the inevitability of weaponization, or in more neutral language, the functionalization of free speech for purposes other than itself.[7] As I hope this essay will show, it can never be plausibly defended as a self-sustaining principle resisting any attempt to weaponize or functionalize it, an *a priori* moral imperative valid under all circumstances.[8] Such an abstraction rests on what can best be called the fetishization of one aspect of a larger and more complicated whole.[9] To make a fetish out of something called "free speech" results from disembedding it, in fact, from two larger contexts. One, which we might call its context of application, considers the concrete cultural, social, or political situations in which it must always be exercised, the institutional and intersubjective settings or "domains"[10] where it can be justified and those where it cannot. The second, which can be called its teleological context, considers the extrinsic functions it is alleged to perform and the purposes it serves, which would be thwarted were it denied. These contexts inevitably overlap, but it is useful to distinguish them for analytic purposes.

The vital importance of certain contexts of application as legitimating or limiting the exercise of unimpeded free speech is widely acknowledged (even, we might add, by many absolutists when push comes to shove). The right is constrained, for example, if something judged to be "the peace" is disturbed or if a gathering, such as a musical performance or religious ritual, demands silence. It can be curtailed when public safety is directly threatened, as in the proverbial cry of fire in a crowded theater (although, of course, the smelling of actual smoke and sight of real flames can justify it). It does not go unpunished when it produces what is considered libel or slander by the legal standards of a community, or violates norms—often, to be sure, contested and in transition—of profanity, obscenity, and, in some cases, blasphemy. It is subjected to rigorous criteria of admissibility in courts of law or punished by judgments of contempt. Nor is it allowed in absolute terms even in the most democratic of settings when Robert's Rules of Order or some such protocols of public debate are observed. Free speech protections also normally do not apply to the unauthorized or unacknowledged use of the words of others or to the violation of certain standards of privacy, including commercial trade secrets. It can be stifled through "gag orders" if it endangers national security or exposes "classified" information. It would not be hard to adduce many other instances of the situational limits on the unimpeded exercise of free speech.

One way in which these constraints are traditionally justified is in terms of conflicting rights, whether granted by specific political choices or reflecting prepolitical claims grounded simply in being "human." Other stipulated rights, often claimed to be equally binding, sometimes even deemed "absolute," to security, safety, privacy, dignity, equality, and the like can be invoked as a check on unlimited freedom of speech. Conflicting legal frameworks can also complicate the ways in which the application of the right to free speech functions. When international codes of law are at odds with those of nation-states, the rights of sovereignty or self-government can be adduced to thwart the intrusion of interference from the outside. Similarly, respecting religious laws can challenge the exercise of what is considered blasphemous speech, such as in contexts where, say, "insulting the Prophet" can even justify violent responses, either from the state or fundamentalist believers. These and many other situational constraints have been litigated ad infinitum and continue to vex legal scholars. Comparative analysis shows how much variation there is across different jurisdictions, despite the universal claims of human rights advocates, when it comes to concrete cases.[11]

Less often considered than contexts of application are the teleological contexts in which free speech is also embedded, and it is these that I want to examine a bit more closely in the service of overcoming its fetishization as an independent value in itself. Whether characterized by the loaded term of "weaponization" or not, they bring to the fore the relative status of free speech as always serving other ends. For analytical purposes, although often blurred in practice, teleological contexts can be divided into three general categories, which can be called "objective," "subjective," and "intersubjective."[12] A possible fourth will be suggested at the close of this essay.

The first telos of free speech, and perhaps the most frequently invoked, is the ascertaining of what is called the objective "truth." It has been a staple of free speech defenses since at least John Milton's *Areopagitica* in 1644.[13] Truth claims, advanced either by credentialed, putatively disinterested communities of experts or in the court of public opinion, need to be justified, and to do so is possible only if relevant justifications can be articulated and found persuasive. Precisely how such truths can be ultimately validated, let alone universally acknowledged, is itself a question that can only be addressed if the unconstrained articulation of arguments on all sides is permitted. To the extent that giving reasons and providing evidence is accepted as the way in which truths are reached, rather than through revelation, received wisdom, or authoritarian fiat, free speech is vital to the process of validation. The prior authority of the speaker is less important—in ideal cases, not important at all—than the persuasive power of the ideas spoken, and everyone has the right to speak freely without regard to his or her status or credentials.[14] Without such freedom the open-ended process of testing claims and considering new arguments is short-circuited, and so too are the chances that the quest for truth will come closer to its goal. No pragmatic claim about the socially useful function of conventional wisdom should impede that quest, for as that most perspicacious of utilitarians, John Stuart Mill, put it, "The usefulness of an opinion is itself a matter of opinion, as disputable, as open to discussion, and requiring discussion as much as the opinion itself."[15]

Here the notion of a community of disinterested scientists tacitly serves as the model for unfettered free speech in the search for truth, whether through procedures of verification or falsification. The metaphor of a Darwinian "survival of the fittest" is often employed to buttress the assumption that truth will ultimately be reached by allowing an unfettered competition of claims. Even critics of the repressive function of toleration in our still unfree society, such as Herbert Marcuse, have acknowledged that "tolerance of free speech is the way of improvement, of progress in liberation, not because there is no objective truth, and improvement must necessarily be a compromise between a variety of opinions, but because there is an objective truth which can be discovered, ascertained only in learning and comprehending that which is and that which can be and ought to be done for the sake of improving the lot of mankind."[16]

But because that goal, *pace* confident rationalists like Marcuse, is often understood to be only asymptotically approachable and the humans who seek it conceded to be fallible, the process of establishing truths is necessarily open-ended and with it the objective function of free speech a permanent condition of its possibility. What is often called "epistemic humility" mandates a recognition of the limits of our quest for certainty. Critique is understood to be inextricably intertwined with truth claims, and any suspension of the right to criticize accepted truth claims jeopardizes the continuing quest for validation. As Mill classically put it in *On Liberty*, "We can never be sure that the opinion we are endeavoring to stifle is a false opinion; and if we were sure, stifling would be an evil still,"[17] because the reasons for arriving at true opinions need to be fully appreciated in addition to the settled truths themselves.

What is to be done once such claims seem to be fully accepted—or at least by virtually everyone—is another matter.[18] Here the function of free speech becomes not so much the discovery of new truths as the protection of those already discovered. Normally, we are reluctant to censor flat earth defenders, even though they are never competitive for positions in geology or astronomy departments (illustrating once again the distinction between free speech and academic freedom). But when it comes to socially sensitive challenges to consensually accepted truth claims—for example, alleged differences in racial capabilities or the denial of the Holocaust—the case for limiting absolute free speech has often seemed stronger. Here, of course, different polities come to different conclusions about those limits, as evidenced by the disparity between the attitudes of America and those of many other countries, beginning with Germany in 1985 and Israel a year later, toward criminalizing Holocaust denial.[19] Restrictive "memory laws" tacitly abandon the assumption that the truth will be reached by the disinterested weighing of competing arguments, acknowledging instead that sometimes a version of "Gresham's Law" operates, in which bad ideas, like bad money, drive out good. Accordingly, skeptics of untrammeled public deliberation, such as the philosopher Brian Leiter, are willing to court charges of paternalism and advocate an "epistemic arbiter," whose sagacious objectivity can presumably cut through the confusion.[20]

What has, in fact, often complicated such efforts is the blurred boundary between objective truths and subjective opinions. There are, of course, many cases of slippage from one category to another. Sometimes allegedly settled truths turn out to be no more than subjective opinions, which are then discredited. Thus eugenic scientists a century ago thought they had discovered verifiable, objective truths about racial differences, whereas we now normally consider them unfounded, indeed pernicious, opinions driven by prejudice. But as demonstrated by the continuing controversy over how to regard Richard J. Herrnstein and Charles Murray's 1994 *The Bell Curve: Intelligence and Class Structure in American Life*, it remains an open question for some, and the proper response to raising it has become a source of vigorous dispute.[21] Conversely, the redescription of objective scientifically confirmed "truths" into mere "opinions" can itself be employed by those with unsavory commercial or political agendas of their own. The campaigns to discredit legitimate research on the carcinogenic effects of smoking and the human causes of climate change show that not every case in which objective truth claims are reduced to subjective opinions can be likened to exposing the pseudoscience of eugenics.

Political implications aside, the slippage between truth seeking and opinion expressing is significant for another reason. Tellingly, in his classic defense of "freedom of thought and discussion" in *On Liberty*, Mill casually mingles objective truths and the opinions of those who may or may not hold them, arguing, for example, that "the opinion which it is attempted to suppress by authority may possibly be true. Those who desire to suppress it, of course, deny its truth; but they are not infallible."[22] Any transition from the putatively disinterested world of scientific and scholarly discovery of truths that transcend personal prejudice to the metaphoric "court of public opinion" implies slippage from the objective to subjective function of free speech. Although still focusing on the collective process of validity testing, the shift from knowledge to opinion inevitably moves the telos of free speech toward the value it has for the subject, which is signaled by calling it "freedom of expression." Article 19 of the Universal Declaration of Human Rights (1948), in fact, explicitly links the two by stating that "everyone has the right to freedom of opinion and expression; this right includes freedom to hold opinions without interference and to seek, receive and impart information and ideas through any media and regardless of frontiers."[23] The International Covenant on Civil and Political Rights (1976) also contains an Article 19, which states: "Everyone shall have the right to hold opinions without interference. . . . Everyone shall have the right to freedom of expression."[24] When the metaphor of the "free marketplace of ideas" is invoked to defend the freedom of expression, the implication is that what survives the competition is not necessarily objective truth but rather a majority consensus of subjective opinions, as is the case with consumer preferences.[25]

Understood in these terms, freedom of speech thus has, in addition to its objective function of justifying truth claims, a second subjective one: fostering the ability of subjects to express their private opinions in public, and ascertaining how widely shared they might become. Such public expression is sometimes even praised for helping make inchoate ideas more coherent, clarifying and fleshing them out, as well as revealing what was hitherto hidden.[26] It implicitly includes the expression of feelings as well as ideas, even if they may sometimes be judged culturally "inappropriate." It also widens the scope of the freedom beyond speech narrowly defined to include nonverbal actions, such as the creation of images and their dissemination through unregulated media.

The right to free expression assumes that communities are made up of persons, individuals, selves, or subjects—each term has its own distinct cargo of meanings—whose interior states of mind and feelings warrant enough respect to justify their public articulation. Its telos is thus the validation of the one whose opinions or feelings are being articulated rather than the search for objective truth. When Mill noted that the threat to free speech came as much, if not more, from the pressure of conventional opinion as state censorship, he observed that "in this age, the mere example of non-conformity, the mere refusal to bend the knee to custom, is itself a service. Precisely because the tyranny of opinion is such as to make eccentricity a reproach, it is desirable, in order to break through that tyranny, that people should be eccentric."[27] Such an argument draws on the assumption that there is an authentic inner self that wants to be heard, a self that is deeper than the superficial outer self that may conform to externally imposed norms. As George Kateb has put it, we have genuine expression "when persons are to some real extent not playing a role or performing a prescribed duty in an institution or a practice, but are as it were independently engaged, even when institutionally situated, in making some essentially mental act of creation or in apprehending one; or in making an unprompted communicative contribution or receiving one."[28] The distinction between role and interior self, to be sure, may well have emerged historically—its birth is sometimes emblematically located in the soliloquies of *Hamlet* or the essays of Montaigne—and has greater purchase in some cultures than others—Western rather than Eastern or bourgeois rather than socialist. But it has become a fundamental assumption of those who understand self-expression as a universal telos of free speech.

Frequently underlying the telos of free expression is what has been called "the autonomy defense,"[29] which draws on a range of related conceptualizations of the subject whose voice seeks to be heard. It has been identified as a self whose quest for self-realization or fulfillment, understood psychologically, requires either direct or sublimated utterance rather than repression. It has also been understood as a more conscious, rational self, whose capacity to argue and provide reasons requires public actualization. Or it has sometimes been conceived as a moral person,[30] whose dignity is recognized only when it is permitted to choose for itself what it wants to say in the public realm.

Whatever the nature of the self whose expression is being defended, the suppression of free speech is widely understood to restrict its full flourishing. Mario Savio, for example, could still draw on the "autonomy defense" thirty years after he led the free speech movement at Berkeley: "Free speech," he argued in 1994, "represents the very dignity of what a human being is.... That's what marks us off from the stones and the stars. You can speak freely.... It is the thing that marks us as just below the angels."[31] Whether or not the realization of human dignity always hangs on the actual exercise of that freedom—are monks who willingly take a vow of silence any less human?—the "autonomy defense" assumes that it can come about only through the making manifest of what is latent, the articulation (or in less forgiving terms, venting) of what has been bottled up. Here a kind of hydraulic model of the self is often assumed: it is healthy to relieve pressure and let it all hang out, no matter what the "it" might be.[32] Otherwise, it suffers the harm of coerced silence.

Or at least, it deserves unimpeded expression if it doesn't in turn cause worse injury to others. Here the famous principle invoked by Mill in *On Liberty* to characterize the limits on individual action of any sort comes into play: "The only purpose for which power can be rightfully exercised over any member of a civilized community, against his will, is to prevent harm to others."[33] Here the injury done to the speaker when his or her right to free expression is abridged is weighed against the harm done to others by the exercise of that very right. Putting aside the ominous implication of what may be done to members of allegedly "uncivilized" communities—and Mill, alas, shared many of the Eurocentric prejudices of his day—what this "harm principle" points to is the third teleological purpose of free speech, which can be called its intersubjective function. Or to its potential dysfunction, as the current debate over "hate speech" makes clear.

Although this is not the place to wrestle in a serious way with the meaning of verbal harm, which goes beyond being offended and, like secondhand smoke, may cause suffering in others besides the intended target, it should be noted how clearly it demonstrates the importance of what speech act theorists since J. L. Austin have called the illocutionary and perlocutionary functions of language as opposed to its locutionary or constative function. That is, what utterances can do or perform rather than merely express or reference must be taken into account in any consideration of their function in specific circumstances. Freedom of speech is, after all, an inadequate defense when invoked to exonerate perjury, fraud, espionage, contempt of court, military insubordination, and other affronts to the norms of certain contexts or domains. Although enabling emotional venting—and thus perhaps defensible on the subjective grounds outlined above—when the intersubjective function of utterances, intended or not, is to demean, humiliate, or intimidate their target, they invite criticism, perhaps, some would argue, suppression. Even if unintended, their ability to undermine the dignity of their target is arguably open to the same challenge. The distinction between sticks and stones, on the one hand, and words or names, on the other, may not always be as watertight as we tell our children.

Precisely when commonplace insults and legitimate criticism cross the threshold into objectionable "hate speech" is, of course, a vexing question. Do I, for example, have the right to shut down or even prosecute an evangelical preacher who screams at me for my sins as an atheist and threatens me with hellfire if I don't repent? Are whole classes of people harmed—say, women in general by pornography—when some of the allegedly harmed class willingly engage in the filming and distribution of their allegedly harmful acts? Does one person who feels offended have the right to deface an artwork that has controversial material? Is there value in being exposed to speech meant to cause harm, and gaining the fortitude, even courage, to survive without calling on the authorities for protection, for example, through trigger warnings at universities? Am I disrespecting the sincerity, indeed perhaps core identities, of those who engage in or positively listen to what makes me uncomfortable, and thus denying them the status of autonomous and responsible agents I would demand for myself?

The answers we give to these and a myriad of other such questions will, of course, vary, but all inevitably acknowledge that the intersubjective, performative functions of speech acts can be as significant as their roles in seeking the truth or expressing subjective opinions. Such performances always take place in specific institutional contexts, domains, or social spaces where they are deemed appropriate or not. To succeed, they will need what speech act theorists call the "felicity conditions" that can produce the outcomes they intend (for example, only the authority of a church or state will give the declaration "I pronounce you man and wife" perlocutionary force). What is permitted to be said on the theatrical stage, where artistic license prevails, might be prohibited in commercial speech, where truth in advertising is mandated. What is allowed on the Internet, where rumors fly, may be forbidden in a courtroom, where hearsay is discounted. The difference, mentioned before, between freedom of speech and academic freedom acknowledges the importance of context in determining limits, if any, on speaking freely.[34]

There are, to be sure, instances when the illocutionary intention of the speaker is less important than the unintended consequences of the speech act, which can sometimes result from a blurring of the domains in which they are performed. In some contexts, to take what may seem like a counterintuitive example, what can be called "love speech" has also been deemed offensive or inciting. It is not by chance that expressions of same-sex affection were once called, in the famous phrase of Lord Alfred Douglas, "the love that dare not speak its name."[35] The self-censorship occurred because the performative force of saying "I love you" in public could apparently extend beyond its immediate target and offend others who heard it. We pride ourselves today at having moved beyond that sensitivity, although there are some bakers who apparently still take offense, while ironically themselves invoking another allegedly absolute right, which protects religious freedom, to defend themselves.

However one weighs the value of self-expression against the cost of injuries to others, there is a more general point that is relevant to our discussion. At the most fundamental level all considerations of freedom of speech, as distinct from freedom of thought or conscience, inevitably imply recognizing its intersubjective function. No issue arises, after all, about regulating whatever someone may shout out in a forest or while taking a shower, as no one can be injured by what they cannot hear. By definition, Robinson Crusoe doesn't have "freedom of speech" until Friday turns up and they begin their halting efforts to communicate. Speaking "freely" implies there is someone who can listen, willingly or not, and can be affected by what you say. The telos of objective truth as the result of a process of judging arguments and evidence involves persuasion, contestation and affirmation, and social interactions, not simply assertion in a void. Although less obvious, the telos of subjective self-expression—as opposed to the retreat into utter silence or an interior monologue—also implies the existence of an audience that witnesses and validates (or not) the public exposure of a hitherto hidden self. Despite its apparent stress on subjective isolation, the autonomy argument tacitly invokes intersubjective recognition. It is tacitly present when the rational self—or moral person—gives itself laws or governs itself rather than simply follows spontaneous impulses. For even the willing application of internal constraints—laws and rules that seem self-determined—implies a subjectivity that is split between desire and obligation, a subjectivity that has tacitly internalized rules from without (as Freud made clear in his explanation of the etiology of the superego). A self, moreover, worthy of being respected for that capacity, a self whose dignity is affirmed by the speech it can exercise freely, is reckoned a free self in the eyes of others, not merely a presocial brute. As in the case of the right to property, which is a social right conveyed by intersubjective recognition and not something that can be reduced to mere possession, the right to free speech, even when based on honoring individual autonomy, inevitably needs external validation. The most negative liberty, prohibiting any interference with the boundaried self, relies on external acknowledgment that such a boundary exists and should be considered inviolable. Otherwise its protection is merely an effect of raw might rather than legitimate right.

Asserting the autonomy of one's self inevitably necessitates, moreover, the possibility if not actuality of the autonomy of others. Demanding that one's own self deserves realization through unfettered expression entails respecting a comparable need in others. When cast in terms of an abstract right, it implies reciprocity, the obligation to listen as well as the opportunity to speak.[36] When opinions are voiced publicly, rather than merely held in private, they tacitly entail the willingness to hear out other opinions in turn (or at least to let others hear them unimpeded). For some democratic theorists, such as Alexander Meikeljohn, they protect a listener's ability to learn from the information supplied by others.[37] The obligation to listen is perhaps most exigent in the special case, so crucial to human rights discourse, of a traumatized or victimized self whose injury is compounded by the silencing of its suffering, and thus cries out to be heard.

Other defenders of free speech who more robustly understand its function in terms of enabling deliberative democracy, such as Robert Post, stress a more active link between personal autonomy and collective self-government.[38] Only when citizens are involved in the process of governing, feeling responsible for the promulgation of the laws that constrain them, can a genuine democracy based on legitimate authority be achieved. According to George Kateb, learning to suffer stoically the outrageous, even offensive speech of others, rather than demanding state censorship, is a mark of civil courage, which "may be part of the character of the good democratic individual, and part, also, of the character of the good democratic citizen."[39]

Even when the essence of democratic interaction is understood to be ongoing dissensus, adversarial contestation rather than collaboration, the role of unregulated speech is vital.[40] Rather than understanding politics as a search for a singular truth, which is frustrated by the interference of ideological and propagandistic distortions calling for the intervention of an "epistemic arbiter," an agonistic version of politics accepts the cacophony of competing claims as a value in itself. It even acknowledges a certain role for shading the truth and perhaps even occasional mendacity in the struggle for power that politics at its most democratic inevitably entails.⁴¹ If commentators like Post and Stanley Fish are right in cautioning us against conflating academic freedom and the freedom of speech, we should also pause before reducing politics to a scholarly debate about truths that once discovered need to be protected against their illegitimate debunking. Analogies to courts of law with their procedural limits on the admissibility of evidence and search for a clear-cut judgment of guilt or innocence are likewise dubious. As shown by the example of criminalizing Holocaust denial, which opened the door for nationalist restrictions on other controversial depictions of the past, good intentions in restricting free speech on the basis of upholding the truth often have disastrous unexpected consequences.⁴²

Perhaps a better way to flesh out this argument will require us to add a fourth function to the tripartite telos of free speech as we have described it. For it can be said to include more than the objective quest for truth, more than the public expression of autonomous interiority, more than the felicitous outcome of intersubjective performativity. It can also be understood as enabling the enrichment of meaning, thus serving more a hermeneutic purpose than an epistemic, expressive, or performative one. Not all speech, after all, aims at producing new knowledge or adjudicating competing truth claims.⁴³ Not all expression reveals subjective interiority. What is performed by language is not always merely a practical outcome, such as the declaration of a war, the humiliation of a foe, or a commitment to a friend. A significant portion—how much is, of course, impossible to measure with any confidence—seeks to reveal or disseminate new ways of interpreting and making sense of the world, as well as unsettling conventional ones. Its locus is what we generally call culture rather than nature, and because there are many different cultures (and subcultures within them), it is pluralist rather than unitary. For all its potential impact on individuals, it transcends their subjective concerns and desires.

It is for this reason that we often grant to speech that is situated in an aesthetic frame the free expression of transgressive—not necessarily pleasing or even beautiful—content that in other contexts would be restricted. What I have elsewhere called "the aesthetic alibi" is, to be sure, sometimes invoked by those who have ulterior, often political motives, which they hide behind the screen of artistic license.⁴⁴ But allowing special freedom to aesthetic expression signifies an awareness of the hermeneutic telos of free speech in general. For the standard of judging and interpreting art is not epistemic, and new, verified knowledge is not its purpose. Its experiments are not the same as those motivating scientific inquiry in its quest for the truth. Nor is its function performative, at least in the sense of producing a direct perlocutionary effect. As W. H. Auden famously put it in opposing its political instrumentalization, "Poetry makes nothing happen."[45] But it does seek to broaden the range and deepen the possibilities of human experience, understood in the widest sense of the term. To the extent that politics itself has an aesthetic dimension—and one can debate whether this is a virtue or a vice[46]—we should recognize the dangers in delegating responsibility to police public discourse to *soi-disant* arbiters of truth or moral rectitude.

Perhaps an even more fundamental manifestation of the function served by unregulated speech in the quest for meaning involves religious speech, in particular prayer.[47] Although of course theological arguments and scriptural revelations are normally couched in terms of truth claims, however persuasive they may be, the activities that we group under the rubric of "prayer" do not. Whether as a request for something desired, an expression of thanks for what has been given, or simply a means of praising God, prayer is a form of communication that relies on an assumption that the world is charged with meaning and that we can partake in it. It has both an expressive and intersubjective dimension, can be either individual or communal, and have an instrumental or simply affirmative end. But at its heart is the belief that creation in general and human existence in particular are not empty of significance. Attempts have often been made to stifle the prayers of believers from stigmatized faiths or punish those in a community who pray in an unsanctioned or sacrilegious manner; from the perspective of believers, blasphemy can be understood as a kind of hate speech directed toward God. But from that of other faiths or those who dissent entirely from religion, it can imply instead an alternative understanding of the meaning of life and creation. Even more than "epistemic humility," what can be called "hermeneutic humility" informs the freedom of speech that has as its telos the expansion and enrichment of the range of meanings available to us, as well as the critique of existing ones, such as those that appear in the idioms of art and religion.

To return in conclusion to the main issue of this essay, alarm at the recent "weaponizing" of freedom of speech on the right is thus not compelling if we take into account the variety of justifications of unregulated speech that go beyond its putative status as an absolute right. Whether serving the search for objective truth, the unconstrained expression of subjective thoughts and feelings, the enabling of intersubjective, performative interactions, or the expansion and evaluation of cultural meanings, the freedom to speak is always already functional. The answer to the alt-right weaponization is therefore not a retreat into an imagined citadel of purity that values freedom of speech as an *a priori* imperative, understood deontologically rather than consequentially. Nor is it the abandonment of free speech as manifesting "repressive tolerance" in favor of restrictions by *soi-disant* wise "epistemic arbiters" who will curb its abuse and prescribe in advance what is harmless and inoffensive. For not only does such a pseudo-solution raise the age-old question of who will determine the identity of said arbiters, but it also risks backfiring when the power to decide passes to those with different definitions of moral goodness and cognitive truth.

Instead, we need to acknowledge the always already instrumental premise of granting speech its unconstrained exercise, while acknowledging that it inevitably has the power to do both good and ill in the world. Once we understand that free speech is fundamentally a means rather than an end in itself, we can focus on the functions it is designed to fulfil in the arenas where it is suited to fulfill them. They are the ultimate reasons that can allow us to justify it, not its intrinsic value prior to its weaponization. Ironically, it may be precisely because it is always already an instrument rather than intrinsically autotelic that it would be hazardous in the extreme to undermine its power. For the laudable goals it serves—the search for objective truth, the expression of subjective thoughts and feelings, the enabling of intersubjective performativity, and the quest for meaning—would ultimately be thwarted without its exercise. In short, we need once again to emulate Amfortas, the legendary guardian of the Holy Grail, and trust that a weapon that may cause wounds also has the capacity to heal them.

NOTES

Introduction

1. For an insightful survey of the ways in which various thinkers from Nietzsche to the present have dealt with this issue, see Hans Joas, *The Genesis of Values*, trans. Gregory Moore (Chicago, 2000). By calling the issue of genesis and validity "perennial," it may seem as if I am stacking the deck against historicist contextualization, but it can also suggest that some difficult questions continue to generate new answers in new contexts (as Hans Blumenberg would argue).

In some respects, the question of how validity relates to genesis parallels the mind/matter problem in metaphysics, analytic philosophy, and cognitive psychology, which, grosso modo, pits dualist advocates of the irreducibility of consciousness against physicalist or materialist monists. The latter employ terms like "grounding," "dependence," or "supervenience" to contest the former's insistence on the autonomy of mental activity. There are, however, important differences. The discourse concerning genesis and validity focuses on concrete historical or cultural contexts and worries about the relativistic implications of genetic explanations. The mind/matter discourse is more abstract and ahistorical, and looks for universal validity in genetic origins, for example, the hard-wiring of human brains rather than the variations of culturally mediated minds.

2. John Diggins, "The Oyster and the Pearl: The Problem of Contextualization in Intellectual History," *History and Theory* 23, no. 2 (May 1984), 151–169.

3. The reconciliation of divine transcendence and historical immanence presented, of course, a constant challenge to Christian theology as well, which sought to avoid the radical gnostic devaluation of the created world. When the search for the "historical Jesus" explicitly called the doctrine of the Incarnation into question in the nineteenth century, one response was to identify God as an entirely "other" beyond human experience.

4. Dipesh Chakrabarty, *Provincializing Europe: Postcolonial Thought and Historical Difference* (Princeton, N.J., 2000).

5. It would be more accurate to say that Western ideas of aesthetic value had been both assimilated and resisted ever since they were first encountered in other parts of the world. See, for example, the checkered reception of Western ideas of beauty in

Japan beginning in the 1870s with the work of Nishi Amane and Tsubouchi Shōyō, which is traced in Michele Marra, ed., *Modern Japanese Aesthetics: A Reader* (Honolulu, 1999). A major issue was the differentiation of "art" from other spheres of life and the elevation of certain formal qualities into allegedly universal principles.

6. See, for example, Paget Henry, *Caliban's Reason: Introducing Afro-Caribbean Philosophy* (New York, 2000); Emmanuel Chukwudi Eze, *On Reason: Rationality in a World of Cultural Conflict and Racism* (Durham, N.C., 2008).

7. Samuel Moyn and Andrew Sartori, eds., *Global Intellectual History* (New York, 2015). See also Amy Allen, *The End of Progress: Decolonizing the Normative Foundations of Critical Theory* (New York, 2016).

8. The issue of scale and commensuration is a problem for global history in general. See Jan de Vries, "Playing with Scales: The Global, the Micro and the Nano," *Past and Present* 242, supplement 14 (November 2019): 23–36.

9. See Edward Baring, "Ideas on the Move: Context in Transnational Intellectual History," *Journal of the History of Ideas* 77, no. 4 (October 2016): 567–587. His chief example is the archive of neo-scholasticism developed by the papacy in late nineteenth-century Europe, which had an impact on continental European thought.

10. Thus, for example, in 1991 the conservative intellectual historian Gertrude Himmelfarb could bemoan the erosion of those values in a conversation with the chair of the National Endowment of the Humanities (and wife of a future American vice president) Lynne Cheney:

HIMMELFARB: I am so disturbed by the enormous emphasis that is put on race, gender, and class. It not only reduces individuals to categories and confines them within those categories; it makes it difficult for them to see themselves as part of a larger, more elevated, more universal whole. It is this sense of universality that is being denied all the time now.
CHENEY: That there is anything universal.
HIMMELFARB: That there is anything universal. One is a woman or one is a black or one is gay, but one is not part of a larger culture, a culture that transcends these particularities.
CHENEY: There is no such thing as the human condition, so we're told. Only your condition and mine and each individual's.
HIMMELFARB: Exactly.

Gertrude Himmelfarb and Lynne V. Cheney, "Conversation: Historian Gertrude Himmelfarb," *Humanities* (May/June 1991), https://www.neh.gov/article/historian-gertrude-himmelfarb.

11. Peter E. Gordon, "Contextualism and Criticism in the History of Ideas," in *Rethinking Modern European Intellectual History*, ed. Darrin M. McMahon and Samuel Moyn (Oxford, 2014), 47.

12. This is not the place to attempt a thorough exploration of Adorno's views on the validity/genesis problem, but an important tension in his positions needs to be

highlighted. He resisted, as Gordon points out, the reduction of truth value to origin, and he frequently criticized the search for foundations in philosophy as comparable to claims of priority by allegedly autochthonous peoples. And yet at the same time, he also argued that there was always a residue of the nonconceptual in concepts, which suggests that synthetic judgments can never entirely shed their origins outside of themselves. Apparently, he was aware that these two positions were at odds and hoped that his friend Alfred Sohn-Rethel might help him overcome the antinomy. See Stefan Müller-Doohm, *Adorno: An Intellectual Biography*, trans. Rodney Livingstone (London, 2008), 220.

13. Gordon, "Contextualism and Criticism," 51.

14. For a discussion of the full range of "psychologistic" challenges to validity claims, see Martin Kusch, *Psychologism: A Study in the Sociology of Philosophical Knowledge* (New York, 1995). "Logicism" has also been used to mean that mathematics is an extension of logic, but here it denotes the antithesis of "psychologism."

15. The search for a mathematical alternative to the polysemic imprecision of vernacular languages is not only a feature of the sciences and social sciences, but also at times the humanities. Several French philosophers, most recently Alain Badiou, have argued that mathematics has ontological meaning. See the discussion in Knox Peden, *Spinoza contra Phenomenology: French Rationalism from Cavaillès to Deleuze* (Stanford, Calif., 2014). Surprisingly, a comparable assumption can be found in certain twentieth-century German thinkers. See Matthew Handelman, *The Mathematical Imagination: On the Origins and Promise of Critical Theory* (New York, 2019), which treats Franz Rosenzweig, Gershom Scholem, and Siegfried Kracauer. At times, the search for a universal ur-language took other forms besides mathematics. See Umberto Eco, *The Search for a Perfect Language*, trans. James Fentress (London, 1995).

16. The idiosyncratic use of the term in the first sense appears in Karl Popper, *The Poverty of Historicism* (London, 1957), where it is used to denigrate pseudoscientific theories of historical development. The more typical use can be found in such works as Friedrich Meinecke, *Die Entstehung des Historismus* (Munich, 1936). When the latter was translated into English, the neologism "historism" was adopted for "historicism."

17. See, most recently, Herman Paul and Adriaan van Veldhuizen, eds., *Historicism: A Travelling Concept* (London, 2020).

18. This is not to deny, of course, that "nature" also experiences temporal changes, such as those evidenced in evolution, just that the pace seems slower than those understood in terms of human history. But, to complicate the opposition still further, there are cataclysmic events in nature that can abruptly undermine the notion of natural stability.

19. Sometimes, as for example in Kant's philosophy, the related but distinct concept of "transcendental" as opposed to "transcendent" signifies a universal mental capacity as opposed to beliefs that derive from a specific culture or tradition. In this version of subjective idealism, context-independent validity is grounded not ontologically but

epistemologically, as a hardwired feature of all human cognition rather than in things themselves.

20. The term is often associated with the Frankfurt School, but it was a tool of earlier figures in the tradition of dialectical thought. For one account, see Andrew Buchwalter, "Hegel, Marx and the Concept of Immanent Critique," *Journal of the History of Philosophy* 29, no. 2 (1991): 253–279.

21. As illustrated by the lively debate set off by the anthropologist E. E. Evans-Pritchard over the rationality of the belief in witches on the part of the Azande people of Central Africa in his *Witchcraft, Oracles and Magic among the Azande* (Oxford, 1937).

22. E. P. Thompson, *The Making of the English Working Class* (Harmondsworth, 1993), 12.

23. The prime example is Charles Taylor, *The Secular Age* (Cambridge, Mass., 2007). For my critique of his argument, see "Faith-Based History," *History and Theory* 48, no. 1 (2009): 76–84.

24. The Catholic phenomenologist Max Scheler was a prominent defender of this position. See Joas, *Genesis of Values*, chap. 6. Scheler, Joas writes, "puts forward the thesis that 'the person alone is the ultimate *bearer* of values, but in no respect whatsoever is the person a *positor* of values.' Although his ethics focuses on the person, for him the objective existence of the world of values cannot be called into question" (98).

25. Karl Popper, *The Myth of the Framework: In Defense of Science and Rationality* (London, 1996).

26. It can also be asked if there is cognitive "progress" or a "learning process" that occurs not only in science but also in philosophy, aesthetics, or ethics. For a consideration of the issues in the first of these areas, see Russell Blackford and Damien Broderick, eds., *Philosophy's Futures: The Problem of Philosophical Progress* (Hoboken, N.J., 2017).

27. Morris Raphael Cohen and Ernst Nagel, *Logic and Scientific Method* (New York, 1934), 388.

28. Reinhart Koselleck, *Sediments of Time: On Impossible Histories*, trans. and ed. Sean Franzel and Stefan-Ludwig Hoffmann (Stanford, Calif., 2018), 8–9.

29. R. G. Collingwood, *The Idea of History* (Oxford, 1994); for a consideration of its argument, see Martin Jay, *Songs of Experience: European and American Variations on a Universal Theme* (Berkeley, 2006), chap. 6.

30. The terms were coined in 1954 by Kenneth Pike. See his *Language in Relation to a Unified Theory of the Structure of Human Behavior* (The Hague, 1971).

31. See David A. Hollinger, ed., *The Humanities and the Dynamics of Inclusion since World War II* (Baltimore, 2006).

32. See Martin Jay, "Vico and Western Marxism," in *Fin-de-Siècle Socialism and Other Essays* (New York, 1988), 67–81.

33. For an account of this debate, see David Simpson, *Situatedness: Or, Why We Keep Saying Where We Are Coming From* (Durham, N.C., 2002). For my response, see

"Speaking Azza," *London Review of Books* 24, no. 23 (November 28, 2002): 32–33. The relationship between language and experience in intellectual history is addressed in John Toews, "Intellectual History after the Linguistic Turn: The Autonomy of Meaning and the Irreducibility of Experience," *American Historical Review* 92, no. 4 (1987): 879–907. The appeal to "experience" as the genetic source of ideas often, however, assumes that the word itself has a univocal meaning. For a challenge to this assumption, see Jay, *Songs of Experience*.

34. For a discussion, see Joas, *Genesis of Values*, chap. 5.

35. This distinction was first developed by Paul Ricoeur, *Freud and Philosophy: An Essay in Interpretation*, trans. Dennis Savage (New Haven, Conn., 1970). He singles out Freud, Marx, and Nietzsche as the three "masters of suspicion" because of their inclination to reduce ideas to their genetic origins.

36. Edmund Husserl, *The Crisis of the European Sciences and Transcendental Phenomenology*, trans. David Carr (Evanston, Ill., 1970).

37. For an influential assessment that he failed, see Jacques Derrida, "'Genesis and Structure' and Phenomenology," in *Writing and Difference*, trans. Alan Bass (Chicago, 1978).

38. For a comparison of their positions, see Margret E. Grebowicz, "Philosophy as Meaningful Science: The Subject and Objective Knowledge in Husserl and Popper," *Philosophical Methodology* (1998), http://www.bu.edu/wcp/Papers/Meth/MethGreb.htm.

39. Daniel Dahlstrom, "Heidegger's Transcendentalism," *Research in Phenomenology* 35 (2005).

40. Dick Pels, *The Intellectual Stranger: Studies in Spokespersonship* (London, 2000), chap. 7.

41. Georg Lukács, *History and Class Consciousness: Studies in Marxist Dialectics*, trans. Rodney Livingstone (Cambridge, Mass., 1971).

42. This is not the place to do justice to this extraordinarily complex issue, but if we generalize from W. E. B. DuBois's celebrated argument about "double consciousness" in *The Souls of Black Folks* (1903), we would have to problematize the possibility of any *soi-disant* vanguard speaking for a minority group as a whole. For insofar as Black Americans have two "souls," it would seem that no metonymic representation can fuse them into a singular, completely coherent unity. And yet, DuBois lauded the role of the "talented tenth" in the struggle for racial justice, which suggested he did recognize the need for a focused leadership. A similar challenge presents itself to diasporic Jews, who also often have double consciousnesses. The Zionist project, we might say, was an attempt to fuse Jewish souls into one, but not without powerful resistance from many who cherished precisely the "alienation" and dual allegiances Zionists sought to overcome.

43. Pels, *The Intellectual as Stranger*, 165, 173.

44. Rainer Forst, *Normativity and Power: Analyzing Social Orders of Justification*, trans. Ciarin Cronin (Oxford, 2017), 3. For a history of the Frankfurt School's efforts

to defend a critical concept of reason, see Martin Jay, *Reason after Its Eclipse: On Late Critical Theory* (Madison, Wis., 2016).

45. Forst, *Normativity and Power*, 4.

46. Walter Benjamin, "The Task of the Translator," in *Selected Writings*, vol. 1, *1913–1916*, ed. Marcus Bullock and Michael W. Jennings (Cambridge, Mass., 1996), 253–263.

47. Intellectual historians are often concerned with precisely this possibility. See, for example, Ann Fulton, *Apostles of Sartre: Existentialism in America, 1945–1963* (Evanston, Ill., 1999); Ethan Kleinberg, *Generation Existential: Heidegger's Philosophy in France, 1927–1961* (Ithaca, N.Y., 2005); Jennifer Ratner-Rosenhagen, *Nietzsche in America: A History of an Icon and His Ideas* (Chicago, 2012).

48. See, for example, the vigorous and ongoing debate launched by Michael Fried's celebrated essay "Art and Objecthood" in *Artforum* in 1967. The essay is republished with significant new material as *Art and Objecthood: Essays and Reviews* (Chicago, 1998). For a representative collection of responses to Fried's work in general, see Jill Beaulieu, Mary Roberts, and Toni Ross, eds., *Refracting Vision: Essays on the Writing of Michael Fried* (Sydney, 2000).

49. For a discussion of the difference between a work's "inventive" impact on later readers and its "originality" in its context of genesis, see Derek Attridge, "Context, Idioculture, Invention," *New Literary History* 42, no. 4 (Autumn 2011), 681–699.

50. For a mobilization of Latour's terminology to defend the capacity of literature to transcend its genetic context, see Rita Felski, "'Context Stinks,'" *New Literary History* 42, no. 4 (Autumn 2011), 573–591.

51. This anthropological reevaluation of "primitive" works that modernists had praised only for their universal formal qualities occurred more or less in the 1980s. See, for example, James Clifford, *The Predicament of Culture: Twentieth-Century Ethnography, Literature and Art* (Cambridge, Mass., 1988).

52. Although a case can be made for the field as a whole, the issues raised by the pitting of genesis against validity perhaps more frequently appear in European intellectual history than elsewhere. It has been easier for ideas whose genesis is located—whether rightly or wrongly—in Europe to assume transcendent status, because their defenders are less likely to be self-conscious about the parochial or marginal status of their origins. Although the recent critique of Eurocentrism has challenged their assumption of "unmarked" hegemony, it has not entirely undermined confidence in claims of universal validity. In addition, Europeanists have been less beleaguered by charges of elitism than, say, their counterparts in American intellectual history, where the pressures from more populist cultural and social history have been stronger.

It would pay more careful study than I can provide here to explore the differences between the American discipline of European intellectual history and its European counterparts. For an account of the French case, see Antoine Lilti, "Does Intellectual History Exist in France? The Chronicle of a Renaissance Foretold," in McMahon and Moyn, *Rethinking Modern European Intellectual History*, 56–73. One important difference is the respected role played by the history of philosophy within the French departments of philosophy, unlike in America. Questions of genesis and validity are as a result more likely to be posed by philosophers than historians, who incline more to study the history of *mentalités* from a broader cultural or social perspective.

53. For a thoughtful comparison of intellectual and cultural history, which concludes by stressing their supplementary value, see Judith Surkis, "Of Scandals and Supplements: Relating Intellectual and Cultural History," in McMahon and Moyn, *Rethinking Modern European Intellectual History*, 94–111. The distinction between "high" or "difficult" texts and their "low" and "simple" alternatives should, of course, be adopted with caution, but it would be no less problematic to conflate them entirely.

54. Randall Collins, *The Sociology of Philosophies: A Global Theory of Intellectual Change* (Cambridge, Mass., 1998), 19.

55. Dominick LaCapra, "Rethinking Intellectual History and Reading Texts," in *Modern European Intellectual History: Reappraisals and New Perspectives*, ed. Dominick LaCapra and Steven L. Kaplan (Ithaca, N.Y., 1982), 47–85. Whereas the documentary treatment of texts sees them as inert vehicles for the transmission of data about the past, the worklike approach treats them as dialogic partners still capable of exerting their influence on later generations, including our own. Latour's notion of texts or artwork as "non-human actors" fits with this approach. As Lynn Hunt notes, "It is no accident that, in America, literary influences first emerged in intellectual history, with its focus on documents that are texts in the literary sense, but cultural historians who work with documents other than great books have not found literary theory to be especially relevant." Hunt, introduction to *The New Cultural History*, ed. Lynn Hunt (Berkeley, Calif., 1989), 15.

56. Compare, for example, the claim by H. Stuart Hughes in his classic study *Consciousness and Society: The Reorientation of European Social Thought, 1890–1930* (New York, 1958) that "the only fitting attitude" for the intellectual historian "is that of the cosmopolitan, detached intellectual" (26), with his admission that "a number of the protagonists of the present study have influenced the presuppositions of the study itself. This duality of function is quite intentional. I should not have chosen to write about these men at all had I not believed that they could help us to a more intelligent consideration of man in society" (25). For a discussion, see Michael S. Roth, "Narrative as Enclosure: The Contextual Histories of H. Stuart Hughes," *Journal of the History of Ideas* 51, no. 3 (1990): 505–515.

57. The importance of transference in Freud's sense of repetition of past feelings and displacement onto current surrogates for all historians has been emphasized by Dominick LaCapra. See, for example, his "Is Everyone a Mentalité Case? Transference and the Culture Concept," *History and Theory* 23, no. 3 (1984): 296–311.

58. This abstention often frustrates critics who insist every historical narrative should be explicitly partisan. For example, the Marxist literary critic Terry Eagleton once called *The Dialectical Imagination* "a masterly account which like most of its author's work suffers from not arguing a case." "In the Twilight Zone," *London Review of*

Books 16, no. 9 (May 12, 1994), https://www.lrb.co.uk/the-paper/v16/n09/terry-eagleton/in-the-twilight-zone.

59. Siegfried Kracauer, *History: The Last Things Before the Last* (New York, 1969). For my gloss on the argument of this book, see Martin Jay, "The Extraterritorial Life of Siegfried Kracauer," in *Permanent Exiles: Essays on the Intellectual Migration from Germany to America* (New York, 1985), 152–197.

60. This formulation is still in common use to describe the task of intellectual historians. See, for example, Daniel T. Rodgers, "Paths in the Social History of Ideas," in *The Worlds of American Intellectual History*, ed. Joel Isaac, James T. Kloppenberg, Michael O'Brien, and Jennifer Ratner-Rosenberg (New York, 2017), 302–323.

61. Ian Hunter, "The Contest over Context in Intellectual History," *History and Theory* 58, no. 2 (June 2019): 185–209.

62. The most detailed presentation of White's argument appears in his *Metahistory: The Historical Imagination in 19th-Century Europe* (Baltimore, 1973). For a succinct summary of his argument, see his essay "Formalist and Contextualist Strategies in Historical Explanation," in *Figural Realism: Studies in the Mimesis Effect* (Baltimore, 2000), 43–65.

63. Ian Hunter, "Hayden White's Philosophical History," *New Literary History* 45, no. 3 (Summer 2014), 331–358, where he claims formalism "seeks to preempt the proposed investigation on purely a priori and potentially sectarian grounds—by declaring that contextual inquiry must itself be transcendentally prefigured—and in part because those who make it are themselves philosophical historians seeking to protect their discipline from historicization" (334).

64. It was still possible for Fredric Jameson in 1981 to argue that various historical struggles "can recover their original urgency for us only if they are retold within the unity of a single great collective story; only if in however disguised and symbolic a form, they are seen as sharing a single fundamental theme—for Marxism, the collective struggle to wrest a realm of Freedom from a realm of Necessity; only if they are grasped as vital episodes in a single vast unfinished plot." Jameson, *The Political Unconscious: Narrative as a Socially Symbolic Act* (Ithaca, N.Y., 1981), 19–20. Forty years later, the signposts of any "single great collective story" seem to have entirely vanished, replaced by a shambolic assortment of disparate narratives, mostly going in a disheartening direction.

65. Hunter, "Contest over Context," 188.

66. Recently, historians have become more willing to reflect on their own personal stories as themselves relevant contexts in need of interpretation. See Jaume Aurell, "Making History as Contextualizing Oneself: Autobiography as Historiographical Intervention," *History and Theory* 54 (May 2015): 244–268.

67. According to Hunter, "what runs through these different iterations of the critique of context is not some common theoretical doctrine but something quite different and far more fundamental: namely, a particular kind of ethical work. This is a work

performed on the self by the self, through which, by suspending the facticity of historical events and records, the ethical labor transforms them into symbols of the dialectical development of the human spirit, and brings the philosophical historian into existence as the personification of that spirit." "Contest over Context," 208.

68. Ibid., 209.

69. Martin Jay, ""Should Intellectual History Take a Linguistic Turn? Reflections on the Habermas-Gadamer Debate," in *European Intellectual History: Reappraisals and New Perspectives*, ed. Dominick LaCapra and Steven L. Kaplan (Ithaca, N.Y., 1982), reprinted in Martin Jay, *Fin-de-Siècle Socialism and Other Essays*.

70. Martin Jay, "Two Cheers for Paraphrase: The Confessions of a Synoptic Intellectual Historian," *Stanford Literature Review* 3 (Spring 1986), reprinted in Jay, *Fin-de-Siècle Socialism and Other Essays*, 52–66.

71. Martin Jay, "Name-Dropping or Dropping Names? Modes of Legitimization in the Humanities," in *Theory Between the Disciplines*, ed. Martin Kreiswirth and Mark Cheetham (Ann Arbor, Michigan, 1990), republished in Martin Jay, *Force Fields: Between Intellectual History and Cultural Critique* (New York, 1993), 167–179.

72. Martin Jay, "The Textual Approach to Intellectual History," in *Force Fields*, 158–166; Martin Jay, "Modernism and the Specter of Psychologism," *Cultural Semantics: Keywords of Our Time* (Amherst, Mass., 1998), 165–180; Martin Jay, "Can There Be National Philosophies in a Transnational World?," in *Essays from the Edge: Parerga and Paralipomena* (Charlottesville, Va., 2011), 162–185.

73. Martin Jay, *Adorno* (Cambridge, Mass., 1985), 14–15.

74. Previously published only as Martin Jay, "Pretensiones desvergonzadas y preguntas abomindables. La historia intellectual come juicio del pasado," *Prismas* (Buenos Aires, Argentina) 11 (2007), 153–157. The translation was by Leonel Livchits. *Prismas*, on whose international board I have sat for two decades, is published by the Centro de Historia Intelectual de la Universidad Nacional de Quilmes.

75. It was first published as Martin Jay, "Historical Explanation and the Event: Reflections on the Limits of Contextualization," *New Literary History* 42 (2011), 557–571.

76. For another discussion of its importance, see Martin Jay "Historicism and the Event," in *Against the Grain: Jewish Intellectuals in Hard Times*, eds. Ezra Mendelsohn, Stefani Hoffman, and Richard I. Cohen (New York, 2014), 143–167.

77. Rather than Hegelian, this model is, if anything, Kantian in its echo of the unsublated dialectic of natural causal determinism and the causality of freedom developed in the first two *Critiques*.

78. Martin Jay, "Intention and Irony: The Missed Encounter Between Hayden White and Quentin Skinner," *History and Theory* 52 (February 2013): 32–48. It was followed by short replies by the two protagonists.

79. Martin Jay, "Walter Benjamin and Isaiah Berlin: Modes of Jewish Intellectual Life in the 20th Century," *Critical Inquiry* 43 (Spring 2017), 719–737.

80. Hans Blumenberg, *Paradigms for a Metaphorology*, trans. Robert Savage (Ithaca, N.Y., 2010).

81. Martin Jay, "Against Rigor: Hans Blumenberg on Freud and Arendt," *New German Critique* 132 (November 2017): 123–144.

82. Hans Blumenberg, *Rigorism of Truth: "Moses the Egyptian" and Other Writings on Freud and Arendt*, ed. Ahlrich Meyer, trans. Joe Paul Kroll (Ithaca, N.Y., 2017).

83. See, for example, Hans Blumenberg, "An Anthropological Approach to the Contemporary Significance of Rhetoric," in *After Philosophy: End or Transformation?*, ed. Kenneth Baynes, James Bohman, and Thomas McCarthy (Cambridge, Mass., 1987), 429–458.

84. Martin Jay, "'Hey! What's the Big Idea?' Ruminations on the Question of Scale in Intellectual History," *New Literary History* 48, no. 4 (August 2017): 617–631.

85. For another spirited defense of the value of an updated "history of ideas" approach, see Darrin McMahon, "The Return of the History of Ideas?," in McMahon and Moyn, *Rethinking Modern European Intellectual History*, 13–31.

86. Martin Jay, "Fidelity to the Event? Lukács' *History and Class Consciousness* and the Russian Revolution," *Studies in East European Thought* 3, no. 4 (November 2018): 195–213.

87. Hunter, "Contest over Context," 209.

88. Martin Jay, "Can Photographs Lie? Reflections on a Perennial Anxiety," *Critical Studies* 2 (September 2016): 6–19. A slightly expanded version will appear in Peter Enneson, ed., *Seeking Stillness: Festschrift for Lambert Zuidervaart* (forthcoming). For my work on visuality, see in particular *Downcast Eyes: The Denigration of Vision in Twentieth-Century Thought* (Berkeley, Calif., 1994); for mendacity, see *The Virtues of Mendacity: On Lying in Politics* (Charlottesville, Va., 2010).

89. Martin Jay, "Sublime Historical Experience: Real Presence and Photography," *Journal of the Philosophy of History* 12 (2018), 432–449.

90. Martin Jay, "Sociology and the Heroism of Modern Life," in *The Cambridge History of Modern Thought*, vol. 2, ed. Peter E. Gordon and Warren Breckman (Cambridge, 2019), 18–43.

91. Martin Jay, "Historical Truth and the Truth of Historians," in *Integrity, Honesty, and Truth Seeking*, ed. Christian B. Miller and Ryan West (Oxford, 2020), 240–273.

92. For an earlier application of this argument in a response to Hayden White and Carlo Ginzburg on the historiography of the Holocaust, see Martin Jay, "Of Plots, Witnesses and Judgments," in *Probing the Limits of Representation: Nazism and the "Final Solution,"* ed. Saul Friedlander (Cambridge, Mass., 1992), 97–107.

93. Martin Jay, "Theory and Philosophy: Antonyms in Our Semantic Field?," *Philosophy and Rhetoric* 53, no. 1 (2020), 6–20.

94. Martin Jay, "For Theory," *Theory and Society* 25, no. 2 (1996), republished in Jay, *Cultural Semantics*, 15–30.

95. For a discussion of this danger, see Martin Jay, "Taking on the Stigma of Inauthenticity: Adorno's Critique of Genuineness," in *Essays from the Edge: Parerga and Paralipomena* (Charlottesville, Va., 2011), 9–21.

96. For a critique of the potential complacency in the reliance on future historical judgment, which tacitly assumes that history somehow progresses toward the light, see Joan Wallach Scott, *On the Judgment of History* (New York, 2020).

Chapter 1

1. Theodor W. Adorno, "Aspects of Hegel's Philosophy," in *Hegel: Three Studies*, trans. Shierry Weber Nicholsen (Cambridge, Mass., 1993), 1–2.

2. David Simpson, *Situatedness, or, Why We Keep Saying Where We're Coming From* (Durham, N.C., 2002).

3. Peter Gordon, "Continental Divide: Ernst Cassirer and Martin Heidegger at Davos, 1929—An Allegory of Intellectual History," *Modern Intellectual History* 1, no. 2 (August 2004): 219–248.

4. Tony Judt, *Past Imperfect: French Intellectuals, 1944–1956* (Berkeley, Calif., 1992); Mark Lilla, *The Reckless Mind: Intellectuals in Politics* (New York, 2003); Richard Wolin, *The Seduction of Unreason: The Intellectual Romance with Fascism from Nietzsche to Postmodernism* (Princeton, N.J., 2004).

5. Martin Jay, *Songs of Experience: Modern American and European Variations on a Universal Theme* (Berkeley, Calif., 2005).

6. F. R. Ankersmit, *Sublime Historical Experience* (Stanford, Calif., 2005).

7. Cited in ibid., 120. Translation emended.

Chapter 2

Note to epigraph: Randall Collins, *The Sociology of Philosophies: A Global History of Intellectual Change* (Cambridge, Mass., 1998), 19.

1. For a convenient summary of the main arguments of Skinner and his school, see the essays collected in James Tully, ed., *Meaning and Context: Quentin Skinner and His Critics* (Oxford, 1988). For another critical account, which distinguishes between Skinner's stress on intentionality expressed through prevailing conventions and Pocock's on linguistic paradigms without authorial intention, see Mark Bevir, "The Role of Contexts in Understanding and Explanation," in *Begriffsgeschichte, Diskursgeschichte, Metapherngeschichte*, ed. Hans Erich Bödecker (Göttingen, 2002), 159–208. Among other distinguished historians and political theorists often included in the Cambridge School are John Dunn, Richard Tuck, Anthony Pagden, Stefan Collini, and David Armitage.

There have, of course, been other prominent exponents of contextualization in intellectual history, for example, Fritz Ringer, who draws on the work of Pierre Bourdieu. For a discussion of his position, see Fritz K. Ringer, "The Intellectual Field, Intellectual History and the Sociology of Knowledge"; Charles Lemert, "The Habits of

Intellectuals"; Martin Jay, "Fieldwork and Theorizing in Intellectual History," and Ringer, "Rejoinder to Charles Lemert and Martin Jay," *Theory and Society* 19, no. 3 (1990).

2. Raymond Williams, *Keywords: A Vocabulary of Culture and Society* (Oxford, 1976). A later edition appeared in 1983, which tacitly revised some of the assumptions criticized by Skinner in "Language and Social Change," in Tully, *Meaning and Context*, 119–132.

3. Skinner, "Motives, Intentions and the Meaning of Texts," in Tully, *Meaning and Context*, 76.

4. Perhaps the one place in which the relativist implications of radical contextualism have vexed historians is in the history of science. In particular, Thomas Kuhn's work a generation ago on scientific revolutions undercut the time-honored notion of scientific progress toward a closer and closer approximation of the truth about the natural world.

5. William H. Sewell, Jr., *The Logics of History: Social Theory and Social Transformation* (Chicago, 2005), 10.

6. John Lewis Gaddis, *The Landscape of History: How Historians Map the Past* (Oxford, 2002), 97.

7. See, for example, Dominick LaCapra, "Rethinking Intellectual History and Reading Texts," in *Modern European Intellectual History: Reappraisals and New Perspectives*, ed. Dominick LaCapra and Steven L. Kaplan (Ithaca, N.Y., 1982).

8. Hayden White, "Formalist and Contextualist Strategies in Historical Explanation," *Figural Realism: Studies in the Mimesis Effect* (Baltimore, 1999), 51.

9. Vincent Crapanzano, "On Dialogue," in *The Interpretation of Dialogue*, ed. Tullio Maranhão (Chicago, 1990), 286.

10. Skinner, "A Reply to My Critics," in Tully, *Meaning and Context*, 281.

11. Dominick LaCapra, *Soundings in Critical Theory* (Ithaca, 1989), 203.

12. Pocock acknowledges this possibility when he says that Burke's critique of the French Revolution can be read in the context of either common law or political economy. See his "The Political Economy of Burke's Analysis of the French Revolution," in *Virtue, Commerce and History: Essays in Political Thought and History, Chiefly in the Eighteenth Century* (Cambridge, 1985), 193–214.

13. In my own work, I have sometimes employed this approach, for example, in my Modern Masters volume *Adorno* (London, 1984), where I sought to situate his work in a force field of constitutive and teleological impulses, including the later impact of deconstruction.

14. Skinner, "Reply to My Critics," 274.

15. Skinner, "Some Problems in the Analysis of Political Thought and Action," in Tully, *Meaning and Context*, 113.

16. Kenneth Minogue raises this issue in his discussion of Skinner's influential work *The Foundations of Modern Political Thought*: "We learn in the *Foundations* much about arguments advanced by this writer or that, but hardly anything about the audience...."

The audience is the great missing character of the *Foundations*, especially in the second volume." "Method in Intellectual History: Skinner's *Foundations*," in Tully, *Meaning and Context*, 189.

17. Martin Jay, "Historicism and the Event," in *Against the Grain: Jewish Intellectuals in Hard Times*, ed. Ezra Mendelsohn, Stefani Hoffman, and Richard I. Cohen (New York, 2014), 143–167.

18. Claude Romano, *Event and World*, trans. Shane Mackinlay (New York, 2009); *Event and Time*, trans. Stephen E. Lewis (New York, 2013).

19. Romano, *Event and World*, 34.

20. Ibid., 38 and 41.

21. Ibid., 46.

22. Ibid., 165.

23. Slavoj Žižek, *The Puppet and the Dwarf: The Perverse Core of Christianity* (Cambridge, Mass., 2003), 160.

24. Romano, *Event and World*, 52. For a discussion of the various meanings of "experience," some of which conform to Romano's definition, see Martin Jay, *Songs of Experience: Modern European and American Variations on a Universal Theme* (Berkeley, 2004).

25. Romano, *Event and World*, 212.

26. Ibid., 62.

27. For a helpful account, see Frederick C. Beiser, *The Fate of Reason: German Philosophy from Kant to Fichte* (Cambridge, Mass., 1987).

28. Hannah Arendt, *The Life of the Mind*, vol. 2, *Willing* (New York, 1978), 110.

29. Romano, *Event and World*, 152.

30. Collins, *Sociology of Philosophies*, 19.

31. Friedrich Nietzsche, *Beyond Good and Evil*, trans. Marianne Cowen (Chicago, 1955), 230.

32. For my attempt to unravel some of them, see Martin Jay, "The Textual Approach to Intellectual History," in *Force Fields: Between Intellectual History and Cultural Critique* (New York, 1993), 158–166.

33. F. R. Ankersmit, *Sublime Historical Experience* (Stanford, Calif., 2005), 280. It should be noted that Derrida himself was somewhat uneasy about the label of a contextualist. In his "Letter to a Japanese Friend" of July 1983, he wrote: "The word 'deconstruction,' like all other words, acquires its value only from its inscription in a chain of possible substitutions, in what is too blithely called a 'context.' For me, for what I have tried and still try to write, the word has interest only within a certain context, where it replaces and lets itself be determined by such other words as 'écriture,' 'trace,' 'différance,' 'supplément,' 'hymen,' 'pharmakon,' 'marge,' 'entame,' 'parergon,' etc. By definition the list can never be closed." In *Derrida and Différance*, ed. David Wood and Robert Bernasconi (Evanston, Ill., 1988), 4. Unlike traditional contextualization, the chain of displaced signifiers that interested him is horizontal, reversible, and infinite.

34. Ankersmit, *Sublime Historical Experience*, 280.

Chapter 3

1. For an introduction to Skinner's work, see Kari Palonen, *Quentin Skinner: History, Politics, Rhetoric* (Cambridge, 2003); for White's, see Herman Paul, *Hayden White: The Historical Imagination* (Cambridge, 2011).

2. Hayden White, *Metahistory: The Historical Imagination in Nineteenth-Century Europe* (Baltimore, 1973); Quentin Skinner, *The Foundations of Modern Political Thought*, vol. 1, *The Renaissance*; vol. 2, *The Age of Reformation* (Cambridge, 1978). Skinner's theoretical essays are collected in vol. 1, *Regarding Method*, of his *Visions of Politics* (Cambridge, 2002).

3. For an overview of the fortunes of the "linguistic turn" in historical studies in general, see Judith Surkis, "When Was the Linguistic Turn? A Genealogy," *American Historical Review* 117, no. 3 (June 2012): 700–722. Interestingly, neither White nor Skinner figures in her account.

4. Palonen, *Quentin Skinner*, 169.

5. White, to be sure, did invoke Austin in his account of "Writing in the Middle Voice," *Stanford Literature Review* 9, no. 2 (Fall 1992): 187, where he claimed that Barthes's notion of intransitive writing somehow was like Austin's notion of the performative dimension of speech acts. Here he tacitly agreed with Skinner's stress on intentionality as entailed in the act, not a motive prior to it, but didn't develop its implications.

6. White more recently has sought to overcome the stark opposition between formalism and contextualism in considering, for example, the approach of the New Historicists. See his "Formalist and Contextualist Strategies in Historical Explanation," in *Figural Realism: Studies in the Mimesis Effect* (Baltimore, 1999), 43–65. But his own work has remained indifferent to contextualist explanations.

7. Michael Roth, "Cultural Criticism and Political Theory: Hayden White's Rhetorics of History," *Political Theory* 16, no. 4 (November 1988): 639–640.

8. Quentin Skinner, "Some Problems in the Analysis of Thought and Action," in *Meaning and Context: Quentin Skinner and His Critics*, ed. James Tully (Oxford, 1988), 111–112. For an argument that says Skinner sometimes confuses the two, see Peter J. Steinberger, "Analysis and History of Political Thought," *American Political Science Review* 103, no. 1 (February 2009): 137.

9. Skinner, "Motives, Intentions, and the Interpretations of Texts," in Tully, *Meaning and Context*.

10. Ibid., 76. Steinberger distinguishes between a stronger and weaker version of Skinner's intentionalist argument, acknowledging that it is the latter that Skinner protests he upholds ("Analysis and History," 138).

11. See Chapter 2. See also Steinberger, "Analysis and History," for several questions concerning the relevance of speech act theory for written texts, which I did not raise.

12. See Jørgen Pederson, "Habermas' Method: Rational Reconstruction," *Philosophy of the Social Sciences* 38 (December 2008): 157–189.

13. To do so, however, might well be construed as less the historian's task than that of the social critic. Habermas, whose rational reconstructions are designed with a normative standard in mind, recognizes the distinction in his essay "History and Evolution," *Telos* 39 (Spring 1979).

14. Louis Althusser, *Politics and History: Montesquieu, Rousseau, Hegel and Marx*, trans. Ben Brewster (London, 1972).

15. Steinberger, "Analysis and History," 142.

16. James Clifford, *The Predicament of Culture: Twentieth-Century Ethnography, Literature, and Art* (Cambridge, Mass., 1988), 270. I cited this passage in *Downcast Eyes: The Denigration of Vision in Twentieth-Century French Thought* (Berkeley, Calif., 1993), 17, as a justification for my construction of an anti-ocularcentric discourse that might not have been consciously intended by some of those who participated in its articulation.

17. In celebrated cases like that of Martin Heidegger, a lively literature has arisen debating the relevance or lack thereof of his Nazi political allegiance for his philosophy.

18. White, *Metahistory*, 37.

19. There is, of course, an immense literature on Socratic irony. For a challenging discussion that contrasts it with Platonic, see Alexander Nehamas, *The Art of Living: Socratic Reflections from Plato to Foucault* (Berkeley, 2000).

20. White, *Metahistory*, 37.

21. White, *Tropics of Discourse: Essays in Cultural Criticism* (Baltimore, 1978), 208.

22. On the issue of terminal points, see my essay "When Did the Holocaust End? Reflections on Historical Objectivity" in *Refractions of Violence* (New York, 2003).

23. Romantic irony was most clearly developed in Friedrich Schlegel's *Über die Unverständlichkeit* of 1800 and elucidated in such works as K. W. F. Solger's *Erwin* of 1815. Often, to be sure, ironic skepticism went along with a residual utopian hope expressed in allegorical terms. For a discussion of these ambiguities, see Marshall Brown, *The Shape of German Romanticism* (Ithaca, N.Y., 1979), 90–105.

24. White, *Metahistory*, 37.

25. See, for example, Paul de Man, "The Concept of Irony," in *Aesthetic Ideology*, ed. Andrzej Warminski (Minneapolis, 1996); Kevin Newmark, *Irony on Occasion: From Schlegel and Kierkegaard to Derrida and de Man* (New York, 2012). Other students of Romantic irony, in particular the version defended by Friedrich Schlegel, have read its implications in less negative terms. See, for example, Gerald N. Izenberg, *Impossible Individuality: Romanticism, Revolution and the Origins of Modern Selfhood, 1787–1802* (Princeton, N.J., 1992), 55–67. He identifies passages in Schlegel's work that contradict his identification of irony with the defeat of meaning, for example, "true irony requires that there be not simply striving after infinity but also possession of infinity" (cited from his *Notebooks* on 58).

26. de Man, "Concept of Irony," 179, 184.

27. Newmark, *Irony on Occasion*, 11.

28. Richard Rorty, *Contingency, Irony, and Solidarity* (Cambridge, 1989), 74. For a discussion of his position, see Brad Taylor, *Rorty and Kierkegaard on Irony and Moral Commitment: Philosophical and Theological Connections* (London, 2006).

29. F. R. Ankersmit, *Sublime Historical Experience* (Stanford, Calif., 2006), 42. The theory of metaphor Ankersmit argues Rorty adopts is derived from Donald Davidson, which he describes as a "catastrophic" use of language involving "an intervention into language from *above* or from *outside* effecting a small rupture in the normal use of language that may, at least for a certain part of language, announce a new dispensation" (37). It is not hard to see parallels with de Man's stress on the importance of parabasis and anacoluthon.

30. Two critics of Romantic irony were Mikhail Bakhtin and Henri Lefebvre, who, to be sure, at certain times in their careers found virtues in a more Socratic alternative, which gets beyond subjective self-indulgence and functions to expose ideological delusion. See the discussion in Michael E. Gardiner, "Post-Romantic Irony in Bakhtin and Lefebvre," *History of the Human Sciences* 25, no. 3 (July 2012): 51–69.

31. White, *Metahistory*, 231.

32. White, *Tropics of Discourse*, 281. Italics in original. In "The Concept of Irony," de Man explicitly invokes catachresis, "the ability of language catachrestically to name anything, by false usage, but to name and thus to posit anything language is willing to posit" (173).

33. White, *Metahistory*, xii.

34. Ibid., 434.

35. White, *Tropics of Discourse*, 23. In reflecting on this argument, Hans Kellner recalls Nietzsche's observation that the will cannot will backward and change the past. See his "Triangular Anxieties: The Present State of European Intellectual History," in *Modern European Intellectual History: Reappraisals and New Perspectives*, ed. Dominick LaCapra and Steven L. Kaplan (Ithaca, N.Y., 1982), 136.

36. Carlo Ginzburg, "Just One Witness," in *Probing the Limits of Representation: Nazism and the "Final Solution,"* ed. Saul Friedlander (Cambridge, Mass., 1992), 87–92.

37. See, for example, the trenchant review of *Metahistory* by John S. Nelson in *History and Theory* 14 (1975).

38. Eva Domanska, "Hayden White: Beyond Irony," *History and Theory* 37, no. 2 (1998): 173–181. One might also argue that by granting the contemporary historian the sovereign power to will a particular emplotment, White was duplicating the elevation of the subjective consciousness in Romantic irony over the undetermined reality facing him.

39. Skinner, "A Reply to My Critics," in Tully, *Meaning and Context*, 270–271.

40. Skinner, "The Missing History: A Symposium," *Times Literary Supplement*, June 23, 1989, 690, cited in Palonen, *Quentin Skinner*, 98.

41. Skinner, "Reply to My Critics," 281.

42. Derrida, *Limited Inc.*, ed. Gerald Graff (Evanston, Ill., 1988), 18.

43. Whether or not the immediate "experience" of actors or witnesses in history is itself the sufficient target for conceptualizing what historians try to recreate is itself a vexed question. I have tried to address it in *Songs of Experience: Modern American and European Variations on a Universal Theme* (Berkeley, 2005), chap. 6.

44. Skinner, "Some Problems in the Analysis of Political Thought and Action," in *Meaning and Context*, 103. He is here characterizing a position that he once erroneously held but has since discarded.

45. Jacques Derrida, *Specters of Marx: The State of the Debt, the Work of Mourning, and the New International*, trans. Peggy Kamuf (New York, 1994). One might also note that many synchronic analyses of the workings of society draw on the ironic implications of unintended consequences, whether for good or ill. Thus, for example, ever since Bernard de Mandeville's *Fable of the Bees*, the idea that private vices can lead to public virtues has justified unregulated market behavior. Ethical theodicies of one sort or another also find a way to turn partial evil into a more general good. In short, the road to heaven can be paved with bad intentions.

46. In intellectual history, to stay with Skinner's main area of interest, the dissolution of a single authorial intention, expressed in his or her textual record, into the maelstrom of different intentions that make up a tradition inevitably involves unintended consequences. This is true not only when the proper name is subsumed in the tradition—say, Locke and liberalism or Machiavelli and republicanism—but even when it is retained, as, for example, in Marxism or Freudianism. Can, after all, the history of Christianity be written without ironic reference to the unrealized intentions of its founding figure?

47. Another way to make this point would be to adopt the distinction made by Jürgen Habermas between "social integration," based on communicative interaction, and "system integration," based on impersonal steering mechanisms like money and bureaucratic rationality. As Seyla Benhabib has noted, "Whereas system integration can occur even when there is a *discrepancy* between intention and consequence, social integration cannot take place unless action consequences are compatible with the intentions of social actors. It follows that whereas action systems can be analyzed, and in fact can *only* be grasped from the external perspective of the third, of the *observer*, social integration must be analyzed from the *internal* perspective of those involved.... In the one case, the consequences of social action proceed 'behind the back of individuals'; in the later case the occurrence of social action needs to be explained via a reconstruction of its meaning as grasped by social actors." *Critique, Norm, and Utopia: A Study of the Foundations of Critical Theory* (New York, 1986), 231. If we assume that historical reconstruction normally entails a dynamic balance between these two perspectives, the necessity of some irony based on unintended consequences is inescapable, but so too is the possibility of outcomes deliberately intended by actors.

Chapter 4

1. George Mosse to the author, Jerusalem, June 4, 1973, in the author's personal collection. Another indication of Berlin's uncomprehending condescension toward Adorno is evident in an anecdote told by Anthony Quinton in his reminiscence of Berlin in *The Book of Isaiah: Personal Impressions of Isaiah Berlin*, ed. Henry Hardy (Woodbridge, 2009), where he recalls, "I think it was Isaiah who overheard him ask one of his lesser refugee colleagues. 'Essen Sie an dem High Table?'" (56). Whether or not this anecdote reveals more about Adorno or about those who found—and in 2009 still find—it amusing is worth pondering.

2. Ramin Jahanbegloo, *Conversations with Isaiah Berlin* (New York, 1992), 49.

3. The reference is worth quoting in full: "Mr. Berlin is here from Oxford on the way to a diplomatic mission in Moscow, which one can reach from England only via South Africa–Constantinople or America-Japan-Vladivostok. He travelled to Canada on an English ship without convey that was attacked twice by German submarines that missed on both occasions, however. They saw the torpedoes explode in the water. The joys of travel. But it is amazing what good spirits Berlin is in, and if what he says regarding England is true, which I have no reason to doubt, then they are truly determined to fight it through over there." Theodor W. Adorno to his father, July 28, 1940, *Letters to His Parents, 1939–1941*, ed. Christoph Gödde and Henri Lonitz, trans. Wieland Hoban (Malden, Mass., 2006), 65–66.

4. Theodor W. Adorno to Max Horkheimer, Hirschegg, August 23, 1951, in Adorno and Horkheimer, *Briefwechsel, 1927–1969*, ed. Christoph Gödde and Henri Lonitz, vol. 4 (Frankfurt, 2006), 41.

5. See Michael Ignatieff, *Isaiah Berlin: A Life* (New York, 1998), 79.

6. Jahanbegloo, *Conversations with Isaiah Berlin*, 22.

7. Cited in Ignatieff, *Isaiah Berlin*, 253. Commenting on this passage, Steven Aschheim contrasts Berlin, who ultimately felt at home in the world, with Benjamin and other émigrés who were deeply alienated from it. See his *At the Edges of Liberalism: Junctions of European, German and Jewish History* (New York, 2012), 18.

8. Of Arendt, Berlin once said, she "produces no arguments, no evidence of serious philosophical or historical thought. It is all a stream of metaphysical associations." Jahanbegloo, *Conversations with Isaiah Berlin*, 82–83. For his anger at Marcuse, see Ignatieff, *Isaiah Berlin*, 253.

9. Isaiah Berlin, "Two Concepts of Liberty," in *Four Essays on Liberty* (Oxford, 1969); Franz Neumann, "The Concept of Political Freedom," in *The Democratic and the Authoritarian State: Essays in Political and Legal Theory*, ed. Herbert Marcuse (New York, 1957), 160–200.

10. See, for example, Joshua L. Cherniss, *A Mind and Its Time: The Development of Isaiah Berlin's Political Thought* (Oxford, 2014). Berlin's role, to be sure, was not always on full public display, as we now know from recently disclosed evidence of his destructive intervention in the career of the Marxist historian Isaac Deutscher. See David

Caute, *Isaac and Isaiah: The Covert Punishment of a Cold War Heretic* (New Haven, Conn., 2013).

11. Jean-Paul Sartre, *Search for a Method* (New York, 1968), 55–56.

12. Isaiah Berlin, *Personal Impressions*, ed. Henry Hardy (Princeton, N.J., 2001). It should be noted that Benjamin confined his impressions to his private writings, adopting a cold impersonality in his published work in which he sought to efface the residues of human warmth through what Adorno once called his "Medusan gaze." Theodor W. Adorno, *Prisms*, trans. Samuel and Shierry Weber (London, 1967), 235. They translate *"Blick"* as "glance," but "gaze" would more accurately capture Medusa's ability to turn someone to stone through her intense stare.

13. Sometimes, of course, proper names come to function as types, in, for example, John Stuart Mill's celebrated contrast of Bentham and Coleridge or George Steiner's pitting of Tolstoy against Dostoyevsky, but the metaphoric resonance is not as powerful as in impersonal binaries, such as the ones discussed in this chapter.

14. Isaiah Berlin, *The Hedgehog and the Fox: An Essay on Tolstoy's View of History*, ed. Henry Hardy (Princeton, N.J., 2013).

15. Ignatieff concludes that his reactions to Nazism and Communism moved him in the direction of the hedgehog during the Cold War: "The fox had discovered that he was a hedgehog after all. He had found 'the one big thing' that was to order his intellectual life thereafter: the theme of freedom and its betrayal." *Isaiah Berlin*, 201. Caute also describes him as a hedgehog because of his obsessive distaste for hedgehogs.

16. Robert Zaretsky, "Sometimes Isaiah Berlin Felt Like a Fox; Sometimes He Felt Like a Hedgehog: On the Sixtieth Anniversary of the Philosopher's Influential Essay," *Jewish Daily Forward*, March 8, 2013, http://forward.com/articles/172000/sometimes-isaiah-berlin-felt-like-a-fox-sometimes/?p=all. The same characterization is made by James Chappel, "The Fox Is Still Running," in Hardy, *Book of Isaiah*, 231–237.

17. Leszek Kolakowski,"The Priest and the Jester," in *Toward a Marxist Humanism: Essays on the Left Today*, trans. Jane Zielonko Peel (New York, 1968), 34. For a further consideration of the category of "jester" or "fool," see Ralf Dahrendorf, "The Intellectual and Society: The Social Function of the 'Fool' in the Twentieth Century," in *On Intellectuals*, ed. Philip Rieff (New York, 1970), 53–56.

18. Perhaps the most significant exception was the running joke he and Scholem shared about a fictitious University of Muri of which they were the only members, but this was a private affair.

19. See, for example, Peter Gay, *Weimar Culture: The Outsider as Insider* (New York, 1968).

20. For a discussion, see Gary A. Abraham, *Max Weber and the Jewish Question: A Study of the Social Outlook of His Sociology* (Urbana-Champaign, Ill., 1992), 8–17.

21. Hannah Arendt, *The Jew as Pariah: Jewish Identity and Politics in the Modern Age*, ed. Ron. H. Feldman (New York, 1978).

22. Indeed, she herself proudly adopted it as a self-designation. See Richard J. Bernstein, *Hannah Arendt and the Jewish Question* (Cambridge, 1997), 21.

23. Howard Eiland and Michael W. Jennings, *Walter Benjamin: A Critical Life* (Cambridge, Mass., 2014), 527, 358–359, 322–323.

24. Theodor W. Adorno, "A l'écart de tous les courants," in *Über Walter Benjamin* (Frankfurt, 1970).

25. Ignatieff reports that in 1950, he learned he was likely to be blackballed for membership in the St. James Club because of anti-Semitism. But rather than denounce it publicly or reject the elitism of clubs per se, he "immediately withdrew his name and was then proposed and accepted for Brooks' club, an even more distinguished establishment just down the street." *Isaiah Berlin*, 176.

26. Aileen Kelly, "A Luminous Personality," in Hardy, *Book of Isaiah*, 109.

27. Noel Annan, "Tributes," in Hardy, *Book of Isaiah*, 10. In his private correspondence, however, there were less attractive indications of what one observer has called "the snobbery Berlin sometimes displays, particularly towards other Jews.... The descriptions he sends to his parents of Jewish fellow passengers on sea voyages are at times positively vicious and provoke the same feeling of unease as his attempts in later life to rid his father's memoir of any taint of Yiddish influence." Jennifer Holmes, "Isaiah Berlin on Himself," in Hardy, *Book of Isaiah*, 239.

28. Ari M. Dubnow, *Isaiah Berlin: The Journey of a Jewish Liberal* (New York, 2013), 51.

29. Susan Sontag, "Camus' Notebooks," in *Against Interpretation* (New York, 1966), 52, 53.

30. Even his close friend Gershom Scholem could recall that when they first met, "Benjamin's attitude towards the bourgeois world was so unscrupulous and had such nihilistic features that I was outraged. He recognized moral categories only in the sphere of living that he had fashioned about himself and in the intellectual world.... Benjamin declared that people like us had obligations only to our own kind and not to the rules of a society we repudiated." *Walter Benjamin: The Story of a Friendship*, trans. Harry Zohn (New York, 1981), 54.

31. For an account of the ways in which Benjamin's bodily experiments were realized in stylistic ones in his autobiographical writings, see Gerhard Richter, *Walter Benjamin and the Corpus of Autobiography* (Detroit, 2000).

32. Mark Lilla, *The Reckless Mind: Intellectuals and Politics* (New York, 2001), 81.

33. Ibid., 92. Compare this assessment with that of Eiland and Jennings in their admiring biography of Benjamin: "With the rejection of Benjamin's submission, the philosophical faculty of the University of Frankfurt brought down on itself a scandal that continues to cast its shadow today.... Presenting an unsurpassed analysis of the historical significance of an ostensibly antiquated artistic form [*Origin of German Trauerspiel*] stands today as one of the signal achievements of twentieth-century literary criticism." *Walter Benjamin*, 233–234.

34. Lilla, *Restless Mind*, 112.

35. Ibid, 199. See also his "Isaiah Berlin Against the Current," *New York Review of Books*, April 25, 2013.

36. Lilla, *Restless Mind*, 209.

37. Ignatieff, *Isaiah Berlin*, 65.

38. Serena Moore, "In the President's Office," in Hardy, *Book of Isaiah*, 118.

39. Russell Jacoby, *Picture Imperfect: Utopian Thought for an Anti-Utopian Age* (New York, 2005), 68–69. Not surprisingly, Jacoby's sympathies are with the "Weimar utopian Jews—intellectuals such as Gershom Scholem, Ernst Bloch, T. W. Adorno and Walter Benjamin" (127).

40. Ibid., 69.

41. Theodor W. Adorno, "Benjamin's *Einbahnstrasse*," in *Notes to Literature*, ed. Rolf Tiedemann, trans. Shierry Weber Nicholsen, vol. 2 (New York, 1992), 322.

42. Eiland and Jennings, *Walter Benjamin*, 484, 485.

43. Russell Jacoby, "Isaiah Berlin—With the Current," *Salmagundi* 55 (1982): 232–241.

44. Walter Benjamin, "The Author as Producer," in *Selected Writings*, vol. 2, *1927–1934*, ed. Michael W. Jennings, Gary Smith, and Howard Eiland, trans. Rodney Livingstone et al. (Cambridge, Mass., 1939), 769.

45. Cited in Ignatieff, *Isaiah Berlin*, 131.

46. Lilla, "Isaiah Berlin Against the Current," 40.

47. Jean Paulhan, *The Flowers of Tarbes, or Terror in Literature*, trans. Michael Syrolinski (Urbana-Champaign, Ill., 2006); Max Weber, "The Social Psychology of the World Religions," in *From Max Weber: Essays in Sociology*, ed. H. H. Gerth and C. Wright Mills (New York, 1958), 285.

48. Ernst Jünger, *The Adventurous Heart: Figures and Capriccios*, ed. Russell Berman, trans. Thomas Friese (Candor, N.Y., 2012).

49. For an example of how such comparative exercises can be frustratingly inconclusive, see Arie Dubnow, "Priest or Jester? Jacob L. Talmon (1916–1980) on History and Intellectual Engagement," *History of European Ideas* 34 (2008): 133–145, which ends by admitting that the question of which characterization is most apt "remains open" (145).

50. Arendt, *Jew as Pariah*, 90.

51. Yuri Slezkine, *The Jewish Century* (Princeton, N.J., 2004).

Chapter 5

1. Primo Levi, *If This Is a Man*, in *The Complete Works of Primo Levi*, ed. Ann Goldstein, trans. Stuart Woolf (New York, 2014), 25.

2. It can, of course, be asked if the cruel absurdity of "L'Univers concentrationnaire," to cite the title of David Rousset's famous 1946 book, was a microcosm of the universe at large, or only an island of malign insanity within it.

3. For a thoughtful analysis of the Book of Job and Primo Levi, see C. Fred Alford, *After the Holocaust: The Book of Job, Primo Levi, and the Path to Affliction* (Cambridge, 2009).

4. Hans Blumenberg, *Rigorism of Truth: "Moses the Egyptian" and Other Writings on Freud and Arendt*, ed. Ahlrich Meyer, trans. Joe Paul Kroll (Ithaca, N.Y., 2018).

5. Hans Blumenberg, *The Legitimacy of the Modern Age*, trans. Robert M. Wallace (Cambridge, Mass., 1983), 117–118. The controversy over Freud's book still rages. For a sampling of recent entries, see Ruth Ginsburg and Ilana Pardes, eds., *New Perspectives on Freud's Moses and Monotheism* (Tübingen, 2006).

6. According to her biographer Elizabeth Young-Brühl, she was given the award "to her great surprise." *Hannah Arendt: For Love of the World* (New Haven, Conn., 1982), 392. As far as I can tell, Arendt never seriously addressed psychoanalysis in her work.

7. For an attempt to discern hidden similarities nonetheless, see José Brunner, "Eichmann, Arendt and Freud in Jerusalem: On the Evils of Narcissism and the Pleasures of Thoughtlessness," *History and Memory* 8, no. 2 (Winter 1982).

8. Often the continuing temptations of sensuality are identified with the appeal of Aaron, Moses's brother, and the worship of the Golden Calf, for example, in Arnold Schoenberg's uncompleted opera *Moses und Aron*. However, Freud did not foreground this dualism in *Moses and Monotheism*.

9. Sigmund Freud, *Moses and Monotheism*, trans. Katherine Jones (New York, 1939), 3.

10. The same sentiment is contained in the similar phrase *Fiat justitia ruat caelum*, with the fall of heaven replacing the perishing of the world. Although sometimes attributed to classical authors, the phrases seem to have been introduced in early modern jurisprudence.

11. Blumenberg, *Rigorism of Truth*, 5.

12. Hannah Arendt, *Eichmann in Jerusalem: A Report on the Banality of Evil* (New York, 1963).

13. Blumenberg, *Rigorism of Truth*, 9, 5.

14. The Organization Todt was primarily an engineering enterprise using forced labor, which had helped build the Autobahn and after 1943 was incorporated into Albert Speer's Armaments and War Administration.

15. For Arendt's role as a public intellectual, see Benjamin Aldes Wurgaft, *Thinking in Public: Strauss, Levinas, Arendt* (Philadelphia, 2016); for a consideration of Freud's interventions, direct and indirect, in public matters, see Eli Zaretsky, *Political Freud: A History* (New York, 2015).

16. According to Odo Marquard, Blumenberg also slept only six nights a week to make up for lost time. See Marquard, "Entlastung vom Absoluten: In Memoriam," in *Die Kunst des Überlebens: Nachdenken über Hans Blumenberg*, ed. Franz Josef Wetz and Hermann Timm (Frankfurt, 1999), 26.

17. See Felix Heidenreich, "Political Aspects in Hans Blumenberg's Philosophy," *Revista de Filosofia Aurora* 27, no. 41 (May-August 2015): 523–539; Angus Nicholls, "Hans Blumenberg on Political Myth: Recent Publications from the Nachlass," *Jerusalem Philosophical Quarterly* 55 (January 2016): 3–33.

18. Hans Blumenberg, "Prospect for a Theory of Non-Conceptuality," in *Shipwreck with Spectator: Paradigm of a Metaphor for Existence*, trans. Steven Rendall (Cambridge, Mass., 1997): 81–102, and *Paradigms for a Metaphorology*, trans. Robert Savage (Ithaca, N.Y., 2010). For accounts, see Rüdiger Zill, "'Substrukturen des Denkens': Grenzen und Perspektiven einer Metapherngeschichte nach Hans Blumenberg," in *Begriffsgeschichte, Diskursgeschichte, Metapherngeschichte*, ed. Hans Erich Bödeker (Göttingen, 2002): 209–258; Birgit Recki, "Der praktische Sinn der Metapher: Eine systematische Überlegung mit Blick auf Ernst Cassirer," in Wetz and Timm, *Die Kunst des Überlebens*, 142–163; David Savage, "Laughter from the Lifeworld: Hans Blumenberg's Theory of Conceptuality," *Thesis Eleven* 94 (2008): 119–131.

19. For one account, see Jan Werner Müller, "On Conceptual History," in Darrin M. McMahon and Samuel Moyn, eds., *Rethinking European Intellectual History* (New York, 2014), 74–93.

20. Blumenberg, *Legitimacy of the Modern Age*; Blumenberg, *Work on Myth*, trans. Robert M. Wallace (Cambridge, Mass., 1985); Blumenberg, *The Genesis of the Copernican World*, trans. Robert M. Wallace (Cambridge, Mass., 1987). Unfortunately, most of his other major works, including *Die Lesbarkeit der Welt* (Frankfurt, 1981); *Lebenzeit und Weltzeit* (Frankfurt, 1986); and *Matthäuspassion* (Frankfurt, 1988); and *Höhlenausgänge* (Frankfurt, 1989), have yet to find their Wallace. In addition to *Shipwreck with Spectator* and *Paradigms for a Metaphorology*, the only other English translations are *Care Crosses the River*, trans. Paul Fleming (Stanford, Calif., 2010) and *The Laughter of the Thracian Woman*, trans. Spencer Hawkins (London, 2015). A selection of his work has, however, recently appeared as *History, Metaphors, Fables: A Hans Blumenberg Reader*, ed. and trans. Hannes Bajohr, Florian Fuchs, and Joe Paul Kroll (Ithaca, N.Y., 2020). For a bibliography of his work and the responses it generated before 1999, see the appendix to Wetz and Timm, *Die Kunst des Überlebens*. There have been several special issues of English-language journals devoted to his legacy, including *Annals of Scholarship* 5, no. 1 (Fall 1987); *Qui Parle* 12, no. 1 (Spring/Summer 2000); and *Telos* 158 (Spring 2012).

21. In one prominent iteration, political theology argues that modern concepts of sovereignty are derived from secularized versions of earlier theological notions of divine will. For two useful compilations that treat this issue, see Creston Davis, John Milbank, and Slavoj Žižek, eds., *Theology and the Political: The New Debate* (Durham, N.C., 2005); Hent de Vries and Lawrence E. Sullivan, eds., *Political Theologies: Public Religions in a Post-Secular World* (New York, 2006). Blumenberg's alternative to the secularization thesis was what he called "re-occupation" in which external forms were retained from earlier periods but were filled with new content, as perennial questions

demanded new answers. These answers were no less "legitimate" than the ones offered before.

22. Blumenberg's critique of Heidegger was apparent in his unpublished *Habilitationsschrift, Die ontologische Distanz* (University of Kiel, 1950).

23. Robert B. Pippen, "Eine Moderne ohne radikale Entzauberung: Zwischen Logos und Mythos," in Wetz and Timm, *Die Kunst des Überlebens*, 99–117.

24. The term "human condition," which needs to be distinguished from the stronger, often normative notion of "human nature," shows a certain commonality with Arendt, whose book with that title was perhaps her most singular achievement. In other respects as well, their arguments invite positive comparisons. See, for example, Elizabeth Brient, "Hans Blumenberg and Hannah Arendt on the 'Unworldly Worldliness' of the Modern Age," *Journal of the History of Ideas* 61, no. 3 (July 2000), 513–530. For a discussion of Blumenberg's development of Husserl's concept of "Lebenswelt" and Gehlen's "Mängelwesen," see Barbara Merker, "Bedürfnis nach Bedeutsamkeit: Zwischen Lebenswelt und Absolutismus der Wirklichkeit," in Wetz and Timm, *Die Kunst des Überlebens*, 68–98.

25. For a discussion of his negative anthropology, which compares his approach with Arendt's, see Hannes Bajohr, "The Unity of the World: Arendt and Blumenberg on the Anthropology of Metaphor," *Germanic Review: Literature, Culture, Theory* 90, no. 1 (2015): 42–59. See also Oliver Müller, *Sorge um die Vernunft: Hans Blumenbergs phänomenologische Anthropologie* (Paderborn, 2005). In *The Legitimacy of the Modern Age*, Blumenberg had emphasized the importance of the nominalist undermining of medieval realism, which led to a contingent world open to the capricious will of an omnipotent God. Abandoning the nominalists' faith in that God, he nonetheless retained their skepticism about the reality of inherent order in the world.

26. "Absoluteness" was one of Blumenberg's key terms, which he used to designate an uncompromising position resisting relativization, for example, the "theological absolutism" of the late Middle Ages in which God's arbitrary and willful omnipotence was posited. Although he normally used it in a negative sense, Blumenberg also spoke approvingly of "absolute metaphors," which resisted being translated into concepts.

27. Blumenberg, *Legitimacy of the Modern Age*, 127–136.

28. The affinity between Blumenberg and pragmatism was noted approvingly by Richard Rorty. For a discussion, see Anthony Reynolds, "Unfamiliar Methods: Blumenberg and Rorty on Metaphor," *Qui Parle* 21, no. 1 (Spring/Summer 2000): 77–103.

29. The once widespread assumption that such a break had occurred with the Greeks has not fared well in recent scholarship. See, for example, Richard Buxton, ed., *From Myth to Reason? Studies in the Development of Greek Thought* (Oxford, 1999); Kathryn A. Morgan, *Myth and Philosophy from the Presocratics to Plato* (Cambridge, 2003). Blumenberg's argument invites comparison with that made by Max Horkheimer and Theodor W. Adorno in *Dialectic of Enlightenment: Philosophical Fragments*, ed. Gunzelin Schmid Noerr, trans. Edmund Jephcott (Stanford, Calif., 2002). They too ar-

gue for the imbrication of myth and logos, but with a far more critical and pessimistic analysis of the implications than Blumenberg's.

30. Hans Blumenberg, "An Anthropological Approach to the Contemporary Significance of Rhetoric," in *After Philosophy: End or Transformation?*, eds. Kenneth Baynes, James Bohman, and Thomas McCarthy (Cambridge, Mass., 1987), 447, 452.

31. For a discussion of the importance of affect for metaphor in Blumenberg, see Rüdiger Zill, "Wie die Vernunft es macht . . . Die Arbeit der Metapher im Prozeß der Zivilisation," in Wetz and Timm, *Die Kunst des Überlebens*, 164–183.

32. Blumenberg, "An Anthropological Approach to the Contemporary Significance of Rhetoric," 440.

33. For the most substantial account of Blumenberg's discussion of myth, including its relation to earlier theories such as those of Ernst Cassirer, and the responses engendered by *Work on Myth*, see Angus Nicholls, *Myth and the Human Sciences: Hans Blumenberg's Theory of Myth* (London, 2015).

34. Hans Blumenberg, "Wirklichkeitsbegriff und Wirkungspotential des Mythos," in *Terror und Spiel: Problem der Mythenrezeption*, ed. Manfred Fuhrmann (Munich, 1971), 11–66. In *Moses and Monotheism*, Freud argued that "religious intolerance, which was foreign to antiquity before this and for long after, was inevitably born with the belief in one God" (21).

35. Blumenberg, "Prospect for a Theory of Nonconceptuality," 94.

36. See Samuel Moyn, "Metaphorically Speaking: Hans Blumenberg, Giambattista Vico, and the Problem of Origins," *Qui Parle* 12, no. 1 (Spring/Summer 2000): 55–76; Robert Pippen, "Modern Mythic Meaning: Blumenberg contra Nietzsche," *History of the Human Sciences* 6, no. 4 (1993), 37–56; Jeffrey Andrew Barash, "Myth in History: Philosophy of History as Myth: On the Ambivalence of Hans Blumenberg's Interpretation of Ernst Cassirer's Theory of Myth," *History and Theory* 50, no. 3 (2011): 328–340.

37. Hans Blumenberg and Jacob Taubes, *Briefwechsel 1961–1981 und weitere Materialen*, ed. Herbert Kopp-Oberstebrink und Martin Treml (Frankfurt, 2013); Götz Müller, "Hans Blumenberg, *Arbeit am Mythos*," *Zeitschrift für deutsche Philologie* 100 (1981), 314–318.

38. Hans Blumenberg, *Präfiguration: Arbeit am politischen Mythos*, ed. Angus Nicholls and Felix Heidenreich (Berlin, 2014). The chapter deals with the effects on Hitler's military plans of his belief in putative prefigurations of the battles he waged. Blumenberg replied to Götz Müller's critique in this volume.

39. There is no mention of him, for example, in Michael L. Morgan and Peter Eli Gordon, eds., *The Cambridge Companion to Modern Jewish Philosophy* (Cambridge, 2007).

40. In May 2015 a conference was held at the Van Leer Foundation in Jerusalem on the theme "Hans Blumenberg in Jerusalem," but from the topics of the papers, it is not clear any significant time was spent on his thoughts on Israel or the conflict with the Palestinians: https://jewishphilosophyplace.com/2015/04/30/conference-hans

-blumenberg-in-jerusalem-philosophical-and-literary-perspectives-van-leer-institute/.

41. The letter, sent to the Catholic theologian Uwe Wolff, is published in *Communio: Internationale Katholische Zeitschrift* 3 (2014).

42. The term was first developed by Anna Freud and often invoked by Theodor W. Adorno in his critique of individual and collective phenomena. For a discussion, see Samir Gandesha, "'Identifying with the Aggressor': From the Authoritarian to Neo-Liberal Personality," in Rüdiger Dannemann, Henry Pickford and Hans-Ernst Schiller, eds., *Der aufrechte Gang im windschiefen Kapitalismus* (Wiesbaden, 2018), 273–297.

43. Blumenberg, *Rigorism of Truth*, 61–62.

44. Whether or not this was fair to Mann, who did in fact often seem to make sense of Nazism by looking into the tangled history of German culture and politics, is less important than his positioning in this anecdote as the non-Jewish critic of excessive theorizing.

45. Freud's own partiality for the truth may well have been more complicated than appears at first glance. It might be said that he was far more interested in the subjective truths—including fantasies—of the patient than the objective truths of what had actually happened in reality. The debate over his revision of seduction theory from an account of real seductions to their role in the psychic imaginary of patients focuses on this distinction. See, for example, Jeffrey Moussaieff Masson, *The Assault on Truth: Freud's Suppression of the Seduction Theory* (New York, 1992). For subtle discussions of the complexities of the role of truth in psychoanalysis, see Samuel Weber, "The Blindness of the Seeing Eye: Psychoanalysis, Hermeneutics, *Entstellung*," in *Institution and Interpretation* (Minneapolis, 1987); John Forrester, *Truth Games: Lies, Money and Psychoanalysis* (Cambridge, Mass., 2000). It also should be remembered that Freud originally called *Moses and Monotheism* "an historical novel."

46. See, in particular, Arendt, "Truth and Politics," in *The Portable Hannah Arendt*, ed. Peter Baehr (New York, 2000), 546.

47. Ibid. For a discussion of the various places in which she interrogated the implications of the motto, see Hannes Bajohr, "Der Preis der Wahrheit: Hans Blumenberg über Hannah Arendts 'Eichmann in Jerusalem,'" *Merkur* 792 (May 2015): 56.

48. Arendt, "Truth and Politics," 556.

49. For a discussion of her thoughts on lying in politics, see Martin Jay, *The Virtues of Mendacity: On Lying in Politics* (Charlottesville, Va., 2010).

50. Hannah Arendt, "Socrates," in *The Promise of Politics*, ed. Jerome Kohn (New York, 2005).

51. Hannah Arendt, *The Life of the Mind*, vol. 1, *Thinking* (New York, 1978), 30. She is paraphrasing Adolph Portmann, with whose argument she is agreeing.

52. Ibid., 113. She did not, however, cite him with full accuracy, as Blumenberg himself later noted. See the discussion in Bajohr, "Unity of the World," 58.

53. Hannah Arendt, "On Humanity in Dark Times: Thoughts about Lessing," in *Men in Dark Times* (New York, 1968), 27.

54. Arendt, *Eichmann in Jerusalem*, 137.

55. Tuija Parvikko, *Arendt, Eichmann and the Politics of the Past* (Helsinki, 2008), 20.

56. The issue of whether the charge of complicity was itself correct, not only from a factual but moral point of view, is addressed with finesse in Dan Diner, *Beyond the Conceivable: Studies in Germany, Nazism and the Holocaust* (Berkeley, Calif., 2006).

57. Blumenberg, *Rigorism of Truth*, 57.

58. Ibid., 5.

59. See Gianni Carchia, "Platonismus der Immanenz: Phänomenologie und Geschichte," in Wetz and Timm, *Die Kunst des Überlebens*, 327–338. It should also be remembered that Arendt never talked of human nature, only of the human condition.

60. For a recent comparison of theories of myth, see Robert Alan Segal, *Theorizing about Myth* (Amherst, Mass., 1999).

61. In fact, in one sense by exposing the latent function of the Eichmann trial as a founding myth of the Israeli state, Blumenberg was tacitly giving ammunition to those who would point out that Zionism excluded players besides Germans and Jews, in particular the Palestinians, who are absent from this particular story. The controversial slogan "A land without people for a people without a land" exemplifies the power of this myth, in which the only "people" are the Jews escaping from the demonic anti-Semitism of a hostile world that had led to the Holocaust. For an illuminating discussion of other Zionist myths and countermyths, see David Ohana, *Origins of Israeli Mythology: Neither Canaanites nor Crusaders*, trans. David Maisel (Cambridge, 2012).

Chapter 6

1. David Armitage, "What's the Big Idea? Intellectual History and the *Longue Durée*," *History of European Ideas* 38, no. 4 (2012): 493–507. He later extended his argument in a book coauthored with Jo Guldi, *The History Manifesto* (Cambridge, 2014), which generated a lively controversy. The fiercest attack was made by Deborah Cohen and Peter Mandler, "*The History Manifesto*: A Critique," *American Historical Review* 120, no. 2 (April 2015): 530–542, followed by a reply by Armitage and Guldi. Cohen and Mandler did not criticize the value of *longue durée* history of ideas as much as the claim that it had fallen out of favor since the 1970s with nefarious political consequences.

2. There is even a compilation of dozens of uses of the phrase by the Three Stooges that can be enjoyed on YouTube: https://www.youtube.com/watch?v=TV1tbKtboaw.

3. The seminal text of 1958 is Fernand Braudel, "History and Social Sciences: The *Longue Durée*," in *Histories: French Constructions of the Past*, ed. Jacques Revel and Lynn Hunt (New York, 1995), 115–145.

4. George Simmel, *The Philosophy of Money*, trans. Tom Bottomore and David Frisby (Boston, 1978), 221. It should not be confused with his more influential idea of the "tragedy of culture."

5. Armitage, "What's the Big Idea?," 494.

6. For my own attempts to grapple with its implications, see "Should Intellectual History Take a Linguistic Turn? Reflections on the Habermas-Gadamer Debate," in *Fin-de-Siècle Socialism and Other Essays* (New York, 1988), 17–36; and "The Textual Approach to Intellectual History," in *Force Fields: Between Intellectual History and Cultural Critique* (New York, 1993), 158–166.

7. This metaphor has often been used by theological fundamentalists who want to jettison the cultural and historical accretions to original doctrine, for example, Adolf von Harnack and Edwin Abbott Abbott.

8. For the specific examples he cites, see Armitage, "What's the Big Idea?," 499.

9. Martin Jay, "Two Cheers for Paraphrase: The Confessions of a Synoptic Intellectual Historian," in *Fin-de-Siècle Socialism*, 52–63.

10. George Boas, *The History of Ideas* (New York, 1969), 3, 22.

11. George Boas, "Idea," in *Dictionary of the History of Ideas: Studies of Selected Pivotal Ideas*, ed. Philip Weiner, vol. 2 (New York, 1973), 542, 548.

12. Arthur O. Lovejoy, *The Great Chain of Being: A Study of the History of an Idea* (New York, 1965), 7. In his 1938 essay "The Historiography of Ideas," he provided a heteroclite list of possible candidates: "Types of categories, thoughts concerning particular aspects of common experience, implicit or explicit presuppositions, sacred formulas and catchwords, specific philosophical theorems, or the larger hypotheses, generalizations or methodological assumptions of various sciences." In *Essays in the History of Ideas* (New York, 1960), 9.

13. Boas, *History of Ideas*, 19. He later adds that the historian of ideas need not concern himself with the question of an author's sincere belief in ideas, although a biographer might.

14. Lovejoy, *Great Chain of Being*, 11.

15. See, for example, Lovejoy's discussion of the influence of Chinese gardens on British Romanticism in "The Chinese Origins of a Romanticism," in *Essays in the History of Ideas*.

16. See, for example, Lovejoy, "Historiography of Ideas," 9.

17. Kenneth Minogue, "Method in Intellectual History," in *Meaning and Context: Quentin Skinner and His Critics*, ed. James Tully (Oxford, 1988), 186.

18. See, for example, Darrin M. McMahon, "The Return of the History of Ideas?," in *Rethinking Modern European Intellectual History*, ed. Darrin M. McMahon and Samuel Moyn (New York, 2013), 13–31.

19. Armitage, "What's the Big Idea?," 497.

20. For one account, see Jan-Werner Müller, "On Conceptual History," in McMahon and Moyn, *Rethinking Modern European Intellectual History*, 74–93. Their most impressive achievement was *Geschichtliche Grundbegriffe: Historisches Lexikon zur*

politisch-sozialen Sprache in Deutschland, 8 vols. (Stuttgart, 1972–1997). Launched in 2005, *Contributions to the History of Concepts* is the leading forum for its development in the English-speaking world.

21. Friedrich Nietzsche, *Genealogy of Morals*, ed. Walter Kaufmann, trans. Walter Kaufmann and R. J. Hollingdale (New York, 1989), 80. Nietzsche's critique of definition in philosophy has also been endorsed by others, for example, Theodor W. Adorno in, among other places, "The Essay as Form," in *Notes to Literature*, ed. Rolf Tiedemann, trans. Shierry Weber Nicholsen, vol. 1 (New York, 1991), 13.

22. Reinhart Koselleck, *Futures Past: On the Semantics of Historical Time*, trans. Keith Tribe (Cambridge, Mass., 1985), 84.

23. The English word "concept" is derived from the past participle of the Latin *concipere*, which means "to take in." Although caution is warranted against assigning semantic priority to such origins, acknowledging them sometimes provides useful reminders of sedimented meanings.

24. Hans Blumenberg, *Paradigms for a Metaphorology*, trans. Robert Savage (Ithaca, N.Y., 2010).

25. For a comparison with Theodor W. Adorno's advocacy of the "nonconceptual," see Martin Jay, "Adorno and Blumenberg: Nonconceptuality and the *Bilderverbot*," in *Splinters in Your Eye: Frankfurt School Provocations* (New York, 2020), 80–97.

26. Hans Blumenberg, "Light as Metaphor for Truth: At the Preliminary Stage of Philosophical Concept Formation," trans. Joel Anderson, in David Michael Levin, ed., *Modernity and the Hegemony of Vision* (Berkeley, 1993, 30–62.

27. In *Paradigms for a Metaphorology*, Blumenberg probed other salient metaphors associated with truth, including "mighty" truth and "naked" truth, as well as the "tribunal" of judging the truth.

28. Hans Blumenberg, "Money or Life: Metaphors of Georg Simmel's Philosophy," *Theory, Culture and Society* 29, nos. 7/8 (2012): 249–262.

29. Ibid., 251.

30. For an example of this insight, see Jürgen Habermas, "The Unity of Reason in the Plurality of Its Voices," in *Postmetaphysical Thinking*, trans. William Mark Hohengarten (Cambridge, Mass., 1992).

31. For a discussion of this distinction, which itself was not always stable in meaning, see Jay, *Songs of Experience: Modern American and European Variations on a Universal Theme* (Berkeley, 2006).

32. For an early use of the distinction, see Paul Ricoeur, "Le paradox politique," *Histoire et vérité* (Paris, 2001): 294–321. For later examples, see Martin Jay, *The Virtues of Mendacity: On Lying in Politics* (Charlottesville, Va., 2010), 205.

33. See Hans Blumenberg, "Foundation and Soil, Bottom and Ground: Hitting Bottom, Getting to the Bottom of Things, Standing on the Ground," in *Care Crosses the River*, trans. Paul Fleming (Stanford, Calif., 2010).

34. J. G. A. Pocock, *Political Thought and History: Essays on Theory and Method* (Cambridge, 2009).

35. Quentin Skinner, "Language and Social Change," in Tully, *Meaning and Context*, 124.

36. Armitage, "What's the Big Idea?," 499.

37. For a discussion of the use of speech act theory by Skinner and his followers, see Jason David BeDuhn, "The Historical Assessment of Speech Acts: Clarifications of Austin and Skinner for the Study of Religions," *Comparative Cultural Studies* 14, no. 1 (2002): 84–113.

38. Franco Moretti, *Distant Reading* (London, 2013). See also his *Graphs, Maps, Trees: Abstract Models for Literary History* (London, 2007). For a trenchant critique, see Christopher Prendergast, "Evolution and Literary History," *New Left Review* 34 (July–August 2005): 40–62. Moretti responds in *Distant Reading*. See also Tom Eyers, "The Perils of the 'Digital Humanities': New Positivisms and the Fate of Literary Theory," *Postmodern Culture* 22, no. 3 (July 2013): 369–386.

39. Matthew L. Jockers, *Macroanalysis: Digital Methods and Literary History* (Urbana-Champaign, Ill., 2013).

40. Dominick LaCapra, "Rethinking Intellectual History and Reading Texts," in *Modern European Intellectual History: Reappraisals and New Perspectives*, ed. Dominick LaCapra and Steven L. Kaplan (Ithaca, 1982), 47–85. The documentary approach to texts sees them as referential media revealing the world, while the "worklike" treats them as complexly indeterminate stimuli to a dialogic encounter that potentially challenges the present and opens the possibility of transforming the status quo.

41. Siegfried Kracauer, *History: The Last Things Before the Last* (New York, 1969), chap. 5. For a similar argument, see Jean Starobinski, *L'oeil vivant: Essais* (Paris, 1961), on which I drew in *Downcast Eyes*, 19–20.

42. Good places to start are Jan Goldstein, ed., *Foucault and the Writing of History* (Cambridge, Mass., 1994), and Thomas R. Flynn, *Sartre, Foucault and Historical Reason: A Poststructuralist Mapping of History*, vol. 2 (Chicago, 2005).

43. Michel Foucault, *The Archaeology of Knowledge and the Discourse of Language*, trans. A. M. Sheridan Smith (New York, 1972), 136–137.

44. Foucault's historical nominalism was perhaps first identified in John Rajchman, *Michel Foucault: The Freedom of Philosophy* (New York, 1985). It meant both an antisubstantialist suspicion of eternal ideas and concepts, which echoed the medieval nominalists' critique of real universals, and a distrust of coherent metanarratives.

45. Foucault, *Archaeology of Knowledge*, 138.

46. For my attempts to explore this issue, see Chapter 2 and "Historicism and the Event," in *Against the Grain: Jewish Intellectuals in Hard Times*, ed. Ezra Mendelsohn, Stefani Hoffman, and Richard I. Cohen (New York, 2014), 143–167.

47. Koselleck, *Futures Past*, 78.

48. Jason Edward, "The Ideological Interpellation of Individuals as Combatants: An Encounter Between Reinhart Koselleck and Michel Foucault," *Journal of Political Ideologies* 21, no. 1 (2007): 54.

Chapter 7

1. Martin Jay, *Marxism and Totality: The Adventures of a Concept from Lukács to Habermas* (Berkeley, Calif., 1984), 84, 103.

2. Slavoj Žižek, "Postface: Georg Lukács as the Philosopher of Leninism," in *A Defense of History and Class Consciousness: Tailism and the Dialectic*, trans. Esther Leslie (London, 2000), 151. The odd epithet "tailism" came from a Russian word, *chvostismus*, which Lenin had used to attack passive, economistic Marxists who linger indecisively in the rear of any revolutionary movement.

3. The comparison is not idle, as Lukács was himself fascinated by Kierkegaard and the difficult choices he made in his life. See Arpad Kadarkay, *Georg Lukács: Life, Thought and Politics* (Cambridge, Mass., 1991), 80.

4. Georg Lukács, "Preface to the New Edition (1967)," *History and Class Consciousness: Studies in Marxist Dialectics*, trans. Rodney Livingstone (Cambridge, Mass., 1971), xv.

5. Lenin, *Collected Works*, vol. 31 (London, 1960–1970), 165. Lenin's epithet "an infantile disorder" appeared in the pamphlet he wrote shortly thereafter called *"Left-Wing" Communism—An Infantile Disorder*, which Lukács read soon after it appeared in June 1920 and took to heart.

6. A still-excellent account can be found in Andrew Arato and Paul Breines, *The Young Lukács and the Origins of Western Marxism* (New York, 1979).

7. See, for example, Michael J. Thompson, ed., *Georg Lukács Reconsidered: Essays on Politics, Philosophy and Aesthetics* (London, 2011); Timothy Bewes and Timothy Hall, eds., *Georg Lukács: The Fundamental Dissonance of Existence: Aesthetics, Politics, Literature* (London, 2011). For an account of the Hungarian government's threat to close the Lukács archive, which is kept in his old apartment in Budapest, see Sándor Kerekes, "The Dress Rehearsal—The Fate of George Lukács and His Archives," *Hungarian Spectrum*, June 17, 2017, http://hungarianspectrum.org/tag/george-lukacs-archives/. Despite an international outcry, it was closed in June 2018.

8. Lukács, *History and Class Consciousness*, 24. He later modified his critique in "Tailism and the Dialectic."

9. See Georg Lukács, *Political Writings: 1919–1929*, ed. Rodney Livingstone, trans. Michael McColgan (London, 1972), 134–147.

10. Fredric Jameson, *Marxism and Form: Twentieth-Century Dialectical Theories of Literature* (Princeton, N.J., 1971), chap. 3; *The Political Unconscious: Narrative as a Socially Symbolic Act* (Ithaca, N.Y., 1981), 34. For a more sustained development of this argument, see his "*History and Class Consciousness* as an 'Unfinished Project,'" *Rethinking Marxism* 1, no. 1 (Spring 1988): 49–72.

11. Lukács, *History and Class Consciousness*, 159.

12. Max Horkheimer and Theodor W. Adorno, *Dialectic of Enlightenment*, ed. Gunzelin Schmid Noerr, trans. Edmund Jephcott (Stanford, Calif., 2002), 191. The crucial issue, of course, is what exactly has been forgotten and must now be remembered: the

origin of commodities in human labor? the domination of nature? the dialectic of recognition?

13. Some critics of *History and Class Consciousness* read Lukács as arguing for the sufficiency of the proletariat's knowledge alone to bring about dereification. And indeed, certain passages in the book support this conclusion, for example, "When the worker knows himself as a commodity his knowledge is practical. *That is to say, this knowledge brings about an objective structural change in the object of knowledge*" (169). But elsewhere he acknowledges that without the organizational leadership of the party, such knowledge alone would not suffice.

14. Lukács, *History and Class Consciousness*, 1.

15. Ibid., xxxviii.

16. For a discussion of its history and implications, see Michael Rosen, "Die Weltgeschichte ist das Weltgericht," in *Internationales Jahrbuch des deutschen Idealismus*, ed. F. Rush (Berlin, 2014).

17. Georg Lukács, "Bolshevism as a Moral Problem," in *Revolution and Counter Revolution, 1918–1921*, trans. Victor Zitta (Mexico City, 1990), 41.

18. Georg Lukács, "Tactics and Ethics," in *Political Writings*, 5–6.

19. Gershom Scholem, "Redemption through Sin," in *The Messianic Idea in Judaism and Other Essays in Jewish Spirituality*, trans. Hillel Halkin (New York, 1995), 78–141. In "Bolshevism as a Moral Problem," Lukács had himself referred disparagingly to Dostoyevsky's character Razuhimin from *Crime and Punishment* for believing that it was possible that we can "lie ourselves through into truth" (41).

20. Maurice Merleau-Ponty, *Humanism and Terror*, trans. John O'Neill (Boston, 1969), 28–29.

21. Jay, *Marxism and Totality*, chap. 1.

22. See, for example, Andrew Feenberg, "Reification and Its Critics," in Thompson, *Georg Lukács Reconsidered*, 172–194.

23. Lukács, *History and Class Consciousness*, 152. Jameson argues that "in some paradoxical or dialectical fashion, Lukács' conception of totality may here be said to rejoin the Althusserian notion of History or the Real as an 'absent cause.'" *Political Unconscious*, 54–55.

24. Lukács, *History and Class Consciousness*, 277.

25. For an account of its different uses in Weber, see Richard Swedberg, *The Max Weber Dictionary: Key Words and Central Concepts* (Stanford, Calif., 2005), 177–179. For a more extensive consideration of its relationship to probability theory and the distinction between its applicability in individual cases and large-scale populations, see Stephen P. Turner and Regis A. Factor, "Objective Possibility and Adequate Causality in Weber's Methodological Writings," *Sociological Review* 29, no. 1 (1981): 5–28. They argue that it shows the importance of *Verstehen* in Weber's conception of causal explanation. Maurice Merleau-Ponty understood the importance of Lukács's debt to Weber in the origins of Western Marxism so much that he called it "Weberian Marxism." See *Adventures of the Dialectic*, trans. Joseph Bien (Evanston, Ill., 1973), 29.

26. See Gary Saul Morson, *Narrative and Freedom: The Shadows of Time* (New Haven, Conn., 1994); Michael André Bernstein, *Foregone Conclusions: Against Apocalyptic History* (Berkeley, Calif., 1994).

27. Lukács, *History and Class Consciousness*, 79.

28. Lucien Goldmann, *Lukács and Heidegger: Towards a New Philosophy*, trans. William Q. Boelhower (London, 1977), xv.

29. Jameson, "*History and Class Consciousness* as an 'Unfinished Project,'" 66.

30. John Rees, introduction to Lukács, *A Defense of History and Class Consciousness*, 22.

31. Ernst H. Kantorowicz, *The King's Two Bodies: A Study in Medieval Political Theology* (Princeton, N.J., 1997).

32. Lukács, *History and Class Consciousness*, 329–330. Italics in original. As Michel Löwy has noted, by the time of "Tailism and the Dialectic," Lukacs had reverted to the claim that the Leninist Party, led by intellectuals, brought class consciousness to the proletariat "from the outside." See his "Revolutionary Dialectics against 'Tailism': Lukács' Answer to the Criticisms of *History and Class Consciousness*," in Thompson, *Georg Lukács Reconsidered*, 67.

33. There are still some holdouts. See, for example, Konstantinos Kavoulakos, "Back to History? Reinterpreting Lukács' Early Marxist Work in Light of the Antinomies of Contemporary Critical Theory," in Thompson, *Georg Lukács Reconsidered*, 151–171.

34. Jean-François Lyotard, *The Postmodern Condition: A Report on Knowledge*, trans. Geoff Bennington and Brian Massumi (Minneapolis, 1984), xxiv.

35. See Nils Gilman, *Mandarins of the Future: Modernization Theory in Cold War America* (Baltimore, 2004).

36. Jameson, "*History and Class Consciousness* as an 'Unfinished Project,'" 57.

37. René Fülöp-Miller, *Mind and Face of Bolshevism: An Examination of Cultural Life in Bolshevik Russia*, trans. F. S. Flint and D. S. Tait (London, 1927), original German edition in 1926; Yuri Slezkine, *The House of Government: A Saga of the Russian Revolution* (Princeton, N.J., 2017).

38. Kadarky, *Georg Lukács*, 203–204.

39. Michel Löwy, *Redemption and Utopia: Jewish Libertarian Thought in Central Europe*, trans. Hope Heany (London, 2017); Anson Rabinbach, *In the Shadow of Catastrophe: German Intellectuals Between Apocalypse and Enlightenment* (Berkeley, Calif., 2001).

40. For one account of struggle to free himself from his religious concerns and his fraught relationship to Bloch, see Harry Liebersohn, *Fate and Utopia in German Sociology, 1870–1923* (Cambridge, Mass., 1988), chap. 6.

41. Hans Blumenberg, *The Legitimacy of the Modern Age*, trans. Robert M. Wallach (Cambridge, Mass., 1983).

42. Žižek, postface to Lukács, *Defense of History and Class Consciousness*, 164.

43. See Martin Jay, "Historicism and the Event," in *Against the Grain: Jewish Intellectuals in Hard Times*, ed. Ezra Mendelsohn, Stefani Hoffman, and Richard I. Cohen

(New York, 2014), 143–167. For an insightful recent treatment of the "political semiotics" of the event, see Robin Wagner-Pacifici, *What Is an Event?* (Chicago, 2017). It has also been defended by Russian theorists such as Vladimir Bibikhin. See Artemy Magun, "The Concept of Event in the Philosophy of Vladimir Bibikhim," *Stasis* 3, no. 1 (2015).

44. Claude Romano, *Event and World*, trans. Shane Mackinlay (New York, 2009). For a discussion of the implications of his argument, see chapter 2 in this volume.

45. As in the case of most binaries, the absolute opposition of Event and historical context cannot be upheld for long, as each entails the other. See Wagner-Pacifici, *What Is an Event?*, chap. 3.

46. Reversing the normal identification of appearances with ephemeral flux and essences (or in Badiou's terminology, Being) with enduring substances, Žižek claims that for Lukács, reified surface appearances, the realm of seemingly intractable "facts," are really much more rigid than the elusive fragility of Events, which surge up from the realm of fluctuation beneath. See his postface to *Tailism and the Dialectic*, 181.

47. George Lichtheim, *Marxism in Modern France* (New York, 1966), 68.

48. When the Event is experienced as entirely traumatic rather than emancipatory, however, Fidelity involves precisely the opposite, as demonstrated by the injunction "never again" in response to the Holocaust.

49. See Georg Lukács, "Hölderlin's Hyperion," in *Goethe and His Age*, trans. Robert Anchor (London, 1968), 136–158. For an account of it as an answer to Trotsky's critique of Stalinist Thermidorian counterrevolution, see Slavoj Žižek, introduction to V. I. Lenin, *Lenin 2017* (London, 2017), lxxvi.

50. For my understanding of Fichte's abiding role in Lukács's argument in *History and Class Consciousness*, see my *Marxism and Totality*, 104–109. For an alternative reading, see Andrew Feenberg, "Reification and Its Critics," in Thompson, *Georg Lukács Reconsidered*.

51. Lukács, *Lenin: A Study on the Unity of His Thought* (Cambridge, Mass., 1971), 88.

52. Ibid., 39.

53. Žižek, introduction to *Lenin 2017*, lii–liii.

Chapter 8

1. Rachel Donadio, "Top Award for Photo Is Revoked," *New York Times*, March 5, 2015, C5.

2. Ibid.

3. Tom Gunning, "What's the Point of an Index?, or, Faking Photographs," *Nordicom Review* 1–2 (2004): 42.

4. Michael Fried, *Why Photography Matters as Art as Never Before* (New Haven, Conn., 2008). For a blistering critique of Fried's argument, see John Roberts, *Photography and Its Violations* (New York, 2014), 45–54. Roberts defends photography's mission to intervene in the conventional perception of the world and create a new "truth-event."

5. See, for example, the essays in Martin Lister, ed., *The Photographic Image in Digital Culture* (London, 1995).

6. For a sample of the arguments for and against, see James Elkins, ed., *Photographic Theory* (New York, 2007).

7. W. J. T. Mitchell, "The Abu Ghraib Archive," in *Cloning Terror: The War on Images, 9/11 to the Present* (Chicago, 2011), 124. For analysis linking digital metadata with the Benjaminian idea of inscription, see Elizabeth Stainforth and David Thom, "Metadata: Walter Benjamin and Bernard Steigler," in *Theorizing Visual Studies: Writing Through the Discipline*, ed. James Elkins and Kristi McClure (New York, 2013), 163–165.

8. This confidence, to be sure, may be misplaced, as Arild Fetveit pointed out to me in a personal communication, when the metadata is itself manipulated.

9. Aaron Meskin and Jonathan Cohen, "Photographs as Evidence," in *Photography and Philosophy: Essays on the Pencil of Nature*, ed. Scott Walden (Malden, Mass., 2008), 75.

10. Walter Benjamin, "Little History of Photography," in *Selected Writings*, vol. 2, *1927–1934*, ed. Michael W. Jennings, Howard Eiland, and Gary Smith, trans. Rodney Livingstone et al. (Cambridge, Mass., 1999), 512.

11. It can, of course, be argued that this is true of all sensual experience, which to one degree or another fashions objects not perfectly equivalent to their external counterparts. As Jonathan Crary shows in *Techniques of the Observer: On Vision and Modernity in the Nineteenth Century* (Cambridge, 1990), the active role of the eye in visual experience came to be appreciated by modern science. The philosophical distinction between phenomena and noumena famously developed by Kant may no longer persuade many critics, but it captures the nonidentity of objects of experience or perception and objects in the world. If our senses already mediate rather than merely record the world, then their technological prostheses are not radically different from them.

12. Roland Barthes, "The Photographic Message," *Image-Music-Text*, trans. Stephen Heath (New York, 1977), 17.

13. See, for example, Kendall L. Watson, "Transparent Pictures: On the Nature of Photographic Realism," in Walden, *Photography and Philosophy*, 48.

14. Roberts, *Photography and Its Violations*, 153.

15. Benjamin, "Little History of Photography," 526.

16. Walter Benjamin, "The Author as Producer," in *Reflections: Essays, Aphorisms, Autobiographical Writings*, ed. Peter Demetz, trans. Edmund Jephcott (New York, 1978), 230.

17. Benjamin, "Little History of Photography," 527. Augurs and haruspices were Roman priests who practiced divination, often from the flights of birds or the entrails of animals who had been sacrificed.

18. This qualification is necessary because not all contemporary art photography relies on techniques that favor artifice over mimesis. There are many examples of photographs that have earned acceptance as works of art without sacrificing their truth claims as indexical traces of actual events in the world.

19. Cited in Howard Eiland and Michael W. Jennings, *Walter Benjamin: A Critical Life* (Cambridge, Mass., 2014), 293.

20. Benjamin, "Little History of Photography," 526.

21. "Les mensonges de la photographie," *Le Siècle*, January 11, 1899, reprinted in Norman L. Kleeblatt, ed., *The Dreyfus Affair: Art, Truth and Justice* (Berkeley, 1977), 212.

22. Jacques Lacan, *Écrits: A Selection*, trans. Alan Sheridan (New York, 1977), 305.

23. There are, of course, other types of speech acts, for example, prayer or the writing of fiction, in which this transcendental premise does not obtain.

24. For a discussion of denial in philosophical and literary as well as psychoanalytical terms, see Wilfred Ver Eecke, *Denial, Negation, and the Forces of the Negative: Freud, Hegel, Lacan, Spitz and Sophocles* (Albany, N.Y., 2006).

25. See Hannah Arendt, "Lying in Politics: Reflections on the Pentagon Papers," in *Crises of the Republic* (New York, 1972), and "Truth and Politics," in *The Portable Hannah Arendt*, ed. Peter Baehr (New York, 2000). For reflections on her argument, see Martin Jay, *The Virtues of Mendacity: On Lying in Politics* (Charlottesville, Va., 2010).

26. Jacques Derrida, *The Truth in Painting*, trans. Geoff Bennington and Ian McLeod (Chicago, 1987), 8–9.

27. Jacques Derrida, "History of the Lie: Prolegomena," in *Without Alibi*, ed. and trans. Peggy Kamuf (Stanford, Calif., 2002). For my gloss on its argument, see Martin Jay, "Pseudology: Derrida on Arendt and Lying in Politics," *Essays from the Edge: Parerga and Paralipomena* (Charlottesville, Va., 2011), 132–148.

28. Derrida, "History of the Lie: Prolegomena," 34, 29.

29. Michel Foucault, *Fearless Speech*, ed. Joseph Pierson (Los Angeles, 2001), 19.

30. Martin Jay, "Visual *Parrhesia*? Foucault and the Truth of the Gaze," in *Essays from the Edge*, 77–89.

31. Gunning, "What's the Point of an Index?," 42.

32. Ariella Azoulay, *The Civil Contract of Photography* (Cambridge, 2012).

33. Derrida, *Truth in Painting*, 47.

34. Gunning, "What's the Point of an Index?," 42.

35. Hagi Kenaan, "Photography and Its Shadow," *Critical Inquiry*, 41, 3 (Spring 2015): 570–571.

36. Benjamin, "Author as Producer," 230.

37. Roberts, *Photography and Its Violations*, 155.

38. Ibid., 158. Italics in original.

39. Arthur Danto, "The Naked Truth," in Walden, *Photography and Philosophy*, 302.

40. My thanks to Arild Fetveit of the University of Copenhagen for his astute reading of an earlier draft of this essay.

Chapter 9

1. Frank Ankersmit, *Sublime Historical Experience* (Stanford, Calif., 2005); Martin Jay, *Songs of Experience: Modern and American and European Variations on a Universal Theme* (Berkeley, 2005). A third partner in our conversation was a younger scholar, Craig Ireland, whose book *The Subaltern Appeal to Experience: Self-Identity, Late Modernity, and the Politics of Immediacy* (Montreal, 2004) appeared a year earlier. Ankersmit's book has generated considerable attention, with some devotees of his earlier narrativist approach, for example, Peter Icke and Keith Jenkins, expressing dismay at what they saw as the betrayal of his better self, and others, for example, Ewa Domanska, applauding his new departure.

2. Calling his approach frankly "romantic," Ankersmit boldly asserts that "the claim that there is a variant of experience preceding and transcending questions of truth and falsity is precisely the main thesis of this book" (*Sublime Historical Experience*, 9). Although the argument that a primordial experience prior to the linguistic judgment of truth or falsehood is plausible, as phenomenologists have long contended, I am less persuaded that it can be said to "transcend" such judgments, at least for the community of historians. For a further discussion of this issue, see David Carr, *Experience and History: Phenomenological Perspectives on the Historical World* (Oxford, 2014), and my review in *Journal of the Philosophy of History* 10 (2016).

3. Martin Jay, "The Manacles of Gavrilo Princip," *Salmagundi* 106/107 (Spring-Summer 1995), reprinted in *Cultural Semantics: Keywords of Our Time* (Amherst, Mass., 1998), 197–204.

4. Jay, Cultural Semantics, 202

5. Ibid., 204.

6. Ankersmit, *Sublime Historical Experience*, 187, 137.

7. Ibid., 121. Thus his evocation of Romeo and Juliet, who escape the constraining contexts of their respective families. Contrary to his explicit rejection of irrationalist mysticism, one reviewer of the book, Michael Roth, skeptically remarks that "it seems to this reader that this is precisely the domain that Ankersmit has been forced to enter, for this is the only alternative he has left himself after rejecting pragmatism, hermeneutics, and the problematics of representation." "Ebb Tide," *History and Theory* 46 (February 2007): 69.

8. Hans Ulrich Gumbrecht, *Production of Presence: What Meaning Cannot Convey* (Stanford, Calif., 2004); Eelco Runia, *Moved by the Past: Discontinuity and Historical Mutation* (New York, 2014), chap. 3. Their positions are not, to be sure, perfectly equivalent. For a discussion of Ankersmit's differences with Runia, see Anton Froeyman,

"Frank Ankersmit and Eelco Runia: The Presence and Otherness of the Past," *Rethinking History* 16, no. 3 (2012): 393–415. In an interview with Marcin Moskalewicz in *Rethinking History* 11, no. 2 (2007): 251–274, Ankersmit said, "I have just read Gumbrecht's book on presence; and there you see much the same things, though Gumbrecht is, I believe, insufficiently aware of all the philosophical complications involved in all of this" (256).

9. For one account of its continuing importance in aesthetic terms, see George Steiner, *Real Presences* (Chicago, 1991). For a discussion of the important distinction between the ontological identity underlying the doctrine of the Holy Eucharist and iconic or imagistic representation, see Catherine Gallagher and Stephen Greenblatt, *Practicing New Historicism* (Chicago, 2000), chap. 3.

10. Ernst H. Kantorowicz, *The King's Two Bodies: A Study in Medieval Theology* (Princeton, N.J., 1957).

11. Louis Marin, *Portrait of the King*, trans. Martha M. Houle (Minneapolis, 1988), 8.

12. Hans Beltung, *Likeness and Presence: History of the Image Before the Era of Art*, trans. Edmund Jephcott (Chicago, 1994).

13. Runia, *Moved by the Past*, 67.

14. Ankersmit, *Sublime Historical Experience*, 182, 184, 185.

15. Ibid., 424. See Roland Barthes, *Camera Lucida: Reflections on Photography*, trans. Richard Howard (Berkeley, Calif., 1981). Runia invokes him in *Moved by the Past*, 100–103.

16. Henri Cartier-Bresson, *The Decisive Moment* (New York, 1952).

17. Ulrich Baer, *Spectral Evidence: The Photography of Trauma* (Cambridge, Mass., 2005), 2.

18. Gérard Wajcman, "De la croyance photographique," and Elisabeth Pagnoux, "Reporter photographique á Auschwitz," *Les temps modernes* 56, no. 213 (2001): 47–83, 84–108.

19. Georges Didi-Huberman, *Images in Spite of All: Four Photographs from Auschwitz*, trans. Shane B. Lillis (Chicago, 2008). For a discussion of the wider controversy over images of the Holocaust, see Janina Struk, *Photographing the Holocaust: Interpretations of the Evidence* (London, 2004).

20. The possibility of turning images produced by "the Nazi gaze" against the intentions of their photographers is suggestively considered by Ulrich Baer, who examines the use made of color photographs from the Łódź ghetto in Dariusz Jablonski's film *Fotoamator*. See *Spectral Evidence*, chap. 4.

21. Didi-Huberman, *Images in Spite of All*, 36.

22. Martin Jay, *Downcast Eyes: The Denigration of Vision in Twentieth-Century French Thought* (Berkeley, Calif., 1993). Didi-Huberman notes that "a characteristic trait of this 'resistance to the image' is its spontaneous adoption of traditional forms of political iconoclasm: outright rejection, the rhetoric of moral censure, the desire to destroy 'idols.'" *Images in Spite of All*, 64. It might also be noted that distrust of photographs for their inability to capture duration, a critique that can be traced back at least to Berg-

son, has often informed historians' responses to them. See Michael S. Roth, "Photographic Ambivalence and Historical Consciousness," *History and Theory, Theme Issue 48: Photography and Historical Interpretation*, ed. Jennifer Tucker (December 2009): 83–86.

23. Pagnoux's phrase is quoted in *Images in Spite of All*, 55.

24. Quoted in ibid., 93.

25. Ibid., 57, 81, 88.

26. Jean-Paul Sartre, *L'imaginaire: Psychologie phenomenologique de l'imagination* (Paris, 1940), 20–28.

27. Didi-Huberman, *Images in Spite of All*, 161.

28. Ibid., 167.

29. Ibid., 169, 170.

30. Ankersmit, *Sublime Historical Experience*, 353, 351.

31. Theodor W. Adorno's assertion in *Negative Dialectics*, trans. E. B. Ashton (New York, 1973): "A new categorical imperative has been imposed by Hitler upon unfree mankind: it arranges their thoughts and actions so that Auschwitz will not repeat itself, so that nothing similar will happen" (365).

32. Frode Molven, "A Proposal for How to Look at the Past: Interview with Frank Ankersmit," Gröningen, December 2007, https://www.scribd.com/document/199536733/Interview-Frank-Ankersmit, 8. Translation emended.

33. Ankersmit, *Sublime Historical Experience*, 265. See also the distinction he draws between LaCapra's focus on trauma as essentially individual, and his own: "In my approach, however, Western civilization itself is the subject of trauma; my question is how Western civilization, *as such*, dealt with its greatest crises when it experienced the traumatizing loss of an old world because one was forced to enter a new one" (351).

34. Ibid., 367–368.

35. Froeyman, "Frank Ankersmit and Eelco Runia," 405.

36. This is not the place to explore Ankersmit's political interventions over the years, but it is significant that for a while he could support Thierry Baudet's right-wing populist Forum for Democracy, which he left only in December 2017.

37. Molven, "Proposal for How to Look at the Past," 4.

38. Ankersmit, *Sublime Historical Experience*, 160.

39. Ibid., 306–309.

40. For an extended discussion of the following argument, see my "Photography and the Event," in Olga Shevchenko, ed., *Double Exposure: Memory and Photography* (New Brunswick, N.J., 2014).

41. Barthes, *Camera Lucida*, 59.

42. Baer, *Spectral Evidence*. For more general considerations of the "event," see Robin Wagner-Pacifici, *What Is an Event?* (Chicago, 2017), and my "Historicism and the Event," in *Against the Grain: Jewish Intellectuals in Hard Times*, ed. Ezra Mendelsohn, Stefani Hoffman, and Richard I. Cohen (New York, 2014), 143–167. Although Ankersmit normally designates the experience of historians rather than the events of

the past as "sublime," he nonetheless does claim that "we can discern in the history of the West several moments where it radically repudiated its previous past in a movement possessing all the characteristics of Hegel's historical sublime. Think, again, of the French Revolution or that other tremendous revolution that was occasioned by the transition from an agrarian and feudal society to a modern industrial society. Few events in Western history have been so intensively discussed by historians." *Sublime Historical Experience*, 366. Although the French Revolution is routinely included among the radical ruptures that count as transformative "events," the long, slow, and uneven process of modernization is not.

Chapter 10

1. For the original debate, its context, and its aftermath, see James Schmidt, ed., *What Is Enlightenment? Eighteenth-Century Answers and Twentieth-Century Questions* (Berkeley, Calif., 1996).

2. Michel Foucault, "What Is Enlightenment?," in *The Foucault Reader*, ed. Paul Rabinow (New York, 1984), 40.

3. Charles Baudelaire, "The Salon of 1846: The Heroism of Modern Life," in *Selected Writings on Art and Literature*, trans. P. E. Charvet (London, 1972), 47–107; Baudelaire, *The Painter of Modern Life and Other Essays*, trans. and ed. Jonathan Mayne (London, 1970). For a discussion of Foucault on Baudelaire and modernity, see Alan Swingewood, *Cultural Theory and the Problem of Modernity* (New York, 1998), 142–144.

4. Reinhart Koselleck, "'Space of Experience' and 'Horizon of Expectation': Two Historical Categories," in *Futures Past: On the Semantics of Historical Time*, trans. Keith Tribe (Cambridge, Mass., 1985).

5. For an argument that Baudelaire's essay on the Salon of 1846 might best be understood itself in terms of a destabilizing irony, see David Carrier, "The Style of Argument in Baudelaire's 'Salon de 1846,'" *Romance Quarterly* 41, no. 3 (1994), 3–14.

6. A comparable point might be made about the modern villain, who is often far more complex and nuanced than his predecessors. The rise of the antihero as the protagonist of much modern fiction was accompanied by what we might call the "antivillain," ironically understood as more interesting than his heroic counterpart. Only in melodrama and the comics, where superheroes abound, are the older black-and-white alternatives still maintained.

7. Foucault, "What Is Enlightenment?," 41.

8. Immanuel Kant, "An Answer to the Question: What Is Enlightenment?," in Schmidt, *What Is Enlightenment?*, 58. This definition, of course, has generated a considerable amount of criticism for its elitist premise, but the point that is relevant here is Kant's assumption that it is a telos still to be realized and unlikely ever to be.

9. Bruno Latour, *We Have Never Been Modern*, trans. Catherine Porter (Cambridge, Mass., 1993).

10. Foucault, "What Is Enlightenment?," 40, 41.

11. Max Horkheimer and Theodor W. Adorno, *Dialectic of Enlightenment,* ed. Gunzelin Schmid Noerr, trans. Edmund Jephcott (Stanford, Calif., 2002).

12. Walter Benjamin, *Charles Baudelaire: A Lyric Poet in the Era of High Capitalism,* trans. Harry Zohn (London, 1973), 74, 76, 97.

13. Any serious account of Benjamin's thoughts on the trope of tragedy without a tragic hero would have to address his discussion of the early modern German *Trauerspiel,* which was not equivalent to classical tragedy, but to do so is beyond the scope of this essay.

14. It also, of course, might be asked if it helps to distinguish modernity from its alleged postmodern successor, but that is a can of worms best left tightly closed in a modest exercise such as this one.

15. John Berger, *Daumier: The Heroism of Modern Life* (London, 2013); Elisabeth Johns, *Thomas Eakins: The Heroism of Modern Life* (Princeton, N.J., 2013); *Manet: The Heroism of Modern Life,* video for National Gallery, Lizzie Barker and Juliet Wilson Bareau (London, 1992).

16. James Meehan, "Marshall Berman, November 24, 1940–September 11, 2013: Chronicler of the Heroism of Modern Life," *Humanity and Society* (2015): 3–12, http://has.sagepub.com/content/early/2015/12/18/0160597615622232.full.pdf.

17. The question of heroism has, in fact, rarely been addressed by sociologists. A quick perusal of the indexes of ambitious general overviews of sociological thought, such as Raymond Aron, *Main Currents of Sociological Thought,* 2 vols., trans. Richard Howard and Helen Weaver (New York, 1965, 1967); Robert A. Nisbet, *The Sociological Tradition* (New York, 1966); Lewis A. Coser, *Masters of Sociological Thought: Ideas in Historical and Social Context* (New York, 1977); Thomas Bottomore and Robert Nisbet, eds., *A History of Sociological Analysis* (New York, 1978); Richard Münch, *Sociological Theory from the 1850s to the Present* (Chicago, 1994), will not find a single entry devoted to it.

18. Hayden White, *Metahistory: The Historical Imagination in Nineteenth-Century Europe* (Baltimore, 1973), 148.

19. Eric Bentley, *A Century of Hero-Worship,* 2nd ed. (Boston, 1957). The first edition appeared in 1944. It is worth nothing that not all attitudes toward the role of heroes in history were as critical. See, for example, the more ambivalent assessment in Sidney Hook, *The Hero in History: Study in Limitation and Possibility* (Boston, 1955).

20. Thomas Carlyle, *On Heroes, Hero-Worship and the Heroic in History,* ed. Carl Niemeyer (Lincoln, Neb., 1966), 1. For a discussion of the nuances of Carlyle's argument and the differences in his attitudes toward figures in his pantheon, see Robert A. Donovan, "Carlyle and the Climate of Hero-Worship," *University of Toronto Quarterly* 42, no. 2 (1973): 122–141.

21. Carlyle, *On Heroes,* 12. Carlyle's general distaste for irony in comparison with Kierkegaard is discussed in Eric J. Ziolkowski, *The Literary Kierkegaard* (Evanston, Ill., 2011), chap. 5.

22. Friedrich Nietzsche, *Untimely Mediations*, ed. Daniel Breazeale, trans. R. J. Hollingdale (Cambridge, 1997), 111. It should be noted, however, that Nietzsche's attitude toward heroism soured during his middle period, when he satirized the narcissistic pathos of heroic fantasies of omnipotence. See Michael Ure, *Nietzsche's Therapy: Self-Cultivation in the Middle Works* (Lanham, Md., 2008), chap. 5.

23. Friedrich Nietzsche, *Beyond Good and Evil*, trans. Marianne Cowan (Chicago, 1955), 200.

24. For an excellent introduction to Jünger and his continuing influence in the postwar era, see Elliot Y. Neaman, *A Dubious Past: Ernst Jünger and the Politics of Literature after Nazism* (Berkeley, Calif., 1999).

25. Sigmund Freud, *Moses and Monotheism*, trans. Katharine Jones (New York, 1939), 138. Freud also suggested to Otto Rank that he write a book on the hero, which became *The Myth of the Birth of the Hero*, trans. F. Robbins and Smith Ely Jelliffe (New York, 1914). The book argued that mythic heroes define themselves by rebelling against the father in a family romance.

26. Georg Wilhelm Friedrich Hegel, *The Philosophy of History*, trans. J. Sibree (New York, 1956), 32.

27. Vladimir Safatle, *Grand Hotel Abyss: Desire, Recognition and the Restoration of the Subject*, trans. Lucas Carpinelli (Leuven, 2016), 116–117. In *Negative Dialectics*, however, Adorno wrote of "the master class joke of the hero and the valet" that it demonstrated Hegel's overrating of the exceptional individual and neglect of his real counterpart. The larger-than-life publicity of geniuses, especially military and political ones, he argued, compensates for the weakness of the latter: "Projections of the impotent longings of all, they function as an *imago* of unleashed freedom and unbounded productivity, as if those might be realized always and everywhere." Theodor W. Adorno, *Negative Dialectics*, trans. E. B. Ashton (New York, 1973), 342.

28. Werner Sombart, *Händler und Helden: Patriotische Besinnungen* (Munich, 1915). For a discussion, see Arthur Mitzman, *Sociology and Estrangement: Three Sociologists of Imperial Germany* (New York, 1973), chap. 22. Sombart's critique of the British as a nation of mere merchants presaged his later demonization of the Jews and embrace of the Nazi "heroic popular community." See Abram L. Harris, "Sombart and German (National) Socialism," *Journal of Political Economy* 50, no. 6 (1942): 805–836.

29. Herbert Spencer, *The Study of Sociology* (London, 1896), 15. For a discussion of Spencer's personal antipathy toward Carlyle, see William Baker, "Herbert Spencer's Unpublished Reminiscences of Thomas Carlyle: The 'Perfect Owl of Minerva for Knowledge' on a 'Poet without Music,'" *Neophilologus* 60, no. 1 (December 1975): 145–152.

30. As Peter Weingart notes in a discussion of the differentiation of sociological from biological claims about human development, "The modernist turn that characterized the work of this 'second generation' of sociologists—Weber, Simmel, Durkheim—centered on their renunciation of the idea of social progress which had dominated sociology through the nineteenth century. One crucial move in this respect was for sociology to abdicate the role of prophet of a future society and to limit itself

to those social phenomena that could be experienced." "Biology as Social Theory: The Bifurcation of Social Biology and Sociology in Germany, circa 1900," in *Modernist Impulses in the Social Sciences, 1870–1930*, ed. Dorothy Ross (Baltimore, 1994), 270.

31. For a short but comprehensive survey of the attempts made by sociologists to analyze modernity, see Donald N. Levine, "Modernity and Its Endless Discontents," in *After Parsons: A Theory of Social Action for the Twenty-First Century*, ed. Renée C. Fox, Victor M. Lidz, and Harold J. Bershady (New York, 2005), 148–166. He identifies several candidates for the primary characteristic posited by different sociologists: functional specialization, individuation, political unification, jural equalization, extension of new forms of discipline, normative universalization, and cultural rationalization, as well as the discontents associated with each.

32. Emile Durkheim, *The Rules of Sociological Method*, ed. George E. G. Catlin, trans. Sarah A. Solovay and John H. Mueller (New York, 1938).

33. For Durkheim's polemic against contractualism, which was directed largely at Herbert Spencer, see *The Division of Labor*, trans. George Simpson (New York, 1933), chap. 7. His understanding of the priority of the community over the individual has sometimes been interpreted as anticipating the evolutionary biological belief that individual members of a species are merely vehicles for the transmission of genetic material, as well as structuralist linguistics. See Talcott Parsons, "Durkheim Revisited: Another Look at *The Elementary Forms of the Religious Life*," in *Beyond the Classics? Essays in the Scientific Study of Religion*, ed. Charles Y. Glock and Phillip E. Hammond (New York, 1973), 156–180.

34. The simple opposition between structuralist and social action approaches to society has, to be sure, often been called into question, with many attempts to see them as reciprocally intertwined, but it is fair to say that Durkheim leaned heavily toward the priority of structure and system over action and agency, especially when the latter was understood in individualist terms.

35. Anomic normlessness was, of course, only one of the explanations Durkheim provided for the etiology of suicide. The others were egoistic and altruistic. See Emile Durkheim, *Suicide: A Study in Sociology*, ed. George Simpson, trans. John A. Spaulding and George Simpson (New York, 1951).

36. Solidarism was a specific political movement during the Third Republic, led by Léon Bourgeois. For a discussion of Durkheim's loose affiliation with its goals, see Steven Lukes, *Emile Durkheim: His Life and Work* (London, 1973), 50–54.

37. See Paul Gerbod, "L'Ethique héroique en France (1870–1914)," *Revue historique* 268, no. 2 (1983): 409–429; Robert A. Nye, *Masculinity and Male Codes of Honor in Modern France* (New York, 1993), 218–222. Restoring ideals of military valor and courage meant reversing a trend that has been traced as far back as the reign of Louis XIV. According to Paul Rabinow, "During his reign there emerged a discourse of discipline and machine-like regulation of the body; the representation of the soldier as a controlled parallelogram of forces replaced that of the heroic warrior." Rabinow, *French Modern: Norms and Forms of the Social Environment* (Chicago, 1995), 117.

38. Emile Durkheim, *The Elementary Forms of the Religious Life*, trans. Joseph Ward Swain (New York, 1968), 328, 333.

39. For a discussion of Durkheim's complex relations to his Jewish identity, see Ivan Strenski, *Durkheim and the Jews of France* (Chicago, 1997).

40. The general recognition among sociologists of the abiding power of religion or its functional equivalents in modernity has long been acknowledged; see, for example, Nisbet, *Sociological Tradition*, chap. 6.

41. Durkheim's disdain for the inner spontaneity of the individual genius was directed against the defense of it made by Gabriel Tarde. See the discussion in Dominick LaCapra, *Emile Durkheim: Sociologist and Philosopher* (Aurora, Colo., 2001), 216–217. He points out that Durkheim sought to go beyond the dichotomy between external, conventional persona and internal, authentic self.

42. For an attempt to do so, see Stjepan G. Meštrović, *The Coming Fin de Siècle: An Application of Durkheim's Sociology to Modernity and Postmodernism* (London, 1991), chap. 5. He claims that Benjamin's "observation that for Baudelaire, modernism exists under the sign of suicide, resonates with Durkheim's claim that suicide is the 'ransom money' of civilization" (75–76), and that "Durkheim was indirectly mirroring Baudelaire's indictment of the modern dandy in his own comments on French Romanticism" (78). David Frisby also notes Benjamin's observation that for Baudelaire suicide was the quintessence of modernity, and adds: "Several decades after Baudelaire's death, the sociologist Emile Durkheim felt compelled to assess the role of 'the different currents of collective sadness' and 'collective melancholy' in causing the 'morbid effervescence' of suicide." David Frisby, *Fragments of Modernity: Theories of Modernity in the Work of Simmel, Kracauer and Benjamin* (Cambridge, Mass., 1986), 263. These are odd arguments insofar as Baudelaire didn't indict dandyism but defended it, and Durkheim never turned suicide into an act of heroic rebellion.

43. For an account of the institutional success of the Durkheimians, see Terry Nichols Clark, *Prophets and Patrons: The French University and the Emergence of the Social Sciences* (Cambridge, Mass., 1973).

44. In his report of a meeting to discuss the crisis of democracy at the Collège in December 1938, Bertrand d'Astorg records without attribution the sentiment that "a country unable to rouse a hero to defend it, or better to cultivate it, is dead. But any system breaking the human will to heroism is criminal." Denis Hollier, ed., *The College of Sociology, 1937–39*, trans. Betsy Wing (Minneapolis, 1988), 195.

45. Comparisons between Weber and Durkheim are more plentiful in the secondary literature than between Simmel and Durkheim. For a good short instance of the former, see Reinhard Bendix, "Two Sociological Traditions," in Reinhard Bendix and Guenther Roth, *Scholarship and Partisanship: Essays on Max Weber* (Berkeley, Calif., 1971). For examples of the latter, see Kurt H. Wolff, "The Challenge of Durkheim and Simmel," *American Journal of Sociology* 63, no. 6 (May 1958): 590–596; Meštrović, *Coming Fin de Siècle*, chap. 4.

46. Weber, to be sure, was also fervently nationalist and defended German imperialism. For a discussion of his theory of leadership in the context of German elitist political thought, see Walter Struve, *Elites against Democracy: Leadership Ideals in Bourgeois Political Thought in Germany, 1890–1933* (Princeton, N.J., 1973), chap. 4. And for a short period during the First World War, Simmel also joined the chorus of German jingoists.

47. For a comparison of their reactions to Nietzsche, see Lawrence A. Scaff, *Fleeing the Iron Cage: Culture, Politics, and Modernity in the Thought of Max Weber* (Berkeley, Calif., 1989), 127–133. For discussions of Weber and Nietzsche, see Robert Eden, *Political Leadership and Nihilism: A Study of Weber and Nietzsche* (Tampa, Fla., 1983); Tracy B. Strong, "Love, Passion, and Maturity: Nietzsche and Weber on Science, Morality and Politics," in *Confronting Mass Democracy and Industrial Technology: Political and Social Theory from Nietzsche to Habermas*, ed. John P. McCormick (Durham, N.C., 2002); Ralph Schroeder, "Nietzsche and Weber: Two 'Prophets' of the Modern World," in *Max Weber, Rationality and Modernity*, ed. Sam Whimster and Scott Lash (London, 1987), 207–221.

48. See Wilhelm Hennis, "Personality and Life Orders: Max Weber's Theme," in Whimster and Lash, *Max Weber, Rationality and Modernity*, 52–74; David Owen, *Maturity and Modernity: Nietzsche, Weber, Foucault and the Ambivalence of Reason* (London, 1994), chap. 7. Owen points out that whereas Nietzsche endorsed turning one's life into a work of art, Weber's personality realized himself through works in the world.

49. Weber's own wrestling with the concept of *Beruf* is traced in Arthur Mitzman, *The Iron Cage: An Historical Interpretation of Max Weber* (New York, 1969). He cites a letter from the young Weber to his fiancée in which he confesses, "I never had any kind of respect for the concept of 'calling,' since I thought I knew I fitted into a large number of positions, to a certain extent" (65). But then he notes that at the end of Weber's life, when he adopted a more realistic notion of politics, "the key concept which binds together aristocracy, charisma and political leadership is *Beruf* (calling)—i.e. precisely that concept from which, in *Wirtschaft und Gesellschaft*, Weber had clearly separated charisma" (247).

50. Friedrich Nietzsche, *The Birth of Tragedy* and *The Genealogy of Morals*, trans. Francis Golffing (Garden City, N.Y., 1956), 160. See Weber, "Politics as Vocation," in *From Max Weber: Essays in Sociology*, ed. Hans Gerth and C. Wright Mills (New York, 1958), where he asserts that "'lack of distance' *per se* is one of the deadly sins of every politician" (115).

51. See the discussion in Joseph W. H. Lough, *Weber and the Persistence of Religion: Social Theory, Capitalism and the Sublime* (New York, 2006), chap. 6.

52. Weber, letter to Edgar Jaffé, September 13, 1907, in W. G. Runciman, ed., *Weber: Selections in Translation*, trans. Eric Matthews (Cambridge, 1978), 385. He cites older Christianity, "before it had lost its integrity," and Kantianism as examples, and he contrasts their idealism with a more modest "ethic of the mean," which accepts man's

nature as it is and puts no pressure on him to behave with ethical heroism. Freud, it should be noted, is included in the latter category.

53. Max Weber, *The Sociology of Religion*, trans. Ephraim Fischoff (Boston, 1964), 156, 273.

54. For the comparison with Durkheim, see, for example, Nisbet, *Sociological Tradition*, 252; Edward Tiryakian, "Emile Durkheim," in Bottomore and Nisbet, *History of Sociological Analysis*, 220. For the comparison with Nietzsche, see Wolfgang J. Mommsen, *The Age of Bureaucracy: Perspectives on the Political Sociology of Max Weber* (New York, 1977), 79.

55. The concept is most elaborately presented in Max Weber, *The Theory of Social and Economic Organization*, ed. Talcott Parsons (New York, 1964), 358–392. For an insightful discussion, see Luciano Cavalli, "Charisma and Twentieth-Century Politics," in Whimster and Lash, *Max Weber, Rationality and Modernity*, 317–333.

56. Parsons's awkward translation of "Herrschaft" as "imperative coordination" has generated considerable comment, as it could just as easily be translated as "domination" or "rulership." See the discussion in Richard Swedberg, *The Max Weber Dictionary: Key Words and Central Concepts* (Stanford, Calif., 2005), 64–66.

57. Weber, *Theory of Social and Economic Organization*, 358–359.

58. For an insightful discussion of routinization, which distinguishes between depersonalized and impersonalized variations, see Wolfgang Schluchter, *The Rise of Western Rationalism: Max Weber's Developmental Theory*, trans. Guenther Roth (Berkeley, 1979), 124–125.

59. Swedberg, *Max Weber Dictionary*, 359. "Berserkers" were Old Norse warriors who went into battle in a trancelike state.

60. The original term *stahlhartes Gehäuse* was rendered as "iron cage" by Talcott Parsons in his influential translation of *The Protestant Ethic and the Spirit of Capitalism*, but it has also been translated as "a shell as hard as steel" or "a steel-hard casing." For a discussion of the controversy over and afterlife of this metaphor, see Swedberg, *Max Weber Dictionary*, 132–133.

61. Harry Liebersohn, *Fate and Utopia in German Sociology, 1870–1923* (Cambridge, Mass., 1988), 124.

62. Mommsen, *Age of Bureaucracy*, chap. 4.

63. The connection with Schmitt was perhaps first suggested by Jürgen Habermas, who originally called him "a legitimate pupil" of Weber and then modified the metaphor to "a natural son." See Stammer, *Max Weber and Sociology Today*, 66. The same volume contains a spirited discussion of Mommsen's argument and the role of nationalism, imperialism, and great-power politics in Weber's worldview. For another analysis of the connection, see Stephen Turner and Regis Factor, "Decisionism and Politics: Weber as a Constitutional Theorist," in Whimster and Lash, *Max Weber, Rationality and Modernity*, 334–354.

64. See, for example, Mitzman, *Iron Cage*, 216–270; Scaff, *Fleeing the Iron Cage*, 106–108; Liebersohn, *Fate and Utopia in German Sociology*, 150–151.

65. Mitzman, *Iron Cage*, 267.

66. Weber, "Politics as Vocation," 127.

67. For a comparison, see Arpád Kardarkay, "The Demonic Self: Max Weber and Georg Lukács," *Hungarian Studies* 9, nos. 1/2 (1994); Liebersohn, *Fate and Utopia in German Sociology*, chap. 6.

68. Weber, "Politics as Vocation," 128.

69. Weber, "Science as Vocation," in *From Max Weber*, 155, 156. The phrase "demands of the day" was Goethe's, as was the idea of a personal "daemon," understood not in the sense of Satanic minion but as a source of spiritual inspiration. See Angus Nicholls, *Goethe's Concept of the Daemonic: After the Ancients* (Rochester, N.Y., 2006).

70. For a selection of these characterizations by intellectuals such as Ernst Troeltsch, Siegfried Kracauer, Karl Mannheim, and Christoph Steding, see Joshua Derman, "Max Weber's Anti-Utopianism in the Eyes of His Contemporaries," *Journal of the History of Ideas* 71, no. 3 (July 2010): 481–503.

71. Liebersohn, *Fate and Utopia in German Sociology*, 151; Scaff, *Fleeing the Iron Cage*, 144–149.

72. See Liebersohn, *Fate and Utopia in German Sociology*, 141–144.

73. See Efraim Podoksik, "Georg Simmel: Three Forms of Individualism and Historical Understanding," *New German Critique* 109 (Winter 2010): 119–145, which argues that there was an often ignored third meaning in his *lebensphilosophische* later work, which understood the individual as a reflection of the totality of life.

74. Simmel, "Individual and Society in Eighteenth-and Nineteenth-Century Views of Life: An Example of Philosophical Sociology," in *The Sociology of Georg Simmel*, ed. and trans. Kurt H. Wolff (New York, 1964), 63.

75. Simmel, "The Social and the Individual Level: An Example of General Sociology," in Wolff, *Sociology of Georg Simmel*, 33.

76. Simmel, "Types of Relationships by Degrees of Reciprocal Knowledge of Their Participants," in Wolff, *Sociology of Georg Simmel*, 321.

77. Simmel, "The Social and the Individual Level," 39.

78. Simmel's approach is often called impressionistic and antisystematic, with a typical description of the characteristics of his style reading as follows: "Different problems more or less simultaneously and without any clear indication of how they are linked, the inclination to eschew careful analysis and detailed argument in favor of pregnant examples and glittering insights, and the playful and inconclusive quality of the inquiry itself, in which aesthetic considerations frequently seem to outweigh the requirements of science." Guy Oakes, introduction to *Georg Simmel: On Women, Sexuality and Love*, trans. Guy Oakes (New Haven, Conn., 1984), 58. Useful introductions to his thought include David Frisby, *Georg Simmel* (Chichester, 1984); Rudolf H. Weingartner, *Experience and Culture: The Philosophy of Georg Simmel* (Middletown, Conn., 1962).

79. For a general analysis of the idea of "society," see David Frisby and Derek Sayer, *Society* (Chichester, 1986), which compares Durkheim and Simmel.

80. Frisby, *Fragments of Modernity*; Swingewood, *Cultural Theory*; Elizabeth S. Goodstein, *Experience without Qualities: Boredom and Modernity* (Stanford, Calif., 2005).

81. Georg Simmel, *The Philosophy of Money*, trans. Tom Bottomore and David Frisby (Boston, 1978). The concept of personal experience underlying Simmel's analysis was more that of transitory *Erlebnis* than cumulative *Erfahrung*, a distinction more explicitly thematized by Benjamin. See Frisby, *Fragments of Modernity*, 63. For my own attempt to sort out different modes of experience, see *Songs of Experience: Modern European and American Variations on a Universal Theme* (Berkeley, Calif., 2005).

82. For an analysis of this interaction, which discusses Simmel and the city he knew so well, see Andreas Killen, *Berlin Electropolis: Shock, Nerves, and German Modernity* (Berkeley, Calif., 2006).

83. Simmel, "The Metropolis and Mental Life," in Wolff, *Sociology of Georg Simmel*, 409–410.

84. For a discussion of the widespread culture of self-armoring in Weimar, especially during the mid-1920s period of the Neue Sachlichkeit, see Helmut Lethen, *Cool Conduct: The Culture of Distance in Weimar Germany*, trans. Don Reneau (Berkeley, Calif., 2002).

85. Simmel, "The Individual's Superiority over the Mass," in Wolff, *Sociology of Simmel*, 32.

86. Simmel, "The Conflict of Modern Culture," in Peter Lawrence, ed., *George Simmel: Sociologist and European* (Sunbury-on-Thames, 1976).

87. Simmel, "The Future of our Culture" (1909), in Lawrence, *George Simmel*, 251.

88. Swingewood, *Cultural Theory*, 146.

89. In his essay collection of 1909, *Soul and Form*, trans. Anna Bostock (Cambridge, Mass., 1974), Lukács adopted the same argument we have traced in Simmel, but after his conversion to Marxism, he explicitly repudiated it, and with it any romanticization of the *Lumpenproletariat* praised by Baudelaire. For an analysis of their relationship, see Liebersohn, *Fate and Utopia in German Sociology*. It should be noted that the German word *Seele*, which is sometimes translated as "soul" and sometimes as "psyche," could be counterposed not only to "form" but also to *Geist*, "intellect" or "spirit."

90. Jürgen Habermas, "Georg Simmel on Philosophy and Culture: Postscript to a Collection of Essays," *Critical Inquiry* 22, no. 3 (Spring 1996): 413.

91. Baudelaire, "Salon of 1846," 105.

92. Foucault, "What Is Enlightenment?," 41.

93. Frisby, *Fragments of Modernity*, 41.

94. As David Kettler and Colin Load note in their discussion of the legacy of Weber and Simmel, "Weimar sociology took its brief from their newly ironic orientation." "Weimar Sociology," in Peter E. Gordon and John P. McCormick, eds., *Weimar Thought: A Contested Legacy* (Princeton, N.J., 2013), 18.

95. Frédéric Vandenberghe, "Simmel and Weber as Ideal-Typical Founders of Sociology," *Philosophy and Social Criticism* 25, no. 4 (1999): 59.

Chapter 11

1. See David D. Roberts, *Nothing but History: Reconstruction and Extremity after Metaphysics* (Berkeley, Calif., 1995). It should be noted that professional philosophers in the recent past, especially in the Anglo-American tradition, have also been loath to spin out speculative philosophies of history. See Kerwin Lee Klein, *From History to Theory* (Berkeley, Calif., 2011).

2. Siegfried Kracauer, *History: The Last Things Before the Last* (New York, 1969).

3. A characteristic expression of this reluctance can be found in Quentin Skinner's declaration: "I am not in general talking about truth; I am talking about what people at different times may have had good reasons by their light for holding true, regardless of whether we ourselves believe that what they held true was in fact the truth.... I am convinced, in short, that the importance of truth for the kind of historical enquiries I am considering has been exaggerated." Quentin Skinner, "A Reply to My Critics," in *Meaning and Context: Quentin Skinner and His Critics*, ed. James Tully (Oxford, 1988), 256.

4. For accounts of the emergence of "scientific" history, see Joyce Appleby, Lynn Hunt, and Margaret Jacob, *Telling the Truth about History* (New York, 1994), part 1; Martha Howell and Walter Prevenier, *From Reliable Sources: An Introduction to Historical Methods* (Ithaca, N.Y., 2001).

5. For a discussion of these different subdisciplines, see Howell and Prevenier, *From Reliable Sources*, chap. 2. Rather, however, than dismissing myth, legend, and fables as merely fallacious, many historians, perhaps beginning with Giambattista Vico, began to read them as symptomatic of cultural mentalities—that is, as hermeneutically legible evidence of past beliefs.

6. Peter Burke, "Historical Facts and Historical Fictions," *Filozofski Vesnik* 2 (1994): 172.

7. Roger Chartier, *On the Edge of the Cliff: History, Language and Practices*, trans. Lydia G. Cochrane (Baltimore, 1996), 6.

8. A salient example, recently revived by Carlo Ginzburg, is the method of the nineteenth-century Italian art historian Giovanni Morelli to identify involuntary, symptomatic clues, such as the way ears were typically rendered, to settle questions of attribution for paintings. Carlo Ginzburg, *Clues, Myths and Historical Method*, trans. John Tedeschi and Ann C. Tedeschi (Baltimore, 1989).

9. The unevenness of the relationship between professionalization and the struggle for objectivity in historical accounts, at least in the American context, is made clear in Peter Novick, *That Noble Dream: The "Objectivity Question" and the American Historical Profession* (Cambridge, 1988). Doubts about the truth claims of historical narratives are, of course, almost as old as the practice of writing them. Peter Burke notes that Lucian already parodied Herodotus and Thucydides in the second century CE. See Burke, "Historical Facts and Historical Fictions," 169.

10. This difference has long been noted, for example, by R. G. Collingwood, who claimed it defeated positivist attempts to write accurately about the past as if it were

an object analyzable from the outside. For an attempt to answer him, see William Dray, *History as Re-enactment: R. G. Collingwood's Idea of History* (Oxford, 1995), 269–270. There is, however, a parallel between history and one scientific subject: stellar astronomy, whose objects of inquiry are long past. For a discussion, see Martin Jay, "Astronomical Hindsight: The Speed of Light and Virtual Reality," in *Refractions of Violence* (New York, 2003), 119–132.

11. For a history of the adoption of that phrase in American historiography, see Georg Iggers, "The Image of Ranke in American and German Historical Thought," *History and Theory* 2 (1962): 17–40.

12. Leopold von Ranke, *The Theory and Practice of History*, ed. Georg G. Iggers and Konrad von Moltke (Indianapolis, 1973), 39.

13. The primacy of the visual model has been detected as far back as the Greek historian Herodotus, who dismissed the value of hearsay. See François Hartog, "Herodotus and the Historiographical Operation," *Diacritics* 22, no. 2 (1992): 83–93. The undistorted mirror can be found in Lucian and was still in use in the seventeenth century. See Reinhart Koselleck, *Futures Past: On the Semantics of Historical Time*, trans. Keith Tribe (Cambridge, Mass., 1985), 133.

14. All of these key terms warrant scare quotes because each has been shown to be the result of a process of historical definition and clarification. See, for example, in the case of "facts," Mary Poovey, *A History of the Modern Fact: Problems of Knowledge in the Sciences of Wealth and Society* (Chicago, 1998); Barbara Shapiro, *A Culture of Fact: England, 1550–1720* (Ithaca, N.Y., 2003); for "event," Martin Jay, "Historicism and the Event," in *Against the Grain: Jewish Intellectuals in Hard Times*, ed. Ezra Mendelsohn, Stefani Hoffman, and Richard I. Cohen (New York, 2014), 143–167.

15. See Robert C. Roberts and Ryan West, "The Virtue of Honesty: A Conceptual Exploration," in *Integrity, Honesty, and Truth Seeking*, ed. Christian B. Miller and Ryan West (New York, 2020), 97–126.

16. Joshua Rasmussen, *Defending the Correspondence Theory of Truth* (Cambridge, 2014).

17. Novick, *That Noble Dream*. The phrase was coined by Theodore Clark Smith and then mocked by Charles Beard in the 1930s. See Wolfgang Natter, Theodore R. Schatzki, and John Paul Jones, eds., *Objectivity and Its Other* (New York, 1995).

18. See David Gross, *Lost Time: On Remembering and Forgetting in Late Modern Culture* (Amherst, Mass., 2000); Paul Ricoeur, *History, Memory, Forgetting*, trans. Kathleen Blamey and David Pellauer (Chicago, 2004); and Frank Ankersmit, *Sublime Historical Experience* (Stanford, Calif., 2005), 319–325, for discussions of the dialectic of forgetting and remembering. Not only is this limitation acknowledged by working historians, who depend on the scattered shards of a past that escaped time's ravages and choose only some of them to build their reconstructions, but it is also part of our everyday understanding of the distinction between normal quotidian existence, which

falls into condign oblivion, and those highly unusual exceptions that are recognized as "memorable" or *a fortiori* "historical."

19. In one of the few missteps in *That Noble Dream*, Novick claims that "in their academic writings scholars strive to present 'the whole truth and nothing but the truth' for a variety of reasons, not least among them fear of the embarrassment which followed being caught doing otherwise" (471).

20. As Ankersmit has noted, representations of the past are never of objects per se, but only of finite aspects of them. Frank Ankersmit, "Truth in History and Literature," *Narrative* 18, no. 1 (2010): 40.

21. See Kracauer, *History*, chap. 5.

22. For a discussion of the rise and fall of the ideal of universal history, see Koselleck, *Futures Past*.

23. Bertrand Russell addressed the paradox as a mathematical problem and claimed that Shandy could have solved it if he had lived forever; but historians, alas, don't have that luxury. For one account of Russell's attempt, see R. J. Diamond, "Resolution of the Paradox of *Tristram Shandy*," *Philosophy of Science* 31, no. 1 (January 1964): 55–58.

24. For a discussion, see chapter 3 of this volume.

25. For a defense of the importance of "side-shadowing," see Gary Saul Morson, *Narrative and Freedom: The Shadows of Time* (New Haven, Conn., 1994); Michael André Bernstein, *Foregone Conclusions: Against Apocalyptic History* (Berkeley, Calif., 1994).

26. See Samuel Weber, "Objectivity Otherwise," in Natter et al., *Objectivity and Its Other*, 33–47.

27. See Dominick LaCapra, *History and Criticism* (Ithaca, N.Y., 1985), chap. 3. He argues that "transference causes fear of possession by the past and loss of control over both it and oneself. It simultaneously brings the temptation to assert full control over the 'object' of study through ideologically suspect procedures that may be related to the phenomenon Freud discussed as 'narcissism'" (72).

28. It was understood as early as J. C. Chladenius in the eighteenth century that not only did historical actors often have different points of view or perspectives, but that historical narrators did as well. See Koselleck, *Futures Past*, 137–140.

29. It turns out that this now famous remark from a conversation during Richard Nixon's trip to China in 1972 may have referred to the events of 1968 rather than the French Revolution of 1789. See Dean Nichols, "Zhou en lai's Famous Saying Debunked," *History Today* (June 15, 2011), https://historynewsnetwork.org/article/140010.

30. Cited in Glen Warren Bowersock, *Fiction as History: Nero to Julian* (Berkeley, Calif., 1994), 12.

31. See, for example, Kalle Pihlainen, "The Eternal Return of Reality: On Constructivism and Current Historical Desires," *Storia della Storiografia* 69, no. 1 (2014): 103–115, for the former, Novick, *That Noble Dream* for the latter. One stresses the cognitive, the other the moral implications of the debunking of an emphatic concept of historical truth.

32. See Richard Vann, "Turning Linguistic: History and Theory and History and Theory, 1960–1975," in *A New Philosophy of History*, ed. Frank Ankersmit and Hans Kellner (Chicago, 1995), 40–69.

33. An extreme version of this argument, occasionally ventured by philosophers, would deny the ontological status of the past as such, arguing instead that all we have are remnants of previous "present" moments in our "present." For a consideration and refutation of this argument, see Michael Dummett, *Truth and the Past* (New York, 2004).

34. As in the case of Ranke, Croce's own position was often simplified by those who cited this slogan. See David D. Roberts, "Croce in America: Influence, Misunderstanding and Neglect," *Humanitas* 8, no. 2 (1995): 3–34; and "The Stakes of Misreading: Hayden White, Carlo Ginzburg and the Crocean Legacy," *Rivista di Studi Italiani* 20, no. 2 (December 2002): 1–30.

35. For a recent discussion of this issue, see Pavel M. Stepantsov, "The Significance of the Issue of Events': Identity under Different Descriptions for Social Theory and Social Philosophy," *International Journal of Social Science and Humanity* 3, no. 3 (May 2013): 259–262.

36. See Roland Barthes, "The Discourse of History," in *The Rustle of Language*, trans. Richard Howard (Berkeley, Calif., 1989), 139.

37. See Hayden White, *Metahistory: The Historical Imagination in Nineteenth-Century Europe* (Baltimore, 1973); *Tropics of Discourse: Essays in Cultural Criticism* (Baltimore, 1978); *Figural Realism: Studies in the Mimesis Effect* (Baltimore, 1999).

38. For a discussion, see David Carr, *Experience and History: Phenomenological Perspectives on the Historical World* (Oxford, 2014), chap. 7.

39. See Gérard Genette, *Narrative Discourse: An Essay in Method*, trans. Jane E. Lewin (Oxford, 1980).

40. Saul Friedlander, *Nazi Germany and the Jews*, 2 vols. (New York, 1998, 2008). It should be noted that as early as the "antilogies" or opposing speeches introduced in Thucydides, historians have ventriloquized different viewpoints in a similar way.

41. For a consideration of this argument, see Hayden White, "Historical Emplotment and the Problem of Truth," in *Probing the Limits of Representation: Nazism and the "Final Solution,"* ed. Saul Friedlander (Cambridge, Mass., 1992), 37–53.

42. R. G. Collingwood, *The Idea of History*, ed. Jan van der Dussen (New York, 1994), 231–249.

43. For one consideration of this dichotomy, see H. Stuart Hughes, *History as Art and as Science: Twin Vistas on the Past* (New York, 1964). It should be noted that for all of his stress on scientificity, Ranke acknowledged that "history is distinguished from all other sciences in that it is also an art. History is a science in collecting, finding, penetrating; it is an art because it recreates and portrays that which it has found and recognized.... The difference is that ... philosophy and poetry move within the realm of the ideal while history has to rely on reality" (*Theory and Practice of History*, 33).

44. See Friedlander, *Probing the Limits of Representation*.

45. Phillip Sydney, *The Defense of Poesie* (Oxford, 1974), 152–153.

46. For a discussion of the emergence of fictionality in the modern novel, see Catherine Gallagher, *Nobody's Story: The Vanishing Acts of Women Writers in the Marketplace, 1670–1820* (Berkeley, Calif., 1994). The intertwining of history and fiction is especially fraught in the case of self-consciously historical novels and counterfactual, alternate history novels.

47. Edmund Husserl, *Experience and Judgment*, trans. James Spencer Churchill (Evanston, Ill., 1975). For a discussion, see Lambert Zuidervaart, *Truth in Husserl, Heidegger, and the Frankfurt School* (Cambridge, Mass., 2017), 117.

48. David Carr, *Time, Narrative, and History* (Bloomington, Ind., 1986), 99. Italics in original.

49. Chartier, *On the Edge of the Cliff*, 17. He attributes the term "laminated" to Michel de Certeau. White, it might be noted, concedes that there is a difference between established "facts" and the narratives woven from them. See White, "Historical Emplotment and the Problem of Truth," in Friedlander, *Probing the Limits of Representation*, 38.

50. Michel de Certeau, *Heterologies: Discourse on the Other*, trans. Brian Massumi (Minneapolis, 1986), 200. For a discussion of the ambivalences in de Certeau's use of falsifiability, see Jeremy Ahearne, *Michel de Certeau: Interpretation and Its Other* (Stanford, Calif., 1995), 35. See also Wim Weymans, "Michel de Certeau and the Limits of Historical Representation," *History and Theory* 43 (2004) for a discussion of the scientific historical impulse in his idiosyncratic method.

51. According to the historian Alan Spitzer, "although the 'whole concept of historical truth' has been called into question, almost everyone claims to know what a lie about the past looks like. In historical debate, lying falls at the near end of a spectrum ranging from willful to unwitting misrepresentation, from the falsification to the misinterpretation of evidence, from arguments in manifest bad faith to well-intentioned incoherence." Alan B. Spitzer, *Historical Truth and Lies about the Past* (Chapel Hill, N.C., 1996), 1.

52. Karl Popper, *The Logic of Scientific Discovery*, trans. Karl Popper (London, 1959); *Conjectures and Refutations* (New York, 1963).

53. Karl Popper, *The Poverty of Historicism* (London, 1957).

54. Carl Hempel, "The Function of General Laws in History," *Journal of Philosophy* 39, no. 2 (1942): 35–48.

55. For an account, see Malachi Haim Hacohen, *Karl Popper: The Formative Years, 1902–1945* (Cambridge, 2000), 207.

56. Jonas Grethlein, "Experientiality and 'Narrative Reference' with Thanks to Thucydides," *History and Theory* 49 (October 2010): 315–335.

57. See Ankersmit, *Sublime Historical Experience*; Eelco Runia, *Moved by the Past: Discontinuity and Historical Mutation* (New York, 2014); Carr, *Experience and History*. See also the literary historian and critic Hans Ulrich Gumbrecht, *Production of Presence: What Meaning Cannot Convey* (Stanford, Calif., 2003). For an exploration of dif-

ferences between Ankersmit and Runia, see Anton Froeyman, "Frank Ankersmit and Eelco Runia: The Presence and Otherness of the Past," *Rethinking History* 16, no. 3 (2012): 393–415. Ankersmit was first known as a narrativist akin in many ways to Hayden White (e.g., Frank Ankersmit, "Wahrheit in Literatur und Geschichte," in *Geschichtsdiscurs*, vol. 5, *Globale Konflikte, Erinnerungsarbeit and Neuorientierungen seit 1945*, ed. Wolfgang Küttler, Jörn Rüsen, and Ernst Schulin [Frankfurt, 1999]), but he became disenchanted with the linguistic turn. For a critique of his later position from an adherent of his earlier one, see Peter Icke, *Frank Ankersmit's Lost Historical Cause: From Language to Experience* (New York, 2012).

58. For an account of the role of experience in historical reasoning, including Ankersmit's notion of sublime historical experience, see Martin Jay, *Songs of Experience: Modern European and American Variations on a Universal Theme* (Berkeley, Calif., 2005), chap. 6.

59. For an account, see Joanna E. Ziegler, "Scholarship as/and Performance: The Case of Johan Huizinga and His Concept of 'Historical Sensation,'" in *Practicing Catholic: Ritual, Body and Contestation in Catholic Faith*, ed. Bruce T. Morrill, Joanna E. Ziegler, and Susan Rodgers (New York, 2006), 247–255.

60. Ankersmit, *Sublime Historical Experience*, 132.

61. Ibid., 161–162.

62. Ibid., 225. Emphasis in original.

63. Runia, *Moved by the Past*, 96.

64. George Steiner, *Real Presences* (Chicago, 1991).

65. Ankersmit, *Sublime Historical Experience*, 233.

66. Runia, *Moved by the Past*, 96. Italics in original.

67. See Thomas Haskell, *The Emergence of Professional Social Science: The American Social Science Association and the Nineteenth-Century Crisis of Authority* (Baltimore, 2000), 237–238; Novick, *That Noble Dream*, 570–572. For Peirce's original argument, see C. S. Pierce, "The Fixation of Belief" (1877) in *Pragmatism: A Reader*, ed. Louis Menand (New York, 1997), 7–25.

68. Collingwood, *Idea of History*, 164.

69. Armand-Augustin-Louis Caulaincourt, *With Napoleon in Russia*, trans. Jean Hanoteau (New York, 1935). The original French version appeared in part in the 1820s.

70. Nancy Streuver, "Topics in History," in *Metahistory: Six Critiques, History and Theory* 19 (1980).

71. Jürgen Habermas, *The Structural Transformation of the Public Sphere: An Inquiry into a Category of Bourgeois Society*, trans. Thomas Burger (Cambridge, Mass., 1992). There is an immense literature on Habermas's notions of the public sphere, communicative rationality, universal pragmatics, and the ideal speech situation. For my own attempt to discuss its implications, which considers objections as well as arguments in its favor, see Martin Jay, *Reason after Its Eclipse: On Late Critical Theory* (Madison, Wi., 2016). What is important to note is that although he began with a theory of justification in which truth was an effect of reaching a consensus, Habermas came to ap-

preciate the importance of practical action in the world to test the validity of such a consensus, action that allows for learning. For a succinct account of this issue, see Zuidervaart, *Truth in Husserl, Heidegger and the Frankfurt School*, chap. 5.

72. Dummett, *Truth and the Past*.

73. Frank Ankersmit, "Truth in History and Literature," *Narrative* 18, no. 1 (2010): 42–43.

74. Thus, for example, de Certeau writes, "This community is also a factory, its members distributed along assembly lines, subject to budgetary pressures, hence, dependent on political decisions and bound by the growing constraints of a sophisticated machinery (archival infrastructures, computers, publishers' demands, etc.). Its operations are determined by a rather narrow and homogeneous segment of society from which its members are recruited. Its general orientation is governed by sociocultural assumptions and postulates imposed through recruitment, through the existing and established fields of research, through the demands stemming from the personal interests of a boss, through the modes and fashions of the moment, etc." (*Heterologies*, 204).

75. Michel Foucault, *Power/Knowledge: Selected Interviews and Other Writings, 1972–1977*, ed. Colin Gordon, trans. Colin Gordon, Leo Marshall, John Mepham, and Kate Soper (New York, 1980).

76. For a history of the professionalization of history, which unlike Novick's focuses on the European rather than American examples, see Rolf Torstendahl, *The Rise and Propagation of Historical Professionalism* (London, 2015).

77. Bernard Williams, *Truth and Truthfulness: An Essay in Genealogy* (Princeton, N.J., 2002), 258.

78. George Orwell, *1984: Text, Sources, Criticism*, ed. Irving Howe (New York, 1963), 109.

Chapter 12

1. Martin Jay, "For Theory," *Theory and Society* 25, no. 2 (April 1996), reprinted in my collection *Cultural Semantics: Keywords of Our Time* (Amherst, Mass., 1998), 15–30.

2. Alvin W. Gouldner, *For Sociology: Renewal and Critique in Sociology Today* (New York, 1973). Gouldner was himself paying ironic tribute to Louis Althusser's *For Marx*.

3. Steven Knapp and Walter Benn Michaels, "Against Theory," *Critical Inquiry* 8 (Summer 1982): 723–742. Similar arguments were made by Stanley Fish during the same era.

4. Paul de Man, *The Resistance to Theory* (Minneapolis, 1986). The specific theory to whose resistance he objected was deconstruction.

5. Jay, "For Theory," in *Cultural Semantics*, 16.

6. Herman Rappaport, *The Theory Mess* (New York, 2001).

7. Nicholas Dames, "The Theory Generation," *N+1* 14 (Summer 2012), https://nplusonemag.com/issue-14/reviews/the-theory-generation/.

8. Putting these familiar terms in quotation marks is necessary to indicate that they too are polysemic with many discrete and often highly charged variations. To do justice to their placement in a semantic force field with "theory" would require carefully unpacking their disparate, even sometimes contradictory, meanings.

9. See, for example, Mark Warren, "What Is Political Theory/Philosophy?," *PS: Political Science and Politics* 22, no. 3 (1989): 606–612.

10. Hasa, "Difference Between Philosophy and Theory," December 7, 2016, https://www.differencebetween.com/difference-between-philosophy-and-vs-theory/.

11. For example, Herbert Marcuse, "Philosophy and Critical Theory," *Negations: Essays in Critical Theory*, trans. Jeremy. J. Shapiro (Boston, 2009), 99–119.

12. Aesthetic questions were not only crucial for post-structuralist and hermeneutic theoreticians but also for those in the Critical Theory tradition, as demonstrated by the influence of Theodor W. Adorno's *Aesthetic Theory*, which was translated into English in 1984 and retranslated only thirteen years later.

13. For one account of the debate, which contains references to the major texts on both sides, see Raoul Moati, *Derrida/Searle: Deconstruction and Ordinary Language*, trans. Timothy Attanucci and Maureen Chun (New York, 2014).

14. For a discussion of Rorty's development, see Neil Gross, *Richard Rorty: The Making of an American Philosopher* (Chicago, 2008). He left the Princeton Philosophy Department in 1982 to take a named chair in the humanities at the University of Virginia and then later Stanford University.

15. Brian Leiter, "Blaming the Victim Is Apparently OK When the Accused in a Title IX Proceeding Is a Feminist Literary Theorist," Leiter Reports: A Philosophy Blog, June 10, 2018, https://leiterreports.typepad.com/blog/2018/06/blaming-the-victim-is-apparently-ok-when-the-accused-is-a-feminist-literary-theorist.html.

16. The term itself was coined by the Hegelian Johann Eduard Erdmann in 1870 to criticize Eduard Beneke, who sought to understand the psychological roots of philosophizing. For an account of the debates it engendered, see Martin Kusch, *Psychologism: A Case Study in the Sociology of Knowledge* (New York, 1995).

17. It is important to note that the implications of its name notwithstanding, "psychologism" extended beyond the reduction of rational thought to psychological emotions. It included the sociology of knowledge, historicist relativism, and the power of cultural contexts. Thus, a theorist like Rorty could protest against the reduction of Heidegger's ideas to his personal history, most notably his Nazi sympathies, and yet still have no use for the universalist or transcendental claims of traditional philosophy.

18. The "culture of critical discourse" was identified with a new elite of humanists and scientists by Alvin W. Gouldner in *The Future of Intellectuals and the Rise of the New Class* (New York, 1979), 28–29. Jürgen Habermas is most often credited with generating interest in the "public sphere" as the institutional basis for "communicative

rationality" in *The Structural Transformation of the Public Sphere: An Inquiry into a Category of Bourgeois Society*, trans. Thomas Burger and Frederick Lawrence (Cambridge, Mass., 1991). Because both of these accounts are historical and sociological, they cannot be seen as pure examples of the critique of psychologism, but they seek to explain how a "space of reasons," to cite the famous phrase of Wilfred Sellars, could be created in which the cultural authority or personal biases of those in the discussion are kept at bay.

19. See Martin Jay, "Modernism and the Specter of Psychologism," in *Cultural Semantics*, 165–180.

20. Morris Raphael Cohen and Ernst Nagel, *Logic and Scientific Method* (New York, 1934), 388. Often understood as anticipated by the classical critique of the *argumentum ad hominem*, it has also been defended by philosophers who cannot be included in the "theorist" category. See, for example, Margaret A. Crouch, "A 'Limited' Defense of the Genetic Fallacy," *Metaphilosophy* 24, no. 3 (July 1993): 227–240.

21. The English translation came out two years later as Julia Kristeva, *Powers of Horror: An Essay on Abjection*, trans. Leon S. Rudiez (New York, 1982). It coincided with renewed interest in the legacy of the renegade surrealist Georges Bataille, whose work had anticipated many of Kristeva's arguments. For a consideration of its importance, see my essay "Abjection Overruled" in *Cultural Semantics*, 144–156. For indications of its continuing relevance, see Rina Arya, *Abjection and Representation: An Exploration of Abjection in the Visual Arts, Film and Literature* (New York, 2014); Rina Arya and Nicholas Chare, eds., *Abject Visions: Powers of Horror in Art and Literature* (Manchester, 2016).

22. In the case of the aesthetic modernism, unlike in its philosophical counterpart, rhetoric was far less of a threat, as the analysis of nonlogical and nonreferential uses of language had always played a central role.

23. Other media through which ideas were refracted—material or sensual—were also foregrounded by theorists who questioned the pristine quality of intellectual argumentation.

24. For an attempt to confront this issue, see my "Can There Be National Philosophies in a Transnational World?," in *Essays from the Edge: Parerga and Paralipomena* (Charlottesville, Va., 2011), 162–176,

25. Bill Readings, "Why is Theory Foreign?," in *Theory Between the Disciplines: Authority, Vision, Politics*, ed. Martin Kreiswirth and Mark A. Cheetham (Ann Arbor, 1990), 97–99.

26. This approach was also adopted by Reinhart Koselleck and his colleagues in the international "conceptual history" movement.

27. The suspicion of this prejudice, especially in a variety of French theories, is traced in Martin Jay, *Downcast Eyes: The Denigration of Vision in Twentieth-Century French Thought* (Berkeley, Calif., 1993). For a discussion of a similar critique of the value of transparency, see Stefanos Geroulanos, *Transparency in Postwar France: A Critical History of the Present* (Stanford, Calif., 2017).

28. Paul Strohm, *Theory and the Premodern Text* (Minneapolis, 2000); Bruce Holsinger, *The Premodern Condition: Medievalism and the Making of Theory* (Chicago, 2005); Andrew Cole, *The Birth of Theory* (Chicago, 2014).

29. For one consideration of this theme, see Isabel Thomas-Fogel, *The Death of Philosophy: Reference and Self-Reference in Contemporary Thought*, trans. Richard A. Lynch (New York, 2011).

30. John McCumber, "Philosophy vs. Theory: Reshaping the Debate," Mondesfrancophone.com, August 25, 2009, https://mondesfrancophones.com/espaces/philosophies/philosophy-vs-theory-reshaping-the-debate/.

31. There are, of course, many examples of respected figures in established philosophy departments who have already heeded this advice. Just to mention a few Berkeley colleagues, past and present: Richard Wollheim, Hubert Dreyfus, Hans Sluga, and Alva Noë.

32. Edward W. Said first introduced this idea in "Travelling Theory," in *The World, the Text and the Critic* (Cambridge, Mass., 1983), 226–247.

33. Ever since the rise of so-called affective criticism, identified with literary critics such as Lauren Berlant, Eve Kosofsky Sedgwick, Rita Felski, and Sharon Marcus, critique and the hermeneutics of suspicion have been under attack. But as in the case of the other "others" of theory listed above, it too cries out for theoretical reflection about its normative investments and hidden premises.

34. For discussions of "weak theory," see the special issue of *Modernism/Modernity*, 25, 3 (September 2018), edited by Paul Saint-Amour, and the responses on the journal's website, which begin here: https://modernismmodernity.org/forums/posts/responses-special-issue-weak-theory-part-i.

Chapter 13

1. Alexander Hall, "Jordan Peterson Announces Free Speech Platform 'Thinkspot,'" *MRC NewsBusters*, June 12, 2019, https://www.newsbusters.org/blogs/techwatch/alexander-hall/2019/06/12/jordan-peterson-announces-free-speech-platform-thinkspot.

2. Among the most powerful critics of the conflation of freedom of speech and academic freedom are Robert Post, *Democracy, Expertise, Academic Freedom* (New Haven, Conn., 2012), and Stanley Fish, *Versions of Academic Freedom: From Professionalism to Revolution* (Chicago, 2014). For a discussion of their positions, including the differences between them, see Martyn Hammersley, "Can Academic Freedom Be Justified? Reflections on the Arguments of Robert Post and Stanley Fish," *Higher Education Quarterly* 70, no. 2 (2016): 108–126. For a defense of unregulated speech in academia, see Erwin Chemerinsky and Howard Gillman, *Free Speech on Campus* (New Haven, Conn., 2017).

3. Cited in Adam Liptak, "How Conservatives Weaponized the First Amendment," *New York Times*, June 30, 2018, https://www.nytimes.com/2018/06/30/us/politics/first

-amendment-conservatives-supreme-court.html. For another account, see Jedidiah Britton-Purdy, "The Bosses' Constitution: How and Why the First Amendment Became a Weapon for the Right," *Nation*, June 12, 2018, https://www.thenation.com/article/the-bosses-constitution/. He argues that it can be traced as far back as "1976 with its decision in *Buckley v. Valeo*, a ruling that gutted Congress's post-Watergate attempts at campaign-finance reform."

4. It has been suggested, however, that the metaphoric use of the term has gone along with the decline of literal violence. See John Kelly, "Everything Is *Weaponized* Now. This Is a Good Sign for Peace," *Slate*, August 30, 2016, https://slate.com/human-interest/2016/08/how-weaponize-became-a-political-cultural-and-internet-term-du-jour.html.

5. For example, Black argued in a dissent in a case dealing with state restrictions on speech, *Beauharnais v. Illinois*, 343 U.S. 988 (1952), that "I think the First Amendment, with the Fourteenth, 'absolutely' forbids such laws without any 'ifs' or 'buts' or 'whereases.'" But, according to Robert Post (personal communication, August 10, 2019), "if you look closely at his opinions, he readily acknowledges—as everybody does—the need for time, place and manner regulations. What he absolutely forbids are laws with the intended purpose of suppressing speech because of its content. That is not absolutism. That is an absolute rule in the service of a particular account of when speech may and may not be regulated."

6. Herbert Marcuse, "Repressive Tolerance," in Robert Paul Wolff, Barrington Moore, Jr., and Herbert Marcuse, *A Critique of Pure Tolerance* (Boston, 1965). For a recent revisiting of some of the issues it raised, see Wendy Brown and Rainer Forst, *The Power of Tolerance: A Debate*, ed. Luca di Blasi and Christoph F. E. Holzhey (New York, 2014). For a recent adoption of Marcuse's position, see Brian Leiter, "The Case Against Free Speech," *Sydney Law Review* 407 (2016): 422–423.

7. Weaponization, to be sure, carries a more pejorative connotation than functionalization, suggesting an ulterior motive beyond the function it alleges to serve. Thus, the alt-right's adoption of the rhetoric of free speech on campuses can be understood not as serving genuine discussion aiming at the truth but as a strategic gambit designed to expose what they claim as the hypocritical liberal and leftist monopoly of existing discussion. What, however, ties weaponization and functionalization together is their common distinction from the absolutist notion that free speech is its own end, no matter the context or consequences.

8. In fact, it is rare to find a total absolutist who brooks no exceptions. As the entry on freedom of speech in the *Stanford Encyclopedia of Philosophy* puts it, "The first thing to note in any sensible discussion of freedom of speech is that it will have to be limited. Every society places some limits on the exercise of speech because it always takes place within a context of competing values." See "Freedom of Speech," last revised May 1, 2017, https://plato.stanford.edu/entries/freedom-speech/.

9. The term "fetishization" is, of course, itself highly loaded and brings with it many layers of meaning from religious, anthropological, economic, and psychological

discourses. Rather than dive into the deep waters that have risen around its various usages, let me stipulate what I intend by it here. For our purposes, it signifies taking a part for the whole, disembedding it from the larger context(s) in which it functions, and isolating it as self-sufficient in its own right. As the classic example of a sexualized foot fetish implies, it involves a displacement of cathected energy away from its actual target to a synecdochic substitute for it.

10. Robert C. Post, *Constitutional Domains: Democracy, Community, Management* (Cambridge, Mass, 1995).

11. For one account, see Ronald J. Krotoszynski, Jr., *The First Amendment in Cross-Cultural Perspective* (New York, 2006).

12. Joshua Cohen argues for a slightly different tripartite alternative: an "expressive interest," which is in the articulation of "thoughts, attitudes and feelings of matters of personal or broader human concern"; a "deliberative interest," which tries to figure out "what is best" or "genuinely worthwhile"; and an "informational interest," which pursues "reliable information about the conditions required for pursuing one's aims and aspirations." See his "Freedom of Expression," *Philosophy and Public Affairs* 22, no. 3 (1993), 207–263.

13. John Milton, *Areopagitica*, ed. Richard C. Jebb (Cambridge, 1918), 43–50.

14. The development of the institutions and practices that accompany this idealized version of rational justification, at least in European history, is classically discussed in Jürgen Habermas, *The Structural Transformation of the Public Sphere: An Inquiry into a Category of Bourgeois Society*, trans. Thomas Burger and Frederick Lawrence (Cambridge, Mass., 1991). His argument has generated many responses, an early compendium of which can be found in Craig Calhoun, ed., *Habermas and the Public Sphere* (Cambridge, Mass., 1992).

15. John Stuart Mill, *On Liberty* (New York, 1956), 27.

16. Marcuse, "Repressive Tolerance," 89.

17. Mill, *On Liberty*, 21.

18. Mill, in fact, optimistically expected that "as mankind improves, the number of doctrines which are no longer disputed or doubted will be constantly on the increase; and the well-being of mankind may almost be measured by the number and gravity of the truths which have reached the point of being uncontested." *On Liberty*, 53. He worried, however, that it would diminish the need to defend such truths through reasoned argument, and he confessed, "I should like to see the teachers of mankind endeavoring to provide a substitute for it" (54).

19. For a trenchant discussion of the rationales for and repercussions of these laws, see Nicolay Koposov, *Memory Laws, Memory Wars: The Politics of the Past in Europe and Russia* (Cambridge, 2018). He notes that at his writing, some twenty-seven countries have restrictive memory laws, but not the United States.

20. Leiter, "Case Against Free Speech," 433ff.

21. The refusal of students at Middlebury College to allow Murray to speak in 2017 occasioned a flood of commentary in the press. For a reflection on the controversy by

a college administrator, see Baishaki Taylor, "Free Speech Conflict: What We Learned at Middlebury College," *Journal of Dispute Resolution* 2 (2018), 23–28.

22. Mill, *On Liberty*, 21.

23. "The Universal Declaration of Human Rights," United Nations, https://www.un.org/en/universal-declaration-human-rights/.

24. "International Covenant on Civil and Political Rights," United Nations Commission on Human Rights, https://www.ohchr.org/en/professionalinterest/pages/ccpr.aspx.

25. The metaphor appears, for example, in Oliver Wendell Holmes's famous dissent to *Abrams v. United States* (1919), whose importance is discussed in Thomas Healey, *The Great Dissent: How Oliver Wendell Holmes Changed His Mind—and Changed the History of Free Speech in America* (New York, 2014). Inevitably, the question has to be asked: what is the relationship between the metaphoric "freedom" of a marketplace of ideas and the supposed freedom of an economic marketplace, especially one inflected by oligopolistic inequalities and the manipulation of preferences through nonrational techniques of persuasion? The ideal of complete laissez-faire is, of course, rarely realized in practice or even defended by economists, except by the most libertarian of theorists, and it is not clear that it would function more effectively in the competition of ideas. Nor it is clear that the trading of commodities in an economic marketplace is equivalent to the weighing of ideas in a discussion, as the former involves scarcity and exchange, while the latter, despite issues of intellectual property, does not. For discussions, see R. H. Coase, "The Economics of the First Amendment: The Market for Goods and the Market for Ideas," *American Economic Review* 64 (1974): 384–391; Raoul Vaneigem, *Rien n'est sacré, tout peut se dire; reflexions sur la liberté d'expression* (Paris, 2015). The latter, by a former Situationist leader, presents an absolutist defense of free speech and radically distinguishes it from freedom of exchange in the marketplace.

26. See, for example, Jonathan Gilmore, "Expression as Realization: Speaker's Interests in Free Speech," *Law and Philosophy* 30 (2011): 517–539.

27. Mill, *On Liberty*, 81.

28. George Kateb, "The Freedom of Worthless and Harmful Speech," in *Liberalism without Illusions: Essays on Liberal Theory and the Political Vision of Judith N. Shklar*, ed. Bernard Yack (Chicago, 1996), 222.

29. Susan J. Brison, "The Autonomy Defense of Free Speech," *Ethics* 108 (January 1998): 312–329.

30. The vexed concept of "person," which has religious as well as legal implications, would have to be carefully unpacked, as it has had implications for everything from the alleged rights of the unborn to those of corporations.

31. Mario Savio, speech at thirtieth anniversary of the Free Speech Movement, cited in *The Free Speech Movement: Reflections on Berkeley in the 1960s*, ed. Robert Cohen and Reginald E. Zelnik (Berkeley, Calif., 2002), 35. Tellingly, the religious source of Savio's free speech purism—he was a lapsed Catholic but was still inspired by the teachings of the Church—is apparent in his evocation of the "great chain of being" premise of medieval cosmology.

32. For a discussion of the pressure release argument, see Thomas I. Emerson, *The System of Freedom of Expression* (New York, 1970).

33. Mill, *On Liberty*, 13.

34. The fear of "weaponizing" free speech in part reflects the blurring of domains, so that the right to speak freely in a political public sphere is inappropriately extended to a university, where academic freedom should prevail. Or the deregulation of commercial speech, which has been restricted to prevent fraudulent claims or health hazards, is defended in the name of generic free speech. For a discussion of this issue, in which ironically the government's role is not to restrict speech but to insist on it, see Robert Post, "Compelled Commercial Speech," *West Virginia Law Review* 117, no. 3 (2015): 867–919.

35. Lord Alfred Douglas, "Two Loves" (published in *The Chameleon*, Oxford, 1894). He may have been referring to relationships between men of different ages, rather than homosexuality in general.

36. For one account of how the reciprocity between rights and obligations is treated, see Alan Gewirth, *Human Rights: Essays on Justifications and Applications* (Chicago, 1983).

37. Alexander Meikeljohn, *Free Speech and Its Relation to Self-Government* (New York, 1948).

38. For the articulation of Post's position and responses to it, see the *Virginia Law Review* 97, no. 3 (May 2011): 477–680.

39. Kateb, "Freedom of Worthless and Harmful Speech," 239.

40. Martin H. Redish, *The Adversary First Amendment: Free Expression and the Foundations of American Democracy* (Stanford, Calif., 2013).

41. See Martin Jay, *The Virtues of Mendacity: On Lying in Politics* (Charlottesville, Va., 2010); Jeremy Elkins and Andrew Norris, eds., *Truth and Democracy* (Philadelphia, 2012).

42. Koposov, *Memory Laws, Memory Wars*.

43. Those like Stanley Fish, who sharply distinguish between academic freedom and freedom of speech, are right to note that a primary mission of research institutions of higher learning is inquiry, which does not give equal weight to all opinions. But they underestimate the ways in which those institutions, especially in the humanities, are also dedicated to hermeneutic rather than epistemic exploration, which can only function when open-ended critique and controversy are permitted. You can cease teaching creationism in biology departments, where evolution has been accepted as a scientific truth, but it would be very problematic to ban, say, psychoanalytic or Marxist interpretations of literature, because their premises are claimed to have been epistemically discredited.

44. See Martin Jay, "The Aesthetic Alibi," in *Cultural Semantics: Keywords of Our Time* (Amherst, Mass., 1998), 109–119. In other words, artistic freedom can be weaponized in the service of political ends, a confusion of domains, but it is not without its own intrinsic merits notwithstanding.

45. W. H. Auden, "In Memory of W. B. Yeats," in *Selected Poetry of W. H. Auden* (New York, 1970), 53. But what it does do, Auden then adds, is survive the poet and reverberate after its moment of enunciation. Auden's dictum has, of course, often been challenged, but it expresses a dimension of artistic freedom worth preserving.

46. For one consideration, see F. R. Ankersmit, *Aesthetic Politics: Political Philosophy beyond Fact and Value* (Stanford, Calif., 1997).

47. George Kateb rightly points out that "judged by the test of truth, which figures provisionally in John Stuart Mill's defense of liberty of thought and discussion, and decisively in Supreme Court First Amendment jurisprudence, theology, like religion, can be said to fail the test. Many religious utterances are demonstrably false." Kateb, "Freedom of Worthless and Harmful Speech," 226.

INDEX

absolutism: in commitment to truth telling, 19, 81–82, 85; concerning truths/norms/values, 1–2, 5, 18, 24, 26, 66; in free speech debate, 25, 205–6, 209, 217, 277n7; moral, 90; or reality's resistance to human intelligence, 85, 87, 89, 92; in rights discourse, 207, 214
academic freedom, 205, 209, 213, 216, 280n43
Adami, Valerio, 133
Adorno, Theodor: Benjamin's and Berlin's friendships with, 62–63, 67, 72; and genesis/validity problem, 3, 220n12; on historical "appreciation," 16, 28; intellectual mapping based on ideas of, 16; and the language of philosophy, 200; and modernity, 157; possession of Klee's *Angelus Novus* by, 62; on reification, 110
advenants, 43, 46–47
advents, 17, 20–21, 41, 120
affective criticism, 276n33
Aleichem, Sholem, 67
alterity. *See* otherness
Althusser, Louis, 51
alt-right. *See* political right
American Civil Liberties Union (ACLU), 204
Ankersmit, Frank, 16, 22–23, 24, 31–32, 46–47, 48, 56, 140–54, 186–87, 189; *Sublime Historical Experience*, 140–41, 144, 151–52, 187, 255n1
Annales School, 40, 94
annals, 178, 182
Annan, Noel, 68
anomie, 162, 163, 261n35
Antifa, 204
Antoni, Carlo, 57

appreciation, of the past from standpoint of the present, 16, 28–33
Aquinas, Thomas, 176
Archilochus, 65
Arendt, Hannah: Benjamin's friendship with, 64; Berlin's antipathy for, 64, 236n8; Blumenberg's critique of, 19, 79–82, 89–91; conventional dichotomies not suitable for, 76; disdain for psychoanalysis, 80; *Eichmann in Jerusalem*, 80, 81–82, 88, 90–91; and "events," 44; "The Jew as Pariah," 76–77; on lies and politics, 132–33, 139; *The Life of the Mind*, 90; *The Origins of Totalitarianism*, 80; pariah/parvenu dichotomy advanced by, 66–69, 76–77; and truth, 82, 89–90
Aristophanes, *The Clouds*, 53
Aristotle, 25, 196
Armitage, David, 20, 93, 95–96, 98, 102, 104, 229n1
art: context and transcendent meaning of, 10–11, 198–99; as an event, 44; free speech and, 216–17; as labor, in Benjamin's thought, 73; psychologistic criticism of, 198–99
Atget, Eugène, 129, 144
Auden, W. H., 217
Auschwitz, 22
Austin, J. L., 37, 49, 102, 197, 212, 232n5
autonomy defense, of free speech, 211–12, 215
Azoulay, Ariella, *The Civil Contract of Photography*, 135

Badiou, Alain, 21, 40, 109, 118–20, 122
Baer, Ulrich, 145
Bakhtin, Mikhail, 39
Balzac, Honoré de, 157

Barthes, Roland, 49, 127, 145, 153, 180, 182
Bataille, Georges, 147
Baudelaire, Charles, 23, 155–61, 163, 170–72, 262n42; "The Painter of Modern Life," 155; "The Salon of 1846," 155, 172
Bechers, Hilla and Bernd, 125
Beltung, Hans, 144
Benda, Julien, 75
Benhabib, Seyla, 235n47
Benjamin, Walter, 18, 62–77; Adorno's friendship with, 63; "The Author as Producer," 73, 128–29; Berlin compared to, 63–77; and events, 40–41; and history, 149–50; intellectual mapping based on ideas of, 16; intellectual style of, 64–77; as Jewish intellectual, 64, 67, 77; life of, 63–64, 67–69, 72, 76; "Little History of Photography," 128–29; and Marxism, 119; and modernity, 157–58, 160–61, 170, 171–72, 262n42; *One-Way Street*, 129; *Origin of the German Trauerspiel*, 67; ownership of Klee's *Angelus Novus* by, 62–77; and photography, 127–30, 137–38, 144, 147; reputation/legacy of, 65; "The Task of the Translator," 10; on traumatic experiences, 142
Bentley, Eric, 159, 160, 170
Bergson, Henri, 96, 98, 142, 163
Berlant, Lauren, 276n33
Berlin, Isaiah, 18, 62–77; Adorno's friendship with, 62–63; Benjamin compared to, 63–77; *Against the Current*, 73; intellectual style of, 64–77; as Jewish intellectual, 64, 68, 77; life of, 63–64, 67–71, 74, 76, 237n15; reputation/legacy of, 65, 68, 72–73
Berman, Marshall, 158
Bernard, Emile, 133
big ideas, 93–105; contexts of, 20, 102; as "events," 45–46, 105; historiography of, 102–5; history of concepts and, 98–99; meanings of, 20, 97, 104; metaphorology and, 99–101; skepticism about, 93–95, 103–5; temporality of, 105; transcendent aspect of, 20, 105
Black, Hugo L., 205
Bloch, Ernst, 17, 36, 44, 46, 119
Blumenberg, Hans, 19–20, 79–92; and absoluteness, 85, 87, 90, 92, 242n26; and anthropology, 84–86, 91; critique of rigorism, 19–20, 79–82, 85, 89–92; *The Genesis of the Copernican World*, 83; influences on, 84; Jewish identity of, 79, 87–88; *The Legitimacy of the Modern Age*, 80, 83; life of, 82–83; and metaphor, 19, 83, 86–87, 90, 99–101, 103; and modernity, 84, 85, 119; and myth, 19, 81–82, 85–89, 91–92; *Nachlass*, 79, 82, 88, 91; reputation of, 82, 83–84; *Rigorism of Truth*, 79, 89, 91; thought of, 84–85; and truth, 19–20, 81–82, 89, 91–92; *Work on Myth*, 83, 87, 89
Blum Theses, 108
Boas, George, 96–97, 104
Boulanger, Georges, 162
Bourke, Richard, 95
Braudel, Fernand, 40, 94, 104
Brecht, Bertolt, 67, 73, 74, 129, 155
Brunner, Otto, 83, 98
Bukharin, Nicolai, 109
Burckhardt, Jacob, 56, 186
Burke, Edmund, 142
Burke, Kenneth, 49
Bush, George W., 3

Calvinism, 164, 173
Cambridge School, 13, 34, 40, 41, 45, 95, 101–2, 229n1
Campbell, Joseph, 91
Camus, Albert, 69
Carlyle, Thomas, 159, 161
Carr, David, 183
Cartier-Bresson, Henri, 22, 128, 145
Cassirer, Ernst, 12, 29, 87
Caulaincourt, Armand-Augustin-Louis, *With Napoleon in Russia*, 188
Certeau, Michel de, 184, 273n74
Cézanne, Paul, 133, 136
Chaplin, Charlie, 67
charisma, 165–67
Cheney, Lynne, 220n3
Chinese Cultural Revolution, 122–23
Chou En-lai, 117, 179
Christianity: function of the relic in, 147, 149; genesis/validity tensions in, 219n3; New Testament events as historical rupture, 42; "real presence" doctrine in, 22, 143, 149, 154, 187

chronicles, 178, 182
Cicero, 53, 180
class consciousness, 9, 114–15
Clifford, James, 51
Cohen, Morris Raphael, 6, 199
Collège de sociologie, 163
Collingwood, R. G., 6, 31, 140, 181, 188
Collini, Stefan, 229n1
Collins, Randall, 12, 34, 45
Communism, 67
Communist Party, 116
Comte, Auguste, 161
concepts, 94–96, 98–105, 247n23. *See also* big ideas; history of concepts; ideas
Confederate States of America, 152
Constant, Benjamin, 73
constructivism, historical, 179–83
context: of big ideas, 12, 102; conventions as constitutive of, 50, 60; events in relation to, 41–42; incommensurability of, 1; of metaphors, 101; relativism based on emphasis of, 1, 3, 30; as theme of intellectual history, 12–14, 29–33; transcendent meaning in relation to, 1–14, 26. *See also* contextualism; genesis
contextualism: "big idea" historiography vs., 20, 94–95; critiques of, 14–16, 36–40, 44–47, 50–51, 61; defenses of, 13–14, 16, 34–36. *See also* historicism
Crapanzano, Vincent, 37
Crary, Jonathan, 253n11
criticality: freedom from particular/contingent constraints as essential to, 3–4; Jewish examples of, 67; transcendence and, 7, 26
Croce, Benedetto, 28, 36, 49, 57, 180
cross-cultural comparison. *See* transcultural comparison
cultural history, 12

Dames, Nicholas, 194
Danto, Arthur, 138
Daston, Lorraine, 95
Daumier, Honoré, 158
Davos Debate, 12, 29
Debord, Guy, 129
deconstruction, 46, 55, 59, 60, 194, 231n33
Deleuze, Gilles, 40, 120
DeLillo, Don, 194

de Man, Paul, 55, 58, 194
Demand, Thomas, 125
Derrida, Jacques: on context of a text/work, 22, 46, 133, 136–37, 231n33; and events, 40, 120; "History of the Lie: Prolegomena," 134; and irony, 56–57; as Jewish intellectual, 77; and ocularcentrism, 96; Searle's conflict with, 59, 197, 201; and temporality, 61; on truth and lies in visual experience, 133–34, 136–37; *The Truth in Painting*, 133–34
Descartes, René, 200
dialectics: of context and transcendent meaning, 14; of genesis and validity, 8–11; Hegel and, 14, 17; jester as example of, 66; of past and present, 18–19, 26
diCorcia, Philip-Lorca, 125
Dictionary of the History of Ideas, 97
Didi-Huberman, Georges, 22, 145–50, 153–54
Diggins, John, 1
digital humanities, 102–3
Dijkstra, Rineke, 125
Dilthey, Wilhelm, 31, 140, 186
discourse analysis, 51
disenchantment of the world, 84, 168
Domanska, Eva, 57, 255n1
Donald Duck, 93
Douglas, Alfred, 214
Dubnow, Ari, 68
DuBois, W. E. B., 223n42
Dummett, Michael, 189
Dunn, John, 13, 229n1
Durkheim, Emile, 23, 158, 161–65, 169–70, 172, 261n35, 262n42

Eakins, Thomas, 158
Eichmann, Adolf, 81–82, 88, 90, 92
Eichmann trial, 19
Eiland, Howard, 72
Eliade, Mircea, 91
emic perspective, 7, 18, 23, 26
end of history, 117
Engels, Friedrich, 108, 109
Enlightenment, 3, 31, 73, 84
Erikson, Erik, 80
ethnic cleansing, 141
etic perspective, 7, 18, 23, 26
Eucharist. *See* real presence

eugenics, 209
Eurocentrism, 2, 212, 224n52
events, 40–47; big ideas as, 45–46, 105; birth as model instance of, 43–44; fidelity to, 109, 118–22; history in relation to, 17, 41–46; Lukács and, 109, 118–23; meaning-bearing function of, 41; metaphysical/religious connotations of, 41; narrative in relation to, 17; photographs as, 146, 153–54; temporality of, 17, 21, 40, 42, 45–46, 105, 120
experience, historical, 24, 31–33, 47, 140, 185–87, 235n43. See also sublime historical experience

falsificationism, 24, 184–85
Febvre, Lucien, 40
Feldman, Ron, 67
Felski, Rita, 276n33
Feyerabend, Paul, 185
Fichte, Johann Gottlieb, 108, 121
First World War, 141, 164
Fish, Stanley, 216, 280n43
Fitzmaurice, Andrew, 95
Fliess, Wilhelm, 38
Floud, Jean, 64
forgetting, 110, 177–78, 268n18
Forst, Rainer, 9–10, 95
Foucault, Michel, 14; archaeological method of, 104; and events, 40, 120; genealogical method of, 21; and history of ideas, 104–5; on knowledge and power, 190, 198, 199; on modernity, 23, 155–58, 160–61, 170, 172; and ocularcentrism, 96; on truth telling and lying, 134
Frankfurt School, 3, 9, 83, 96
Franzen, Jonathan, *The Corrections*, 194–95
freedom of expression, 210–11
free speech, 204–18; absolutist defenses of, 25, 205–6, 209, 217, 277n7; academic freedom distinct from, 205, 209, 213, 216, 280n43; contexts of, 206–7; fetishization of, 206; hermeneutic functions of, 216–17, 280n43; intersubjective functions of, 212–16; liberalism's championing of, 204, 205; objective functions of, 207–10, 214; other rights and concerns cited in restrictions of, 25, 205, 206–7, 212–16; political right's championing of, 204–5, 217–18; religion and, 217; subjective functions of, 209–12, 214–15; teleological functions of, 25–26, 206, 207–18; weaponization of, 25, 205–6, 207, 217–18, 277n7

Frege, Gottlob, 198
Freud, Sigmund: Blumenberg's critique of, 19, 79–82, 89; factors contributing to the thought of, 38; and heroic individuals, 159–60; *Moses and Monotheism*, 79–81, 86–87, 91, 159–60, 244n45; and rationalization, 101; and subjectivity, 214; transference concept of, 179; and truth, 81, 244n45; Weber and, 165
Fried, Michael, 125
Friedlander, Saul, 181
Frisby, David, 172–73
Froeyman, Anton, 151
Fromm, Erich, 80
Frye, Northrup, 49
Fülöp-Miller, René, *Mind and Face of Bolshevism*, 118
fusion of horizons, 26, 39

G (journal), 129
Gadamer, Hans-Georg, 15, 26, 39
Gaddis, John Lewis, 36
Galison, Peter, 95
Geertz, Clifford, 12, 35
Gehlen, Arnold, 84
genesis: art works and, 10–11; as basis for validity claims, 7–8, 26–27; Christian theology and genesis/validity issue, 219n3; of concepts, 98–99; dialectical relationship between validity and, 8–11; global intellectual history not compatible with focus on, 2–3; of photographs, 22; standpoint theory and, 11; validity of ideas/values in relation to their, 1–11, 26, 219n1. See also context
genetic fallacy, 6, 199
Genette, Gerard, 181
Gentile, Giovanni, 57
George, Stefan, 159, 167, 168
Ginzburg, Carlo, 57
global intellectual history, 2–3
Gnosticism, 85
Goldmann, Lucien, 114
Gordon, Peter, 3–4, 29, 33
Gouldner, Alvin, 193
Gramsci, Antonio, 9

"great man" theories, 159–60, 161
Gresham's Law, 209
Gumbrecht, Hans Ulrich, 143
Gundolf, Friedrich, 167
Gunning, Tom, 124, 135, 137; "What's the Point of an Index? or, Faking Photographs," 135
Gursky, Andreas, 125
Guys, Constantin, 155

Habermas, Jürgen: Gadamer's debate with, 15; and modernity, 156, 172; rational reconstruction in the work of, 51; on social vs. system integration, 235n47; and theory of communicative rationality, 9, 96, 189–90, 272n71; on transcendent appeals, 3–4
Hamann, Johann Georg, 64, 73
Hardy, Henry, 68
hate speech, 204, 212–13, 217
hedgehog/fox dichotomy, 65–66, 237n15
Hegel, G. W. F.: Benjamin's and Berlin's opinions of, 64, 72; comic paradigm of philosophy of, 160; and dialectic, 14, 17, 110; genesis/validity tensions in, 30; and heroic individuals, 160, 169, 173; historical judgments of, 28; and the language of philosophy, 200; Lovejoy on, 98; Lukács and, 108; narrative patterns in work of, 57–58; transcendent meaning of history in work of, 14, 21; and world history, 23, 111, 160, 173
Heidegger, Martin: Benjamin's and Berlin's opinions of, 64, 72; Cassirer's debate with, 12, 29; and events, 40–41, 44; and the language of philosophy, 200; and modernity, 84; reception of, 75; and technology, 85; transcendental assumptions in work of, 8; and truth as unconcealment, 23, 127, 130, 138, 142; and Van Gogh's *Old Shoes with Lacings*, 133
Heine, Heinrich, 55, 67, 68
Hempel, Carl, 185
Herder, Johann Gottfried, 73
hermeneutics of suspicion, 8, 56, 115, 202, 223n35, 248n44, 276n33
heroism: comic conception of, 160–61; Durkheim on, 162–63; of modern life, 23, 155–61, 171–73; romantic conception of, 159–61; Simmel on, 168–72; skepticism about, 161–63; sociological analyses of, 161–73, 259n17; types of, 23, 159–61; and villainy, 258n6; Weber on, 164–68, 173
Herrnstein, Richard J., *The Bell Curve*, 209
Herzen, Alexander, 73
Hess, Moses, 108
Hessel, Franz, 65
Himmelfarb, Gertrude, 220n3
historians. *See* historiography
historical materialism, 107–9, 116, 130
historicism, 4, 20, 56–57, 75, 164, 185. *See also* contextualism
historiography: community/institutions of practitioners of, 23–24, 27, 187–91, 273n74; constructivist fallacy in, 24, 179–83; falsificationism in, 24, 184–85; genesis/validity tensions in, 23–24; institutional justificationism in, 24, 187–91; ironic mode in, 17–18, 52–61; learning process in, 183; Lukács and, 109–11, 122; micro- and macrohistory, 2, 178, 183, 185; new experientialism in, 24, 185–87; philosophy distinguished from, 13, 25, 174; positivist/hyperrealist fallacy in, 24, 175–79; professionalization of, 174, 190–91; realist fiction as template for, 108, 109, 112, 114, 117; scientific approaches in, 174–76, 270n43; status of experience in, 24, 31–33, 47, 235n43; temporality of, 61; thought patterns underlying, 14, 29, 52, 54, 57–58, 180, 189; and truth, 174–92. *See also* intellectual history
history of concepts, 6, 20, 83, 98–101, 105
history of ideas: Foucault's practice of, 104–5; Lovejoy's practice of, 96–98, 246n12; social basis of, 13, 20; transhistorical, 20. *See also* big ideas; ideas; intellectual history
history/the past: dialectic of the present and, 18–19, 26; "events" in, 17, 40–47; experiences of, 24, 31–33, 47, 140, 185–87, 235n43 (*see also* sublime historical experience); institutional/professional evaluation of, 23–24, 27, 187–91; ironic perspective on, 17–18; Lukács's conception of, 109–14; nature vs., 4; otherness of, 16, 32, 33, 34; presentist uses of, 5, 16, 28–29, 31, 34, 49; recapturing of, 17–18, 24, 34–37, 49–50, 61, 175–79; ruptures in continuity of, 17, 21, 40, 42, 104–5, 119–20, 161, 186. *See also* historiography

Hitler, Adolf, 88
Hobbes, Thomas, 45, 48
Höfer, Candida, 125
Hölderlin, Friedrich, 151
Holocaust: Blumenberg and, 79, 82, 88; denials of, 182, 209, 216; explicability/ inexplicability of, 78–79, 88, 90, 92, 141, 147–48; Freud and, 80; historical experiences of, 152–53; historic sites dedicated to, 141; Jewish intellectuals and, 77, 79; narrative voice in accounts of, 181; visual representations of, 145–50
Horkheimer, Max, 63, 88, 110, 157
Hughes, H. Stuart, 225n56
Hugo, Victor, 158
Huizinga, Johan, 32, 46–47, 142, 186
Hungary, 107, 108, 117
Hunt, Lynn, 225n55
Hunter, Ian, 13–15, 17, 21
husband/lover dichotomy, 69–71
Husserl, Edmund, 8, 83, 84, 85, 181, 182, 198

Icke, Peter, 255n1
ideal types, 23, 164
ideas: concept of, 96–98; emotions associated with, 97–98; life-history of, 98; and unit-ideas, 97–98. *See also* big ideas; concepts; history of ideas
identity politics, 7, 26, 29
ideology, 3, 38–39
Ignatieff, Michael, 237n15
illocutionary force, 4, 17, 35, 37, 39, 42, 49–50, 102, 131, 135, 212–13
image-word relationship, 133–37, 147
immanence: defined, 5; expansive concept of, 5; scientific perspective contrasted with, 5–6; transcendence within, 8–10
immanent critique, 5
incommensurability: contextual, 200; cultural, 7, 18; linguistic, 7, 200; of norms and values, 71, 190; scientific, 6; temporal, 18, 33, 180–81
the individual. *See* heroism; subjectivity
institutional justificationism, 24, 187–91
intellectual history: agonistic model of, 14–15; Anglo-American, 30–31; Berlin as practitioner of, 70, 74–75; defined, 12; European vs. American, 224n52; evaluative nature of, 12–13; "events" in, 45; genesis/context emphasized in, 13–14; genesis/validity (context/transcendent meaning) tensions in, 12–14, 29, 224n52; intentionality's role in, 51–52; ironic mode in, 235n46; metaphorical oppositions deployed in, 18–19, 65–77; narrative tropes in, 14; philosophy compared to, 74; philosophy in relation to, 13, 25; practice of, 12–13; relationship of present to past in, 16, 28–33; thought patterns underlying, 18–19. *See also* historiography; history of ideas
intellectuals: defined, 12, 34, 45; purportedly transcendent perspective of, 9. *See also* Jewish intellectuals
intentionality: critiques of, 59; disregard for, 51; historical grasp of, 17, 34–35, 49–52, 58–61; ideology as obstacle to ascriptions of, 38–39; irony in relation to, 17–18, 60; and lying, 132, 134–35; of photographs, 128, 136–37; texts in relation to, 50
International Covenant on Civil and Political Rights, 210
Ireland, Craig, 255n1
Irigaray, Luce, 96
irony: defined, 52; dramatic, 53–55, 58, 61; features of, 52–53; intentionality in relation to, 17–18, 60; liberal, 56; as mode of historiography, 17–18, 52–61; as mode of intellectual history, 235n46; and modernity, 23, 156–58, 160–61, 170–73; as narrative trope, 17, 52; nihilistic implications of, 56–57, 61; paradoxical, 55–58, 60–61; Romantic, 55, 233n23, 233n25, 234n30; in Skinner's work, 58–59; Socratic, 52–55, 58, 61; temporality of, 54, 60; in White's work, 17, 52, 54–58
Iser, Wolfgang, 83

Jacoby, Russell, 71, 73
Jameson, Fredric, 109, 114, 118, 226n64
Jauß, Hans Robert, 83
Jay, Martin: *The Dialectical Imagination*, 225n58; *Downcast Eyes*, 96, 147, 233n16; "The Manacles of Gavrilo Princip," 141–42; *Marxism and Totality*, 96, 106; *Reason after Its Eclipse*, 96; *Songs of Experience*, 95–96; *The Virtues of Mendacity*, 96

Jenkins, Keith, 255n1
Jennings, Michael, 72
Jewish intellectuals: Benjamin and Berlin as examples of, 64, 67–68, 77; Derrida as example of, 77; responses of, to the Holocaust, 79; in twentieth century, 77
Johns Hopkins University, 96
Jonas, Hans, 79
Judt, Tony, 31
Jünger, Ernst, 75, 159

Kadarky, Arpad, 119
Kafka, Franz, 67
Kagan, Elena, 205
Kant, Immanuel: and aesthetic experience, 135; and antinomies of thought, 108, 110; on freedom and causality, 44; and modernity, 156; moral philosophy of, 90; phenomena-noumena distinction of, 58; on psychologism, 198; relationship of philosophy and theory in, 196; and the sublime, 142; transcendentalism of, 14, 135, 221n19; on the will, 57
Kantorowicz, Ernst, 115
Kateb, George, 211, 215
Kein, Petr, 141
Kenaan, Hagi, 137
Kierkegaard, Søren, 40–42, 55, 58, 118–19
king's two bodies, 115, 143
Klee, Paul, *Angelus Novus*, 62
Kloppenberg, James, 95
Koch brothers, 204
Kolakowski, Leszek, 66
Koselleck, Reinhart, 6, 20, 21, 83, 98–99, 105, 156
Kracauer, Siegfried, 12, 13, 147, 149, 174
Kraus, Karl, 66
Kristeva, Julia, 199
Kuhn, Thomas, 6, 183, 185, 230n4
Kun, Bela, 107

Lacan, Jacques, 131–32, 135, 147, 148
LaCapra, Dominick, 12, 17, 29, 37, 103, 150
Lahr, Bert, 93
Lakatos, Imre, 185
Landgrebe, Ludwig, 83
languages, incommensurability of, 7, 200
Lanzmann, Claude, 145–47; *Shoah*, 146, 147
Latour, Bruno, 11, 156, 225n55

Lawrence, D. H., 159
Lazare, Bernard, 67
Lebensphilosophie, 8, 169
Leibniz, Gottfried Wilhelm, 86
Leiter, Brian, 197–98, 209
Lenin, Vladimir, 107–8, 113, 121; *Philosophical Notebooks*, 107
Leninism, 122–23
Leninist Party, 114–15, 117
Leo, Heinrich, 14
Levi, Primo, *If This Is a Man*, 78, 92
Levinas, Emmanuel, 96
Levine, Donald, 261n31
liberalism: Berlin and, 64, 66; and free speech, 204, 205; Locke as wellspring of, 61; and transcendental approach, 31
Lichtheim, George, 120
Liebersohn, Harry, 167
Lilla, Mark, 31, 70–71, 74
linguistic turn, 15, 29, 31, 48, 95, 180, 181, 185, 197, 199
Lissitsky, El, 129
literary realism, 109–10, 112, 114, 117, 120, 122, 181, 182, 194
Locke, John, 45, 61
locutionary meaning, 35, 102, 131, 212
longue durée, 93–94, 104
Louis XIV, 143
Lovejoy, Arthur, 96–98, 246n12
Lowenthal, Leo, 119
Löwith, Karl, 84, 119
Löwy, Michel, 119
Lukács, Georg: "Bolshevism as a Moral Problem," 112; and class consciousness, 9, 114–15; composition and reception of *History and Class Consciousness*, 106–8, 118; conversion to Marxism and political engagement of, 106–7, 111–12, 118–19; *History and Class Consciousness*, 14, 21, 106–23; issues concerning thought of, 108–9; *Lenin*, 121; and objective possibilities, 109, 114–18, 121–22; and realism, 108, 109, 112, 114, 117; reification concept of, 107, 110–11; self-criticism by, 108, 121; Simmel and, 172; "Tactics and Ethics," 112; "Tailism and the Dialectic," 106, 108, 115, 119, 121, 249n2; and Weber, 109, 114, 168, 250n25; and world history, 21, 109–14, 116–17, 121

Luxemburg, Rosa, 76, 113–14, 122
lying: errors contrasted with, 131; ethical dimension of, 134, 135; historiographical, 271n51; intention as aspect of, 131–32, 134–35; photography and, 22, 124–39; in politics, 96, 132–33, 139; speech act theory and, 130–31, 134–35; temporality of, 132–33, 136; truth in relation to, 132. *See also* truth; validity
Lyotard, Jean-François, 40, 96, 117, 120, 193

MacCumber, John, 201
Machiavelli, Niccolò, 45, 48
macrohistory, 2, 178, 183, 185
Magritte, René, 134
Maistre, Joseph de, 73
Manet, Edouard, 158
Mann, Thomas, 88
Marcus, Sharon, 276n33
Marcuse, Herbert, 64, 206, 208
Marin, Louis, 143
marketplace of ideas, 210, 279n25
Marquard, Odo, 83
Marx, Karl: alienation concept of, 107; Benjamin's and Berlin's interest in, 64; on fetishization of commodities, 136; historical materialism of, 109, 110; Jewish heritage of, 68; Lukács's emulation of, 106, 111, 112–13; on Napoleon III, 158; *Theses on Feuerbach*, 173. *See also* Marxism
Marxism: deconstruction aligned with, 31; historical materialism of, 116; Lukács and, 106, 108, 111; and standpoint theory, 7, 9. *See also* Western Marxism
mathematics, 4, 221n15
McMahon, Darrin, 95
Meikeljohn, Alexander, 215
Mémoire de camps (exhibition), 145–46
memory: historiography limited by, 110, 177–78, 268n18; photographs as stimuli to, 153; trauma and, 142
Merleau-Ponty, Maurice, 250n25; *Humanism and Terror*, 112
metanarratives, 117
metaphorology, 19–20, 90, 99–101
metaphors: Blumenberg's theory of, 19, 83, 86–87, 90, 99–101, 103; contexts of, 101; oppositions based on, 18–19, 65–77
metaphysics. *See* philosophy

Meyer, Ahlrich, 79, 82
microhistory, 2, 178, 183, 185
Mies van der Rohe, Ludwig, 129
Mill, John Stuart, 73, 208, 210
Milton, John, *Areopagitica*, 207
mind/matter problem, 219n1
Minogue, Kenneth, 230n16
Mitchell, W. J. T., 126
modernity: Blumenberg and, 84, 85, 119; characteristics of, 156, 261n31; disenchantment as feature of, 84, 168; Durkheim and, 162–63; Heidegger and, 84; heroization of, 23, 155–61, 171–73; irony and, 23, 156–58, 160–61, 170–73; philosophy associated with, 201; postmodernity vs., 200–202; and secularization, 144; Simmel and, 168–72; sociology and, 23, 158, 161–73, 260n30, 261n31; villainy and, 258n6; Weber and, 164–68
Moholy-Nagy, László, 129
Molven, Frode, 150
Mommsen, Wolfgang, 167
money, 94, 100
montage, 73, 74, 129–30, 137, 146, 147
Montaigne, Michel de, 211
Moretti, Franco, 103
Moscow Trials, 112
Moses, 19, 80–81, 86–87
Mosse, George, 62
Muirhead, Russell, 25
Murray, Charles, *The Bell Curve*, 209
myth: attack on, by truth-telling drive, 19, 81; Blumenberg and, 19, 81–82, 85–89, 91–92; significance of, 19; as subject of sublime historical experience, 151

Nagel, Ernest, 6, 199
naive realism, 24, 54–55, 58, 176–80, 184, 185
names, ideas/philosophies identified with, 15, 51, 235n46, 237n13
Nancy, Jean-Luc, 40
Napoleon III, 158
narrative: the event as challenge to, 17; Lukács's historical method and, 109–10, 112–13, 122; prefigural patterns in, 14, 29, 52, 54, 57–58, 180, 189; temporalities in, 180–81; voice in, 181
Nazism, 87, 141, 150

neo-Hegelianism, 108
neo-Kantianism, 97, 114, 164, 169
Neue Sachlichkeit, 128, 129, 138
Neumann, Franz, 64
New Criticism, 50
new experientialism, 24, 185–87
New Historicism, 232n6
New Left, 117
Newmark, Kevin, 55
new romanticism. *See* new experientialism
N-gram, 102–3
Nietzsche, Friedrich: *Beyond Good and Evil*, 45; critique of definition by, 98, 104; dialectic of genesis and validity in work of, 8; and "events," 41, 45, 47; genealogical method of, 21; *Genealogy of Morals*, 165; and heroic individuals, 23, 159, 162, 164–65, 168–70, 172, 260n22; on knowledge and power, 198; and the language of philosophy, 200; on modernity, 164; and myth, 87; on relation of personal life and thought, 76
Nixon, Richard, 117
Nizan, Paul, 75
nostalgia, 151–52
novelty: the event as, 17, 42–44; transcendent aspect of, 17; and utopia, 44
Novick, Peter, 176

Obama, Barack, 118
objective possibility, 109, 114–18, 121–22
ocularcentrism, 96, 147, 200, 233n16
Organization Todt, 83, 240n14
origins. *See* context; genesis
Orwell, George, *1984*, 192
otherness: of the past, 16, 32, 33, 34; of viewpoints, 7, 18
Oxford English Dictionary, 99

Pagden, Anthony, 229n1
Palonen, Kari, 48
pariah/parvenu dichotomy, 66–69, 76–77
particularity, vs. universality, 1–3
Parvikko, Tuija, 90
the past. *See* history/the past
Paulhan, Jean, 75
Peirce, C. S., 127, 148, 187, 190
Pels, Dick, 8, 9
perlocutionary effect, 35, 42, 50, 131, 212, 217

Peterson, Jordan, 204
philosophy: assumptions underlying, 25; Berlin and, 74; criticisms of, 202; genesis/validity tensions in, 198–99, 202; historiography distinguished from, 13, 25, 174; institutional role of, 196–98, 202; intellectual history in relation to, 13, 25, 74; modernity associated with, 201; psychologism disparaged by, 198, 202; rhetorical and linguistic issues in, 199–200; theory in relation to, 24–25, 196–203; transcendent claims of, 16, 24–25; visual metaphors in, 97
photography: as art, 125, 127–29; of Auschwitz, 22; Barthes's concepts of *studium* and *punctum* in, 145, 153; Benjamin's Marxist critique of, 128–30, 138; digital revolution in, 125–26; etymology of, 137; as "event," 146, 153–54; intentionality and, 128, 136–37; mimetic/indexical quality of, 22, 125–27, 137–38, 148; and sublime historical experience, 22, 144–54; temporality of, 136, 138; and truth/lying, 22, 124–39; validity and genesis of, 21–22; veiling vs. tearing functions of, 148
Pippen, Robert, 84
Plato, 52–53, 85, 90, 91, 189, 198
Plunkett, David, 25
Pocock, John, 13, 34, 95, 102
Poetics and Hermeneutics, 83
Polish Resistance, 146
political right: free speech championed by, 204–5, 217–18; universal standards championed by, 3, 220n3
political theology, 84, 241n21
politics: free speech and, 215–16; lying and, 96, 132–33, 139; roles of truth and opinion in, 89–90. *See also* identity politics
Popper, Karl, 6, 8, 184–85
positivism, 5, 8, 13, 58, 64, 162, 175–79, 185
possibility, events in relation to, 17, 41–44, 47
Post, Robert, 215–16
postcoloniality, 2
postmodernity, 117, 157, 180, 200, 202
post-structuralism, 31, 148, 200
prayer, 217

presentism: critiques of, 5, 16, 29, 31, 34, 49; defenses of, 36–37, 49; inevitable traces of, 178–79
priest/jester dichotomy, 66
Princip, Gavrilo, 141–42, 153
producer/rentier dichotomy, 73–75
psychologism, 4, 8, 16, 25, 198–99, 202, 274n16, 274n17
Pynchon, Thomas, 194

Rabinbach, Anson, 119
Raenger-Patsch, Albert, *Die Welt ist Schön*, 128
Rank, Otto, 260n25
Ranke, Leopold von, 13–14, 56, 176, 180, 270n43
Rappaport, Herman, 194
rationality. *See* reason/rationality
rational reconstruction, 51–52
Readings, Bill, 193, 199
realism. *See* literary realism; naive realism
real presence, 22, 143, 146, 149, 154, 187
reason/rationality: counter-Enlightenment critique of, 73; dialectic of genesis and validity in use of, 9–10; historiographical assumptions concerning, 39; and psychologism, 198–99, 274n18; rhetoric and, 86, 189; Weber on, 39, 101, 166–68
Rees, John, 115
Reich, Wilhelm, 80
reification, 107, 110–11, 113, 116–18, 128, 129, 139, 172
relativism: challenges to, 3–4, 6, 8; contextualization as basis of, 1, 3, 30; historical constructivism as, 180, 182
religion, and free speech, 217
rhetoric: Blumenberg on role of, 19, 84, 85–86, 99–100; history based on, 14, 48–49, 58, 186, 188–89; philosophy in relation to, 199; politics in relation to, 89–90; and rationality, 86, 189; Skinner and, 48–49; theory in relation to, 199; White and, 14, 48–49, 58, 189
Rickert, Heinrich, 164
right, political. *See* political right
rigorism, 19–20, 79–82, 89–92
Rimbaud, Arthur, 156
Ringer, Fritz, 75
Roberts, John, 128, 138
Romano, Claude, 17, 41–47, 120

Romanticism, 3
Ronell, Avital, 197
Rorty, Richard, 31, 56, 197, 201
Rosenfeld, Sophia, 95
Rosenzweig, Franz, 149
Roth, Michael, 49
Rothacker, Erich, 83, 98
Rousseau, Jean-Jacques, 151
Ruff, Thomas, 125
Runia, Eelco, 143, 144, 145, 149, 151, 186–87
Russian Revolution, 106, 107, 109, 112, 117–18, 120

Sabbatianism, 112
Safatle, Vladimir, 160
Sartre, Jean-Paul, 65, 148
Savio, Mario, 211–12
Schapiro, Meyer, 133
Scheler, Max, 222n24
Schelling, F. W. J., 98
Schiller, Friedrich, 30, 52; "Resignation," 111
Schlegel, August, 55
Schlegel, Friedrich, 55, 233n23, 233n25
Schmitt, Carl, 40, 75, 84, 119, 167
Scholem, Gershom, 62–63, 67, 112, 149
science: cumulative knowledge achieved by, 6; falsificationism in, 184–85; historiography as, 174–76, 270n43; immanent grounding of, 8; immanent perspective contrasted with, 5–6; Kuhn's contextualization of, 6, 230n4; transcendent perspective contrasted with, 5
Scott, Joan, 31, 140
Searle, John, 37, 49, 59, 102, 197, 201
Sebald, W. G., *Austerlitz*, 144
Second International, 108, 113–14
Second World War, 159
Sedgwick, Eve Kosofsky, 276n33
Sewell, William, Jr., 35–36, 40
Shakespeare, William: *Hamlet*, 211; *Othello*, 53
Shapiro, Ben, 204
Sherman, Cindy, 125
Shroud of Turin, 144
side-shadowing, 114, 179
Sidney, Philip, 182
Siegel, Jerrold, 95
Simmel, Georg: on concept formation, 94; "The Conflict of Modern Culture," 171; on heroes, 23, 164, 168–72; on individual-

society relationship, 171; "The Individual's Superiority over the Mass," 171; intellectual style of, 265n78; and *Lebensphilosophie*, 8, 169–70; "The Metropolis and Mental Life," 170; and modernity, 23, 158, 161, 168–72; *The Philosophy of Money*, 94, 100, 170
Simpson, David, 29
situatedness, 4, 7–8, 14, 25, 29
skepticism, 5, 37, 56, 59
Skinner, Quentin, 13, 17, 34–35, 37–39, 42, 45, 48–51, 58–61, 95, 102, 142; *Foundations of Modern Political Thought*, 48, 230n16
Slezkine, Yuri: *The House of Government*, 118; *The Jewish Century*, 77
social facts, 162, 164, 169, 172
sociological tragedy, 171
sociology: genesis/validity tensions in, 23; and heroism, 161–73, 259n17; and modernity, 23, 158, 161–73, 260n30, 261n31
Socrates, 52–53, 90
Sombart, Werner, 161, 164
Sontag, Susan, 69, 76
Sophists, 89, 198
Sophocles: *Antigone*, 160; *Oedipus Rex*, 53
speaking as/for, 7–9, 26–27, 223n42
speech acts: agonistic, 39; Habermas and, 3–4; of historical figures, 17, 50, 51, 58–60; iterability of, 60; and lying, 130–31, 134–35; photographs likened to, 22; theory of, 35, 37, 39, 42, 49–50, 102, 197, 212
Spencer, Herbert, 161, 169
Spengler, Oswald, 159
Spinoza, Baruch, 44
Spitzer, Alan, 271n51
Stalin, Joseph, 121
standpoint theory, 7–9
Steinberger, Peter, 51
Sterne, Laurence, *Tristram Shandy*, 178
Stone, Sasha, 128, 129
structuralism, 40–41
Struth, Thomas, 125
sublime historical experience, 140–54; aesthetic–rather than epistemological–character of, 31–32, 140; communal character of, 152–53; and context, 46–47; emotion as characteristic of, 142, 152; immediacy as characteristic of, 142–43; myth as subject of, 151; new experientialism and, 186; otherness of the past revealed in, 16; overview of, 22–23, 31; photography as vehicle for, 22, 144–54; powerful conjunction of present and past at root of, 142–43, 149, 151, 153–54; resistance of, to meaning/explanation, 24, 141–42, 144, 145, 149, 153, 255n2
Sugimoto, Hiroshi, 125
suicide, 158, 162, 163, 261n35, 262n42
Surrealism, 129

Talbot, William Henry Fox, 137
Talmon, Jacob, 70
Taubes, Jakob, 83, 87
Taylor, Charles, 95
temporality: of big ideas, 105; of events, 17, 21, 40, 42, 45–46, 105, 120; of historiography, 61; incommensurabilities involving, 18, 33, 180–81; of irony, 54, 60; of lies, 132–33, 136; narrative and, 180–81; of photographs, 136, 138
Les temps modernes (journal), 145–47
texts: authorial intention and interpretation of, 50; context in relation to, 46; documentary vs. worklike qualities of, 12, 103, 225n55, 248n40; features of, 95
textualism, "big idea" historiography vs., 20, 94–95
the good, values contrasted with, 4, 5
theory: criticisms of, 202–3; defense of, 194–96; genesis/validity tensions in, 202; institutional role of, 193–95, 197–98; others of, 195–96; philosophy in relation to, 24–25, 196–203; psychologism embraced by, 199; rhetorical and linguistic issues in, 199–201; theological argument compared to, 201
Theory and Society (journal), 193
Theresienstadt concentration camp, 141–43
thick description, 12, 35
Thinkspot (website), 204
Thompson, E. P., 5
Three Stooges, 93
time. *See* temporality
Tocqueville, Alexis de, 73
Toews, John, 31

Tolstoy, Leo, 65, 188
Tönnies, Ferdinand, 101, 164
tragedy of culture, 171
transcendence/transcendent meaning: big ideas and, 20, 105; context/origins in relation to, 1–14, 26; criticality's appeal to, 7, 26; defenses of, 5; defined, 5; events as structured by, 17; generational, 6–7, 20; within immanence, 8–10; institutions as site for, 24; Kantian distinctions pertaining to, 221n19; Lukács's view of, 111–12; nonabsolute, 6–7, 26; presentism associated with, 30; in standpoint theory, 9; as theme of intellectual history, 12–14, 29–33. *See also* validity
transcendental phenomenology, 8
transcultural comparison, 1–2, 7, 10. *See also* big ideas
traumatic experience, 22, 120, 142, 145, 150, 153, 215
Troilo, Giovanni, 124–25, 135, 139
Trotsky, Leon, 121
Trump, Donald, 118, 204
truth: Arendt and, 82, 89–90; Blumenberg and, 19–20, 81–82, 89, 91–92; certainty vs., 4; correspondence theories of, 140, 176, 179, 182; critique of absolute commitment to, 19–20, 79–82; free speech defended as means to, 207–10; historians' moral commitment to, 24, 191–92; historiography and, 174–92; institutional/professional evaluations of, 23–24, 27, 187–91; lying in relation to, 132; photography and, 22, 124–39; as unconcealment, 23, 127, 130, 138, 142. *See also* lying; validity
Tuck, Richard, 13, 95, 229n1
Turgenev, Ivan, 73

unit-ideas, 97–98
Universal Declaration of Human Rights, 210–12
universality: Enlightenment thinkers associated with, 3; in language, 4, 221n15; particularity in relation to, 1–2; political right as champion of, 3, 220n3
University of California, Berkeley, 204, 211
utopianism, 3, 30, 44, 71, 73, 74, 107, 108, 114, 120

Vaihinger, Hans, 97, 104
Valéry, Paul, 65
validity: art works and, 10–11; dialectical relationship between genesis and, 8–11; genesis as basis for claims of, 7–8, 26–27; of ideas/values, in relation to their genesis, 1–11, 26, 219n1; inventive fecundity as counterpart to, 11; issues in "speaking as" and "speaking for," 7–9, 26–27, 223n42; of photographs, 21–22; standpoint theory and, 10–11; world history as judge of, 111–12, 117, 121. *See also* lying; transcendence/transcendent meaning; truth
values: the good contrasted with, 4, 5; incommensurability of, 190
Van Gogh, Vincent, *Old Shoes with Lacings*, 133
Varnhagen, Rahel, 67
Vico, Giambattista, 7, 48, 54, 73, 87
vitalism, 70, 159, 160, 163, 164, 166–68, 170, 171, 173

Wagner, Richard, 159
Wajcman, Gérard, 145
Wall, Jeff, 125
Wallace, David Foster, 194
Wallace, Robert M., 83
Weber, Max: and charisma, 165–67; "disenchantment" concept of, 84, 168; on heroes, 164–68, 173; and ideal types, 23, 164; on Jews as pariahs, 67; Lukács and, 109, 114, 168, 250n25; and modernity, 23, 84, 158, 161, 172; "objective possibility" concept of, 109, 114; "Politics as Vocation," 167–68; on prophets, 75, 165; and rationality, 39, 101, 166–68; "Science as Vocation," 167, 172, 173; and thick description, 35
Weil, Simone, 76
Weingart, Peter, 260n30
Western Marxism, 96, 106, 108, 250n25
White, Hayden, 14, 17, 18, 29, 31, 36–37, 48–49, 52, 54–59, 61, 142, 159, 180, 189, 232n5, 232n6; "The Absurdist Moment in Contemporary Literary Theory," 56–57; *Metahistory*, 48, 52, 57; *The Tropics of Discourse*, 57
Wiesel, Elie, *Night*, 78–79
Williams, Bernard, 191
Williams, Raymond, 34, 102

Wittfogel, Karl August, 109
Wittgenstein, Ludwig, 5, 49, 98–99, 185
Wolin, Richard, 31
word-image relationship, 133–37, 147
world-historical perspective, 21, 23, 109–14, 116–17, 121, 160, 173
World Press Photo, 124, 127, 130, 135, 139

Yiannopoulos, Milo, 204
Yugoslavia 141

Zaretsky, Robert, 66
Zionism, 67, 82, 87, 91, 223n42
Žižek, Slavoj, 21, 42–43, 76, 106, 109, 119, 122–23

ACKNOWLEDGMENTS

In the genesis of any book, an author is likely to incur more debts than can ever be adequately acknowledged. In the case of a collection of essays drawing on a lifetime—or at least, a lengthy career—spent pondering a variety of related issues, the challenge of recalling them all and doing justice to the acts of generosity they represent is even more insurmountable. But the imperative to try is for all that no less valid. So with preemptive apologies to those I've forgotten or inadvertently neglected, let me give it a shot.

It has been my great good fortune to have been taught by, had collegial relations with, or served as mentor to several generations of gifted and accomplished modern European intellectual historians teaching in America. The generation above me—most notably John Clive, Peter Gay, H. Stuart Hughes (my dissertation director), Georg Iggers, Leonard Krieger, Frank Manuel, George Mosse, Fritz Ringer, Carl Schorske, and Fritz Stern—either directly trained me or indirectly offered admirable models to emulate. Those of my own generation, loosely defined, whose careers more or less overlapped with mine have been frequent and valued interlocutors, never failing to astonish me with the range of their interests, command of difficult ideas and multiple contexts, and willingness to criticize constructively each other's work. The list is long, and would be even longer if it included colleagues from abroad, let alone the myriad philosophers, political theorists, sociologists, literary critics, anthropologists, and even economists who practice intellectual history without a license, and often with great skill. But as this is probably the last chance I will get publically to express my gratitude for their role in the vibrant scholarly community to which I've belonged for a half century, I hope you will indulge my recording their names: Walter Adamson, Celia Applegate, Andrew Arato, David Armitage, Steven Aschheim (an Israeli, but a frequent enough visitor to qualify as one of the tribe), Keith Baker, David Bates, Jonathan Beecher, Frederick Beiser, David Biale, Paul Breines, James Clifford, Lee Congdon, Robert Darnton, Christian Emden,

Michael Ermarth, David James Fischer, Stefanos Geroulanos, Mary Gluck, David Gross, Malichi Hacohen, Jeffrey Herf, Judith Hughes, Jonathan Israel, Gerald Izenberg, Margaret Jacob, Russell Jacoby, Peter Jelavich, William Johnston, Tony Judt, Alan Kors, Lloyd Kramer, Dominick LaCapra, Anthony La Vopa, Harry Liebersohn, Mark Lilla, Colin Loader, Peter Loewenberg, David Luft, Eugene Lunn, Harold Mah, Tracie Matysik, Allan Megill, Mark Micale, Cecilia Miller, Jan-Werner Müller, Jerry Z. Muller, Anthony Pagden, Mary Pickering, Mark Poster, Moishe Postone, Anson Rabinbach, John Randolph, Camille Robcis, David Roberts, Paul Robinson, Sophia Rosenfeld, Michael Roth, Jerrold Seigel, Marci Shor, Matthew Specter, Peter Stansky, Michael Steinberg, Judith Surkis, John Toews, Enzo Traverso, Steven Vincent, Hayden White, Robert Wohl, Richard Wolin, and John Zammito. Some on this list have been close friends for many years, others more occasional interlocutors; some have plowed the same fields, others adjoining or even distant ones; some have been generous respondents to my work (and vice versa), others have been critics and been criticized in turn. But in all cases, I have profited enormously from their contributions to the vibrant field I've been proud to call my own for more than five decades.

Having had the extraordinary opportunity to spend those years teaching at a major research university in a department always ranked among the best in our field, I have witnessed with pleasure and admiration the maturation of many rising—or fully arisen—leaders of our little corner of the scholarly universe. Some were undergraduates at Berkeley: Carolyn Dean, Nils Gilman, Ethan Kleinberg, Benjamin Lapp, Suzanne Marchand, and Darrin McMahon. Others did their graduate degrees in our department (or in Rhetoric, where I also directed a handful of dissertations): John Abromeit, Jennifer Allen, Sonia Amadae, Paige Arthur, Amos Bitzan, Nicholaas Barr Clingan, Abner Ben-Amos, Michael Bess, Theodore Bogacz, Julian Bourg, Warren Breckman, Alice Bullard, Eliah Bures, Rita Chin, Carolyn Dean, David Delano, Ari Edmundson, Grahame Foreman, Lawrence Frohman, Martin Gammon, Elisabeth Goodstein, Peter Gordon, Lohren Green, Richard Gringeri, Michael Gubser, Andrew Jainchill, Richard Kim, Eiko Kuwana, James Kwak, Benjamin Lazier, Dirk Moses, David Moshfegh, Samuel Moyn, Gregory Moynahan, David Myers, Elliot Neaman, Elias Palti, Knox Peden, Melissa Ptacek, Terence Renaud, Emanuel Rota, Jonathan Sheehan, Abraham Socher, David Sorkin, Alexander Soros, Eliyahu Stern, Noah Strote, Ania Wertz, Benjamin Wurgaft, and Jonathan Zatlin. Even those who have made careers outside of the university often continue to be part of the larger fellowship that has emerged from their common training. I am delighted to dedicate this collection in enormous gratitude for their contributions, present and future, to European intellectual history in general and to the ongoing education of this one contributor to it in particular.

The more proximate genesis of each of the essays in this collection also merits acknowledgment. Chapter 1 appeared as "Pretensiones desvergonzadas y preguntas abominables. La historia intellectual come juicio del pasado," *Prismas* (Buenos Aires, Argentina) 11 (2007). Chapter 2 appeared as "Historical Explanation and the Event: Reflections on the Limits of Contextualization," *New Literary History* 42 (2011). Chapter 3 appeared as "Intention and Irony: The Missed Encounter between Hayden White and Quentin Skinner," *History and Theory* 52 (February 2013). Chapter 4 appeared as "Walter Benjamin and Isaiah Berlin: Modes of Jewish Intellectual Life in the 20th Century," *Critical Inquiry* 43 (Spring 2017). Chapter 5 appeared as "Against Rigor: Hans Blumenberg on Freud and Arendt," *New German Critique* 132 (November 2017). Chapter 6 appeared as "Hey! What's the Big Idea? Ruminations on the Question of Scale in Intellectual History," *New Literary History* 48, no. 4 (August 2017). Chapter 7 appeared as "Fidelity to the Event? Lukács' *History and Class Consciousness* and the Russian Revolution," *Studies in East European Thought* 3, no. 4 (November 2018). Chapter 8 appeared as "Can Photographs Lie? Reflections on a Perennial Anxiety," *Critical Studies* 2 (September 2016). Chapter 9 appeared as "Sublime Historical Experience, Real Presence and Photography," *Journal of the Philosophy of History* 12 (2018). Chapter 10 appeared as "Sociology and the Heroism of Modern Life," in *The Cambridge History of Modern Thought*, vol. 2, eds. Peter E. Gordon and Warren Breckman (Cambridge, 2019). Chapter 11 appeared as "Historical Truth and the Truth of Historians," in *Integrity, Honesty, and Truth-Seeking*, eds. Christian Miller and Ryan West (Oxford, 2020). Chapter 12 appeared as "Theory and Philosophy: Antonyms in Our Semantic Field?" *Philosophy and Rhetoric* 53, no. 1 (2020). These publications were often generated by invitations to give named lectures, attend conferences, or contribute to essay volumes, and their validity, such as it is, was enhanced by the scrutiny of many acute readers. Thanks are thus due to Frank Ankersmit, Warren Breckman, Paul Breines, Andrew Feenberg, Rita Felski, Arild Fetveit, Peter Gordon, Daniel Gross, Peter Uwe Hohendahl, Ethan Kleinberg, Christian Miller, Samuel Moyn, Robert Post, Quentin Skinner, Nancy Snow, Marek Tamm, Herbert Tucker, Ryan West, Hayden White, and Eugen Zeleňák.

I have also benefited from my interactions with colleagues in Berkeley's History Department, most notably John Connelly, John Efron, Richard Herr, Carla Hesse, Stefan-Ludwig Hoffmann, David Hollinger, Thomas Laqueur, Jonathan Sheehan, and Randolph Starn, and with my co-conspirators in the Critical Theory Program, Dan Blanton, Wendy Brown, Judith Butler, Robert Kaufman, and Hans Sluga. Material support for research was generously provided until I retired in 2016 by the Sidney Hellman Ehrman Chair. I also very much appreciate the opportunity to join the distinguished book series *Intellectual History of the Modern Age*, edited by Angus Burgin, Peter Gordon, Joel Isaac, Karuna Mantena, Samuel Moyn, Jennifer Ratner-Rosenhagen, Camille Robcis, and Sophia Rosenfeld (special thanks to Peter and Sam for shepherding the book through the vetting process). I appreciate the suggestions of two anonymous readers for the Press. Robert Lockhart and Lily Palladino have been steady editorial presences, and I've benefited from the copyediting of Lori Rider and the preparing of the index by David Luljak.

Finally, it is always an unalloyed pleasure to acknowledge with love as well as gratitude the support, affection, and indulgence of my family. My daughters Shana and Rebecca, their husbands Ned and Grayson, and my four grandchildren, Frankie, Sammy, Ryeland, and Sidney, as well as my sister Beth, remain constant sources of strength and warmth in my life. And it is especially gratifying yet again to offer a modest verbal repayment, however inadequate, of the inestimable debt I owe in so many ways to my partner in thoughtcrimes, ideal reader, and beloved wife, Catherine Gallagher.

www.ingramcontent.com/pod-product-compliance
Lightning Source LLC
Chambersburg PA
CBHW051209300426
44116CB00006B/494